The Creative Argument

The Creative Argument

RHETORIC IN THE REAL WORLD

WITH READINGS

Thomas Girshin

Hackett Publishing Company, Inc.
Indianapolis/Cambridge

For further information, please address
  Hackett Publishing Company, Inc.
  P.O. Box 44937
  Indianapolis, Indiana 46244-0937

  www.hackettpublishing.com

Cover design by E. L. Wilson
Interior design by E. L. Wilson and Elana Rosenthal
Composition by Aptara, Inc.

Library of Congress Control Number: 2023951590

ISBN-13: 978-1-64792-165-1 (pbk.)
ISBN-13: 978-1-64792-173-6 (PDF ebook)
ISBN-13: 978-1-64792-174-3 (epub)

The paper used in this publication meets the minimum requirements of
American National Standard for Information Sciences—Permanence of Paper
for Printed Library Materials, ANSI Z39.48–1984.

♾

Contents

Preface for Instructors

The Creative Argument is a combination textbook and anthology that supports student-centered learning of argumentation in real contexts. Drawing on nearly twenty works of creative nonfiction, literary journalism, and scholarly argument, the book provides students simultaneously with a theoretical framework and an essay that exemplifies, and sometimes even subverts, that framework. This juxtaposition should lead students to the kind of thinking-through a typical textbook may not prompt.

Current argumentation textbooks draw primarily on canned, made-to-order arguments that, while they clearly illustrate the concepts, don't have the complexity to allow students to see how these principles might operate in a more realistic context. For example, the traditional argumentation textbook might provide the following example of an argument.

Although the motor vehicle industry is protesting loudly, the recently implemented 54.5 mpg fuel efficiency standard is a good idea. First, it will reduce out-of-pocket expenses for most Americans. Second, it will help cut greenhouse gas emissions. Finally, it will help keep U.S.-made cars competitive with more fuel-efficient foreign vehicles. (Example 1)

As an illustrative example, this argument is convenient. The textbook can ask its readers to, for instance, diagram this argument, linking claims and reasons. It can ask its readers what kind of an argument this is, or what pattern of inference it is developing. Students will have little trouble doing any of these things with proper guidance, as long as they are analyzing this or a similarly simple argument. When it comes to analyzing and writing more complex arguments, however, students will continue to have difficulty without reference to more complex examples.

Rarely do we encounter an argument as simple and overt as the above in our everyday reading or conversations. Here, for example, is the opening paragraph from a recently published *New York Times* op-ed on the same topic.

> The Obama administration's stringent fuel efficiency standards are intended to reduce auto pollution and drive up gas mileage. They are the biggest single step any nation has taken to fight global warming. The rules worked well, at first. They no longer do. They can be fixed. (Example 2; Becker & Gerstenzang, "Stalling on Fuel Efficiency," 3.10.16)

This is relatively straightforward, but even so it is significantly less rhetorically transparent than Example 1. Students might have difficulty finding the claim in

Example 2, even after some practice with the typical argumentation textbook. For one thing, unlike Example 1, Example 2 doesn't lay out all its claims, subclaims, and reasons in the opening paragraph. You'd have to read further for these. Moreover, it's difficult to be certain which sentence(s) in Example 2 represent the resolution and which represent other parts of the argument. Identifying these elements in a larger work like Bill McKibben's *Eaarth* or a work of literary journalism like Vladimir Pozner's "Gasoline" presents further challenge.

The Creative Argument takes a rhetorical analysis approach to identifying and explaining relevant principles and strategies of argumentation, which serves to provide both concrete examples of argument strategies as well as specific principles for analyzing and building effective arguments. Each chapter proceeds as the study of an extraordinary published argument—from Gorgias's *Encomium of Helen*, to Malcolm X's "The Ballot or the Bullet," to Jennine Capó Crucet's "What We Pack." Drawing on these examples, the book provides a comprehensive and digestible introduction to argumentation as a process of reasoned decision-making. That is, this book concentrates on a subset of persuasion in which participants agree to exchange reasons for their claims as a way to come to the best possible outcome under the circumstances. Rather than focusing on "winning" or manipulating audiences into agreement, the book presents argumentation as a method of influencing the thoughts and actions of others through the transparent exchange of claims and reasons.

This book is useful to any instructor who wants to emphasize the role of argumentation in writing, whether that is in undergraduate courses in argumentation (in communication studies, English, or writing departments) or a first-year writing course (FYW).

Although it is written as an introductory text—that is, it presumes no prior knowledge of argumentation—this book nevertheless introduces some helpful tools for more advanced work in argumentation and argument. It provides (1) a theory of argumentation, (2) a technical approach to creating and analyzing arguments, and (3) a technical lexicon for talking and writing about argument.

Each chapter provides three Ps: Prime, Pause, and Probe, which are opportunities for students to engage with the text on several levels. Placed at the start of a chapter, before the example text, the Prime is meant to help students activate their prior knowledge so that they read the example text more actively. Some Prime questions simply ask readers to consider how familiar they already are with some concept or context in a given text, while others ask students to take note of some element of the text, drawing on what they already know.

Pause gives students an opportunity for reflection on some major concept introduced in the text, to help students think about the example text like rhetoricians. Situated directly after the example text or at transition points throughout the chapters, Pause asks students to step back from the text and take time to process some of what they read.

Probe asks students to go deeper, to ask questions that have no easy answer but lead to more complex and insightful questions. Open-ended questions situated at the end of each chapter, Probe asks students to explore their understanding of core concepts in each chapter and apply these concepts to new contexts. Probe questions may also be expanded into stand-alone formal writing assignments.

Taken together, the three Ps not only give students opportunities to engage more actively with the text but also can function as formative feedback from students, giving instructors a window into student learning. By reviewing (but not grading) student responses to the three Ps, instructors can learn what students understand, what they seem to be struggling with, what misconceptions they may have, and what opportunities for development exist. To maximize the three Ps as formative feedback, instructors may wish to collect some of these responses anonymously, or to use them as a pre/posttest, soliciting responses to the same question(s) before and after some form of intervention to measure learning.

The textbook is designed to support student learning in a variety of contexts, and toward diverse learning outcomes. Thus, while the chapters do build on one another, especially the early chapters, the book has multiple entry points, allowing instructors to choose varied paths through it, depending on their course goals and outcomes. The instructor manual provides different options for such paths, organized by the type of course. It is available for request at hackettpublishing .com/creative-argument-resources.

The first five chapters of the book introduce the fundamental principles of argumentation as a process of decision-making, drawing on informal logic, outline the basic building blocks of an argument, and demonstrate how these work together to form complex arguments.

Chapters 6 through 8 more directly support the making of arguments, including both how to respond to other arguments and how to use evidence, including visual evidence, to effectively support your claims.

Chapters 9 through 13 foreground six of the most common patterns of inference: arguments from example, comparison or analogy, cause to effect, sign, commonplaces, and form. These chapters provide stellar examples of each of these inference patterns in published works, with analysis following that demonstrates how a given inference pattern governs a particular essay.

The final four chapters introduce validity and fallacies in informal logic, and the three spheres in which argumentation may occur: the personal sphere, the technical sphere, and the public sphere.

One benefit of such an approach, which proceeds from an example of a published argument, is that it teaches students greater flexibility in argumentation. Published examples are more complex and nuanced than examples invented for the purpose of illustration. This greater complexity gives students and teachers more opportunity to both see the various ways a rhetorical device may be used, for example, and gain greater flexibility in strategies of argument. Using published examples makes clear that argumentation is never simply putting ready-made pieces together, but a complex task of identifying and responding to rhetorical situations.

Ultimately *The Creative Argument* teaches students how to draw on principles and practices of argumentation to make compelling, nuanced, and varied arguments, fitted to the demands of the task, time, place (or medium), and audience. The book helps support students to become knowledgeable, agile writers equally at ease writing a policy proposal as they are an autobiographical essay.

Chapter 1
How Arguments Begin

Key Terms

argumentation

audience

uncertainty

controversy

justification

cooperative enterprise

risk

Key Points

- Argumentation is a way of making decisions by providing supporting reasons.
- Argumentation involves providing justification for claims.
- Argumentation is audience-dependent, meaning that an audience must accept claims and their reasons for them to work.
- Argumentation is rooted in uncertainty: we argue only about that which we cannot know for certain.
- Argumentation is a cooperative enterprise.
- Argumentation involves some degree of risk.

PRIME

As you read, consider the decisions you and those close to you had to make as you navigated the college admissions process. What did you tend to base your decisions on?

What We Pack

Jennine Capó Crucet (2019)

It was a simple question, but we couldn't find the answer in any of the paperwork the college had sent: How long was my family supposed to stay for first-year student orientation? This may seem easy enough to answer now, but this was 1999 and Google wasn't yet a verb, and we were a low-income family (according to my new school) without regular internet access. I was the first in my family to go to college, which made me a first-generation college student as well as a first-generation American, because my parents were born in Cuba. We didn't know that families were supposed to leave campus almost immediately after they unloaded your stuff from the car.

Together we made the trip from my hometown of Miami to what would be my new college home in upstate New York. Shortly after arriving on campus, the five of us—both of my parents, my younger sister, my abuela, and me—found ourselves listening to a dean end his welcome speech with the words: "Now, parents, please, go. Your child is in good hands. Time to cut the cord. Go home."

Almost everyone in the audience laughed, but not me, and not my parents. They turned to me and said, "What does he mean, go?" My abuela asked my sister in Spanish, "What? What's he saying?" a new note of panic in her voice because my sister had stopped translating. She didn't know how, exactly, to translate the dean's joke. She turned to me like something was my fault and said, "But orientation's just started." I was just as confused as they were. We thought we all needed to be there for first-year orientation—the whole family, for the whole week. My dad had booked their hotel room until the day after my classes officially began. They'd used all their vacation time from work and had been saving for months to get me to school and go through what we'd thought of as our orientation. This confusion isn't the most common or problematic issue first-generation college students and their families face—not by a long shot—but it shows just how clueless and out of our element we were. Another example: Every afternoon during that week, we had to go back to the only department store we could find, the now defunct Ames, for some stupid thing we hadn't known was a necessity, something not in our budget, things like shower shoes, a bathrobe, a plastic soap holder (we hadn't realized the bathroom situation would be a communal one—in fact, we hadn't thought about the bathroom situation at all), extra-long twin sheets, mesh laundry bags. Before the other families left, we carefully watched them because they looked at ease, like they knew what they were doing, and we made new shopping lists with our limited vocabulary: Those things that lift up the bed, we wrote. That plastic thing to carry stuff to the bathroom.

My family followed me around as I visited department offices during course registration. "Only four classes?" they asked, assuming I was mistakenly taking my first semester too easy. And I'd agreed: Like most high schoolers, I'd taken six classes every year, so four seemed like nothing—this kind of assumption being one of the more common first-generation college student mistakes, one I thankfully didn't make.

They went with me to the campus store to buy my books, and together we learned what the stickers on worn copies promised: Used Saves. They walked me to orientation events they thought they'd also be attending and to buildings I was supposed to be finding on my own. They waited outside those buildings so that we could all leave from there and go to lunch together. The five of us wandered each day through the dining hall's doors. "You guys are still here!" the over-friendly person swiping ID cards said after day three. "They sure are!" I chirped back, learning via the cues of my hallmates that I was supposed to want my family gone. But it was an act: I wanted them there. We sat together at meals—amid all the other students, already making friends—my mom placing a napkin and fork at each seat, setting the table as we did at home.

I don't remember the moment they drove away. I'm told it's one of those instances you never forget, that second when you realize you're finally on your own, a feeling of fear mixed with freedom, and also, I'm told, with relief. But for me, the memory of that moment just doesn't exist—perhaps because, when you're the first in your family to go to college, you never truly feel like you're there on your own.

I'd applied to only two places for college, the University of Florida and Cornell University, because applying to college was (and is) an expensive process, and I didn't know about fee waivers. My decision to apply specifically to Cornell—a choice that would eventually change the course of my life— might as well have occurred randomly. I was waiting in a high school guidance counselor's office for a schedule change as she silently sorted through a pile of college-related junk mail (she wasn't the college counselor, and that year, as far as I knew, my high school didn't have one). When I saw a cover image flash by—that of a tree bursting red with color, in the height of its fall foliage—I blurted out, "What's that one?" and lurched forward to put my hand on top of it, to stop her sorting. She handed it to me as an afterthought, without even looking up, and the rest of the brochures—all these other possible versions of my future—went into her recycling bin. I learned from that viewbook that Cornell was the first of the Ivy League schools to admit women and people of color. I thought that was cool, and that was enough to make me want to try and get accepted (but not necessarily go). This single experience, coming before easy access to the internet, constituted the bulk of my college research process. There was a paper application inside that viewbook, which I would eventually fill out and send off with all the other pieces of information Cornell required, including an application fee.

By some measures, most of them financial, my choice to attend Cornell was not a smart one. And when I say "my," I mean "me and my entire family," because the decision never felt wholly my own to make, as I understood that my choice would impact my parents' lives in drastic ways none of us could fully anticipate. What I did know was that, thanks to my good grades and various state initiatives meant to entice students to stay in the state for college, I had an excellent financial aid package from the University of Florida (UF): full tuition, room and board covered, the additional scholarships I'd earned through other channels all landing in my pocket to cover books and other expenses. I could afford to have a car. I could come home on weekends if I wanted. I was about to be the first in my family to go to college, and it wouldn't cost us a cent. Thanks to rolling admissions, I knew by October that I'd been admitted, and by November, I was stockpiling Gator paraphernalia. Then, in April, I got into Cornell. I now know that their financial aid package was also strong, but it didn't feel that way then: There was a subsidized loan of four thousand a year that was in my name, and in addition to that, there was an "expected family contribution" (or EFC) of a few thousand dollars—a gap in my aid package that my parents were expected to cover and that could (and would) change each year.

The questions for us became: Did I need to go to the more expensive school? Would it really make a tangible difference in my life? I had the privilege of supportive parents who, while they definitely wanted me closer to home, had been convinced by both me and the school trying to recruit me that going to Cornell was an investment in a future that—though we couldn't quite picture it—we somehow intuited we'd be foolish to pass up. We didn't know what exactly we were investing in, only that the result of this investment was whoever I was going to be. I look back on it now and cannot believe what I did to my parents: They remortgaged their home, which they'd already paid off (hence the financial aid office seeing it as a resource they could tap) to cover what Cornell calculated they could afford.

Recently I called my mom in Miami to ask her why in the end they agreed to let me turn down a free ride to UF.

"Don't you remember?" she said. "We went to that Cornell recruitment thing at that man's house in Coral Gables. He was a lawyer or something. Me and your father couldn't sleep that night. We were talking, thinking, okay, we're two stupid people—not stupid, you know what I mean—and these people, they were just . . . we wanted that for you, for you to have all that, be all that."

"But isn't that wrong, the way that event made you feel? Wasn't that manipulative?"

"Of course it was! That's how the world works! You know that," she said.

I only remember the inside of that house in Coral Gables (which is one of the Miami area's wealthiest neighborhoods, and which is in fact its own city). The host had a whole room in his house just for his family's books—a room I now know is called a study—and jutting out from one of the built-in bookshelves was a desk, and on top of that was the family's computer. He'd used the internet to pull up that morning's issue of the *Cornell Daily Sun*, the campus newspaper. He'd let me sit at the desk and read it while the rest of the house hummed with laughing and talking. And floating just under the talking, classical music, which emanated from speakers I couldn't see, only feel. I remember looking around, trying and failing to find them.

I couldn't understand back then that attending Cornell would plug me into a kind of access and privilege I didn't yet have a name for. But my parents, having worked trade jobs their whole lives, knew better.

My mother said, "Do you really think you'd be where you are now if you'd gone to UF?"

I can't say where I'd be had I not asked a bored counselor to hand me a brochure she was about to throw away. All I can possibly know is where I am now, which is far from home, living dependent free, in a landlocked state, writing books and working as a newly tenured professor at a Big Ten school in a city where I am related to absolutely no one. My best friend from high school, who graduated second in our class and was supposed to be my Gator roommate, went to UF and loved it.

She finished a semester early, married her high school boyfriend, and has two gorgeous children and an amazing house. She has rewarding friendships (she's substituted me as her BFF with a woman whose life on Instagram looks equally amazing—by which I mean she seems to own a boat). She has a fulfilling career. She has a loving relationship with her parents and sees them all the time. There is no "but" here.

At Cornell, the woman in the dorm room next to mine was from Iowa, from a family of pig farmers; she'd almost gone to the University of Iowa instead of Cornell. She ended up transferring there after our first year. As she put it, she just didn't need Cornell (and its accompanying price tag) for what she wanted to do with her future, though I'm sure there was more to it than that. The girls in my hall—myself included, all of us from the East Coast—teased her mercilessly for being from Iowa and for coming from a pig farming background, behavior of which I am now ashamed. (At the Lincoln farmers' market, there is always a vendor selling a T-shirt that says IOWA HAS BAD CORN, and I think that might be the meanest it gets out here when it comes to teasing people from Iowa. Also, the irony of the fact that I recently needed to take a class in Omaha on half-hog butchery—to write a compelling, believable scene for a new short story set in Miami—just to learn things my former hallmate likely came to college already knowing is not lost on me.) A year away showed her what she actually needed from her college experience, and when she chose to transfer, I couldn't help but think she'd outsmarted a system into which I'd naively fallen without a firm sense of what to expect or demand from it.

What I still find remarkable is that a decision I made at seventeen, with very little information or guidance, has gone on to shape my entire life. Maybe this feels remarkable to me because it's a lasting characteristic of the first-gen college student identity, which can carry with it the knowledge of a shadow life, one where you're equally happy having done something or gone somewhere else. Or maybe the decision still feels astonishing to me because I initially chose to attend a completely different university, its two biggest draws being that it was essentially free and that my best friend would be there—two reasons that seemed good to me and to my family, in part because none of us knew what we could or should expect from the college experience. Perhaps what needs the most consideration when college commitments are being made is not which college, but what you feel you need from a school, and that's a tricky set of qualities to recognize (and an even trickier thing to trust) when you're the first in your family to set off down that path. When I walked around UF's campus, a visit I made with my mom after having already tentatively committed to the school, I didn't feel anything, except some vague unease. I couldn't explain it, and I'm glad I didn't rationalize it away.

I'm glad my parents didn't ask me to try to articulate what, exactly, felt wrong for me about the place.

They were teaching me to trust my gut.

I don't know why UF didn't feel like the right college home for me, but that feeling was strong enough to make me sign on for some major financial commitments at a school more than a thousand miles away at the ripe old age of eighteen, a school that may not have been right for me either, but which felt more right than my other option. I want to be clear: Debt was not something I took on lightly, and it would probably be harder for me to make the same decision today that I made in 1999, with the amount of debt feeling even more insurmountable because of fears about what the job market would look like when I finished. And excellent opportunities abound at public universities across the United States (I teach at one now, and I have amazing students who I know will go on to change the world). But at that Cornell recruitment reception, there was this vague promise being held out to me, to my family—not just of economic opportunity, but of the opportunity to transcend the limits of my imagination about who I might someday be. But only the economic one was visible from the minute we drove into that neighborhood to meet other students admitted to Cornell, many of them from private high schools, many of them seeing the financial aid as irrelevant to their decision: They'd be paying most if not all of the cost anywhere they went. For them, whatever came next was worth that cost, and that was the promise my family and I could recognize and want for ourselves.

A promise is not the same as a guarantee, but we couldn't yet tell the difference.

When I started high school, my mother took me to the orthodontist. I had inherited my parents' jacked-up teeth, and at the time when most of my friends were getting their braces removed, we were there to potentially start the whole ordeal, finally in an economic position that let us take on the debt of braces. After poking around in my mouth and taking impressions of my teeth, the orthodontist declared that I did not need braces—my bite was a little off but mostly fine, so braces weren't necessary; they'd be purely for cosmetic reasons.

Because we'd already identified ourselves as the kind of people who would need help affording orthodontics, the doctor thought this news would come as a relief to my mother. It did not. She started crying, and I was confused. (I was fourteen and happy to hear I could dodge the discomfort my friends had endured.)

"If she needed them, it would be easier in my head to pay for it," she said. "Everyone is getting braces, someday they'll all be people with straight teeth. I don't want her to have crooked teeth when she's thirty." She pointed toward her own mouth.

My mother wanted to give me an advantage she never had, and this desire in and of itself counts as a need. Yes, it was rooted in unfairness—in her knowledge that people would make assumptions about me based on something superficial—but it was too deep in her gut to ignore. She needed to be someone who could give her daughter this gift.

I should mention that my mother has a beautiful, almost perfect smile. Her own braces came as an adult, after a car accident pushed all her teeth in. I never really noticed they were still a little crooked, though now that we live far from each other, it's something that, when I first see her after months apart, I can't help but notice.

My braces came off my junior year. I am in my thirties now and still sometimes wear my top retainer: I grind my teeth in my sleep, unconsciously undoing the work of making them straight. The bottom retainer no longer fits at all because I lost it for a couple of years, and when I found it in a move and went to pop it in, my teeth had already shifted too much, perhaps because of the wisdom tooth still in my lower jaw (though I hear that's a myth), or maybe the nail-biting I can't curtail, or perhaps just time. In fact, my bottom teeth are almost back to where they started despite those braces.

What a waste of all that metal, that pain, and that work. With that gift came the commitment to honor and maintain it, and perhaps because I was the first in my family to have such a gift, I didn't know that things never stop shifting, that getting the chance at something better doesn't automatically guarantee it.

A couple of weeks into my first semester of classes at Cornell, after my parents finally abandoned me far above Cayuga's waters, I received the topics for what would be my first college paper, in an English course on the modern novel. I might as well have been my abuela trying to read and understand them; the language felt that foreign. I called my mom at work and in tears told her that I had to come home, that I'd made a terrible mistake, that I should've gone to UF, where everyone seemed to be having a lot more fun than I was.

She sighed into the phone. I heard the chatter of her two-way radio behind her, electricians asking questions about permits and supply deliveries, asking my mom (who the workers called Base, since she worked from an office) for updates. She turned down the volume and said, "Just read me the first question. We'll go through it a little at a time and figure it out."

I read her the topics slowly, pausing after each sentence, waiting for her to say something, just an mmhmm or the conversational throw-me-a-bone of okay. The first topic was two paragraphs long. I remember it had the word *intersectionalities* in it. And the word *gendered*. I waited for her response and for the ways it would encourage me, for her to tell me I could do this, but I knew from my mother's total silence that, like me, she'd never before heard these words: my first insight into how access to certain vocabularies was a kind of privilege.

Of course, I didn't know to call this privilege, not yet.

"You're right," my mother said after a moment. "You're screwed."

Parents who've gone to college themselves know that at this point they should encourage their kid to go to office hours, or to the writing center, or to ask the professor or a TA for clarification—that it's not just a student's right but their responsibility as budding scholars to do so. But my mom thought I was as on my own as I feared. While my college had done an excellent job recruiting me, I had no blueprint or road map for what I was supposed to do once I made it to campus, how I was going to spend the next four years. I'd already embarrassed myself by doing things like asking my RA what time the dorm closed for the night. As far as I knew, there'd been no mandatory meeting geared toward first-generation students like me. Aside from a check-in with my financial aid officer, where she explained what work-study was (I didn't know and worried it meant I had to join the army or something) and where she had me sign for my loan, I'd been mostly keeping to myself to hide the fact that I was a very special kind of lost: What seemed obvious to many students left me flailing. This was a feeling shared by my parents, who had no idea what they were supposed to say, who couldn't suggest I just come home for the weekend, and who didn't know to offer solutions that seemed obvious to people who've been to college themselves. This, too, is a kind of privilege: the resource of people—people who love you—who have navigated a version of the very system you are now navigating.

"I mean, I literally have no idea what any of that means," my mom said. "I don't even know how it's a question."

I folded the sheet with the paper topics in half and put it in my desk drawer.

"I don't know what you're gonna do," my mom almost laughed. "Maybe— have you looked in the dictionary?"

I started crying harder, my hand over the receiver.

"You still there?" she eventually asked.

I murmured, "Mmhmm."

"Look, just stick it out up there until Christmas," she said. "We have no more vacation days this year. We can't take off any more time to go get you."

"Okay," I swallowed (my OK having that sharp *a*, a still present relic of my Miami accent that only okay, on the page, accurately represents). I started breathing in through my nose and out through my mouth, calming myself. "I can do that," I said.

My mom laughed for real this time and said, "Mamita, you don't really have a choice."

She didn't say this in a mean way. She was just telling me the truth. "This whole thing was your idea, remember?"

It sounded almost like a threat—and there it was: the beginning of a kind of resentment many first-generation college students come to know, one born from our families' frustrations at no longer knowing how to help us. Yes, it had been my idea. I'd argued with them that going away to Cornell would be the best thing for the whole family in the long run, but none of us could predict how vast the distance would come to feel, how it would move me into a different class of people—out of the class that had forged me—and that this shift would remain a painful source of tension from that moment on.

The racket of radios started up again—so much static and screaming— and my mom told me she had to go, that she needed to get back to work.

So I got back to work, too, and Get back to work became a sort of mantra for me. I tackled the paper with the same focus that had landed me at Cornell in the first place. I did okay on it, earning a B-/C (I never found out how a grade could have a slash in it, but now that I'm an English professor I understand perfectly what he meant with that grade). The professor had covered the typed pages with handwritten comments and questions, which I took as a bad thing rather than as a sign of his engagement with my work and the kind of attention my tuition dollars were affording me, and so I never followed up with him about my paper as I should have. It was in his endnote (the first one I had ever received in my academic career, looking like its own small essay) where he listed the various campus resources available to me—the writing center, his office hours—that I first learned of their existence.

My mom didn't ask outright what grade I earned on the paper. She eventually stopped asking about assignments altogether. And I learned from my peers that grades were something I didn't have to share with my parents the way I had in high school. My report card had transformed into a transcript, a euphemism I'd deploy in December when my mom asked when my school would be sending her the former.

My grades were the first of many elements of my new life for which they had no context. With each passing semester, what I was doing became, for them, as indecipherable as that paper topic.

They didn't even know what questions to ask, which is also the quintessential condition of the first-generation college student experience—though I wouldn't begin to understand this until long after I'd earned my degree. The question my parents were really asking when they wondered if I "needed" to go to the more expensive school was: Which option has the potential to open the most doors, and how much can we afford to hope she'll walk through them? It's a more complex question. And they knew more than I did that there wasn't a straightforward answer, in part because of the word *potential*, which acknowledges the lack of guarantees, and in part because the answer depended on what I'd make out of whichever version of my education we bought into. My college education eventually taught me to pursue harder, more complex questions, that asking harder questions is one of the most important things a person can do. I was learning, with each seemingly more baffling paper topic, how to think critically—a skill I use on itself, to ask whether or not I could've learned it just as thoroughly without going into debt.

My parents know for a fact that going to the more expensive school was the best investment they ever made in me. But I can admit that I'll never know for sure. And I know enough to recognize my ambivalence as a sign that perhaps proves them right.

Introduction

If you just picked up this book—maybe it is your first reading assignment in a class on argumentation or academic writing—you may be surprised at this choice in an opening text: a personal essay about going away to an elite university in the Northeast as a first-generation Cuban American college student from Miami.

For one thing, the essay is about the personal experience of a "regular" person (though Capó Crucet is a professor as she writes it, she is drawing mostly on her experience as a student), uses "I," and does not seem to be about big ideas like politics or religion. In short, it doesn't match what we typically think of when we think of arguments and argumentation.

Where are the furious declarations of who's right and who's wrong? Where are the barbed remarks, the attacks, where is the vitriol?

Well, perhaps you don't see the state of argumentation in the United States as all that bad. But even still, this might hardly seem like an argument.

Despite what you may have seen on daytime TV talk shows or viral social media videos, or even on political debate stages, argumentation is not about getting your way or proving someone else wrong. Instead, **argumentation** is a two-thousand-year-old tradition of reasoned decision-making. We use argumentation to make decisions when we're not quite sure about how we should understand something or what we should do.

> Argumentation is a way of making decisions when we can't be certain about the outcomes.

So if we want to see whether or not this is a good example of an argument, let's start there. Is Capó Crucet's essay meant to help anyone make a decision? If so, whom, and how?

Certainly, Capó Crucet is talking about a decision she and her family made when she was a high school senior—to attend the more expensive Cornell University over the University of Florida closer to home. Lots of high school students and their families must make similar decisions every year. And so, it is reasonable to think the essay might help someone reading the piece in a similar situation make their own decision.

What if someone picks up this book, reads Capó Crucet's piece, and thinks, "Well, she went to an Ivy League university out of state, so that's what I'm going to do too"? Does that mean this is an argument? The article did seem to influence that reader's decision. If you see a commercial with your favorite athlete eating some brand of cereal, you may be influenced to buy that cereal too, but is that the result of argumentation? Is it an example of reasoned decision-making? Probably not. Being influenced by what someone says or does is not the same thing as coming to a conclusion based on reasoned decision-making.

The Basic Characteristics of Argumentation

Argumentation is a process of reasoned decision-making, so let's take a look at what that process looks like, starting with the basic characteristics of argumentation.

When we talk about argumentation as a means of decision-making, we proceed from five related characteristics.

1. Audience
2. Uncertainty
3. Justification for claims
4. Cooperation
5. Risk

These characteristics are the topic of this chapter. If these five characteristics are present, then we are talking about argumentation, but if not, then we have something else.

Here's a simple example, before we get back to Capó Crucet. Let's say you and your friends want to see a movie this Friday night but can't decide which one. Most of you want to watch the new Tarantino film, which just came out on Netflix, but one of your friends says that Tarantino is derivative and flashy, privileging style over story (your friend is a bit over the top).

Let's apply the five characteristics of argumentation to this example one by one, to see if you and your friends are engaged in argumentation.

Audience

We start with **audience**. The twentieth-century rhetorician Chaïm Perelman defines audience as "the gathering of those whom the speaker wants to influence by his or her arguments." For me, the word that stands out in this definition is *gathering*. That's a strange word in this context. So why does Perelman use it?

Gathering implies an action on the part of the speaker or writer. We tend to think of audience as the people in front of us when we speak—independent of what it is we are saying. Audience is just whoever happens to be there when we talk or whoever reads what we have written. But there are several reasons why this doesn't work. For one, when we make an argument we tend to have a purpose, something we want people to accept, and not everyone sitting in front of you or reading your work has the potential to be moved by your words. Some people may be dead set against you from the start, and no amount of reasoning will change their minds. Others may be 100 percent behind you from the start, and so don't need to hear the argument you're making. Others still may not be paying much attention, or unable to understand. If you start putting together your argument trying to influence each of these groups equally, you'll be in a difficult position. It's inadvisable to try to reach everyone in front of you, or everyone picking up your work, if you know you have no chance of changing their minds or affecting their attitudes.

Rather, you want to target your work to those who have the potential to be influenced by it; you want to move them into a space where they are actively considering your claims and evidence, willing to change their minds if compelled to. So when Perelman uses the word *gathering*, then, he is implying this action on the part of the writer or speaker—that they are actively working to select or build their audience.

This implies something very important about argumentation: when we argue, we are not dealing with universal truths (something we'll take up again in the next characteristic of argumentation, uncertainty). If we were, our audience would always be everyone, because universal truths by definition affect everyone equally. Instead, our arguments are subject to the willing acceptance of an audience. It is the audience who decides whether or not our arguments have merit, whether or not they should be accepted.

> Argumentation does not lead to universal truths, but rather beliefs that are willingly accepted by an audience. The knowledge produced by argumentation, whether it is what is the best policy to adopt or how we should understand some historical event, is always subject to change and reinterpretation.

However, audience acceptance does not mean that every argument is as good as another. If you are making the case that the moon is made of green cheese to a group of first graders and many of them believe you, that does not mean you have made a good argument. There are many standards and values dictating what the qualities of good arguments are, based on a two-thousand-year-old tradition of testing and discussion.

To go back to our example, most of your friends already want to see the same movie. Chances are, the one friend who doesn't like Tarantino is willing to be convinced, because they have already suggested they want to see a movie with you all, and they haven't yet left. So, in this case, they would be the only person you want to influence with your arguments. They are your audience.

To make your arguments to your other friends, the ones who want to see the same film as you, is not an effective use of time, because they already agree with you—it's preaching to the choir.

> Who is Capó Crucet's audience? Whose thoughts or actions is she trying to influence?

Instead, you should direct your arguments to the friend who doesn't quite see things your way, but who is willing to engage in further conversation about it.

Uncertainty

If you had all agreed from the start to watch the same movie, then there would be no need for an argument. You would just pull it up on Netflix and press play. It is only because one of your friends disagreed with the decision to see the Tarantino movie that the discussion about which movie to see continues. As a group, you are not certain which movie you will watch. We argue, therefore, about things about which we are uncertain.

Uncertainty, as a characteristic of argumentation, is the recognition that some decision must be made, but multiple decisions are possible. If we knew with certainty what the outcome would be—whether because we all agree ahead of time or because we are not in a position to make a decision, or for some other reason—then argumentation would be unlikely. We typically engage in argumentation only when we are unsure about the outcome.

Uncertainty also implies that things could be otherwise. We are in the realm of what Aristotle called the possible (*to dynaton*). No matter the outcome, we recognize that it could be otherwise. If we end up agreeing that we will watch the Tarantino film, it is with the understanding that other possibilities exist, and vice versa. This is important because it emphasizes that arguments are never universal, never complete. Even when we come to agreement, it does not mean we won't have the same disagreement in the future, in light of new evidence, for example.

Because we don't know how the argument will turn out, and we don't know what the best decision is in a given situation, the audience is asked to make a jump from what we agree we know to what cannot be known for sure. In our simple case, all the friends are being asked to agree, without having seen it, that the Tarantino film is the best one to see that night, based on any arguments you make with evidence drawn from his previous films, even though it cannot be known for certain that they will enjoy that film, or that they would not enjoy another film more.

> We engage in argumentation under conditions of uncertainty, when we aren't sure how something will turn out.

When such a difference of opinion exists among participants in some discussion, the technical term for this is *controversy*. A **controversy** is a genuine difference of opinion that matters to the participants and that they wish to see resolved. Often, controversies are presented as questions that have no clear and immediate resolution.

In our example case, not all of you agree about which movie to see, which is a difference of opinion responding to the question, "Which movie should we see tonight?" Those of you involved in the discussion care about which movie you will see, and you want to agree so that you can go to the movies. So we have a controversy.

Justification for Claims

Because we are asking something of our audience, we must give them reasons for doing so. We are essentially providing **justification** for our claims, a rationale for accepting a claim that is inherently uncertain.

We know now that argumentation is audience-dependent. Therefore, a claim is considered justified when the reasons provided are acceptable to a reasonable person exercising critical judgment—one open to agreeing or disagreeing depending on the reasons presented.

Justification is not proof, though you may have frequently been told you must prove your claims. We will talk more about proof when we talk about the distinction between formal and informal argumentation in Chapter 2. For now, it is enough to remind you that, because arguments are audience-dependent and uncertain, they can never be proven in a final way.

Justification is subjective, dependent on the acceptance of a particular audience. One audience can accept a set of arguments, while another may reject it.

Justification is also provisional. The same audience may accept an argument one day and then reject it the next (or vice versa), as they become aware of new arguments.

Finally, justification varies in degree of strength; an audience may find your reasons merely plausible, highly probable, or somewhere in between. Again, no matter how probable some justification may appear, it is never certain.

All these elements of justification apply to our situation if you and your friend continue to give reasons for your preferences. If your friend who doesn't like Tarantino were simply to have said they don't like him and that's that, it would be unlikely for an argument to proceed, because they are not offering any justification for claims. But because they gave reasons for not liking Tarantino (derivative, style over story), they show a willingness to provide justification, and because they remain involved in the discussion, they imply a willingness to hear reasons for your own claims that run counter to theirs.

Cooperative Enterprise

This willingness to hear claims and reasons that differ from your own point of view is another basic characteristic of argumentation. Argumentation is a **cooperative enterprise**. This means that, unlike the popular notion of arguments as a kind of fighting with words, true arguments always begin with a foundation of agreement. Before you can begin an argument with someone, you have to agree on all kinds of things—that you have a disagreement to work out, that you want to work it out using reasons and not force, and that you share a common goal of reaching the best possible decision under the circumstances. These agreements are typically made implicitly—they go without saying—but it's hard to have an argument without them.

In our example case, you and your friends have agreed to discuss which movie to see, and to accept the decision the group makes. All arguments also, at minimum, share a frame of reference, some level of agreement on which their disagreement is built, a common language and mostly agreed-upon definitions, procedural assumptions and expectations such as what counts as evidence, and a common set of values such as respect for the audience.

Even when each participant in the argument wants to "win," to persuade the other of their opinion, as long as they are willing to accept the outcome of the debate, they are still engaged in a cooperative enterprise. In fact, many scholars of argumentation believe that the adversarial elements of argument—the desire of opposing debaters to win the argument—are a way to achieve the common goal of the best possible decision. When we have a stake in the outcome we are motivated to make the best possible argument we can, and so we work harder to identify critical pieces of evidence and try to make the most compelling claims. Also, when an audience knows that the people involved in an argument are all trying to make the best argument they can, they are more confident in the outcome. Think about it this way: if you are arm wrestling your cousin and it's clear you let them win, no one watching will really believe your cousin is stronger than you. But if it's clear you both tried your hardest, then people will likely believe that the winner of that contest is the stronger.

Similarly, if your friend really does not want to see the Tarantino film, they will try to make as strong a case against it as they can, and so we are likely to hear many of the most relevant and strongest arguments against seeing the film, just as you are more likely to make relevant and strong arguments for seeing the film to the extent that you genuinely want to see it. And if in the end your friend is convinced to watch it despite their unwillingness at the start of the discussion, then there is more confidence among you and your friends that you have made the right decision, because if the decision was in the end endorsed by so contrary a friend, then the decision must be a good one.

Risk

Arguments also carry an element of **risk**. For one, you risk being shown to be wrong. Some people—people who value learning and inquiry—don't mind being wrong. The biologist Stuart Firestein says he welcomes it, because being wrong leads to new questions, opportunities to create new knowledge, while being right just confirms what he already knows. But for most of us, especially in everyday situations, being wrong is uncomfortable.

You have to believe the argument is worth having given the risks associated with it. Again, because arguments are audience-dependent, you can never be sure of what the outcome of any given argument will be. You may be highly confident in the argument you are making, but you still may lose.

All arguments, when engaged with genuine openness, present risks to the participants of being shown to be wrong. If you go into an argument as a means of decision-making, rather than just winning at all costs, then you must accept the possibility that the audience will choose a position other than the one you argue for. If you are truly open to the argument, you also have to accept the risk of having to change your mind—hard as that may be.

So, perhaps you present your best arguments to your friend, but your friend likewise makes some excellent arguments and gives you some things to think about that hadn't occurred to you before. Or perhaps someone else steps in and brings up something about one of Tarantino's films or about the director himself that you didn't know about, or else raises the possibility that a comedy would be more fun to watch as a group. Because the outcome of an argument is always uncertain, there is always the possibility that you may have to change your mind.

While the possibility that you may have to change your mind may appear risky under certain circumstances (think about when changing your mind would imply changing the way you've always thought of yourself, or losing face among your friends, or having to go back to square one on a research project), this openness to changing one's mind is also one of the greatest opportunities of argumentation, because it allows us to discover truths we didn't have available to us before. This is the great power of argumentation, and why it is at the center of any democratic institution.

> **PAUSE**
>
> Take five minutes to remember a recent argument you have been involved in, and consider whether or not it meets the five conditions of argumentation: audience, uncertainty, justification for claims, cooperation, and risk.

Argumentation in Capó Crucet

Capó Crucet's piece is not a typical argument, so much so that it might not even seem like an argument to you upon first reading it. Maybe it just seems like she's

sharing her experience. When we consider the extent to which the basic characteristics of argumentation apply here, though, we see that she is indeed making
an argument, even though it's not a simple one.

Characteristic of Argumentation	Questions to Consider	Possible Answers
Audience	Who is Capó Crucet's audience? Whose thoughts or actions is she attempting to influence?	High school students considering where to go to college? Their parents? Her own parents? Herself? The general public?
Uncertainty	What decision(s) is the audience being asked to make? What are the potential options?	Which college to attend? Which college was right for Capó Crucet to have attended? What is the value of a college education? Do Ivy League schools deserve their elite status? What does success look like?
Justification for claims	What reasons does Capó Crucet provide in her essay? Is she telling us a story just to tell us a story, or as insight into an experience that might help us make some decision?	Capó Crucet's parents' reasons for supporting her decisions? Capó Crucet's own reasons, at the time and looking back? Capó Crucet's analysis of the value of college education?
Cooperation	What evidence is there in Capó Crucet's essay that she values the opinions of her audience? What common ground does she appear to point to?	The complexity of Capó Crucet's personal story? The experience of whether or not to attend college, or which college to attend, which may be shared with many of her readers? The common stake we all have in higher education?
Risk	Does Capó Crucet seem vulnerable at all in this essay? What risks does she appear to be taking?	Being shown to be wrong? Having her personal experience dismissed? Recognizing that she made a wrong decision? Alienating readers to whom she might be close, or whose opinions she cares about?

Looking across these categories, it seems unlikely that Capó Crucet is making an argument about whether or not someone should attend Cornell University, or whether Ivy League schools do or do not deserve their elite status. If she were doing that, she'd be providing different kinds of reasons, like the economic outlook for graduates of these institutions, for example. I don't think she's making an argument about whether or not Cornell was the right choice for her, because it's not clear why her audience would be interested in such a limited question. Rather, using her personal experience as evidence (something we'll consider further in Chapter 7), she seems to be asking us to consider what it is exclusive universities like Cornell are selling, particularly to first-generation college students. Implicitly, she's also asking us to consider the ethics of such a sales pitch.

Conclusion

It's hard to overlook the negative connotation the word *argument* carries in everyday usage—argument is often seen as something we should avoid. Maybe you're thinking that, because of this negative connotation, we should use different words, like debate, or reasoning, or dialogue. I've decided to use argument in this book for a couple of reasons. For one, this book is meant to introduce you not just to the concept of and strategies for effective argumentation but to a scholarly field as well. The technical language a scholarly field uses is an important part of learning about that field, and how to participate in that field. Argument and argumentation are the technical terms used in the field, so I've decided to use them as well.

The other reason I choose to use the words *argument* and *argumentation* throughout this book is that I think there is a problem in thinking of argument as a bad thing. When we think of argument as a bad thing, we tend to avoid some pretty necessary and often interesting conversations. How many of you grew up with rules—spoken or unspoken—about bringing up arguments at holiday gatherings? How many of you were asked to avoid bringing up politics or religion at the Thanksgiving table (or climate change, the theme of the essay in Chapter 6, "Attack and Defense")? The justification for avoiding these conversations is understandable: they can lead to shouting, or hurt feelings, or alienation between family and friends. My hunch, though, and the arguments of scholars such as Patricia Roberts-Miller, is that it's not having the conversations that leads to these negative outcomes but rather not knowing how to have the conversations in a productive way. When we enter into argumentation as a type of problem-solving through discussion, when we enter it as a cooperative enterprise, provide reasons for our claims, and are willing to take the risks that the uncertainty of audience acceptance presents, then argumentation makes things better. This book isn't a primer on how to engage in arguments with family and friends productively—there are other books out there on that. But I expect as you read this book, read and write arguments, and participate in productive discussions, you'll start to see the elements of argumentation in your everyday life more and more. You'll also likely see where someone is trying to pass off something as an argument, even when it really isn't. Noticing these things will not only make you a better arguer, but it will raise the standard of argument you're willing to accept.

PROBE

Consider the five conditions of argumentation in Capó Crucet. You may use the table above as a resource.

Chapter 2
Formal Logic and Its Limits

Key Terms

encomium

formal logic

deductive reasoning

premises

conclusion

analytic logic

syllogism

categorical syllogism

disjunctive syllogism

disjunct

conditional syllogism

antecedent

consequent

Key Points

- Formal logic proceeds with certainty, draws conclusions that contain no new information, and needs no reference to the outside world.
- The most common form of deductive logic is the syllogism, and three common types of syllogism are the categorical, the disjunctive, and the conditional.
- Each type of syllogism has a shortcut for determining validity.
- Informal logic is the basis of most everyday arguments.

PRIME

As you read, underline anything in Gorgias's speech that is even a little bit familiar to you—for example, any names, places, events, and so on, that you've heard before, even if in a different context.

Encomium of Helen

Gorgias of Leontini (5th Century BCE)

[1] What is becoming to a city is manpower, to a body beauty, to a soul wisdom, to an action virtue, to a speech truth, and the opposites of these are unbecoming. Man and woman and speech and deed and city and object should be honored with praise if praiseworthy and incur blame if unworthy, for it is an equal error and mistake to blame the praisable and to praise the blamable. [2] It is the duty of one and the same man both to speak the needful rightly and to refute [the unrightfully spoken. Thus it is right to refute] those who rebuke Helen, a woman about whom the testimony of inspired poets has become univocal and unanimous as had the ill omen of her name, which has become a reminder of misfortunes. For my part, by introducing some reasoning into my speech, I wish to free the accused of blame and, having reproved her detractors as prevaricators and proved the truth, to free her from their ignorance.

[3] Now it is not unclear, not even to a few, that in nature and in blood the woman who is the subject of this speech is preeminent among preeminent men and women. For it is clear that her mother was Leda, and her father was in fact a god, Zeus, but allegedly a mortal, Tyndareus, of whom the former was shown to be her father because he was and the latter was disproved because he was said to be, and the one was the most powerful of men and the other the lord of all.

[4] Born from such stock, she had godlike beauty, which taking and not mistaking, she kept. In many did she work much desire for her love, and her one body was the cause of bringing together many bodies of men thinking great thoughts for great goals, of whom some had greatness of wealth, some the glory of ancient nobility, some the vigor of personal agility, some command of acquired knowledge. And all came because of a passion which loved to conquer and a love of honor which was unconquered. [5] Who it was and why and how he sailed away, taking Helen as his love, I shall not say. To tell the knowing what they know shows it is right but brings no delight. Having now gone beyond the time once set for my speech, I shall go on to the beginning of my future speech, and I shall set forth the causes through which it was likely that Helen's voyage to Troy should take place.

[6] For either by will of Fate and decision of the gods and vote of Necessity did she do what she did, or by force reduced or by words seduced [or by love possessed]. Now if through the first, it is right for the responsible one to be held responsible; for god's predetermination cannot be hindered by human

premeditation. For it is the nature of things, not for the strong to be hindered by the weak, but for the weaker to be ruled and drawn by the stronger, and for the stronger to lead and the weaker to follow. God is a stronger force than man in might and in wit and in other ways. If then one must place blame on Fate and on a god, one must free Helen from disgrace.

[7] But if she was raped by violence and illegally assaulted and unjustly insulted, it is clear that the raper, as the insulter, did the wronging, and the raped, as the insulted, did the suffering. It is right then for the barbarian who undertook a barbaric undertaking in word and law and deed to meet with blame in word, exclusion in law, and punishment in deed. And surely it is proper for a woman raped and robbed of her country and deprived of her friends to be pitied rather than pilloried. He did the dread deeds; she suffered them. It is just therefore to pity her but to hate him.

[8] But if it was speech which persuaded her and deceived her heart, not even to this is it difficult to make an answer and to banish blame as follows. Speech is a powerful lord, which by means of the finest and most invisible body effects the divinest works: it can stop fear and banish grief and create joy and nurture pity. I shall show how this is the case, since it is necessary to offer proof to the opinion of my hearers: I both deem and define all poetry as speech with meter. [9] Fearful shuddering and tearful pity and grievous longing come upon its hearers, and at the actions and physical sufferings of others in good fortunes and in evil fortunes, through the agency of words, the soul is wont to experience a suffering of its own. But come, I shall turn from one argument to another. [10] Sacred incantations sung with words are bearers of pleasure and banishers of pain, for, merging with opinion in the soul, the power of the incantation is wont to beguile it and persuade it and alter it by witchcraft. There have been discovered two arts of witchcraft and magic: one consists of errors of soul and the other of deceptions of opinion. [11] All who have and do persuade people of things do so by molding a false argument. For if all men on all subjects had [both] memory of things past and [awareness] of things present and foreknowledge of the future, speech would not be similarly similar, since as things are now it is not easy for them to recall the past nor to consider the present nor to predict the future. So that on most subjects most men take opinion as counselor to their soul, but since opinion is slippery and insecure it casts those employing it into slippery and insecure successes. [12] What cause then prevents the conclusion that Helen similarly, against her will, might have come under the influence of speech, just as if ravished by the force of the mighty? For it was possible to see how the force of persuasion prevails; persuasion has the form of necessity, but it does not have the same power. For speech constrained the soul, persuading it which it persuaded, both to believe the things said and to approve the things done. The persuader,

like a constrainer, does the wrong and the persuaded, like the constrained, in speech is wrongly charged. [13] To understand that persuasion, when added to speech, is wont also to impress the soul as it wishes, one must study: first, the words of astronomers who, substituting opinion for opinion, taking away one but creating another, make what is incredible and unclear seem true to the eyes of opinion; then, second, logically necessary debates in which a single speech, written with art but not spoken with truth, bends a great crowd and persuades; [and] third, the verbal disputes of philosophers in which the swiftness of thought is also shown making the belief in an opinion subject to easy change. [14] The effect of speech upon the condition of the soul is comparable to the power of drugs over the nature of bodies. For just as different drugs dispel different secretions from the body, and some bring an end to disease and others to life, so also in the case of speeches, some distress, others delight, some cause fear, others make the hearers bold, and some drug and bewitch the soul with a kind of evil persuasion.

[15] It has been explained that if she was persuaded by speech she did not do wrong but was unfortunate. I shall discuss the fourth cause in a fourth passage. For if it was love which did all these things, there will be no difficulty in escaping the charge of the sin which is alleged to have taken place. For the things we see do not have the nature which we wish them to have, but the nature which each actually has. Through sight the soul receives an impression even in its inner features. [16] When belligerents in war buckle on their warlike accoutrements of bronze and steel, some designed for defense, others for offense, if the sight sees this, immediately it is alarmed and it alarms the soul, so that often men flee, panic-stricken, from future danger [as though it were] present. For strong as is the habit of obedience to the law, it is ejected by fear resulting from sight, which coming to a man causes him to be indifferent both to what is judged honorable because of the law and to the advantage to be derived from victory. [17] It has happened that people, after having seen frightening sights, have also lost presence of mind for the present moment; in this way fear extinguishes and excludes thought. And many have fallen victim to useless labor and dread diseases and hardly curable madnesses. In this way the sight engraves upon the mind images of things which have been seen. And many frightening impressions linger, and what lingers is exactly analogous to [what is] spoken. [18] Moreover, whenever pictures perfectly create a single figure and form from many colors and figures, they delight the sight, while the creation of statues and the production of works of art furnish a pleasant sight to the eyes. Thus it is natural for the sight to grieve for some things and to long for others, and much love and desire for many objects and figures is engraved in many men.

[19] If, therefore, the eye of Helen, pleased by the figure of Alexander, presented to her soul eager desire and contest of love, what wonder? If, [being] a god, [love has] the divine power of the gods, how could a lesser being reject and refuse it? But if it is a disease of human origin and a fault of the soul, it should not be blamed as a sin, but regarded as an affliction. For she came, as she did come, caught in the net of Fate, not by the plans of the mind, and by the constraints of love, not by the devices of art.

[20] How then can one regard blame of Helen as just, since she is utterly acquitted of all charge, whether she did what she did through falling in love or persuaded by speech or ravished by force or constrained by divine constraint?

[21] I have by means of speech removed disgrace from a woman; I have observed the procedure which I set up at the beginning of the speech; I have tried to end the injustice of blame and the ignorance of opinion; I wished to write a speech which would be a praise of Helen and a diversion to myself.

PAUSE

Gorgias says he's trying to save Helen's reputation in this speech, arguing that she doesn't deserve such disgrace. What are one or two things that you think have an undeservedly bad reputation?

Introduction

Helen had a bad reputation in ancient Greece. Gorgias says her name was an "ill omen" (§2). Wife of the Spartan king Menelaus, Helen is taken (precisely how is the conjecture of Gorgias's *Encomium*) by Paris back to Troy, which precipitates the Trojan War that is the subject of Homer's epic *The Iliad*. Since then, the name of Helen was thought unlucky in ancient Greece, so much so that Aeschylus, in his play *Agamemnon*, puns on her name by writing, "Who named that bride of the spear and source of strife with the name of Helen? For, true to her name, a Hell she proved to ships, Hell to men, Hell to city."

Just as it is today in the United States, rhetoric was big business in ancient Greece, highly valued then and now in marketing, politics, and academia. If a rhetorician in ancient Greece wanted to make a name for himself, he might make a sophisticated speech praising something most people thought was insignificant or deserved censure. We have speeches like this praising things like flies and foolishness. A speech like this was known as an **encomium**, and many took up the cause of Helen, trying to restore her good name.

Gorgias's encomium is one such example—though as the most renowned rhetorician of his time, he hardly needed the recognition. Gorgias writes, "By introducing some reasoning into my speech, I wish to free the accused of blame." The key word here is reasoning, *logeion* in the original Greek, which means calculation or computation, but which is best understood as something like **formal logic**.

Today, formal logic is studied most commonly in classes in mathematics, and there's a good reason for this. Like mathematics, formal logic deals in certainties. Two plus two does not sometimes equal four and sometimes equal elephant. It is certain that two plus two equals four, in part because two isn't roughly two, but exactly two. As we discussed in the previous chapter, we rarely—if ever—encounter such certainty in argumentation. In fact, if ever two people share this kind of certainty, there's no reason to argue. That's why it is unusual for people to argue about whether or not two plus two really does equal four (though, under some circumstances, they might).

Formal Logic

Formal logic is a type of reasoning, known as deductive reasoning, and the most important form of deductive reasoning is the syllogism. Some people associate deductive reasoning with moving from the general to the specific, but that isn't correct. One can use deductive reasoning to move from general to specific or from specific to general. For example:

> All people breathe oxygen (general).
> Gorgias is a person (specific).
> Therefore Gorgias breathes oxygen.

This is an example of deductive reasoning. But you can flip those two premises around to begin with the specific statement and it would still be an example of deductive reasoning. **Deductive reasoning** simply means that you have a relationship between a set of premises and a conclusion in which the conclusion follows with certainty from the premises. Deductive reasoning begins with a set of premises and draws necessary conclusions based on that set of premises. This means that the conclusion is an inescapable consequence of the premises—there cannot be another outcome without changing the premises.

Premises are explicit statements or propositions that serve as the basis for another statement. The statement inferred from the premises is called the **conclusion**. When you drop a stone into a pond, you expect it to sink. This expectation is based on a couple of premises, namely, that anything denser than water will sink, and that a rock is denser than water. The conclusion that the rock is going to sink is based on these premises. In formal logic, the conclusion must follow from the premises—there's no other possibility. If you threw a rock in the water and it didn't sink, you wouldn't just think, "Huh, fancy that," and move on. You would need to revise your premises.

Because in deductive reasoning the conclusion follows necessarily from the premises, you don't really learn anything from deductive reasoning most of the time—certainly you don't learn anything about the relationship the conclusion enjoys with the premises. This is called **analytic logic**, which needs no reference to the outside world, and in which the conclusions contain no new information that was not already in the premises. If you throw a rock into the water a hundred times, you'll expect the rock to sink on the last throw just the same as you had with the first. You didn't learn anything new about the rock sinking—in fact, all the information present in the conclusion was already inherent in the premises. Deductive reasoning just sort of moves information around, rather than creating really new knowledge.

One last thing about deductive reasoning before we get back to Gorgias's *Encomium*. Deductive reasoning is what is called analytic: it means neither the conclusion nor the premises need to reference the outside world. In fact, most of the time when you learn formal logic you don't use statements at all, but letters. For example:

$$p \rightarrow q$$

This premise is read "If p, then q." Both p and q could stand for any two things that have a consequential relationship to one another. If it rains (p), then we'll get wet (q). If the Cavs score more points than the Warriors (p), then the Cavs will win (q). From the point of view of formal logic, the content of the premises is not important. What is important is the relationship.

Formal Logic in Gorgias's *Encomium of Helen*

Now, Gorgias makes a number of statements that serve as premises, so that he can use logic to clear Helen's name. Overall, his argument is that there are a limited number of circumstances that would have forced Helen to leave Sparta for Troy. If we account for each of these reasons, one by one, we will move from the uncertain to the certain. Gorgias relies on a series of syllogisms to get there. A **syllogism** is a specific type of deductive reasoning consisting of at least two premises and a conclusion that follows with certainty from those premises.

Gorgias begins his speech with a series of rather complicated syllogisms. Let's just start with the first one. A speech is good, he says, when it is truthful. Then, he says that if something is good, it should be seen as good (praised if praiseworthy).

The implication is that a truthful speech should be praised. Let's set this up as a series of premises followed by a conclusion to see this more clearly:

> A speech is good when it's truthful.
> If something is good, it should be praised.
> Therefore, a truthful speech should be praised.

This three-part arrangement is the basic structure of a syllogism. The first two lines serve as the premises for the third line, which is the conclusion that follows. Now, before I said that deductive reasoning proceeds from the premises to the conclusion with certainty. Does that hold up here, with this example?

Maybe not. One could say that a speech is not just good when it's truthful, or that sometimes a truthful speech might actually be bad, or that praising the good is a bad idea. But here's the thing: in deductive reasoning we are not saying that the premises are always true. In fact, we don't really care about the truth value of any given set of premises or the conclusion that follows. Rather, in deductive reasoning we are concerned only with the relationship between the premises and the conclusion.

Another way of putting this is that in deductive reasoning, the conclusion is always true *if the premises are true*. So the above premises might not be true. In that case, the conclusion might not be true either. But the important thing to remember in deductive reasoning is that if the premises are true, then the conclusion *must* be true. So *if* a speech is good when it is truthful, and *if* something is good it should be praised, then it follows with certainty that a truthful speech should be praised.

Gorgias, then, when he says that a speech should be praised when it is truthful, is relying on the deductive logic of a perfectly sound syllogism. From this syllogism, he moves on to others:

> That which comes from the gods is praiseworthy.
> Helen's beauty comes from the gods.
> Helen's beauty is praiseworthy.

And,

> The victim of physical force is not to blame.
> Speech has the power of physical force.
> Helen was the victim of speech.
> Therefore, Helen is not to blame.

This basic syllogistic form—two or more premises and a conclusion that follows with certainty from the premises—is used by Gorgias again and again.

Categorical Syllogisms

All of the above examples, moreover, are a specific type of syllogism, known as the **categorical syllogism**. A categorical syllogism arranges the world into categories and then classifies individual entities as either within those categories, or not. Another way to think about this is to imagine the world divided up into preset boxes, so that everything in the world could, theoretically, be arranged into those boxes.

To see more clearly how Gorgias's syllogisms are categorical syllogisms, we'll have to change the wording a bit.

> All truthful speech is good.
> All good things should be praised.
> Therefore, all truthful speech should be praised.

This is essentially what Gorgias states, only rearranged a little, and with the word *all*, which is implied in Gorgias's statement, made explicit. The word *all* is important here, because categorical syllogisms are either universal or partial. They don't account for degrees. You can't, in a categorical syllogism, use fractions or percentages, numbers, or even relative terms like majority. For example,

> Two-thirds of the cats in my house eat mice.
> Fluffy is a cat in my house.
> Therefore . . .
> What? We don't know, do we? You can't say with certainty.

That's why the only possible options for a categorical syllogism are "All," "None/No," or "Some."

> All truthful speech is good.
> All good things should be praised.
> Therefore, all truthful speech should be praised.

Or,

> No truthful speech is good.
> All good things should be praised.
> Therefore, no truthful speech should be praised.

Or, finally,

> Some truthful speech is good.
> All good things should be praised.
> Therefore, some truthful speech should be praised.

The validity of categorical syllogisms varies with the content of the syllogism. The rules for determining validity in categorical syllogisms are complex. If this were a book devoted to formal logic, we would need to go through them in detail. But since this is a book about informal logic, it is enough to know the shortcut. As I write above, categorical syllogisms divide the world up into circles or boxes and then arrange things within, or exclude them from, those boxes. So we can use diagrams to check the validity of any categorical syllogism. **If you can use the premises of the syllogism to conclusively mark something inside or outside the diagram, you'll know you have a valid syllogism. If not, you'll know the syllogism is invalid.**

We begin with a first premise. This time, let's use "All cats in this house eat mice."

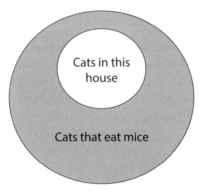

Then, adding in the second premise, we determine whether or not we have enough information to mark an X for the thing in question, in this case, Fluffy. I know Fluffy is a cat in this house, and so I can mark an X for Fluffy in that corresponding circle, telling me that this is a valid categorical syllogism.

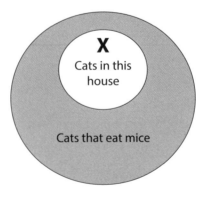

What happens when we change the first premise to "Some cats in this house eat mice"? We will have to alter the arrangement of the circles.

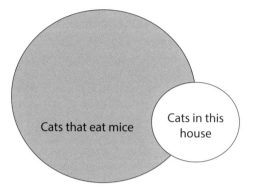

I know that some of the cats in this house eat mice, and I know that Fluffy is a cat in this house, but I don't know whether to put her in the part of the "cats in this house" circle that overlaps with the larger circle of cats that eat mice, or whether to put her in the part of the circle that excludes cats that eat mice. This tells me that this is an invalid syllogism.

On the other hand, if we return to the example from Gorgias, we can craft a valid categorical syllogism using *all* as the term of inclusion.

> All good things should be praised.
> All truthful speech is good.
> Therefore, all truthful speech should be praised.

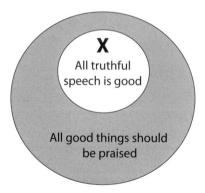

Because there is overlap between the "good things should be praised" circle and the "truthful speech is good" circle, we know that some truthful speech should be praised.

Disjunctive Syllogisms

Gorgias moves on from this first series of arguments rather abruptly, introducing in §6 another form of syllogism, the disjunctive. The **disjunctive syllogism** is another common form of deductive logic, in which a series of options or possibilities are presented, and the selection of one of these options or possibilities automatically rejects all others. Here is what Gorgias says:

> For either by will of Fate
> and decision of the gods
> and vote of Necessity
> did she do what she did,
> or by force reduced
> or by words seduced
> <or by love possessed>.

So in essence Gorgias is arguing that it was either (1) Fate/the Gods/Necessity, or (2) physical force, or (3) words, or (4) love, that compelled Helen to leave with Paris. Ultimately, he makes the case that it doesn't matter which of these was responsible because they all have greater force than Helen, and the weaker person cannot be blamed for being overpowered by the stronger.

This combination of *either* X *or* Y has led the disjunctive syllogism to be known as the either/or syllogism. Here's an example of how it works. Let's say you are running late for work, and you can either take the Bridge Street Tunnel or the Tunnel Street Bridge. The tunnel is more out of your way but tends to have less traffic, while the opposite is true for the bridge. Whichever way you choose to go, once you've made that decision, once you've gone through the tunnel or crossed that bridge, you've given up your opportunity to make the other choice. You can't take the bridge then go back around and take the tunnel—not without making yourself even later, of course.

We can state this as a syllogism this way:

> Either I will take the Bridge Street Tunnel to work, or I'll take the Tunnel Street Bridge.
> I take the Tunnel Street Bridge.
> Therefore, I did not take the Bridge Street Tunnel.

> In a disjunctive syllogism, accepting one possibility automatically means rejecting the other.

So that's how a disjunctive syllogism works. Once you've determined that one possibility, or **disjunct**, is the case, then the other disjunct is automatically not the case. The acceptance of one possibility always implies the rejection of the other, and vice versa.

Now, in the above example this is pretty clear, because it's obvious that one person cannot simultaneously take a bridge and a tunnel. The "or" in this either-or is what's known as *exclusive*. But there are plenty of contexts in which the "or" may not be exclusive, in which both possibilities could occur without the one excluding the other. For example, you might tell a friend on the way to lunch that you'll have either the salad or the sandwich, but decide upon ordering that, you know what, you're going to have both. So while affirming one disjunct—the bridge—automatically denies the other in the above example, affirming either disjunct in this current example doesn't tell us anything definitively about the other disjunct. That's why this is not a valid syllogism.

> Either I will have the sandwich for lunch, or I will have the salad.
>
> I will have the sandwich.
>
> Therefore, I will not have the salad.

Your having the sandwich does not, with certainty, imply that you won't also have the salad. The important thing to remember here is that, while like with categorical syllogisms there is a complex system for determining validity when it comes to disjunctive syllogism in formal logic, for our purposes it is most effective to **consider the context to decide whether or not the two disjuncts are mutually exclusive**. If they are, affirming one to deny the other, or vice versa, is a valid form of syllogism. But if they are not, then denying or affirming one or the other disjunct does not determine with certainty the status of its counterpart, and it is thus not a valid syllogism.

Let's go back, then, to Gorgias's disjunctive syllogism. Helen's actions, Gorgias is arguing, could have been precipitated only by a limited number of possibilities—we can call these disjuncts now. Either it was (1) Fate, (2) Force, or (3) Speech. Now, it is up to us as savvy rhetoricians to decide whether or not these are mutually exclusive. That is, if we affirm that it was, for example, Fate that caused Helen's actions, then does that automatically preclude Force or Speech from being the cause? This is tricky, and could be addressed in two ways. One way would be to—recalling from the previous chapter that argument is determined by the audience—research how this syllogism would have appeared to Gorgias's contemporaries, two and a half millennia ago. Another, more expedient direction is to look to the text itself. When we do that, we see that Gorgias is really splitting these three choices into two choices. He's saying it was either something bigger than humans (Fate, the Gods, Love) that caused Helen to leave Sparta, or else it was something human (physical force or speech). Put this way, it seems obvious that this is an exclusive "or," that something can't be simultaneously both greater than human and limited to the human. It's one or the other. So that makes this a valid syllogism.

Conditional Syllogisms

The final common type of syllogism we see in Gorgias's speech is known as a **conditional syllogism**. In a conditional syllogism we are presented with two premises. The first premise in a conditional syllogism consists of an "if-statement," called the **antecedent**, and a "then-statement," called the **consequent**. The second premise confirms or denies part of the first premise. The conclusion follows from the two premises, as with all syllogisms.

> In a conditional syllogism, you present an if-then statement, and either accept the if- statement or deny the then- statement to come to a conclusion. So long as you either accept the if- statement (the antecedent) or deny the then-statement (the consequent), you have a valid syllogism.

For example,

> *Antecedent*
> Premise 1: If the Cavs score more points than the Warriors by the end of the game,
>
> *Consequent*
> then the Cavs will win the game.
>
> Premise 2: The Cavs did score more points than the Warriors by the end of the game.
> Conclusion: Therefore, The Cavs won the game.

Because of this structure, conditional syllogisms are sometimes called if-then syllogisms. Here's another example:

> *Antecedent*   *Consequent*
> If unemployment in Alandria is above 10 percent, then immigration will fall.
> Unemployment is above 10 percent.
> Therefore, immigration will fall.

Now, what if I do not accept the antecedent as in both of the following examples, but rather deny the consequent? Will that still work?

> *Antecedent*
> If the Cavs score more points than the Warriors by the end of the game,
>
> *Consequent*
> then the Cavs will win the game.
> The Cavs did not win the game.

Therefore, the Cavs did not score more points than the Warriors by the end of the game.

That works, right? Let's look at another one.

> *Antecedent*   *Consequent*
> If unemployment in Alandria is above 10 percent, then immigration will fall.
> Immigration did not fall.
> Therefore, unemployment in Alandria is not above 10 percent.

That seems to work as well.

So far, then, we can see that a valid conditional syllogism is one in which either we accept the antecedent or deny the consequent. What about the converse? What happens when we deny the antecedent?

> *Antecedent*   *Consequent*
> If unemployment in Alandria is above 10 percent, then immigration will fall.
> Unemployment is not above 10 percent.
> Therefore, immigration will not fall.

That seems to work on first glance, but the conclusion in this case does not follow with certainty from the premises. This is because immigration could fall for other reasons. We know that immigration will fall if unemployment is above 10 percent, but that does not mean necessarily that the converse is true. Perhaps unemployment remains below 10 percent in Alandria, but conditions become favorable in neighboring countries as well, which leads to a decline in immigration anyway. Or perhaps conditions in neighboring countries decline, but Alandria implements measures to prevent immigration by force. Both of these cases might lead to a decline in immigration in Alandria despite unemployment remaining below 10 percent.

The same goes for accepting the consequent.

> *Antecedent*   *Consequent*
> If unemployment in Alandria is above 10 percent, then immigration will fall.
> Immigration has fallen.
> Therefore, unemployment in Alandria is above 10 percent.

Well, as we can see in the prior hypotheticals, not necessarily, right? There are a number of other possibilities that could lead to a decline in immigration that have nothing to do with the unemployment rate in Alandria.

So in most cases, then, **accepting the antecedent or denying the consequent in a conditional syllogism leads to a valid conclusion, while the converse, denying the antecedent or accepting the consequent, leads to invalid conclusions**.

I say in most cases because, as with the other types of syllogisms covered here, there are some complex rules governing validity in conditional syllogisms. You'll notice I did not use our first example of a game between the Cavs and the Warriors. This is because, if you try it quickly, you'll see that denying the antecedent in that particular case does seem to lead to a valid conclusion. The reason for this is that the antecedent in that case is really "if and only if the Cavs score more points than the Warriors by the end of the game." This "if and only if" is actually another syllogism sneaking into our conditional syllogism, and makes it an exception to the rules of validity for conditional syllogisms.

The vast majority of the time, though, the rules of validity above do govern conditional syllogisms. If you're ever not sure, see if you should necessarily replace the "if" in the antecedent with "if and only if."

Gorgias uses conditional syllogisms throughout his *Encomium of Helen*. He says, "If then one must place blame on Fate and on a god, one must free Helen from disgrace" (§6). Gorgias does not go on to definitively accept the antecedent or to deny the consequent, leaving these possibilities to hang with the others he puts forth in the speech. Nevertheless, the implications of Gorgias's speech make it necessary to accept the antecedent if we accept this version of Helen's removal from Sparta.

Limitations of Formal Logic

And that should satisfy us as readers. Gorgias has used a series of different kinds of syllogisms to do what he set out to do, to "free the accused from blame" (§2). He has shown that regardless of whether it was a human force, or a force greater than the human, Helen herself was not liable for her leaving Sparta with Paris. The syllogistic reasoning was solid, proceeding from premises to conclusions that follow from those premises with certainty.

And yet, despite the validity of the reasoning, we don't finish the piece with quite the level of certainty we might expect. For one thing, Gorgias ends the speech by stating that his purpose was not really to "free the accused from blame," as he said above, but rather to "write a speech [as] a diversion to myself" (§21). That is a strange way to end it, undermining the seriousness of his sustaining arguments. And there's also this line earlier on: "All who have and do persuade people of things do so by molding a false argument" (§11). Well now, that's a strange thing to say in a speech that relies so heavily on the certainty of logical

> Gorgias ends his piece in a strange way if he's trying to make an earnest argument, which leads many scholars to think he's really got another purpose in mind—to point out the power of persuasion.

deduction. It suggests that maybe Gorgias's real purpose is separate from praising Helen, or even defending her. Perhaps it is rather to say something about the limits of formal logic.

For a long time, formal logic was seen in the Western tradition as the model for all argumentation. The European Enlightenment, for example, was founded in large part on the promise of introducing formal logic into all spheres of human existence: philosophers used formal logic to probe individual consciousness, mathematicians worked to prove the viability of Christianity, and rhetoricians sought to mold civic life after the certainty of logic. But, beginning especially in the twentieth century, the role of formal logic in argumentation has undergone a significant revision. Today, no one expects arguments to be founded on formal logic, and in fact the use of formal logic in contemporary argumentation is rare. After all, as I mention above, there are some pretty significant limitations to formal logic: it doesn't need to have any correspondence to reality, allows no degrees of probability, and leads to conclusions that have no new information. How often does the reality of a statement not matter to an audience? How often is it helpful to have no degrees of probability, but only "all," "some," or "none"? And how often is it helpful for our conclusions to have no information that was not already present in the premises?

Perhaps more importantly, as Gorgias implies in his speech, the certainty that is seemingly available in formal reasoning is only the appearance of certainty. As Gorgias puts it, "*all* who have and do persuade people of things do so by molding a false argument." All. Gorgias isn't saying that some persuasion is rooted in knowledge and therefore true and other persuasion is rooted in opinion and therefore false, but rather that *all* persuasion is rooted in opinion. Opinion is, obviously, not fact; is changeable and subject to influence; and is, in short, not certain. The certainty implied by Gorgias's use of the syllogism has the appearance of certainty, then, but isn't really certain.

I think that's Gorgias's main point, in fact: that for the most part we don't need certainty, that we make decisions all the time without it, that appearances are actually the basis of our knowledge most of the time. And he's not suggesting this is a limit of human knowledge, that we are always mistaken, always making decisions based on things that are not really certain. On the contrary, Gorgias suggests that speech can be used to make things appear all kinds of ways, and that this appearance "has the form of necessity" (12). In other words, **persuasion and certainty are basically the same**. Most of the time, our knowledge is partial and subject to revision, and this is a good thing, because it is the basis for our continuing to find new solutions and new questions, and to make new arguments.

This is roughly the consensus of contemporary perspectives on argumentation, and the view this book takes as well.

A basic understanding of deductive reasoning and an awareness of common forms of syllogism are helpful, because some of the thought patterns and errors of formal reasoning are sometimes seen in informal reasoning. Nevertheless, the focus of this book is on informal, rather than formal, reasoning. In informal reasoning, that is, in everyday argumentation, interpretation is important. We can't replace the key terms in most arguments with placeholder variables because those terms are subject to interpretation, which is itself sometimes the subject of controversy.

Take, for example, the recent Supreme Court decision in *Trump v. Hawaii*, to allow the Trump administration to restrict travel into the United States by people from seven different countries. Much of the controversy there, at least in court arguments, was about how to interpret the executive order as written. One of the key lines of argument Hawaii pursued was that Trump's anti-Muslim and anti-immigration tweets while president should be considered in interpreting the executive order. But Chief Justice John Roberts, in presenting the court's opinion, concluded that because the text of the order itself spoke only to "national security" and not "animus toward Islam," the order should be upheld. How one should interpret the text of the executive order—in other words, the *meaning* of the p's and q's—was the source of controversy in this case, and this is often the case in arguments today.

Here's another example. Perhaps you have heard of CRISPR, a new genetic manipulation technique that has the potential to change the genetic makeup not only of an individual but also, because the genetic change could be passed on to that individual's offspring, of future generations as well. Many who argue against the use of CRISPR technology make the case that it presents too much power for people to yield, and that using it is akin to playing God. Well, "playing God" is not neutral language in this case. We can't just replace it with another similar term or phrase (or even less so a variable like p) and keep the argument the same. There is a connotation attached to the phrase "playing God" that becomes part of the argument. To change the language is to change the argument.

In addition, unlike in deductive logic, in real arguments the conclusion does contain new information. Supreme Court decisions, for example, become precedent, which means they form a new status quo, a new way of understanding a particular question or controversy. The opinion of the court becomes more than a restating of prior interpretations; it becomes rather a new interpretation that did not exist before. Similarly, in the case of genetic manipulation, the opinions of various experts and stakeholders present premises that were not previously available, and thus they lead to conclusions that were not wholly contained in the premises themselves. One set of premises must be weighed against others. Moreover, because the premises don't always fit neatly with one another, the conclusion rarely, if ever, follows with certainty from the premises in day-to-day argumentation. Rather, the conclusion only follows with a degree of probability. It is possible, for example, that genetic manipulation could have unforeseen disastrous consequences—this is the premise of many science fiction novels and films. But when scientists do this kind of work, they tend to do so only when they see these consequences as minimally probable.

Why then, you might ask, would we accept conclusions that are only probable and not certain? Well, as we see in the above examples, certainty is rare in the real world. And yet, we cannot avoid acting altogether—even inaction is an action in certain circumstances.

More importantly, the conventions of argumentation developed over the last couple thousand years do provide a degree of reliability that we can count on. When we follow these conventions—which are the subject of this book—we can be sure we're making decisions effectively.

Conclusion

So let's recap. Informal logic, which is the basis of argumentation, deals with uncertainty, while formal logic deals with certainty. The study of argumentation today, then, deals little with formal logic, which is analytic, and draws conclusions that contain no new information and need no reference to the outside world. The most common form of deductive logic is the syllogism, and three common types of syllogism are the categorical, the disjunctive, and the conditional.

Type of Syllogism	Valid	Invalid
Categorical	Can be diagrammed with certainty	Cannot be diagrammed with certainty
Disjunctive	When disjuncts are truly mutually exclusive	When disjuncts are not truly mutually exclusive
Conditional	Accept the antecedent Deny the consequent	Deny the antecedent Accept the consequent

While once seen as the model for all reasoning, formal logic has come under increasing challenge over the course of the twentieth century. As a result, formal logic is no longer presented as the basis of argumentation. Instead, argumentation today is concerned primarily with informal logic, which is messier than the study of formal logic, but more appropriate to the way people actually make decisions by exchanging reasons. While formal logic is rooted in certainty, informal logic is rooted in probability. When we give up the certainty of formal logic, we have the possibility of learning new information. When founded on sound principles, informal logic is a reliable aid in decision-making.

PROBE

Think of an argument you might make in everyday life, whether with friends, in class, with family, or at work. See if you can develop an argument that uses only valid deductive logic; in other words, your conclusions must follow from your premises with certainty.

Chapter 3
The Basic Building Blocks of Argument

Key Terms

claim

statement

truth value

evidence

warrant

claim of fact

claim of definition

claim of quality

claim of policy

Key Points

- Arguments begin when two people or groups of people disagree on something they care about.
- Another precondition of argument is the desire by each party for the others' willing assent.
- The final precondition of argument is an agreement that the controversy is better addressed through the exchange of reasons than in any other way.
- At their most basic, arguments are made up of a claim, evidence, and an explicit or implicit warrant, which links the two.
- There are four basic types of claims: fact, definition, quality, and policy.

PRIME

As you read Kerry's speech, underline at least three sentences in which Kerry seems to be giving reasons for accepting some course of action, adopting some position, or understanding something a particular way.

Vietnam Veterans against the War Statement

John Kerry (1971)

Thank you very much, Senator Fulbright, Senator Javits, Senator Symington, Senator Pell.

I would like to say for the record that—and also for the men behind me who are also wearing the uniform and their medals—that my sitting up here is really symbolic. I'm not here as John Kerry. I'm here as one member of a group of 1,000, which is a small representation of a very much larger group of veterans in this country. And were it possible for all of them to sit at this table, they would be here and have the same kind of testimony.

I would simply like to speak in very general terms. I would like to talk representing all those veterans and say that several months ago in Detroit we had an investigation at which over 150 honorably discharged, and many very highly decorated, veterans testified to war crimes committed in Southeast Asia.

These were not isolated incidents but crimes committed on a day-to-day basis with the full awareness of officers at all levels of command. It's impossible to describe to you exactly what did happen in Detroit—the emotions in the room and the feelings of the men who were reliving their experiences in Vietnam.

But they did. They relived the absolute horror of what this country, in a sense, made them do.

They told the stories of times that they had personally raped, cut off ears, cut off heads, taped wires from portable telephones to human genitals and turned up the power, cut off limbs, blown up bodies, randomly shot at civilians, razed villages in the fashion reminiscent of Genghis Khan, shot cattle and dogs for fun, poisoned food stocks, and generally ravaged the countryside of South Vietnam in addition to the normal ravage of war and the normal and very particular ravaging which is done by the applied bombing power of this country.

We call this investigation the "Winter Soldier Investigation." The term Winter Soldier is a play on words of Thomas Paine's in 1776 when he spoke of the Sunshine Patriot and summertime soldiers who deserted at Valley Forge because the going was rough.

And we who have come here to Washington have come here because we feel we have to be winter soldiers now. We could come back to this country; and we could be quiet; we could hold our silence; we could not tell what went on in Vietnam. But we feel because of what threatens this country, the fact that the crimes threaten it, not redcoats but the crimes which we're committing are what threaten it; and we have to speak out.

I would like to talk to you a little bit about what the result is, of the feelings these men carry with them after coming back from Vietnam. The country doesn't know it yet but it's created a monster, a monster in the form of millions of men who have been taught to deal and to trade in violence, and who are given the chance to die for the biggest nothing in history; men who have returned with a sense of anger and a sense of betrayal which no one has yet grasped.

As a veteran, and one who feels this anger, I'd like to talk about it. We're angry because we feel we have been used in the worst fashion by the Administration of this country. In 1970 at West Point, Vice President Agnew said, "Some glamorize the criminal misfits of society while our best men die in Asian rice paddies to preserve the freedoms which those misfits abuse."

And this was used as a rallying point for our effort in Vietnam.

But for us, his boys in Asia whom the country was supposed to support, his statement is a terrible distortion from which we can only draw a very deep sense of revulsion; and hence the anger of some of the men who are here in Washington today.

It's a distortion because we in no way considered ourselves the best men of this country; because those he calls misfits were standing up for us in a way that nobody else in this country dared to; because so many who have died would have returned to this country to join the misfits in their efforts to ask for an immediate withdrawal from South Vietnam; because so many of those best men have returned as quadriplegics and amputees, and they lie forgotten in Veterans Administration hospitals in this country which fly the flag which so many have chosen as their own personal symbol.

And we cannot consider ourselves America's best men when we were ashamed of and hated what we were called to do in Southeast Asia. In our opinion, and from our experience, there is nothing in South Vietnam, nothing which could happen that realistically threatens the United States of America. And to attempt to justify the loss of one American life in Vietnam, Cambodia, or Laos by linking such loss to the preservation of freedom, which those misfits supposedly abuse, is to us the height of criminal hypocrisy, and it's that kind of hypocrisy which we feel has torn this country apart.

We are probably much more angry than that and I don't want to go into the foreign policy aspects because I'm outclassed here. I know that all of you have talked about every possible alternative to getting out of Vietnam. We understand that. We know that you've considered the seriousness of the aspects to the utmost level and I'm not going to try and deal on that. But I want to relate to you the feeling which many of the men who've returned to this country express because we are probably angriest about all that we were told about Vietnam and about the mystical war against communism.

We found that not only was it a civil war, an effort by a people who had for years been seeking their liberation from any colonial influence whatsoever, but also we found that the Vietnamese, whom we had enthusiastically molded after our own image, were hard put to take up the fight against the threat we were supposedly saving them from.

We found that most people didn't even know the difference between communism and democracy. They only wanted to work in rice paddies without helicopters strafing them and bombs with napalm burning their villages and tearing their country apart. They wanted everything to do with the war, particularly with this foreign presence of the United States of America, to leave them alone in peace; and they practiced the art of survival by siding with whichever military force was present at a particular time, be it Vietcong, North Vietnamese, or American.

We found also that all too often American men were dying in those rice paddies for want of support from their allies. We saw firsthand how monies from American taxes was used for a corrupt dictatorial regime. We saw that many people in this country had a one-sided idea of who was kept free by our flag, as blacks provided the highest percentage of casualties. We saw Vietnam ravaged equally by American bombs as well as by search and destroy missions, as well as by Vietcong terrorism; and yet we listened while this country tried to blame all of the havoc on the Vietcong.

We rationalized destroying villages in order to save them. We saw America lose her sense of morality as she accepted very coolly a My Lai and refused to give up the image of American soldiers that hand out chocolate bars and chewing gum. We learned the meaning of "free-fire zones," "shoot anything that moves," and we watched while America placed a cheapness on the lives of Orientals. We watched the United States' falsification of body counts, in fact the glorification of body counts. We listened while month after month we were told the back of the enemy was about to break.

We fought using weapons against "oriental human beings," with quotation marks around that. We fought using weapons against those people which I do not believe this country would dream of using were we fighting in a European theater—or let us say a non–third-world-people theater. And so we watched while men charged up hills because a general said, "That hill has to be taken." And after losing one platoon or two platoons they marched away to leave the hill for the reoccupation by the North Vietnamese; we watched pride allow the most unimportant of battles to be blown into extravaganzas; because we couldn't lose, and we couldn't retreat, and because it didn't matter how many American bodies were lost to prove that point. And so there were

Hamburger Hills and Khe Sahns and Hill 881's and Fire Base 6's, and so many others.

And now we're told that the men who fought there must watch quietly while American lives are lost so that we can exercise the incredible arrogance of Vietnamizing the Vietnamese.

Each day to facilitate the process by which the United States washes her hands of Vietnam, someone has to give up his life so that the United States doesn't have to admit something that the entire world already knows, so that we can't say that we've made a mistake. Someone has to die so that President Nixon won't be, and these are his words, "the first President to lose a war."

And we are asking Americans to think about that because how do you ask a man to be the last man to die in Vietnam? How do you ask a man to be the last man to die for a mistake? But we're trying to do that, and we're doing it with thousands of rationalizations, and if you read carefully the President's last speech to the people of this country, you can see that he says, and says clearly:

> But the issue, gentlemen, the issue is communism, and the question is whether or not we will leave that country to the Communists or whether or not we will try to give it hope to be a free people.

But the point is they're not a free people now—under us. They're not a free people. And we cannot fight communism all over the world, and I think we should have learnt that lesson by now.

But the problem of veterans goes beyond this personal problem, because you think about a poster in this country with a picture of Uncle Sam and the picture says "I want you." And a young man comes out of high school and says, "That's fine. I'm going to serve my country." And he goes to Vietnam and he shoots and he kills and he does his job or maybe he doesn't kill, maybe he just goes and he comes back. When he gets back to this country he finds that he isn't really wanted, because the largest unemployment figure in the country—it varies depending on who you get it from, the Veterans Administration 15 percent, various other sources 22 percent—but the largest figure of unemployed in this country are veterans of this war. And of those veterans 33 percent of the unemployed are black. That means 1 out of every 10 of the nation's unemployed is a veteran of Vietnam.

The hospitals across the country won't or can't meet their demands. It's not a question of not trying. They haven't got the appropriations. A man recently died after he had a tracheotomy in California, not because of the operation but because there weren't enough personnel to clean the mucous out of his tube and he suffocated to death.

Another young man just died in a New York VA hospital the other day. A friend of mine was lying in a bed two beds away and tried to help him, but he couldn't. They rang a bell and there was no one there to service that man, and so he died of convulsions.

Fifty-seven percent—I understand 57 percent of all those entering VA hospitals talk about suicide. Some 27 percent have tried, and they try because they come back to this country and they have to face what they did in Vietnam, and then they come back and find the indifference of a country that doesn't really care, that doesn't really care.

And suddenly we are faced with a very sickening situation in this country because there's no moral indignation, and if there is it comes from people who are almost exhausted by their past indignancies, and I know that many of them are sitting in front of me. The country seems to have lain down and accepted something as serious as Laos, just as we calmly shrugged off the loss of 700,000 lives in Pakistan, the so-called greatest disaster of all times.

But we are here as veterans to say that we think we are in the midst of the greatest disaster of all times now because they are still dying over there, and not just Americans, Vietnamese, and we are rationalizing leaving that country so that those people can go on killing each other for years to come.

Americans seem to have accepted the idea that the war is winding down, at least for Americans, and they have also allowed the bodies, which were once used by a President for statistics to prove that we were winning this war, to be used as evidence against a man who followed orders and who interpreted those orders no differently than hundreds of other men in South Vietnam.

We veterans can only look with amazement on the fact that this country has not been able to see that there's absolutely no difference between a ground troop and a helicopter crew. And yet, people have accepted the differentiation fed them by the Administration. No ground troops are in Laos, so it's alright to kill Laotians by remote control. But believe me, the helicopter crews fill the same body bags and they wreak the same kind of damage on the Vietnamese and Laotian countryside as anyone else, and the President is talking about allowing that to go on for many years to come. And one can only ask if we will really be satisfied when the troops march in to Hanoi.

We are asking here in Washington for some action, action from the Congress of the United States of America which has the power to raise and maintain armies and which by the Constitution also has the power to declare war. We've come here, not to the President, because we believe that this body can be responsive to the will of the people; and we believe that the will of the people says that we should be out of Vietnam now.

We're here in Washington also to say that the problem of this war is not just a question of war and diplomacy. It's part and parcel of everything that we are trying as human beings to communicate to people in this country: the question of racism, which is rampant in the military; and so many other questions also: the use of weapons; the hypocrisy in our taking umbrage in the Geneva Conventions and using that as justification for continuation of this war, when we are more guilty than any other body of violations of those Geneva Conventions—in the use of free-fire zones, harassment interdiction fire, search and destroy missions, the bombings, the torture of prisoners, the killing of prisoners—accepted policy by many units in South Vietnam. That's what we're trying to say. It's part and parcel of everything.

An American Indian friend of mine who lives on the Indian nation of Alcatraz put it to me very succinctly. He told me how as a boy on an Indian reservation he had watched television and he used to cheer the cowboys when they came in and shot the Indians. And then suddenly one day he stopped in Vietnam and he said, "My God, I'm doing to these people the very same thing that was done to my people"—and he stopped. And that's what we're trying to say, that we think this thing has to end.

We're also here to ask—We are here to ask and we're here to ask vehemently, Where are the leaders of our country? Where is the leadership? We're here to ask: Where are McNamara, Rostow, Bundy, Kilpatrick, and so many others? Where are they now that we the men whom they sent off to war have returned? These are commanders who have deserted their troops and there is no more serious crime in the law of war. The Army says they never leave their wounded. The Marines say they never leave even their dead. These men have left all the casualties and retreated behind a pious shield of public rectitude. They've left the real stuff of their reputations, bleaching behind them in the sun in this country.

And finally, this Administration has done us the ultimate dishonor. They've attempted to disown us and the sacrifices we made for this country. In their blindness and fear, they have tried to deny that we are veterans or that we served in Nam. We do not need their testimony. Our own scars and stumps of limbs are witness enough for others and for ourselves. We wish that a merciful God could wipe away our own memories of that service as easily as this Administration has wiped their memories of us.

And all that they have done and all that they can do by this denial is to make more clear than ever our own determination to undertake one last mission: to search out and destroy the last vestige of this barbaric war, to pacify our own hearts, to conquer the hate and fear that have driven this country these last ten years and more—and more.

And so, in thirty years from now our brothers go down the street without a leg, without an arm or a face, and small boys ask why, we will be able to say "Vietnam" and not mean a desert, not a filthy obscene memory but mean instead the place where America finally turned and where soldiers like us helped it in the turning.

Thank you.

PAUSE

Consider some differences of opinion you have observed on social media recently. These may be controversies among friends, or nationally. Did the participants seem to care about the outcome? How did they respond? Remember to use the specialized definition of controversy from Chapter 1.

Introduction

Kerry's statement against the Vietnam War is a powerful, complex, and even controversial speech, given during a time of rising discontent with U.S. military involvement in Vietnam. The person giving the speech is John Kerry, whom we now know as a former senator from Massachusetts and a secretary of state under President Barack Obama, but who in 1971 had just been honorably discharged from the navy to pursue a congressional seat. And the speech is being given in front of the Senate Foreign Relations Committee but also televised live on NBC News, meaning that Kerry had to be conscious of multiple audiences. I could go on and mention the political context, including Nixon's critique of Kerry, or international relations and the ongoing Cold War, but even without this it should be clear that Kerry had to be aware of a lot of factors regarding his argument, beyond thesis statements and finding sufficient supporting sources. In fact, I could ask you to go through Kerry's speech and underline the thesis statement, and while that would be a challenge here, we'd still have captured so little of Kerry's argument, about the conditions for argumentation, and about the basic building blocks of an argument, which is the focus of this chapter.

So let's begin by asking what brings Kerry to testify before the Senate Foreign Relations Committee about the U.S. military involvement in Vietnam. The Vietnam War was hardly the first war to spark major domestic controversy—there has been opposition to war for probably as long as there has been war. But nevertheless, by the end of 1967, resistance to the Vietnam War grew into a full-fledged movement, with massive protests, several activist groups, and the support of major figures like Martin Luther King Jr. and Muhammed Ali. Numerous groups arose to protest the war, and the Vietnam anti-war movement was the first in which organized student activism played a significant role. John Kerry had just been to the Winter Soldier Investigation, which—before it was a Marvel film—was a media event in Detroit sponsored by Vietnam Veterans against the War (VVAW), publicizing testimony from Vietnam veterans about atrocities they saw, or had themselves committed, while in Vietnam.

Controversy like that surrounding the Vietnam War is the fertile soil of argument. Simply put, arguments occur when two people disagree about something. Many people in the United States supported the Vietnam War, while many others opposed it. Of course it's not as simple as that—some people may have supported it at one time and grown to oppose it, or supported the effort but not the methods, or opposed it for legal reasons, or ethical reasons, or strategic reasons, and so on. Nevertheless, arguments do not occur when everyone is in agreement about something. The first precondition for argument, then, is disagreement with explicit or implicit reasons (even if the reasons are unexamined). The technical term for this, as we learned in Chapter 1, is controversy.

> Arguments begin when two people or groups of people disagree on something they care about.

When Arguments Are Likely to Occur

But controversy on its own is not sufficient for argument to occur—after all, people don't see eye to eye on all kinds of things, but these don't always develop into arguments. For example, let's say that you and a friend want to go to a movie tonight. You live in a small town with only one theater, and that theater only has two screens, one of which is showing a comedy, the other a drama.

> Review: What kind of syllogism is this an example of? See Chapter 2 if you need a reminder.

Your friend says to you, "Let's go see the drama—I'm really looking forward to it."

"I was hoping to see the comedy," you reply, "but I'm going to the movies again this weekend, so sure, let's go see the drama."

In this case, there is implicitly a question about which movie to see and there is disagreement, but no argument develops because only one of the parties—your friend—cares much about the disagreement. The controversy surrounding the Vietnam War, on the other hand, was one of the most heated of the second half of the twentieth century. As Kerry alludes to in his speech, Nixon saw the war as a proxy for a larger war on communism, for example. Implicitly, policy arguments related to the Vietnam War responded to controversies like, "How should the United States respond to the spread of communism globally?" Though not everyone was united against the war, demonstration after demonstration against the war shows that many people cared deeply about ending the war. It's not enough, then, simply to disagree on something: the people involved in the disagreement have to care about the outcome.

So the first two preconditions of argumentation, the things that have to be in place for an argument to occur, are

1. disagreement or controversy, and
2. consequence: meaning that the outcome matters to the participants.

But even if we satisfy both of these, we don't necessarily end up with an argument, because disagreement is not always resolved through argumentation. For example, maybe you and your friend disagree about which movie to see, and maybe you both care enough about it that neither one of you is willing to give up their preference immediately. But you might want to see the comedy so badly that you offer to pay for their ticket if they come with you to see the comedy. Your friend agrees. Did you just engage in argumentation?

Well, let's recall from Chapter 1 that argument is reason-giving, which is justification for claims so that assent is freely given. In the above case, you essentially paid your friend to agree with you, which means his assent was not *freely* given. When you buy or otherwise coerce an audience's acceptance of your claim, you are employing a type of force. Now, you may recall Gorgias in the previous chapter saying that persuasion is akin to force, but that isn't the same as using force—physical force, for example—to avoid engaging in argumentation altogether. Many rhetoricians have argued that persuasion is a way to avoid the use of force—including war—to come to mutual, rather than coerced, agreement. Kerry likewise wanted to convince those watching his speech that continued war in Vietnam was not in their best interests, and to do so by gaining their willing assent.

> Argumentation happens when a reasonable discussion—meaning it proceeds through claims and support for those claims—occurs in response to a controversy that the parties involved care about.

The third precondition for argumentation, then, is the desire by each party for the others' willing assent. This is an important foundation for argumentation, because (1) the argument cannot continue if someone is coerced, and (2) it provides greater likelihood that the result of the exchange is the best possible outcome under the circumstances. When many people engage in conversation about something like military involvement in another country, provide arguments to support outcomes they truly care about, and are free to both form their own opinions and promote their point of view, the chances are greatest that the best decision will be identified and made.

All the characteristics related to argumentation covered in Chapter 1 still apply here, including the idea that arguments can only proceed in the context of uncertainty. This is similar to saying that arguments begin with disagreement, as we already know, because we don't typically disagree on things about which we are certain—no one argues, for example, about who the first president of the United States was, or the capital of Angola. But uncertainty as a precondition of argumentation puts a condition on that disagreement, placing it in the context of what is broadly agreed upon. That is, even if you don't know that George Washington was the first U.S. president, or that Luanda is the capital of Angola, or even if you think one thing but your friend thinks another, the disagreement that proceeds from that lack of knowledge does not lead to argument, because there is a much easier way to solve the dispute: research. So the fourth precondition of argument is that all the parties involved agree that there is no better way to resolve their disagreement. In the case of Kerry's speech, although Nixon had, as commander in chief, the power to send U.S. troops where he saw fit, Congress had the "power of the purse strings." That is, Congress could vote to fund the military operations or not. This balance of power meant that there was no easier way to settle the dispute, and that the disagreement had to be addressed through persuasion.

To review, then, the preconditions for argumentation are (1) disagreement or controversy, (2) an outcome that matters to the participants, (3) desire by each party for the other's willing assent, and (4) an agreement that the controversy is better addressed through the exchange of reasons than in any other way.

Claims and Evidence

Okay, so we have the preconditions for argument met. What happens next? That is, what are the main elements of arguments themselves? How do we actually put an argument together? Well, let's return to our movie example to see if that can't answer some of our questions.

You might say to your friend, I really want to see the comedy. Your friend might reply that they prefer the drama. This meets our preconditions for argument, doesn't it? After all, (1) you disagree, (2) it's something you care about, (3) neither of you wants to force the other to go, and (4) there isn't an easier way to settle the difference.

Well, that depends on what happens next. Your friend might ask you why you want to see the comedy, and you might say you are in the mood to laugh tonight. There's no real evidence your friend could present to try to persuade you, because it is a matter of personal preference and mood. Instead, your friend might just give in, or resort to cajoling, or try to make a deal, or call the whole thing off. None of that would constitute argumentation, and an argument would not proceed.

What is a claim? A **claim** is

1. a **statement**: a sentence that clearly expresses a fact, an opinion, or a point of view. The sentence "Washington, D.C., is the capital of the United States" is a statement, but "What is the capital of the United States?" is not.

that has

2. **truth value**: meaning that it can be shown to be either true or false. The sentence "I like unicorns better than mermaids" typically does not have truth value because it is simply a personal preference. "Unicorns are real creatures that live in European forests," however, does have truth value. It can be shown to be either true or false. Again, truth value does not mean something is true, or even that we know whether or not it is true, just that it is theoretically possible to determine whether or not it is true.

and that

3. responds to a controversy. "Lyndon Johnson was president when U.S. ground forces in Vietnam peaked," for example, is not a claim because if it is ever met with uncertainty, it can be looked up easily, quickly ending any controversy. "Lyndon Johnson was a highly effective leader in times of war," however, is a claim because the implicit question (was Johnson an effective wartime leader?) is open to legitimate differences of opinion.

So, while controversy, consequence, willing assent, and uncertainty are necessary preconditions for argument, they are not sufficient on their own. This is because arguments are exchanges of claims and justifications for those claims. Argumentation is the practice of reason-giving, and when the reasons run out, so does the argument.

Argumentation happens, then, when a reasonable discussion—meaning it proceeds through claims and support for those claims—occurs in response to a controversy that the parties involved care about. Another example might help make this clearer. Let's say, this time, that you and your friend are not deciding on which movie you want to see tonight; instead you are two analysts for a venture capital fund deciding on which film to invest in. In this case, if you want to invest in the comedy, and your colleague wants to invest in the drama, the succeeding conversation will likely constitute an argument. Your colleague might say that dramas are more popular than comedies and point to some data that supports this statement. But you might respond that while dramas are marginally more popular, they are also riskier, more likely to bomb at the box office. You might talk about who's committed to what roles in each film, what the overall budget is, when the release date is, and so on. In short, you may end up having an argument, a process of reasoned decision-making, involving the exchange of claims and support for those claims.

In its most simplistic representation, then, an argument is made up of a claim, support for that claim (typically called **evidence**), and a third element, called a **warrant**, connecting the claim with its evidence.

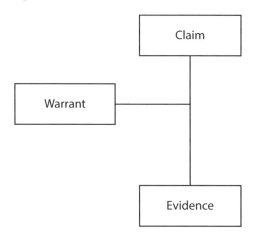

This is a descriptive representation of an argument, one that goes back to Stephen Toulmin's book *The Uses of Argument*. If you recall back to Chapter 2, we made the distinction between formal and informal reasoning, stating that in formal reasoning the conclusion follows with certainty from the premises, while in informal reasoning the conclusion follows only with probability. And we went on in that chapter, and continue in this one, emphasizing how important uncertainty is in informal argumentation—that in fact arguments cannot proceed without uncertainty. Well, this uncertainty is at the heart of Toulmin's model of argument, which he based on his analysis of how people argue in everyday situations.

> Warrant defines the relationship between the claim and the evidence in an argument.

The reality is that, again, we rarely if ever argue about claims that follow with certainty from their premises. On the contrary, we argue when claims and evidence are related in uncertain ways. In the above example, you and your colleague as film analysts cannot predict with certainty which film is a better investment, the comedy or the drama. The relationship between the claim and the evidence or data that supports it is uncertain.

This uncertainty is what allows argumentation to proceed as a method of reason-asking-and-giving. Again, we can see this in the previous example. What happens when you question your colleague's use of data showing that dramas are more popular than comedies?

"Wait a minute," you might say. "The data showing that dramas are more popular is only part of the picture. You're looking at the average. But the data also shows that some dramas are very popular, while others are very unpopular. So while dramas are slightly more popular overall, any one drama might be unpopular, and so is riskier."

You didn't question the data here, right? If you had, you might have said, "Where did you get those figures? I have completely different numbers from the Motion Picture Association." So the evidence is not at issue. And the claim has already been questioned when you two disagreed about which film to invest in. You could think of that original claim as "We should invest in a drama." That's the claim that started the disagreement, which led to your colleague providing the above data. So the claim isn't at issue here either. Rather, what is at issue is the relationship between the claim and the data. You look at the same data as your colleague does, but it doesn't lead you to the same conclusion. **This relationship between claim and evidence is called the warrant, and it is one potential source of uncertainty in an argument.**

Let's look at a few simple examples first, before we return to Kerry's speech to flesh this out a little more.

> Claim: Selena Gomez is more popular than Ariana Grande.
>
> Evidence: Selena Gomez has more Instagram followers.
>
> Warrant: The number of social media followers is a measure of popularity.

> Claim: Drake is the best musician of our day.
>
> Evidence: Drake was the most streamed artist in 2021.
>
> Warrant: Popularity is a measure of an artist's quality.

> Claim: You should listen to the Ed Sheeran song "Bad Habits."
>
> Evidence: It was the most downloaded song of 2021.
>
> Warrant: You are likely to enjoy songs that other people enjoy.

As you can see in all these examples, warrants are not guaranteed to be reasonable links between claims and evidence. In fact, much of the time people argue, they argue over warrants. While popularity may be a way to measure a musical artist's quality, one could just as easily argue that it isn't: that, for example, critical acclaim is a better measure, or theoretical soundness, or creativity. Similarly, some people may not like a song, even if it is widely popular. Perhaps they don't like the genre, or they tend to like more obscure artists. If you're arguing about how the evidence relates to the claim, you're arguing about the warrant.

Rarely do people label the parts of their argument or state explicitly that they are making a claim, or providing evidence, or stating their warrant. Rather, these elements of an argument are either produced organically in the course of a discussion, or else called for by the writing situation, in the case of written arguments.

Claims, Evidence, and Warrants in Kerry's Speech

Now that we have a description of the basic building blocks of argumentation, let's go back to Kerry's speech and see if we can recognize some of these there. Like any complex argument, Kerry provides a dynamic and wide-ranging set of claims and reasons for accepting those claims in his speech. He makes at least three major claims in his speech: (1) that U.S. involvement in the Vietnam War was morally unjust, (2) that U.S. involvement in the Vietnam War was legally unjustified, and (3) that the United States should immediately withdraw all troops from Vietnam. Since we can only cover a small slice of Kerry's robust argument in this chapter, let's identify his main argument and point to some evidence Kerry draws on to support it.

Since Kerry is making three claims in this speech, how can we know which is his main argument, and which are subordinate? As arguments proceed, participants offer multiple claims. To identify which claim is the main one, it is helpful to ask which claims support other claims presented in the argument, and which seems to be the one getting support. Two of Kerry's claims seem to support the third claim, that the United States should immediately withdraw all troops from Vietnam. That is, the argument seems to be that because (1) U.S. involvement in Vietnam is morally unjust and also because (2) U.S. involvement is legally unjustified, (3) the United States should immediately withdraw all troops from Vietnam. Claims 1 and 2 are actually reasons for claim 3: they are evidence supporting the main argument. A warrant linking claim 3 with the evidence offered in claim 1 might be that the United States has an express commitment to participating only in just wars.

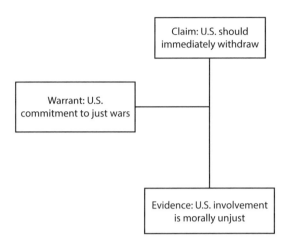

Much more analysis of claims and evidence in Kerry's speech is possible. For example, Kerry also presents testimony from U.S. soldiers about the many war crimes they committed while in Vietnam. What claim might this serve as evidence for? What might a reasonable warrant be? Does Kerry state the warrant explicitly, or leave it up to the audience to determine?

The Four Types of Claim

There are four types of claim: fact, definition, quality or value, and policy.

The first basic type, the **claim of fact**, involves description. These claims concern matters that, in theory, can be described and verified independently by others. They may relate to the past, present, or future. Take this claim of fact, for example: "Women make $.79 for every dollar a man in the United States makes." This is a claim, as opposed to an observation, because it is not easy to check this with certainty. Should we measure this as an average of all workers, or does it make more sense to account for variations in education or position? Should hours worked figure into this measurement, since women are often expected to do more at home? The claim "Al Gore received more popular votes than Bush in 2000" is also a claim of fact. What counts as a vote? What got counted? These questions were the very things at issue when the case ended up before the U.S. Supreme Court in *Bush v. Gore*. Even something as seemingly objective as average salaries or total number of votes, then, can be controversial and the subject of dispute.

The second type, **claims of definition**, involves meaning or interpretation. Like with claims of fact, people are sometimes confused about how definitions can be subject to argument. Don't you just look it up if you aren't sure? Well, you can certainly look up a definition, but definitions are not neutral. Take, for example, the argument "Capital punishment is murder." Looking at the definitions of both of the key terms in this claim in the dictionary would not get you any closer to certainty about whether or not to accept the claim. And the language used is very important. There is a very big difference between my saying that capital punishment is murder and capital punishment is justified retribution. Both imply putting an end to a convicted person's life, but with very different connotations. Claims of this type place concepts in categories and provide perspective.

A **claim of quality** or value, the third basic type of claim, involves judgment. Judgment represents an appraisal or evaluation (good or bad, right or wrong, etc.). The evaluation can be absolute (the federal government's response to the crisis was unsatisfactory) or comparative (economic growth is more important than environmental protection), and it can involve instrumental (in what they lead to; self-quarantine measures are tough but necessary for the greater good) or terminal values (in and of themselves; this peach-mango sorbet is delicious).

Lastly, claims of the fourth type, **claims of policy**, involve action. These types of claims are probably the most common, especially in public debate. They are assertions about what should or should not be done. They are characteristic of deliberative bodies such as Congress, but also of informal deliberations among friends. For example, "The Senate should review the president's judicial nominee" is a claim of policy, but so is "You should buy a car with AWD."

How Arguments Proceed

In the above example we saw how when someone questions the relationship between the evidence and the claim, you end up with the opportunity to present a new claim. Let's go back to our example of two colleagues deciding whether to invest in a drama or a comedy. Let's call them Judy and Jermaine.

Judy: We should invest in the drama. (Claim)

At this point, Jermaine can just accept that claim, and the argument is over, or he can ask for reasons and the argument would proceed.

Let's imagine Jermaine wants to know what reasons Judy has for making this claim.

Jermaine: Why do you say that?

Here, Judy can respond by either providing evidence, or making a new claim that supports her overall claim.

Judy: Dramas are more popular than comedies.

Although this serves as a reason, Jermaine is not satisfied with just a claim alone and wants evidence.

> Jermaine: How do you know?
>
> Judy: Of the top ten most popular movies last year, more were dramas than comedies.

Jermaine can now choose to accept Judy's evidence and agree with her suggestion that they invest in the drama, or choose one of three other options: (1) disagree with the claim, (2) disagree with the evidence, or (3) disagree with the implied relationship between the claim and the evidence.

You can see what this exchange looks like in the diagram below.

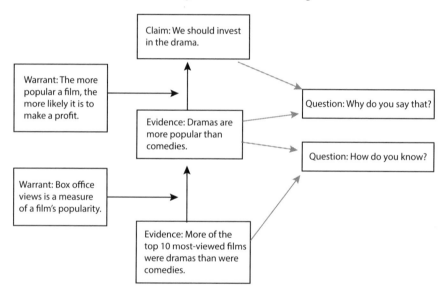

Conclusion

The parts of an argument become evident when we think about how a conversation would proceed when it meets the preconditions of arguments. This is an important point: although argumentation is a complex field with a long history, it is as much descriptive as it is prescriptive. That is, much of what we know today as the principles of effective argumentation were developed by observing how people tend to have discussions that lead to effective decisions. Since what we know about argumentation is learned by observing the way people behave in certain situations, we recognize that argumentation is a dynamic field that changes over time.

Arguments begin when we have a difference of opinion, or controversy, and we care about the outcome. Not only that, but we—for ethical or practical reasons—agree that we want to settle the controversy by having a conversation rather than by exerting force or outside influence on one another. When that happens, we begin to exchange claims, statements that have truth value and respond to a controversy. When we provide a reason or reasons that support our claim, we are providing evidence. And the relationship between the claim and the evidence is the warrant. These are terms that have been assigned to the basic parts of arguments as they occur in natural settings.

Of course, arguments can become much more complicated quickly. Our example of the two colleagues shows how, just by scratching the surface of an argument, we can see numerous claims and reasons being developed by both participants. We'll work on similar diagrams in the next chapter.

PROBE

Return to the claims you underlined as you read Kerry's speech (Prime). Choose one and consider what a warrant that links this claim with its evidence might be. Is the warrant stated, or left unstated?

Chapter 4

Analyzing Arguments

Key Terms

satire

scanning

statement

indicator or cue

standardizing

diagramming

complementary reasons

reservation

inferential leap

backing

Key Points

- Because drawing on formal logic alone may not give you a complete understanding of the reasonableness of a given argument, other strategies for analyzing arguments are common.
- Common strategies for analyzing arguments include scanning, standardizing, and diagramming.
- Breaking arguments down into their claims, evidence, warrants, and backing following Toulmin's model can help us understand how an argument is functioning in context.

PRIME

As you read, underline at least three claims that you find to be unreasonable. Consider how these claims affect the way you read the piece overall.

A Modest Proposal

Jonathan Swift (1729)

It is a melancholy Object to those, who walk thro' this great Town, or travel in the Country, when they see the *Streets*, the *Roads* and *Cabbin-Doors* crowded with Beggars of the Female Sex, followed by three, four, or six Children *all in Rags*, and importuning every passenger for an alms. These *Mothers*, instead of being able to work for their honest livelihood, are forced to employ all their Time in stroling to beg Sustenance for their *helpless Infants* who, as they grow up, either turn *Thieves* for want of Work, or leave their *dear native Country, to fight for the Pretender in Spain*, or sell themselves to the *Barbadoes*.

I think it is agreed by all Parties, that this prodigious Number of Children in the Arms, or on the Backs, or at the Heels of their Mothers, and frequently of their Fathers, is in the present deplorable State of the Kingdom, a very great additional Grievance; and therefore whoever could find out a fair, cheap and easy method of making these children sound and useful members of the common-wealth, would deserve so well of the publick, as to have his statue set up for a preserver of the nation.

But my intention is very far from being confined to provide only for the children of professed beggars: it is of a much greater extent, and shall take in the whole number of infants at a certain age, who are born of parents in effect as little able to support them, as those who demand our charity in the streets.

As to my own part, having turned my thoughts for many years, upon this important subject, and maturely weighed the several schemes of our projectors, I have always found them grossly mistaken in their computation. It is true, a child just dropt from its dam, may be supported by her milk, for a solar year, with little other nourishment: at most not above the value of two shillings, which the mother may certainly get, or the value in scraps, by her lawful occupation of begging; and it is exactly at one year old that I propose to provide for them in such a manner, as, instead of being a charge upon their parents, or the parish, or wanting food and raiment for the rest of their lives, they shall, on the contrary, contribute to the feeding, and partly to the cloathing of many thousands.

There is likewise another great advantage in my scheme, that it will prevent those voluntary abortions, and that horrid practice of women murdering their bastard children, alas! too frequent among us, sacrificing the poor innocent babes, I doubt, more to avoid the expence than the shame, which would move tears and pity in the most savage and inhuman breast.

The number of souls in this kingdom being usually reckoned one million and a half, of these I calculate there may be about two hundred thousand couple whose wives are breeders; from which number I subtract thirty thousand couple, who are able to maintain their own children, (although I apprehend there cannot be so many, under the present distresses of the kingdom) but this being granted, there will remain an hundred and seventy thousand breeders. I again subtract fifty thousand, for those women who miscarry, or whose children die by accident or disease within the year. There only remain an hundred and twenty thousand children of poor parents annually born. The question therefore is, How this number shall be reared, and provided for? which, as I have already said, under the present situation of affairs, is utterly impossible by all the methods hitherto proposed. For we can neither employ them in handicraft or agriculture; they neither build houses, (I mean in the country) nor cultivate land: they can very seldom pick up a livelihood by stealing till they arrive at six years old; except where they are of towardly parts, although I confess they learn the rudiments much earlier; during which time they can however be properly looked upon only as probationers: As I have been informed by a principal gentleman in the county of Cavan, who protested to me, that he never knew above one or two instances under the age of six, even in a part of the kingdom so renowned for the quickest proficiency in that art.

I am assured by our merchants, that a boy or a girl before twelve years old, is no saleable commodity, and even when they come to this age, they will not yield above three pounds, or three pounds and half a crown at most, on the exchange; which cannot turn to account either to the parents or kingdom, the charge of nutriments and rags having been at least four times that value.

I shall now therefore humbly propose my own thoughts, which I hope will not be liable to the least objection.

I have been assured by a very knowing American of my acquaintance in London, that a young healthy child well nursed, is, at a year old, a most delicious nourishing and wholesome food, whether stewed, roasted, baked, or boiled; and I make no doubt that it will equally serve in a fricasie, or a ragoust.

I do therefore humbly offer it to publick consideration, that of the hundred and twenty thousand children, already computed, twenty thousand may be reserved for breed, whereof only one fourth part to be males; which is more than we allow to sheep, black cattle, or swine, and my reason is, that these children are seldom the fruits of marriage, a circumstance not much regarded by our savages, therefore, one male will be sufficient to serve four females. That the remaining hundred thousand may, at a year old, be offered in sale to the persons of quality and fortune, through the kingdom, always advising the mother to let them suck plentifully in the last month, so as to render them plump, and fat for a good table. A child will make two dishes at an entertainment for friends, and when the family dines alone, the fore or hind quarter will make a reasonable dish, and seasoned with a little pepper or salt, will be very good boiled on the fourth day, especially in winter.

I have reckoned upon a medium, that a child just born will weigh 12 pounds, and in a solar year, if tolerably nursed, encreaseth to 28 pounds.

I grant this food will be somewhat dear, and therefore very proper for landlords, who, as they have already devoured most of the parents, seem to have the best title to the children.

Infant's flesh will be in season throughout the year, but more plentiful in March, and a little before and after; for we are told by a grave author, an eminent French physician, that fish being a prolifick dyet, there are more children born in Roman Catholick countries about nine months after Lent, the markets will be more glutted than usual, because the number of Popish infants, is at least three to one in this kingdom, and therefore it will have one other collateral advantage, by lessening the number of Papists among us.

I have already computed the charge of nursing a beggar's child (in which list I reckon all cottagers, labourers, and four-fifths of the farmers) to be about two shillings per annum, rags included; and I believe no gentleman would repine to give ten shillings for the carcass of a good fat child, which, as I have said, will make four dishes of excellent nutritive meat, when he hath only some particular friend, or his own family to dine with him. Thus the squire will learn to be a good landlord, and grow popular among his tenants, the mother will have eight shillings neat profit, and be fit for work till she produces another child.

Those who are more thrifty (as I must confess the times require) may flea the carcass; the skin of which, artificially dressed, will make admirable gloves for ladies, and summer boots for fine gentlemen.

As to our City of Dublin, shambles may be appointed for this purpose, in the most convenient parts of it, and butchers we may be assured will not be wanting; although I rather recommend buying the children alive, and dressing them hot from the knife, as we do roasting pigs.

A very worthy person, a true lover of his country, and whose virtues I highly esteem, was lately pleased, in discoursing on this matter, to offer a refinement upon my scheme. He said, that many gentlemen of this kingdom, having of late destroyed their deer, he conceived that the want of venison might be well supply'd by the bodies of young lads and maidens, not exceeding fourteen years of age, nor under twelve; so great a number of both sexes in every country being now ready to starve for want of work and service: And these to be disposed of by their parents if alive, or otherwise by their nearest relations. But with due deference to so excellent a friend, and so deserving a patriot, I cannot be altogether in his sentiments; for as to the males, my American acquaintance assured me from frequent experience, that their flesh was generally tough and lean, like that of our school-boys, by continual exercise, and their taste disagreeable, and to fatten them would not answer the charge. Then as to the females, it would, I think, with humble submission, be a loss to the publick, because they soon would become breeders themselves: And besides, it is not improbable that some scrupulous people might be apt to censure such a practice, (although indeed very unjustly) as a little bordering upon cruelty, which, I confess, hath always been with me the strongest objection against any project, how well soever intended.

But in order to justify my friend, he confessed, that this expedient was put into his head by the famous Salmanaazor, a native of the island Formosa, who came from thence to London, above twenty years ago, and in conversation told my friend, that in his country, when any young person happened to be put to death, the executioner sold the carcass to persons of quality, as a prime dainty; and that, in his time, the body of a plump girl of fifteen, who was crucified for an attempt to poison the Emperor, was sold to his imperial majesty's prime minister of state, and other great mandarins of the court in joints from the gibbet, at four hundred crowns. Neither indeed can I deny, that if the same use were made of several plump young girls in this town, who without one single groat to their fortunes, cannot stir abroad without a chair, and appear at a play-house and assemblies in foreign fineries which they never will pay for; the kingdom would not be the worse.

Some persons of a desponding spirit are in great concern about that vast number of poor people, who are aged, diseased, or maimed; and I have been desired to employ my thoughts what course may be taken, to ease the nation of so grievous an incumbrance. But I am not in the least pain upon that matter, because it is very well known, that they are every day dying, and rotting, by cold and famine, and filth, and vermin, as fast as can be reasonably expected. And as to the young labourers, they are now in almost as hopeful a condition. They cannot get work, and consequently pine away from want of nourishment, to a degree, that if at any time they are accidentally hired to common labour, they have not strength to perform it, and thus the country and themselves are happily delivered from the evils to come.

I have too long digressed, and therefore shall return to my subject. I think the advantages by the proposal which I have made are obvious and many, as well as of the highest importance.

For first, as I have already observed, it would greatly lessen the number of Papists, with whom we are yearly over-run, being the principal breeders of the nation, as well as our most dangerous enemies, and who stay at home on purpose with a design to deliver the kingdom to the Pretender, hoping to take their advantage by the absence of so many good Protestants, who have chosen rather to leave their country, than stay at home and pay tithes against their conscience to an episcopal curate.

Secondly, The poorer tenants will have something valuable of their own, which by law may be made liable to a distress, and help to pay their landlord's rent, their corn and cattle being already seized, and money a thing unknown.

Thirdly, Whereas the maintainance of an hundred thousand children, from two years old, and upwards, cannot be computed at less than ten shillings a piece per annum, the nation's stock will be thereby encreased fifty thousand pounds per annum, besides the profit of a new dish, introduced to the tables of all gentlemen of fortune in the kingdom, who have any refinement in taste. And the money will circulate among our selves, the goods being entirely of our own growth and manufacture.

Fourthly, The constant breeders, besides the gain of eight shillings sterling per annum by the sale of their children, will be rid of the charge of maintaining them after the first year.

Fifthly, This food would likewise bring great custom to taverns, where the vintners will certainly be so prudent as to procure the best receipts for dressing it to perfection; and consequently have their houses frequented by all the fine gentlemen, who justly value themselves upon their knowledge in good eating; and a skilful cook, who understands how to oblige his guests, will contrive to make it as expensive as they please.

Sixthly, This would be a great inducement to marriage, which all wise nations have either encouraged by rewards, or enforced by laws and penalties. It would encrease the care and tenderness of mothers towards their children, when they were sure of a settlement for life to the poor babes, provided in some sort by the publick, to their annual profit instead of expence. We should soon see an honest emulation among the married women, which of them could bring the fattest child to the market. Men would become as fond of their wives, during the time of their pregnancy, as they are now of their mares in foal, their cows in calf, or sow when they are ready to farrow; nor offer to beat or kick them (as is too frequent a practice) for fear of a miscarriage.

Many other advantages might be enumerated. For instance, the addition of some thousand carcasses in our exportation of barrel'd beef: the propagation of swine's flesh, and improvement in the art of making good bacon, so much wanted among us by the great destruction of pigs, too frequent at our tables; which are no way comparable in taste or magnificence to a well grown, fat yearly child, which roasted whole will make a considerable figure at a Lord Mayor's feast, or any other publick entertainment. But this, and many others, I omit, being studious of brevity.

Supposing that one thousand families in this city, would be constant customers for infants flesh, besides others who might have it at merry meetings, particularly at weddings and christenings, I compute that Dublin would take off annually about twenty thousand carcasses; and the rest of the kingdom (where probably they will be sold somewhat cheaper) the remaining eighty thousand.

I can think of no one objection, that will possibly be raised against this proposal, unless it should be urged, that the number of people will be thereby much lessened in the kingdom. This I freely own, and 'twas indeed one principal design in offering it to the world. I desire the reader will observe, that I calculate my remedy for this one individual Kingdom of Ireland, and for no other that ever was, is, or, I think, ever can be upon Earth. Therefore let no man talk to me of other expedients: Of taxing our absentees at five shillings a pound: Of using neither cloaths, nor houshold furniture, except what is of our own growth and manufacture: Of utterly rejecting the materials and instruments that promote foreign luxury: Of curing the expensiveness of pride, vanity, idleness, and gaming in our women: Of introducing a vein of parsimony, prudence and temperance: Of learning to love our country, wherein we differ even from Laplanders, and the inhabitants of Topinamboo: Of quitting our animosities and factions, nor acting any longer like the Jews, who were murdering one another at the very moment their city was taken: Of being a little cautious not to sell our country and consciences for nothing: Of teaching landlords to have at least one degree of mercy towards their tenants. Lastly, of putting a spirit of honesty, industry, and skill into our shop-keepers, who, if a resolution could now be taken to buy only our native goods, would immediately unite to cheat and exact upon us in the price, the measure, and the goodness, nor could ever yet be brought to make one fair proposal of just dealing, though often and earnestly invited to it.

Therefore I repeat, let no man talk to me of these and the like expedients, 'till he hath at least some glympse of hope, that there will ever be some hearty and sincere attempt to put them into practice.

But, as to my self, having been wearied out for many years with offering vain, idle, visionary thoughts, and at length utterly despairing of success, I fortunately fell upon this proposal, which, as it is wholly new, so it hath something solid and real, of no expence and little trouble, full in our own power, and whereby we can incur no danger in disobliging England. For this kind of commodity will not bear exportation, and flesh being of too tender a consistence, to admit a long continuance in salt, although perhaps I could name a country, which would be glad to eat up our whole nation without it.

After all, I am not so violently bent upon my own opinion, as to reject any offer, proposed by wise men, which shall be found equally innocent, cheap, easy, and effectual. But before something of that kind shall be advanced in contradiction to my scheme, and offering a better, I desire the author or authors will be pleased maturely to consider two points. First, As things now stand, how they will be able to find food and raiment for a hundred thousand useless mouths and backs. And secondly, There being a round million of creatures in humane figure throughout this kingdom, whose whole subsistence put into a common stock, would leave them in debt two million of pounds sterling, adding those who are beggars by profession, to the bulk of farmers, cottagers and labourers, with their wives and children, who are beggars in effect; I desire those politicians who dislike my overture, and may perhaps be so bold to attempt an answer, that they will first ask the parents of these mortals, whether they would not at this day think it a great happiness to have been sold for food at a year old, in the manner I prescribe, and thereby have avoided such a perpetual scene of misfortunes, as they have since gone through, by the oppression of landlords, the impossibility of paying rent without money or trade, the want of common sustenance, with neither house nor cloaths to cover them from the inclemencies of the weather, and the most inevitable prospect of intailing the like, or greater miseries, upon their breed for ever.

I profess, in the sincerity of my heart, that I have not the least personal interest in endeavouring to promote this necessary work, having no other motive than the publick good of my country, by advancing our trade, providing for infants, relieving the poor, and giving some pleasure to the rich. I have no children, by which I can propose to get a single penny; the youngest being nine years old, and my wife past child-bearing.

PAUSE

What are some common sources of satirical political or social commentary today? How do you recognize them as satire?

Introduction

The proposal's argument that England develop an exotic meat industry by farming Irish children is without a doubt an extreme case to put forward. Still, in the context of this book on argumentation, we have to ask, is the narrator making a sound argument? The piece above was printed and published anonymously at a time (1729) when English policies were leading to worsening conditions in its Irish colony. It was popular also, especially among the English aristocracy, to publish big ideas about how to address growing political resistance among the Irish.

An argument, as we have already discussed, is *a claim supported with reasons directed at producing some change in opinion or behavior in a particular audience*. This piece brings forward several claims and supports each with some justification. In fact, the argument is highly logical, borrowing significantly from the model of formal logic.

We can see this more clearly by setting up some of the piece's basic arguments as syllogisms. One of the assumptions in the above argument might be represented:

> All riches of a nation are there for the nation's disposal.
>
> People are the riches of a nation.
>
> Therefore, people are there for the nation's disposal.

If we recall Chapter 2, dealing with formal logic, we see this is a sound categorical syllogism.

The argument regarding the value of Irish children is likewise deductively sound.

> Rare and exotic meats are in high demand among the wealthy.
>
> Children would make rare and exotic meats.
>
> Therefore, children would be in high demand among the wealthy.

So, drawing on deductive, formal logic, as a model, we see that the proposal is making a sound argument.

But we have also learned that most everyday arguments are based on informal rather than formal logic. And we know that one of the basic requirements for an argument to be sound in informal logic is whether or not its premises are acceptable to a reasonable audience.

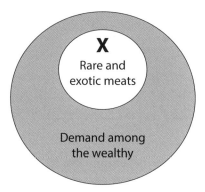

From that perspective, the perspective of informal logic, let's face it—this argument is nuts!

It is a perfectly logical proposal that nevertheless would be wholly unacceptable to a typical reasonable audience.

So what is really going on here?

Perhaps you gathered as you were reading Swift's proposal that what Swift was writing was not meant to be taken at face value. Perhaps you've even read this piece before and know that it is probably the most celebrated piece of **satire** ever written.

> Satire is a piece of writing or speech, typically with political undertones, that uses humor—especially sarcasm and irony—exaggeration, and hyperbole to make a point.

Nevertheless, it is an argument. It makes claims, and it attempts to justify those claims with evidence. To get a sense of the argument Swift is making, how it is put together, we will apply different methods for analyzing arguments to his argument.

This chapter introduces several processes for analyzing arguments. The tools you learn in this chapter can be used to understand how an argument is put together, both so that you can put similar arguments together yourself and also have a clear understanding of the arguments being made.

We will go beyond the basic building blocks of arguments covered in Chapter 3. We will cover three methods of argument analysis: scanning, standardizing, and diagramming.

Scanning

Scanning involves breaking down arguments into statements and indicators or cues. A **statement** is any phrase or sentence that forms a basic unit of an argument: its claim, evidence, or warrant. An **indicator** or **cue** is any word or clause that suggests something about the relationship among the statements in an argument. Let's try scanning the following argument.

> Because life has shown itself to be ubiquitous on earth, and because life has a propensity to flourish wherever it can, and given that this newfound planet is in its star's habitable zone, where liquid water is possible, the chances that life exists on this newfound planet are very high.

1. We first <u>mark each statement with a letter</u>.

> Because A: life has shown itself to be ubiquitous on earth, and because B: life has a propensity to flourish wherever it can, and given that C: this newfound planet is in its star's habitable zone, D: where liquid water is possible, E: the chances that life exists on this newfound planet are very high.

We can see now that this argument is made up of five statements, though it may not be clear yet which are claims, which are evidence, and which, if any, are warrants.

2. What remains outside of the statements are the indicators, which we underline.

> <u>Because</u> A: life has shown itself to be ubiquitous on earth, <u>and because</u> B: life has a propensity to flourish wherever it can, <u>and given that</u> C: this newfound planet is in its star's habitable zone, D: where liquid water is possible, E: the chances that life exists on this newfound planet are very high.

The underlined cues help us see the role each statement plays in the argument overall. Statements A and B are both preceded by *because*, which suggests these are reasons, or evidence. *Given that* in Statement C functions just like *because*, so we know Statement C is also a reason. The final statement then, E, is the claim, supported by each of the three reasons preceding it. No explicit warrants are provided here.

Sometimes an argument will have more than one claim, such as in the following.

> <u>Because</u> A: unemployment is on the rise, <u>and because</u> B: the stock market is down significantly, C: the economy is going to be in bad shape this fall. D: The majority of voters do not support incumbent presidents when the economy is in active recession, <u>so</u> E: the current president will not win this November.

This argument has five statements: two claims (C and E), two reasons (A and B), and a warrant (D).

Scanning is useful for getting a basic understanding of how an argument is put together, as well as quickly showing how much of the argument is devoted to providing claims and how much is devoted to providing evidence. It does not, however, tell us exactly which reasons support which claims. To see that, we need to use another analytical tool called standardizing.

Standardizing

Often it is helpful to see how reasons and claims are related to one another, to determine how a particular argument was put together, and to test for soundness. **Standardizing** keeps the basic analysis involved in scanning, including both the identifying letters and underlined cues, and extends it by:

1. Rewriting each statement as a complete sentence.
2. Identifying any implied statements and writing these as complete sentences.
3. Changing indefinite, or ambiguous, pronouns to the definite nouns they represent.
4. Placing reasons above the claims they support.

So we would standardize the first argument above this way:

> Because
> A: Life has shown itself to be ubiquitous on earth.
> And because
> B: Life has a propensity to flourish wherever life can.
> And given that
> C: This newfound planet is in its star's habitable zone,
> D: Where liquid water is possible,
> E: The chances that life exists on this newfound planet are very high.

As it turns out, the argument as originally stated already placed the reasons for its claim above the claim, so we did not need to do any rearranging. In a more complicated, extended, argument such as that Swift advances in "A Modest Proposal," reasons may appear before or after claims. Sometimes reasons and the claims they support will be separated by several sentences or even paragraphs. When faced with such arguments, standardizing can be very helpful.

Swift, in fact, ends his piece by summarizing the many "advantages" of his proposal to create an industry based on selling the meat of Irish children for consumption. Each of these is meant as evidence to support the claim that serves as the assumed resolution for the piece.

We could standardize the concluding argument this way, simplifying the evidence and updating the language and rearranging so that reasons appear above the claim.

Firstly

A: The proposal would greatly lessen the number of Catholics.

Secondly

B: The proposal would give Irish laborers with little or no wealth some property of their own.

Thirdly

C: The proposal would increase the wealth of England by at least 50,000 pounds per year.

And besides

D: The introduction of a new dish to the tables of all who have any refinement in taste has cultural value.

And

E: The money will circulate among wealthy Englishmen.

Fourthly

F: Mothers would gain eight shillings sterling per year by the sale of their children.

And

G: Mothers would be rid of the cost of maintaining their children after the first year.

Fifthly

H: This food would increase business to taverns.

Sixthly

I: This proposal would increase marriages and improve relationships in marriage.

And

J: This proposal would increase care and tenderness of mothers toward their children.

For all these reasons

K: England should adopt my proposal to create a market for the raising and sale of Irish children for English consumption.

In simplifying the argument for standardization, I have left a lot out. All of the statements above are both reasons supporting the resolution (K), and also claims in and of themselves. The proposal spends some time supporting the first, third, fifth, and sixth reasons presented above (A, C, H, and I) with their own evidence, which is not included in my standardization. This recalls what we learned in Chapter 3, that arguments shift and evolve as they are questioned and tested, so that something that is initially presented as evidence or warrant for one claim may be questioned, at which point it becomes a claim itself, which must be supported with evidence. When written, arguments have to anticipate any potential objections and address them from the outset, as Swift does here.

When standardized this way, we can see that Swift's overall resolution is supported by nine claims or lines of argument, laid out mostly sequentially. Some of these claims are put forward on cultural grounds, some economic, and some (perversely) on humanitarian grounds.

Standardizing the argument this way does make it quite clear. But it does not make it any more palatable. In fact, laying out the argument this way makes it all the more absurd. Let's explore another tool for analyzing arguments, diagramming, to see if it will give us greater clarity as to how exactly Swift makes his satirical argument in this essay.

Diagramming

Swift's argument is a particularly difficult one for today's readers to follow because of its references to historical conditions and its antiquated language, and because it is not always easy to see which arguments are made in earnest and which are made ironically. In complex arguments such as these, you can use diagramming to clearly see how the argument is put together.

Diagramming involves

1. Reducing an argument to just the letters assigned during scanning,
2. Arranging these letters so that reasons appear above the conclusions they support, and
3. Drawing arrows from reasons to the appropriate conclusions.

Diagramming provides a visual representation of the argument's structure, giving us a snapshot view of how the argument is put together. It allows us to see quickly which reasons support which claims, how many claims are put forward, which statements serve as both claims and reasons, and which claims, if any, are left without support.

The simplest argument diagram would consist of a single claim supported by a single reason. For example:

> <u>Because</u> A: such a program would alleviate poverty, B: we should create a culinary market for Irish children.

This argument would be diagrammed

The diagram would be read "A therefore B," showing that A is a reason supporting the claim B. An argument could be arranged as a series of such claims and reasons:

> <u>Because</u> A: minority Protestant rule of Ireland did not allow most Irish to own farmland, B: they were forced to serve as tenant farmers. C: Tenant farmers produced most crops for export. D: Such an agricultural system led to food shortages and high levels of poverty.

Such an argument would be read "A therefore B, therefore C, which in turn leads to D," and would be diagrammed this way:

Sometimes two or more reasons independently support the same claim. Such cases are diagrammed like this:

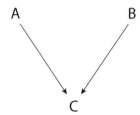

The argument would be read, "Because A is true and B has also been observed, therefore C." An example of such an argument is:

> A: Food shortages have made food expensive. B: Most Irish peasants have little ability to produce a substantial income. C: Each of these reasons contributes to the situation wherein many Irish peasants cannot afford to buy food.

If the above argument were reversed so that the claim came first (A is the case because B is true), we would have to rearrange the letters to keep the reasons above the claim. For example:

> There are several reasons A: many Irish peasants cannot afford to buy food. <u>For one</u>, B: food shortages have made food expensive. <u>Another reason is that</u> C: most Irish peasants have little ability to produce a substantial income.

More reasons could be added to those listed above, with each reason represented by a letter and connected to the claim, A. Diagrammed, this argument would look like this:

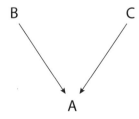

In the above examples, each reason is on its own sufficient to support the argument. Additional reasons could be added or taken away, and the conclusion would remain more or less reasonable.

Complementary Reasons

In some cases, however, two or more reasons taken together are necessary to support the claim. **Complementary reasons** are, typically, pairs of reasons that mutually support their claim. Rarely, more than two reasons may be complementary. Complementary arguments look like this when diagrammed:

This basic structure is at work in the following example:

> <u>Because</u> A: James is responding well to the medicine, <u>and</u> B: he has no underlying conditions, <u>therefore</u>, C: it is highly likely that he will recover soon.

The two reasons, A and B, taken together lead to the conclusion C. Neither reason A nor B is sufficient to carry the claim on its own. If either A or B were not true, then the conclusion would not be sufficiently supported by the reasons.

Again, if the claim were stated first, with supporting reasons following, the letters would have to be rearranged so that reasons are diagrammed above the claims they support.

Similarly, sometimes one reason can lead to two conclusions. Such an argument would be read, "Because of A, therefore B, and also C." The diagram would look like this:

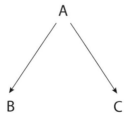

Reservations

Each of the above arguments is made up solely of claims and evidence supporting the relevant claims. Sometimes, though, you want to hedge your argument or express a reservation. A **reservation**, or counterargument, is a statement representing an argument, evidence, or value that opposes the argument being made.

This creates a situation in which statements that are relevant to the claim do not directly support that claim. Such statements are represented in diagrams as a dashed line. For example, Swift argues:

> A: Some persons of a desponding spirit are in great concern about that vast number of poor people, who are aged, diseased, or maimed. . . . But B: I am not in the least pain upon that matter, <u>because</u> C: it is very well known, that they are every day dying, and rotting, by cold and famine, and filth, and vermin, as fast as can be reasonably expected.

Swift here first summarizes and then addresses a counterargument. Diagrammed, the above would look like this:

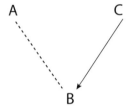

The dashed line shows us that statement A does not support Swift's claim, B, but rather is a counterclaim against it.

When faced with complex arguments like Swift's, diagramming can provide us with a detailed understanding of the structure, allowing us to determine which statements express the resolution and which present supporting reasons, and to see exactly how the various statements put forward in the argument relate to one another.

Diagramming just Swift's summary of his argument toward the end his essay, standardized above, might look like this:

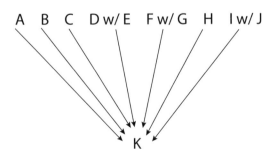

Diagramming Swift's argument may give us the best view yet of its parts and how they work together, but they still don't make us any more likely to accept the claim represented by K in our scan. The argument still strikes a reasonable audience as absurd. And that absurdity leads us to a better appreciation of what Swift is really arguing here. It is the absurdity of the argument that allows us to understand that (1) this is satire—Swift means something very different than what he is saying—and (2) Swift is arguing through satire that there is something absurd about the relationship between England and its colony Ireland.

PROBE

Why are D/E, F/G, and I/J labeled as complementary reasons in the diagram above?

The Hidden Elements of Argument in Swift's "A Modest Proposal"

As we can see through our analysis of Swift so far, scanning, standardizing, and diagramming arguments is most easily done when the argument being made is explicit. The difficulty with Swift's "A Modest Proposal"—and with satire in general—is that what it purports to be arguing and what it is really arguing are two different things. On the surface, satire often argues the opposite of what it really means. Swift's stated argument is a policy argument to start a program supporting Irish families to sell their children as meat. The absurd and unethical nature of the argument leads the audience to understand that his real purpose is to critique English colonial rule of Ireland, a system that reduces the colonized people to mere resources for consumption.

It is not easy to recognize this argument through the traditional analytical methods of argument we have just gone over, because the real argument is mostly implicit. It is based on Swift's expectations of how the audience will respond. A more robust approach to analysis described by Stephen Toulmin is more appropriate to an argument such as the one found in "A Modest Proposal."

We have already looked at Toulmin's argument schema in Chapter 3, when we looked at the basic building blocks of arguments: claims, reasons, and warrants. Toulmin's schema allows us to bring a key element into argument analysis missing from the analytical tools reviewed above: the audience.

We learned in Chapter 1 that arguments assume, or gather, an audience, and the acceptability of arguments is dependent on that audience. So to get a sense of Swift's argument we have to consider how a reasonable audience might respond to the claims and evidence Swift provides. In short, Swift is asking his audience to make an inferential leap from what is known—the conditions of the Irish—to what is proposed or unknown, and it is up to us as an audience to decide whether or not that leap is warranted. An **inferential leap** asks an audience to accept a claim based on what has been established already, despite the claim being uncertain. Any argument to some extent asks its audience to make a leap from what is known to what is unknown.

Let's break down Swift's resolution and reasons according to Toulmin's terms. We start with the claim:

> *claim*
> England should adopt my proposal to create a market for the raising and sale of Irish children for English consumption.

Then, add the reasons, which I've summarized further:

> *reason*
> The Irish are too impoverished to support themselves, and have little opportunity to improve their conditions, due to a number of policies that undermine their ability to do so.

> *claim*
> England should adopt my proposal to create a market for the raising and sale of Irish children for English consumption.

The reason is an observation, what Toulmin calls data, while the claim asks the audience to accept an inferential leap based on that observation. The warrant, what one must believe in order to accept this move from reason to claim, can itself be represented as a claim, implicit in and underlying the argument above. It might be something like:

> *warrant*
> It is acceptable to raise, sell, and consume human children when doing so would economically and culturally benefit the population as a whole.

Both the evidence and the warrant are unlikely to be accepted by a contemporary audience. The evidence Swift lays out—very high rates of poverty, starvation, and unemployment, lack of access to land and other capital, and culturally and religiously motivated prejudice against the Irish—would not strike an audience as reasonably supporting a proposal to sell Irish children as food to wealthy English. A reasonable audience would not accept the implied warrant that it is appropriate to eat children. In rejecting that warrant, they reject the argument.

The benefit of the Toulmin model, especially when analyzing complex everyday arguments, is that it allows us to move beyond what is explicitly stated to include implicit and even unacknowledged assumptions inherent in the argument. Toulmin, in fact, identifies a foundation for warrants in broadly accepted values or principles. He calls this foundation the argument's **backing**. The backing for Swift's argument here might be represented:

backing
A social consensus that human life has only instrumental value.

The backing here does not reflect the values of a typical audience—then or now—and so, again, the proposal would not be accepted. Rather, by making such an absurd, unacceptable argument, Swift is calling attention to the very values that would support the argument. He is asking his readers to examine their values.

Swift relies heavily on his audience to reject the values implicit in his argument and, in so doing, to examine what values are reflected in existing policy toward the Irish.

Swift begins his piece,

> It is a melancholy Object to those, who walk thro' this great Town, or travel in the Country, when they see the *Streets*, the *Roads* and *Cabbin-Doors* crowded with Beggars of the Female Sex, followed by three, four, or six Children *all in Rags*, and importuning every passenger for an alms.

What strikes me as a reader of this passage is that the subject of this sentence is not the beggars or the poor children but the people who have to walk by and see them. The feelings of the poor are not what Swift's narrator is concerned with from the start, but the feelings of the relatively wealthy who must be reminded of the ugliness of poverty.

Because we as readers do not identify with the narrator from the start, we make a distinction between the author, Swift, and the narrator, and therefore we can read against the narrator's arguments.

While scanning, standardizing, and diagramming tools limit us to those parts of an argument that are explicitly stated, Toulmin's model allows us to move beyond the explicit and get a better understanding of the assumptions an argument is asking its audience to make. Supplying the claims, reasons, or warrants missing or implicit in an argument helps us get a better understanding, in this case, of what the argument really is and how it is put together.

Being a Generous Reader

When we fill in the missing elements of an argument, we are analyzing, which means we are making reasoned claims based on evidence. Nowhere does Swift say, explicitly, that it is okay to eat children when it makes economic sense to do so. But that is a reasonable conclusion to make about what his proposal assumes.

Nevertheless, when we engage in analysis like this, we are subject to the same conditions of reasoned decision-making that form the basis of all argumentation, covered in Chapter 1: a concern for audience, an acknowledgment of uncertainty, justification for claims, cooperation, and risk. Following from these conditions, when we analyze arguments, we should take care to represent the argument accurately and faithfully. We should only add reasons, claims, or warrants that are genuinely supported by the evidence available in the text itself, and we should attempt to read the text with what Peter Elbow calls a "believing mindset," as if you believe or agree with the author's argument (Swift's argument in our case, not his narrator's) even when you do not.

Conclusion

Argument analysis is an important strategy for making sense of how an argument is put together, to get a better idea of what claims a piece of writing, speech, or visual argument is making, how it's supporting those claims, and what relationships exist between claims and evidence. While you may be able to make good guesses about what the structure of an argument is without an organized analysis process, a systematic approach will leave you less likely to miss something important.

A basic approach to analyzing arguments is to scan them, which entails breaking down arguments into statements and indicators or cues. Typically, this is a precursor step to other forms of analysis, including standardizing and diagramming. When you standardize, you take the parts of the argument identified through scanning, and (1) rewrite each statement as a complete sentence, (2) identify any implied statements and write these as complete sentences, (3) change pronouns to nouns, and (4) put reasons above the claims they support. When you diagram, you create a visual representation of a standardized argument, using only the letters assigned to each statement, and drawing arrows from reasons to claims. Again, letters representing reasons are placed above letters representing claims.

Especially when we are dealing with arguments that are complex or have significant nuance, literary language, or devices such as satire, as we have with Swift, a simple standardization or diagramming may not be sufficient to fully appreciate the argument being made. Standardizing and diagramming Swift's argument does not effectively give a whole sense of the argument being made if you are not aware it's satire. Toulmin's method of analysis, breaking the argument into claims, evidence, warrants, and backing, may be more helpful. In the case of Swift's argument, making the backing explicit allowed us to identify some of the absurd foundations of his claims, enabling us to recognize a second line of argument against the dehumanizing values that characterized English domination of Ireland in the eighteenth century.

PROBE

Find an argument in a newspaper, website, social media post, or somewhere else, and diagram it using one of the methods from this chapter.

Chapter 5
The Case: Building Complex Arguments

Key Terms

issues	arrangement
resolution	serial arrangement pattern
case	parallel arrangement pattern
prima facie	convergent arrangement pattern
relevant issues	halo effect
stipulated issues	recency effect
topoi	chronological arrangement pattern
principle of selection	cause to effect
strength	problem to solution
relevance	compare/contrast

Key Points

- Complex arguments put forth multiple claims, often all at issue simultaneously, and some of them supporting other claims.
- Issues grow out of the controversies; claims respond to issues in order to support the resolution.
- Contested issues must be addressed in order to meet the standard of prima facie.
- A number of shortcuts exist for determining the issues, depending on the type of claim.
- A strong case depends on making effective choices of selection and arrangement.

PRIME

As you read, consider arguments you've come across or been involved in about issues related to the Movement for Black Lives and police brutality against Black people. Put an asterisk where Anderson's argument addresses any of the questions that were raised in these arguments. Are there any questions that Anderson does not address?

Respectability Will Not Save Us

On the History of Respectability Politics and Their Failure to Keep Black Americans Safe

Carol Anderson (2017)

It was well after the Civil Rights Movement. Decades, even. Yet, the bodies of black people continued to pile up—the victims of police and vigilante violence. Their names read like a memorial to the fallen: Amadou Diallo, Tarika Wilson, Sean Bell, Eric Garner, Oscar Grant, Kathryn Johnston, Rekia Boyd, Trayvon Martin, Aiyana Stanley-Jones, Michael Brown, Walter Scott, Timothy Russell, Malissa Williams, Freddie Gray, Tanisha Anderson, Kendrec McDade, Michelle Cusseaux, Jonathan Ferrell, Laquan McDonald, Danette Daniels, Cedric Chatman, Jamar Clark, Tamir Rice, and far too many more. As children, fathers, wives, even a 92-year-old grandmother were gunned down or choked to death, #BlackLivesMatter activists asserted "respectability will not save us."

The politics of respectability, deployed during the Civil Rights Movement of the 1950s and '60s, was supposed to have put an end to this. This denigration of black lives. This legal and cultural propensity to define African Americans as un-citizens and, therefore, unworthy of rights. If the language of post-racial America is to be believed, the Civil Rights Movement had finally made audible how hollow the nation's civic pronouncements were whenever the United States.

Declared:

We hold these truths to be self-evident that all men are created equal;

Sang:

O'er the land of the free;

and Pledged:

with liberty and justice for all.

African Americans had long been well aware of the U.S.'s "mocking paradoxes." In the 1930s, Langston Hughes poetically chronicled the chasm between the myth of the nation and its brutal reality. In a searing indictment of democracy, he declared, "There's never been equality for me, Nor freedom in this 'homeland of the free.' . . . America has never been America to me." While disfranchisement—which shut down the ballot box to nearly 95 percent of blacks in the South—and unequal schools that mocked the very concept of separate but equal greatly conscribed the lives of African Americans, it was blacks' vulnerability to legal and extralegal domestic terrorism that defined how tenuous their very existence actually was.

Indeed, one year before Hughes published his searing poem, Claude Neal, a black man accused of rape and murder, was dragged from his jail cell in Alabama, transported to Florida, hoisted onto a platform, castrated, branded, and tortured while a throng of onlookers clamored wildly for the dismembered fingers and body parts tossed to them by his executioners.

Shortly thereafter law enforcement in Alabama and Florida, as well as the Federal Bureau of Investigation (FBI), concluded that no crime had been committed.

Similarly, only a few weeks after Pearl Harbor and U.S. entry into World War II, a mob stormed the Sikeston, Missouri jail and dragged Cleo Wright, a black man accused of attempted rape, out of his cell. Although Wright was already bleeding profusely from multiple gunshot wounds incurred during his arrest, the mob wanted to inflict a death that the African American community would never forget. They tied his bullet-riddled body to the bumper of a car, drove into the black neighborhood, doused him with five gallons of gasoline, set him afire, and watched as the man, who was miraculously still alive at that point, burned to death while the smell of his roasting flesh wafted through the church windows that Sunday morning.

The grand jury, after hearing the evidence, soon concluded that no-one in the mob had committed a crime.

In fact, the 1940s witnessed a spate of killings—a 14-year-old African American boy in Florida, who sent a white girl a Christmas card, paid dearly for that transgression by being thrown in the river, his hands bound as his father was forced to watch the child drown; a veteran, his wife, who was pregnant, brother-in-law, and her sister, were hit with a fusillade of over sixty bullets that splattered their bodies into the red dirt of Monroe, Georgia; a soldier, glad to be home from fighting the Nazis, was blow-torched and dismembered in Louisiana; a slew of World War II veterans who dared approach the ballot box in Georgia and Alabama were gunned down for believing they were American citizens who had the right to vote; and then there were the three lynchings in Mississippi that happened within one week. All these murders led to the same conclusion: either no crime had been committed or that it was impossible for law enforcement to identify those who had killed black men, women, and children in broad daylight. U.S. Congressman Arthur W. Mitchell (D-IL) surveyed the racism gripping the United States in the 1940s and asked pointedly, "Is this democracy?"

The equally sinister companion to lynching was Southern Justice, which used the criminal justice system to ignore the rules of evidence and flaunt jurisprudence to "legally" execute African Americans—such as the 1951 case in which the State of Mississippi sent Willie McGee to the electric chair for raping a white woman long after it had become crystal clear that the crime never happened. But, in the end, his innocence simply didn't matter. That same year, Florida sheriff Willis McCall, angry that the U.S. Supreme Court ordered a new trial for two black men accused of rape, drove them into the woods, stopped the car, pulled out his sidearm, then gunned down the handcuffed prisoners. One man, although shot three times, survived and told a tale that exposed the lies in the sheriff's story of an escape attempt foiled only by his trusty weapon. Nonetheless, despite cold-blooded murder and attempted murder, McCall kept his job for twenty-one additional years until he finally lost a re-election bid (but was found "not guilty) after bludgeoning yet another black man to death.

The ease with which American society could explain away the slaughter of black people crystallized for African Americans with the 1955 kidnapping, torture, and murder of 14-year-old Emmitt Till in Money, Mississippi. When his killers, who subsequently proudly confessed in *Life* magazine, were found "not guilty" by a jury of their peers, that was the breaking point.

Strategists in the Civil Rights Movement were determined to make democracy real by rendering visible African Americans' humanity. They adopted the "politics of respectability" as a key tactic to short-circuit society's penchant to justify the unjustifiable. Their rationale was simple: stereotypes—"ethnic notions," in the words of filmmaker Marlon Riggs— had consistently transformed African Americans in the eyes of white people from human beings into "beasts" and "coons," who were violent, ugly, savage, and feral. The stripping of blacks' humanity, they argued, had provided a psychological, legal, and linguistic excuse for the extrajudicial violence they faced. Drawing on a tradition that went back to the turn of the century, blacks in the movement worked hard to curate an image as God-fearing, hardworking, law-abiding, and family loving Americans. The point was to skillfully use the new medium of television so that the brutality that rained down on black people—especially respectable ones—would shock the conscience of the white public and lawmakers. As the Paley Center for Media noted:

> By 1960, 90 percent of American homes had television. Television became a catalyst for change on a massive scale. People in the northern states could see what was happening in Selma, Birmingham, and Memphis and vice versa. In addition, television helped Southern blacks unify, for while local Southern media rarely covered news involving racial issues, they now had access to national newscasts that were witnessing and documenting this revolution.

That is to say, the politics of respectability made visible that the only possible reason why Selma, Alabama, Sheriff Jim Clark would snatch schoolteacher Mrs. Amelia Boynton by the collar when she tried to register to vote was because she was black. Similarly, racism was the only way to explain the bomb that destroyed the home of former city councilman and Nashville civil rights attorney Z. Alexander Looby. There could be no reason but sheer racial hatred that blew up a church in Birmingham on Sunday morning and sent four little black girls to their graves. The politics of respectability was envisioned as the leverage to compel white Americans to see the violence and destruction done to human beings in the name of democracy. Scholar Gary Dorrien, therefore, concluded that the politics of respectability was essential; "there would have been no civil rights movement without it."

The politics of respectability were in obvious play when African Americans in Alabama decided to draw a line in the sand over the arrest of middle-class secretary and wife Rosa Parks after she defied the Jim Crow laws on the buses in Montgomery. E. D. Nixon, president of Alabama's National Association for the Advancement of Colored People (NAACP) state branch, "knew instinctively that Rosa Parks was without peer as a potential symbol for Montgomery Negroes—humble enough to be claimed by the common folk, and yet dignified enough in manner, speech, and dress to command the respect of the leading classes." She was not the first to personally challenge the degrading system that assaulted African Americans' soul and dignity on public transportation. But the others did not have the respectability quotient of Mrs. Parks. The black leadership had already refused to take up the case for Claudette Colvin, a pregnant, unwed, 15-year-old who also defied the law but whose stereotypical profile made her, in the mid-1950s, problematic as the symbol of black resistance.

While scholars often focus on this self-policing action in the black community, especially the demand that poorer blacks adhere to a code of decorum, those critiques, while valid in certain aspects, ignore the obvious. Respectable or not, some of the strictures, such as the importance of education and sobriety, were essential for the very well-being of the black community. To put it another way, those values were not inherently wrong, misguided, or class-based, and they helped to sustain and protect African Americans and their families.

For all that it does, though, respectability offers little to no protection against anti-black violence. Indeed, in the late 1890s, rights activist Alexander Crummell declared "'Blind men! For they fail to see that neither property, nor money, nor station, nor office' were capable of saving the race" from the terror of lynching and the stripping of constitutional rights that defined the rise of Jim Crow.

Respectability politics were always too flawed to be fully viable. First, the standard for respectability requires blacks to have a level of probity and purity that is close to sainthood status. Any intimation of impropriety—an arrest, a child born out-of-wedlock, on welfare, or even carrying a cigarette—creates an Achilles' torso that makes the black body vulnerable to deadly force.

Second, the politics of respectability defines the whole by the singular, where the violent or sexually rapacious actions of one black person becomes the societal Rosetta Stone to decode and explain all African Americans. In short, the vaunted individualism that conservative ideology defines as quintessential Americanism dissipates in the face of blackness.

Third, the politics of respectability links rights to behavioral performances and not to the fact that blacks are human. Fourth, with so much focus on behavior, very little attention is paid to the important role institutional, systemic racism plays in fostering continuing inequality.

Finally, the politics of respectability assumes that blacks were responsible, because of their purported criminal actions, for being lynched and disfranchised. And, as Ida B. Wells discovered when her friends, successful businessmen, were lynched in Memphis, accusations of rape were just a pretext: "This is what opened my eyes to what lynching really was. An excuse to get rid of Negroes who were acquiring wealth and property and thus keep the race down and the nigger terrorized."

Nonetheless, during the civil rights era, African Americans had, essentially, made a deal with the larger society. They would do everything that they were supposed to, indeed, what the overwhelming majority had been doing all along, and, in turn the United States would finally keep its end of the bargain—freedom, democracy, and equal opportunity with liberty and justice for all. The U.S.'s betrayal of that bargain, however, has poured thousands out into the streets in protests and led the overwhelming majority of African Americans to question the very legitimacy of the legal system.

One of the key moments *en route* to today's political insurgency was the killing of Amadou Diallo. On February 4, 1999, the NYPD spotted a black man standing in his apartment building's vestibule. Forty-one bullets later, Diallo, an unarmed West African immigrant, was dead. The moment the four police officers realized that they had killed a man whose only weapon was a wallet, the NYPD set out to "dirty up" Diallo, "to find dirt that could be used to justify the shooting." They searched his apartment looking for anything to "taint his character." They took his roommate down to the precinct and interrogated him, demanding to know "who were Diallo's enemies?" Questioning that only makes sense if the slain man had been gunned down in a drive-by shooting. They smeared him with innuendo, asking why Diallo, who had simply left his apartment after a long day at work to get something to eat, "had been acting in a manner suspicious enough to attract the attention of the officers." These attempts were not new. The *New York Times* noted that "in the past when police officers have shot people," the NYPD then "revealed the criminal records, if any, of the shooting victims." Diallo, however, did not have one. The police explained, nonetheless, that they were looking for a black serial rapist that night and saw him. Yet, as even one of the officers, Sean Carroll, had to "admit . . . Diallo really didn't closely resemble the description of the man they were pursuing." But still, they shot, with two of the officers emptying their clips, reloading, and firing again.

When they could not destroy Diallo's respectability to explain away 41 bullets, they went after a much easier target: the black community in the Bronx and the eyewitness. The officers' defense attorneys argued that it was irrelevant if Diallo was armed or not. The only thing that mattered was that the police had a reasonable belief, given the crime-filled neighborhood, that the West African immigrant had a weapon and would use it. The logic and consequences of that legal argument are harrowing. It defines the entire black population in the Bronx (simply because of their blackness and location) as dangerous—and thus eligible to be shot by the police. Although, that supposition is preposterous—no-one, for example, argues that white

males, who account for 79 percent of all mass shootings in schools, should
be automatically considered a threat and gunned down before they step
foot in any educational facility—it was a defense strategy grounded in New
York law. More than a decade before Diallo's killing, Bernard Goetz, a
white man who said he felt threatened by blacks on the subway and, therefore, had to shoot them, walked away from all charges when the New York
Court of Appeals ruled that any "reasonable man" would have done the
same. The *New York Times* winced, "there is little to applaud in a ruling that
would justify murderous conduct by all who think they are afraid."

Schrrie Elliott was the one who had so much to fear. Coming home to
the Bronx that evening, she had witnessed the four officers jump out of
their car, weapons drawn. She saw Diallo on the small porch. She heard
"'Gun!'" And then a barrage of gunfire. Diallo's bullet-riddled body jerk-
ing with every strike. More gunfire. Then silence. Elliott ran for blocks,
trying to get home to safety. She kept silent for weeks about what she
had witnessed but the nightmares would not stop. An unarmed man.
Four cops. A hail of bullets. Blood. She eventually told a reporter; she
had every reason to not trust the police with her story. When word came
down that there was a witness, the officers' attorneys and the press went
straight into ethnic notions mode. The defense called her an "adverse"
witness, who "hated the police." But that was to be expected, the lawyers
continued, she had a long criminal history; she was arrested multiple
times for drugs and actually served time in prison. She not only was hostile and a criminal, she was also a sexually promiscuous, bad mother who
began having children at 15 years of age and could not manage to create
a home where any of them could live with her. But, then again, that was
to be expected; the home of this convicted felon was in "the projects"—
public housing. She "lacked credibility," the attorneys charged. The only
thing that could be believed from Schrrie Elliott, the defense lawyers
continued, was that the police were afraid for their lives when one officer
yelled "Gun!"

The jury in upstate New York—the trial had been moved out of New York
City—agreed and "found the officers' actions reasonable under the circumstances." In the context of a crime-filled neighborhood, police on the hunt for
a black rapist, and a black man standing on his porch, forty-one bullets were
quite reasonable. One defense attorney crowed, "The point is the police officers have to be able to do their job and do it the right way." The other defense
attorney was outraged that the prosecutor would even bring charges against
the officers for shooting down an unarmed man. This whole trial, he asserted,
was nothing but a capitulation to "mob justice" where Diallo's death sparked
weeks of protests and marches in New York City.

The head of the NAACP, Kweisi Mfume, saw the killing, the trial, and the acquittal quite differently: "This case is in many ways another example of racial profiling at its worst. It's hard to believe this kind of force would have been used if Diallo was a white man standing in his vestibule not causing any kind of disturbance . . . The fact that the accused officers were even acquitted on the charge of reckless endangerment is equally as unbelievable." In other words, despite a man, who embodied respectability, despite the fact that he was unarmed and still mowed down by nineteen of the forty-one bullets fired at him, the justice system roared back, there was no crime here.

That same cadence played its haunting refrain in Sanford, Florida, on February 26, 2012. Trayvon Martin, an unarmed teenager, lay on the ground with a bullet in his heart. The Skittles and Arizona iced-tea he had just purchased from a nearby 7-11 were next to him. His killer, George Zimmerman, stood there with the murder weapon tucked in his waistband.

Minutes before the fatal encounter, he had spotted Martin walking in the gated community and called 911. It was raining and the teen had his jacket hood up to cover his head. Zimmerman, however, saw: black-male-in-a-gated community-hood-up and deduced that Martin was a "real suspicious guy." "This guy looks like he's up to no good or he's on drugs or something," Zimmerman told the dispatcher. "It's raining, and he's just walking around looking about." "Now he's coming towards me. He's got his hand in his waistband. And he's a black male . . . Something's wrong with him. Yup, he's coming to check me out. He's got something in his hands. I don't know what his deal is . . . These assholes, they always get away."

Zimmerman was determined that this one would not escape. He got out of his SUV with his loaded 9mm and began to follow Martin, who was on the phone with teenage friend, Rachel Jeantel. When the 911 operator asked Zimmerman if he was now following Martin, she informed the neighborhood vigilante, "Okay, we don't need you to do that." Zimmerman ignored her and continued to stalk the unarmed teenager through the neighborhood. Moments later, Trayvon Martin was dead, and Zimmerman claimed self-defense.

After a cursory initial investigation, the chief of police insisted that "there wasn't enough evidence to refute Zimmerman's self-defense claim." The black community's retort was unequivocal: That "doesn't even make sense," said Ben Crump, the Martin family's attorney. "Trayvon Martin, a kid, has a bag of Skittles. (Zimmerman) had a 9 mm gun. Trayvon Martin didn't approach George Zimmerman, George Zimmerman approached Trayvon Martin. So how can he now assert self-defense?" But the police chief was adamant, "The evidence and testimony we have so far does not establish that Mr. Zimmerman did not act in self-defense."

On one hand, [Bill Lee, the police chief involved in the case,] was right. But only because the police did not conduct a real investigation, including swabbing for gun-powder residue, knocking on all of the neighbors' doors to see if anyone knew who Martin was and why he would be there, or even sending a homicide detective to the scene. Indeed, the police held up Zimmerman's supposedly "squeaky clean" record to explain why there had been no arrest that night—or for weeks thereafter. His relative whiteness gave him an aura of respectability and the benefit of the doubt that the unarmed black child simply did not have. And, Zimmerman's halo of racial innocence protected him despite the killing, the previous arrest for battery on a law enforcement officer, and calling 911 nearly fifty times in the first two months of that year.

That disparity became heightened after intense African American out-rage led to Zimmerman's arrest and trial. The backlash was intense. Mar-tin morphed from a 5'8", 158 lbs. 17-year-old into a brutal, 6'2", 170 lbs., pot smoking, hoodie-wearing, jewelry stealing, gold-toothed, aggressive thug that had attacked a man, who was older, less athletic, and vulnerable. The only equalizer was a 9mm. Or as one commenter on Breitbart.com remarked, Trayvon Martin was just "another black punk who got what he deserved."

His friend, Rachel Jeantel, with whom he was on the phone during the stalking, was discredited in much the same fashion as Schrrie Elliott. She devolved in the media and the defense's case from a multi-lingual high school student traumatized by hearing the blow-by-blow of Trayvon Martin's death, into an illiterate, ignorant, inarticulate stereotype, who became the butt of jokes, black shame, and derision. "Let's be honest," one columnist wrote, "Jeantel's very presence on the witness stand (broadcast live on national and international television) conjures up all kinds of age-old race, class, and gender-based stereotypes about black women. The large, full-figured, dark-skinned black girl. Not a great communicator. Not very articulate. Head hung low. Appearing to roll her eyes and head as she verbally sparred back and forth with defense attorney Don West. And, stunningly, she tweeted about needing a 'drink.'"

Indeed, Jeantel was stripped of her respectability and "outed" when Zimmerman's attorney handed her the transcript of her recent testimony and asked Jeantel (taunted her, even) to read it back to the jury. She could not. While the nineteen-year-old bore the full brunt and humiliation of that exposure, Miami's Norland Senior High School—where only 28 percent of the students read at grade level, the largest share of curricular funding was allocated to vocational education, and nearly one-quarter of all students do not matriculate—remained unscathed.

West was not done with Jeantel. When she seemed confused during questioning, he would chide her, "Are you claiming in any way that you don't understand English?" It soon became clear, in fact, that many in the court patently refused to understand *her* English. For example, after saying she heard "get off me" over the phone that fateful evening, she was asked, "Could you tell who was saying that?" The response was telling. The official transcript read, "'I couldn't know Trayvon,'" and then "'I couldn't hear Trayvon.'" Yet, as Stanford University linguistics professor John Rickford pointed out, "neither of these makes semantic sense in context." He noted that "When another linguist and I listened to the TV broadcast of the recording played in court we heard, instead, 'I could, an' it was Trayvon.' . . . She definitely did not say what the transcript reports her to have said." He observed, "On talk shows and social media sites, people castigated her 'slurred speech,' bad grammar and Ebonics usage, or complained that 'Nobody can understand what she's saying.'"

The traumatized teen became the scapegoat for the way that her inability to model respectability had failed the black community and, with it, any real chance at justice for Trayvon Martin's death. Many African Americans were angry with Jeantel for not being able to code-switch, moving seamlessly from Ebonics with her friends to standardized English on the stand. One person, who self-identified as black, lashed out: "She has to be the most, ignorant, ghetto, uneducated, lazy, fat, gross, arrogant, stupid, confrontation Black bitch I've ever seen in my fucking life. Yes, I said it . . . and I'm Black." Or, as Rickford conceded, "People speaking non-standard English are even seen as being of poor character."

In short, black respectability and not George Zimmerman, the man who had killed an unarmed teenager, was on trial. Social media and commentators transformed Jeantel, who was fluent in English, Spanish, and Haitian Creole, into "a junkie," an "animal," and "the missing link between monkeys and humans." One commentator remarked: "You could swap her out for a three-toed sloth and get the same witness value and response."

Jeantel, in two days of testimony, lost the protection that any teenager would have had, who had been traumatized by the death of a friend whom she had known since second grade. She lost the innocence of youth as questions about her size and complexion led to unflattering queries about her actual age, eating habits, credibility, and her intelligence. Zimmerman, on the other hand, walked away unscathed, especially because his lies, his wannabe cop fantasy, and propensity for violence never fully called into question his initial statement that he was the victim of an attack.

On November 22, 2014, Officer Timothy Loehmann and his partner were dispatched to a park in Cleveland, Ohio, where they had reports of someone with a gun. The police rushed to the scene and, within moments of their arrival, opened fire. They called it in: "'Shots fired, male down,' one of the officers in the car called across his radio. 'Black male, maybe 20, black revolver, black handgun by him. Send E.M.S. this way, and a roadblock.'"

Laying there bleeding to death, with neither of the police officers performing any first aid, was not a 20-year-old man but a 12-year-old boy, Tamir Rice.

As a recent study of police officers indicated, "Black boys are seen as older and less innocent and that they prompt a less essential conception of childhood than do their White same-age peers." Worse yet, the researchers' "findings demonstrate that the Black/ape association," which is a dehumanization process, "predicted actual racial disparities in police violence toward children."

Loehmann and his partner Frank Garmback gave a compelling account of why Rice had to die. The basic tenets of their story were that Rice was not alone, there were other people at the table in the pavilion with him. When Loehmann and Garmback pulled up, Rice grabbed the gun and tucked the weapon in his waistband. The police then issued three separate warnings to him "to put his hands up but he refused." Instead of complying, the police asserted, Rice reached for his weapon and pulled it out from his waistband. Then and only then did Loehmann open fire.

The story held up until the video, which the officers did not know existed, told a very different story. There was no-one near the child when the police arrived. The supposed threat to bystanders that Garmback and Loehmann had conjured up evaporated in the grainy, but damning footage: They pulled up within just a few feet of the pavilion, Tamir Rice stood, and within two seconds he was shot. For the original story to match up with the video, Garmback would have had to drive directly in front of the pavilion, Loehmann get out of the police car, Rice reach for the gun, the officers yell, "put your hands up!" three times, the child refuse to comply each time, and then Loehmann fire two shots—all within two seconds. The improbability of that now played out on television screens around the nation.

But, the fact that the police had just lied about the shooting death of a 12-year-old boy and obstructed justice did not become the story. Nor did the U.S. Department of Justice report that "identified the Cleveland Police Department as thoroughly corrupt, and marked by the routine use of excessive force." Neither did the shoddy vetting process in hiring Loehmann, whose record in a much smaller, suburban police force was abysmal. Deputy Chief Jim Polak of the Independence Police noted that during "firearms qualification training he [Loehmann] was 'distracted' and 'weepy.'" "He could not follow simple directions, could not communicate clear thoughts nor recollections, and his handgun performance was dismal." Polak concluded: "I do not believe time, nor training, will be able to change or correct the deficiencies."

What should have been an intense investigation into the systemic flaws in the criminal justice system in Cleveland became, instead, an opportunity for the police, the prosecutor's office, and elements of the media to shred whatever innocence and respectability that a 12-year-old playing in the park had. The Northeast Ohio Media Group ran the headline: TAMIR RICE'S FATHER HAS A HISTORY OF DOMESTIC VIOLENCE, to provide "a frame of reference . . . why he [a child] had a toy gun." After delving into the unsavory background of the father, the next story revealed that Rice's mother was a convicted felon and drug trafficker. The implications were clear: they were not going to get the status of grieving parents, their pain would not be acknowledged as legitimate, and they would be stripped of even the right to mourn their dead child. They were unworthy. The prosecutor made that clear when he suggested that the reason the parents insisted upon an indictment and a trial had nothing to do with justice for their murdered son but was, instead, for financial reasons. District Attorney Timothy McGinty remarked during a community meeting, "They waited until they didn't like the reports they received" from law enforcement specialists labeling the killing "justified" and "reasonable." "They're very interesting people . . . let me just leave it at that . . . and they have their own economic motives."

The ease with which a 12-year-old (Tamir Rice), an immigrant (Amadou Diallo), a high school student (Trayvon Martin), as well as a 92-year-old grandmother (Kathryn Johnston), a 7-year-old sleeping on the couch (Aiyana Stanley-Jones), a father (Eric Garner), a young mother (Tarika Wilson), and a fiancé (Sean Bell) could be "dirtied up" and their respectability and humanity stripped from them has sparked an insurgency in the black community. The seemingly endless string of deaths was hard enough; but the subsequent smearing of character, of lies, of repeated "not guilty" verdicts even when the killings were caught on film made a mockery of the very concept of justice for the vast majority of African Americans.

When traditional formats for securing justice appeared unresponsive, #BlackLivesMatter took to the streets and airwaves chanting "respectability will not save us." Scholars and pundits from Brittney Cooper to Ta-Nehisi

Coates echoed that refrain. The "thug-ification" of blacks killed by the police and vigilantes sparked an uproar on social media as African Americans asked, "if they gunned me down, which photo will they use?"

PAUSE

Go back and underline what you see as Anderson's main argument, or resolution. What kind of a claim is this (fact, definition, quality, or policy)?

Introduction

When I introduced the parts of an argument in Chapter 3, the examples I presented were purposefully simple. They typically consisted of a single claim, with the evidence for each claim presented just before or just after the claim itself. And when more than one argument was presented on the same topic, the argument nevertheless proceeded sequentially; that is, only a single controversy was being debated at a time.

But as the essays that precede each chapter in this book show—and Anderson's powerful essay above is no exception—real arguments rarely are so simple. Rather, real, everyday arguments typically make multiple claims, with several controversies being debated simultaneously. In this chapter, we will see the structure of these more complex arguments, to see how they are built and to learn strategies for building our own.

Controversies to which Anderson responds:

- What is the historical context for Black Lives Matter (BLM)?
- Which, if any, of the high-profile killings of African Americans by police appear to be justified?
- Does a politics of respectability demand a higher burden from African American communities and individuals than it does from white communities?
- To what extent did the civil rights movement result in a nation that is fundamentally fair to all citizens, regardless of race?
- To what extent does a politics of respectability work to guarantee the fundamental rights to life, liberty, and the pursuit of happiness promised in the U.S. Declaration of Independence?

Let's begin by taking a closer look at Anderson's essay. This is a complex argument that makes several claims, lays out several lines of justification, and responds to several controversies at once. The piece addresses a core tenet of the Black Lives Matter (BLM) movement, a movement that has itself been made controversial by opponents who have coined phrases such as "all lives matter" and "blue lives matter." While those opposed have forwarded few arguments beyond hashtags, Anderson's essay provides a historical context for the BLM movement's move away from respectability politics to activism.

The essay also addresses the controversy of whether or not a number of high-profile killings of African Americans were justified under the circumstances. Anderson takes a close look at the homicides of Amadou Diallo, Trayvon Martin, and Tamir Rice as test cases for the claim that the politics of respectability can protect Black people from state-sanctioned physical violence. Anderson also takes on the issue of whether or not a politics of respectability puts disproportionate pressure on Black communities to adhere to a stricter standard of behavior than white communities. The essay addresses the controversy of whether or not the civil rights movement resulted in a country that is fundamentally fair to all citizens, regardless of race. Ultimately, the essay responds to the controversy: To what extent does a politics of respectability work to guarantee the fundamental rights to life, liberty, and the pursuit of happiness promised in the U.S. Declaration of Independence?

As you recall from Chapter 3, arguments begin in response to a particular controversy. Any given controversy is itself made up of related questions. These too must often be answered in order to respond effectively to the larger controversy. The technical term for these subordinate questions is an issue. **Issues** are questions that grow naturally out of the controversy and that must be answered in order to address the controversy. For example, a simple controversy such as "What should we have for dinner tonight?" necessarily raises questions such as what we have available, and what we had for dinner last night, or for lunch today. Even if implicitly, these questions must be addressed using claims in order to support the **resolution**, or the overall response to the controversy. A resolution in this case might be, we should have vegetable stew for dinner tonight.

This simple argument could be represented in a diagram that shows a resolution as raising several issues, and claims that respond to the issues and support a resolution.

The controversy begins the argument, and the issues grow naturally out of the controversy. The left side of the diagram represents the implicit or explicit context of the argument: it is important to be clear about what controversy you are addressing, and it is important to identify all the issues inherent to that controversy and respond appropriately. The right side of the diagram represents the argument itself: the resolution, and the claims that support it.

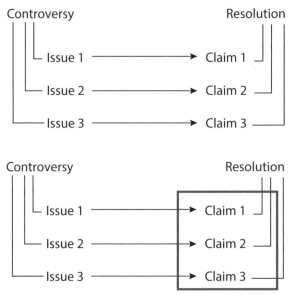

The case is represented by the right side of the diagram.

Taken together, the elements on the right side of the diagram are called a **case**: the set of claims and supporting evidence assembled in support of, or in opposition to, a resolution, for a particular audience.

When we engage in complex arguments, whether as part of a speech, in written policy documents, or in feature articles like Anderson's, we are working to build a case that our audience will find more compelling than opposing cases.

> Prima facie, literally at first face, refers to an argument's initial burden of proof. This is the standard at which an argument appears reasonable, before any refutation or counterargument.

Whether these opposing cases are explicitly argued, as in a debate, or implied by our case, they are inherent in the controversy. Any controversy can always be responded to with a number of different resolutions, and so it is part of your job when making an argument to identify the best possible resolution, and show why it is preferable to its alternatives.

In the diagram above, we see one claim responding to one issue, but this is simplified. In everyday arguments, a single claim may respond to several issues. Conversely, one issue may spark multiple claims.

At a minimum, a case has to respond to the issues of a given controversy. This is known as the standard of prima facie. Literally meaning "first face" in Latin, **prima facie** is the most basic standard of a case, and it is the perception that a case is responding to the relevant issues. This is the point at which an audience will consider a case on its merits or not. If a case does not appear to an audience to meet the standard of prima facie, the audience may not be willing to consider it at all.

I say relevant issues because even though issues are inherent in a controversy and must be addressed to carry a resolution, not all issues will come up in every situation. If you engage in the same argument ten times with ten different groups, you may find that some groups raise one set of questions, while other groups raise different questions. All of these questions, if they emerge naturally out of the controversy, are potential issues, but in an argument you only have to address the questions that do come up, or are likely to.

Take, for example, the controversy "How should the United States respond to growing climate threats?" A resolution may be: The United States must deploy a combination of both mitigation and adaptation strategies to address climate change.

Now, an audience of climate skeptics will raise very different issues in response to this argument than an audience of climate scientists or a mixed audience of policymakers. Regardless of which issues are raised, any question inherent in a controversy is an issue, even if it is not asked or pointed out during the course of a given argument.

> When building a case, you should focus on the issues that are likely to come up with the anticipated audience and the purpose of the argument: focus on how decisions are likely to be made.

Issues raised during an argument, as well as those likely to be asked by an audience (whether to themselves or aloud), are known as **relevant issues**.

Issues not raised during an argument are known as **stipulated issues**, which, as suggested above, will vary from audience to audience and situation to situation.

Strategy for building a case, then, should focus on the issues that are likely to come up with the anticipated audience and the purpose of the argument: how decisions are likely to be made.

Controversy: How should the United States respond to growing climate threats?

Relevant Issues (likely to come up in a discussion among policy experts)	Stipulated Issues (unlikely to come up in a discussion among policy experts)
To what extent are growing climate threats a problem?	Is climate change caused by human activity?
What are the immediate causes of these threats?	Does the United States have a role to play in addressing climate change?
How quickly will mitigation efforts make an impact?	Are the effects of climate change more negative than positive?
What is the cost of implementing mitigation and adaptation measures when compared with doing either one separately or with doing nothing?	Should the United States do more to address climate change abroad?

Determining the Issues

Remember that if a case does not address the issues, it does not meet the standard of prima facie, the minimum standard of an effective argument. So, given a controversy, how can we determine what the issues are? This is probably the most important question when building a case. Chances are, if you are reading this book as a college student, you have already written a number of arguments, and when you've been successful, you have probably addressed most of the issues in these arguments, most of the time. So how did you determine what the issues are?

Well, as we have already seen, issues grow naturally out of a controversy, so it is quite likely that a number of the relevant issues could be determined by taking a careful look at the controversy itself and determining key words and phrases in the resolution. Fully addressing those key terms would go a long way in addressing the issues. You have probably done this when building a case in the past.

> One way to determine the issues in a controversy is to take a careful look at the controversy itself and determine key words and phrases in the resolution.

You probably have also considered the underlying context of the controversy, considering things like what is appropriate, what is possible or could be otherwise, and how you will know what is the right time to make a particular argument. These questions are, in fact, recurring issues used by the ancient Sophists such as Gorgias (whom you read in Chapter 2).

You could also do research on the controversy by reviewing a sample of what has been argued about the controversy in academic journals, newspapers, online periodicals, and other sources, and see what issues other arguments have addressed. Whatever issues have been agreed upon can be put aside. By addressing the issues that remain, the relevant issues, you are likely to have met the standard of prima facie.

Shortcuts for Determining Issues

These are all effective methods of determining issues, some or all of which you have likely drawn on in the past. As systematic methods for determining issues, they are a bit time-consuming, and they don't help you recognize if you've missed any relevant issues. Luckily, there is also a shortcut for determining whether or not a case meets the standard of prima facie. In Chapter 3 we determined that there are four basic types of claim: fact, definition, quality, and policy. Certain questions tend to come up again and again with each type of type of argument. These are known as **topoi**, or standard issues for a given type of claim. By knowing the issues, you can be more efficient in analyzing the controversy and resolution, including the underlying context, and in researching other arguments in response to the same controversy.

Fact

Claims of fact have two topoi:

1. What are the criteria that determine whether or not the statement is true?
2. Have these criteria been satisfied?

Ex. The death penalty does not deter crime.

1. A generally lower crime rate as a result of the death penalty.
2. Lower crime rates in states with the death penalty than in states without it, so long as the states are similar in other ways.

Definition

Claims of definition have three topoi:

1. Is the interpretation relevant? That is, does the interpretation effectively consider the context for the controversy—is it appropriate?
2. Is the interpretation fair? A fair interpretation considers all the parts of whatever is being interpreted. It does not leave out key aspects.
3. How do we choose among competing interpretations? What makes one interpretation more compelling, effective, or appropriate than another?

Ex. The death penalty is murder.

1. To what extent is state-sponsored killing murder?
2. Murder is not a neutral term. Are there key aspects to what we commonly agree constitutes murder that are not present in the administration of the death penalty? Are there key aspects of the administration of the death penalty that are not present in what we commonly agree is murder?
3. All things considered, what makes murder the best definition of the death penalty? Is another definition better?

Quality

Claims of quality have three topoi:

1. Is the condition truly good or bad as alleged?
2. Has the value been properly applied to the situation at hand?
3. How do we choose among competing values?

Ex. The death penalty is unjust.

1. The death penalty is truly unjust, because it affects certain populations disproportionately.
2. Black people are more likely to oppose the death penalty than white people. Crimes with white victims are more likely to seek the death penalty than crimes with Black victims. Black people tried in death penalty cases are less likely to be tried by a jury of their peers.
3. The death penalty only compounds the original crime.

Policy

Claims of policy have four topoi:

1. Is there a problem?
2. Who, or what, is to credit or blame for the problem?
3. Will the proposal solve the problem?
4. On balance, will things be better off with the proposal?

Ex. The United States should abolish the death penalty.

1. The death penalty places an undue cost on government resources.
2. Administrative costs, including personnel costs, are significantly higher with death penalty cases.
3. Abolishing the death penalty will significantly reduce administrative costs.
4. The money saved on death penalty cases may be put toward crime prevention measures that have been shown to work.

By following these shortcuts, you can be sure you're addressing all the relevant issues in a given controversy, and you can probably save yourself some time also. It is not necessary to follow the order of the topoi, but all the topoi must be addressed to meet the standard of prima facie.

Choices of Selection

Even if you stick to the relevant issues in a given controversy, you still have a lot of choices to make about what to include in your case and what to ignore. This is because there are always more potential claims than can be made in a given argument, and there is always more potential evidence than can be raised. We are necessarily limited by time for a speech or debate, or word count for an article or essay, and always by our own attention span and that of our audience. Thus, every argument is a reflection of choices about which claims and which evidence to use. This is known as the **principle of selection**, and it is the first consideration when building a case.

The principle of selection is not simply a reflection of conscious decisions made by someone as they build a case. Often, we do not control what we notice and what we don't, what we understand and what we don't, what knowledge we have access to and what we don't. This is the notion of point of view, which is the foundation of argumentation: it is the reason we get better decisions from the process of argumentation than if we proceed with untested beliefs. Newman P. Birk and Genevieve B. Birk provide a useful example to illustrate this principle of partial access to knowledge:

> Suppose . . . a lumberjack, an artist, and a tree surgeon are examining a large tree in the forest. Since the tree itself is a complicated object, the number of particulars or facts about it that one could observe would be very great indeed. Which of these facts a particular observer will notice will be a matter of selection, a selection that is determined by his interests and purposes. A lumberjack might be interested in the best way to cut the tree down, cut it up and transport it to the lumber mill. . . . The artist might consider painting a picture of the tree, and his purpose would furnish his principle of selection. The tree surgeon's professional interest in the physical health of the tree might establish a principle of selection for him. (*Understanding and Using Language*)

The principle of selection is even at play as we read this passage, first published in 1972. I found myself noticing the use of masculine pronouns throughout, for example, something I would be unlikely to notice were I reading this in 1972. Because of the principle of selection, no single perspective has access to the whole truth. Rather, knowledge is directly related to point of view.

In Anderson's essay the principle of selection allows her to notice trends that may not be noticeable to others with less information and training. Her history of research on the topics of race and violence—she is the author of numerous articles and books on the subjects—gives her access to a wealth of data and knowledge not accessible to nonexperts. From this, she is able to select the claims that are most likely to lead her audience to willingly accept her resolution.

Strength

Since we must make choices about what to include—and exclude—from our arguments, and since the purpose of argumentation is reasoned decision-making, we want to select our strongest arguments and evidence so that we have the best chance of coming to the best decision. **Strength** is a measure of the effectiveness of a particular argument or evidence pertaining to how likely it is to affect a particular audience. To determine the strength of a particular argument or bit of evidence, you have to know something about the audience and what types of arguments and evidence they are most ready to accept. Typically, arguments are strongest when they draw on or refer to shared, or common, knowledge. It is important to keep in mind that common knowledge varies from audience to audience. What is common knowledge to an audience of medical professionals about the health risks of tobacco use is not the same as what common knowledge would be on the same subject to a group of athletes. Both audiences may have similar views on tobacco use, but with varied degrees of knowledge on the subject. If you are familiar with the audience, you will have a good sense of what may constitute common knowledge about your subject. If not, you would be well served by an audience analysis (see inset). At the very least, you will want to meet the standard of prima facie, by addressing all the issues relevant to the resolution.

Anderson has access to many examples that reflect the argument she is making, that often when an African American is the victim of police brutality, they subsequently become a victim of a rhetorical campaign to remove them of respectability. She chooses to focus on Amadou Diallo, Trayvon Martin, and Tamir Rice, but she could as well have focused on Sandra Bland, Freddie Gray, or Michael Brown, among others. The cases Anderson chooses are strong cases because the circumstances powerfully reflect the claim she is making, and they are well-known cases that received a significant amount of media attention. In at least some of the cases, photographic or video evidence is available, which tends to be strong for all audiences. In fact, many credit the existence of video evidence in transforming the debate around police brutality and race altogether.

Audience Analysis

1. Determine your audience's attitude toward your point of view, and what you want their attitude to be after you have made your argument. Are they likely to share your point of view, have an opposing view, or not have a clear point of view on the subject at all?
2. Determine what reasons your audience has for holding the point of view they do. It may be that they hold different values, have different information, or are not aware of the controversy.

Relevance

In addition to strength, relevance is an important consideration when building a case. **Relevance** is a measure of the extent to which a piece of evidence actually does support the claim it is meant to support, or a measure of the extent to which a claim supports a resolution. The greater the relevance of a particular bit of evidence, the more likely an audience is to accept the claim based on the evidence. For example, if I am making the argument that the United States must deploy a combination of both mitigation and adaptation strategies to address climate change, and for evidence I present compelling evidence that neither mitigation (reducing emissions) nor adaptation (instituting policies and strategies to better live with climate change) alone will be sufficient on their own, an audience is likely to accept my resolution if they accept my evidence claims. These evidence claims have a high degree of relevance. However, if I instead present evidence that the United States has made significantly less progress on climate change than the European Union in the last several years, an audience may not accept my resolution even if they do accept the evidence, which means this evidence does not have a high degree of relevance. Similarly, the more likely an audience is to accept my resolution if they accept my claim, the more relevant that claim is.

Number

In building our case, we must also consider how many arguments to make across the range of possible arguments, and how many pieces of evidence to bring forward. I list above three other cases, among many, that Anderson could have drawn upon in her essay. Why not use all of these, in addition to the three main cases she focuses on? Why not talk about all six, or nine, or nineteen?

Well, one reason already mentioned is space and time. In a larger work, like a book, Anderson may very well draw on all or many of these cases. But in a shorter essay, Anderson is forced to limit her examples and the scope of her arguments. It is a convention of an essay to be short, and narrow in scope. There is also the attention span of her audience: an audience reading a piece online (this was published on the online blog space LitHub) does not expect to spend more than an hour—at the most—reading a piece. In fact, studies of online reading show that people spend much less time than that on a single piece.

> When you offer too many claims, the strength of any one of the claims becomes diluted, and your resolution suffers.

In addition to these limits, there are also rhetorical considerations. If you choose to draw on too many examples, the audience may start to lose confidence in your claim. This may seem counterintuitive, but when your claims go on and on, the strength of any one of the claims becomes diluted, and your resolution suffers. There is also a danger, if you introduce too many claims, that your argument will suffer on the level of ethos: you might be seen by your audience as someone more interested in winning their argument than in collaboratively working with your fellow debaters and your audience to achieve the best possible outcome in response to the controversy. If your audience sees you this way, they will be less likely to trust you and your arguments—even if the arguments themselves are strong.

Finally, if you draw on too many arguments, you increase your chances of presenting contradicting claims. If you argue, for example, that you did not steal Jessie's pencil, and you weren't even in the room when it happened, and you don't even like pencils, preferring pens, and you already have several pencils of your own, and what's more, even if you had taken the pencil, you weren't stealing, you were just borrowing, well, you've set yourself up for a difficult cross-examination. You've introduced several inconsistencies into your argument, when focusing on just one or two claims would have made it stronger.

In legal contexts there are other, more technical reasons for limiting the range of your arguments. One such reason is known as opening the door. If either party in a legal dispute makes an argument during court proceedings that introduces evidence that had been deemed inadmissible prior to the trial, that evidence becomes admissible.

Choices of Arrangement

In addition to choices of selection, building a case involves choices of **arrangement,** or the relationship patterns evident in a case. These choices include those strictly concerned with form, as well as those concerned with the content of the claims. The three main forms for arranging arguments are serial, parallel, and convergent. Many different arrangement options exist for the content of arguments, and we'll cover a few in this chapter.

Form

Arrangement choices on the level of form have to do with the structure of the argument. These are broadly applicable, regardless of the content of the argument you are making, though of course you as a rhetor have to decide which arrangement pattern is going to work best for your specific argument.

Serial

In a **serial arrangement pattern**, each argument leads directly to the next, so that each argument is dependent on the one before it. This is also sometimes called a subordinative arrangement pattern.

Claim 1 ⟶ Claim 2 ⟶ Claim 3 ⟶ Resolution

Let's take, for example, the controversy "What is the cause of the increase in wildfires in California?" One possible resolution in response to this controversy is that the increase in wildfires in California is due to poor management of forests. My first claim here is that California has reduced its forest management budget since the mid-1900s. My second claim is that, because of this reduction in spending, insufficient resources were available to clear excess brush and dead trees. My final claim is that, because the forests have increased fuel for fires, forest fires can burn hotter for longer, and can spread more easily. All of these lead to my resolution that the increase in wildfires in California is due to poor management of forests.

Serial Arrangement Pattern

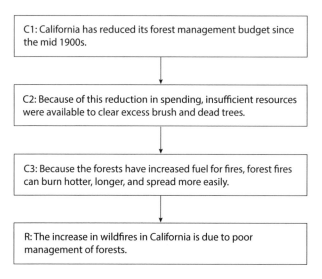

C1: California has reduced its forest management budget since the mid 1900s.

C2: Because of this reduction in spending, insufficient resources were available to clear excess brush and dead trees.

C3: Because the forests have increased fuel for fires, forest fires can burn hotter, longer, and spread more easily.

R: The increase in wildfires in California is due to poor management of forests.

The strength of a serial arrangement pattern is that having a set of claims, one leading directly to the next, can build a strong sense of inevitability. Such an arrangement pattern invites a storylike presentation, a narrative that can be very compelling to an audience.

On the other hand, serial arrangement patterns are vulnerable to attack because if any single claim in the chain is refuted, then the whole argument breaks down. If my opponent responds to my argument above with evidence that only a small percentage of California's forests are managed by the state, that would undermine my first claim. As a result, my second and third claims become much less relevant, and the whole case falls apart.

Parallel

Parallel arrangement patterns consist of multiple claims, each independently supporting a resolution. Because each claim supports the resolution independently, this is sometimes also called a multiple arrangement pattern.

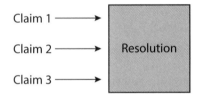

I could choose to arrange a case in response to the same controversy above using a parallel arrangement pattern, but my resolution would have to change from the resolution above. My resolution is that climate change has caused an increase in wildfires. To support this resolution, I would forward three claims. My first claim would be that decreased rainfall over the last several years has increased the fuel available for fires. My second claim is that increased average temperatures over the last several years have also increased the fuel available for fires. My third claim is that longer and more extreme periods of sustained heat have increased the fire season. All of these support the resolution that climate change is causing an increase in wildfires.

Parallel Arrangement Pattern

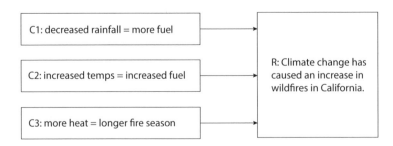

Unlike with the serial arrangement pattern, each of these claims is sufficient on its own to support the resolution. The strength of this arrangement pattern, then, is that some portion of the underlying claims can be refuted and the resolution can still be compelling to an audience. In our example above, even if it turns out that one of the claims is not accurate—that, say, rainfall has not actually decreased—the other two claims still support the resolution.

On the other hand, one downside of the parallel arrangement pattern is that it does not have the same momentum that a serial arrangement pattern has, lacking a narrative quality.

Convergent

In a **convergent arrangement pattern**, multiple claims work together to support the resolution, so that no single claim is sufficient. Rather, it is the convergence of the claims that leads to the resolution. This is sometimes called a coordinative arrangement pattern.

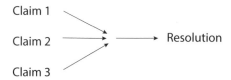

Such an arrangement pattern might serve a resolution in response to the controversy "How can we decide whether to dedicate our resources to combating racism or to protecting our environment?" A resolution might be: Environmental justice greatly overlaps with racial justice, given the history of institutional racism that has led to people of color living in areas with unhealthy environmental conditions. My first claim here might be that racially motivated housing policies have led to highly segregated living conditions. My second claim might be that highly polluting entities, such as power plants, chemical plants, and landfills, tend to be located where land is cheap and there is the least local resistance. My third claim might be that inequitable education and economic conditions have caused people of color to have significantly less access to financial and legal resources to fight placement of highly polluting plants.

Convergent Arrangement Pattern

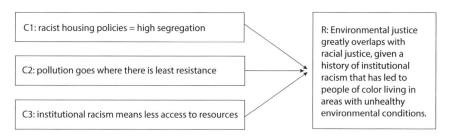

The convergent arrangement pattern differs from the parallel arrangement pattern in that no single claim here is sufficient to support the resolution. Rather, it is the combination of the claims, the way they first support one another, that leads to support of the resolution.

The convergent arrangement pattern differs from the serial arrangement pattern in that the order of the claims does not matter: I could replace claim 1 and claim 3, for example, and still make a similar argument. In a serial arrangement pattern, the order of claims is essential.

Like a serial arrangement pattern, the convergent arrangement pattern can have a momentum to it—the way the claims come together produces a force greater than any one of the claims on their own. The convergent arrangement pattern likewise is vulnerable to the same kinds of attacks as a serial arrangement pattern, though to a lesser degree. Depending on the content of the argument, a case arranged in a convergent pattern may be able to withstand losing one or more of its claims, so long as the other claims together are sufficient to carry the resolution.

A potential drawback of the convergent arrangement pattern is that its reliance on complex relationships may be confusing to audiences. It's important, then, to make sure the relationships are clearly described.

Selection and Arrangement of Content

Order of Claims

Looked at purely logically, order makes no difference in the validity of most arguments, with serial arrangement patterns being an exception. Most of the time, though, from the perspective of logic it does not matter which claim in a case is made first, which second, and so on. But in real, everyday arguments, made to real audiences, order matters quite a bit.

When you put together a case, then, you have to at least consider which of your arguments to lead with and which to close with. If you are arranging your case serially, then these choices are largely made for you. If you are using an arrangement pattern other than serial, however, you could choose to

1. Put your strongest arguments first. Putting your strongest argument first may get your audience to pay attention right away, to become more inclined to weigh all your arguments more seriously, and to look more favorably on your remaining arguments (what is known as **halo effect**). However, if your case ends with all your weakest arguments, the audience is likely to leave with a negative view of your case.

2. Put your strongest arguments last. Putting your strongest argument last may have the benefit of leaving your audience with the best impression of your case, since they will remember your strongest argument most clearly (what is known as **recency effect**). However, if you begin with your weakest arguments, the audience may not be paying as careful attention by the time you get to your strongest arguments, and in fact they may have already dismissed your case by then.

3. Put your strongest arguments at the front and at the end. This is known as the Nestorian arrangement and tends to be the most commonly advised route. Putting a strong argument at the front of your case may produce the halo effect, and ending with another strong argument may produce the recency effect. Altogether, this may have the most favorable effect on your audience.

Depending on the circumstances, it may be useful to present your strongest arguments at the beginning of your case, the end of your case, or at both the beginning and the end. No matter the circumstances, you do not want to bury your strongest arguments in the middle of your case.

Counterclaims and Reservations

It is a good idea to include counterclaims and reservations in your case if you are presenting to a knowledgeable audience, or an audience that is likely to go out and do more research on their own. A knowledgeable audience may already know the available counterclaims, and by not addressing them you not only miss a chance to strengthen your case but also may make your audience think you either are not as knowledgeable as they are or are purposely leaving these out of your case. They may decide you are not being honest, or you are more interested in winning the argument than in coming to the best possible outcome based on reasoning and the evidence. A highly motivated audience may come to similar conclusions if they find out about counterclaims you left out after hearing or reading your case and doing research on their own.

On the other hand, if an audience is not likely to know about counterclaims already, and is not likely to go out and do research to find these out on their own, then you may safely choose to make your case without addressing counterclaims. As you know, one of the principles of argumentation is cooperation. Purposely leaving out counterclaims may go against this principle if you know the counterclaim is likely to lead your audience to a different conclusion. However, if the counterclaim is a minor one and not likely to change anyone's mind, then it can be left unaddressed. You'll have to exercise good judgment here.

Familiarity

Typically, you want to identify arguments that are likely to be most familiar to your audience, building from the most familiar to the least familiar. We can see this principle at work in Anderson's argument, which begins with the most recent cases of police violence against Black people, cases with which her audience is likely to be already familiar, and then moves to less familiar cases prior to the civil rights movement.

Patterns

Above we considered the order of claims based only on form: serial, parallel, and convergent. But we also have to take into consideration the content of claims, and there are a number of common patterns for arranging claims on the level of content.

Chronological

The **chronological arrangement pattern** is both well known and misunderstood. Often, people inexperienced with analyzing arguments mistake any argument as chronological if it follows a logical pattern. *An argument should be labeled chronological only if the passage of time is what primarily determines what follows what.* A logbook, beginning in the morning and chronicling all the events of the day, is obviously chronological. A serial argument detailing the events that led to your being late for work is also arranged chronologically.

Cause/Effect

Arranging a case from **cause to effect** means that you first describe the factors that directly contribute to an event or phenomenon, and then describe the event or phenomenon itself. In this arrangement pattern, you are making the case that there is a causal relationship between the factors you describe and the event or phenomena that follows. See Chapter 11 for more on cause and effect arguments.

Problem/Solution

To arrange a case from **problem to solution** you first describe a perceived problem, lack, or shortcoming, and then make a case for solving the problem or addressing the lack or shortcoming. This is a common arrangement pattern for policy arguments.

Compare/Contrast

A **compare/contrast** arrangement pattern either identifies the similarities across apparent differences (compare), differences across apparent similarities (contrast), or both. A case may be arranged by comparison, describing the ways in which two objects, places, actions, people, phenomena, or ideas are similar. A case may also be arranged by contrast, pointing out the ways in which two objects, places, actions, people, phenomena, or ideas are different. A single case may also do both of these things, first comparing then contrasting, for example.

Arrangement in Anderson's Argument

Let's take a closer look at Anderson's argument to see how she has arranged her case. I identified above several issues to which Anderson is responding. I list below the claims Anderson puts forward in responding to these issues.

1. A politics of respectability fails to guarantee fundamental civil rights because it cannot protect Black people from state-sanctioned physical violence.
    a. In several high-profile cases respectability politics worked against Black victims of police violence.
    b. Because the humanity of the Black victims was not taken for granted, any Black American who failed to meet a very high standard of respectability was considered justifiably killed.

2. A politics of respectability puts disproportionate pressure on Black communities to adhere to a stricter standard of behavior than white communities.
    a. Respectability politics were born out of the civil rights movement to remind white people of the humanity of Black people, as a way to address systemic injustice.
    b. Black people were thus put in the position of having to demonstrate their humanity, rather than it being taken for granted.
    c. This put a significant and unfair burden on Black people and the Black community to adhere to a strict standard of behavior.

3. The civil rights movement did not succeed in creating a country that is fundamentally fair to all citizens, regardless of race.
    a. Following the abolition of slavery, a pattern of brutal murders of Black Americans in which law enforcement and the justice system were complicit show that the rights of Black Americans to live without fear of physical violence were not protected.

Anderson selects powerful claims and evidence, which are highly relevant to her resolution, in order to form the basis of her case. And she makes choices about arrangement that will allow her to make her case most effectively. Knowing the potential of serial arrangement patterns to build momentum, she chooses this arrangement pattern for the major claims of her piece. At the same time, recognizing the vulnerability of serial arrangement patterns to attack, she provides lots of evidence to support each one of these major claims and draws on a variety of arrangement patterns to present this evidence, as you can see in the diagram below.

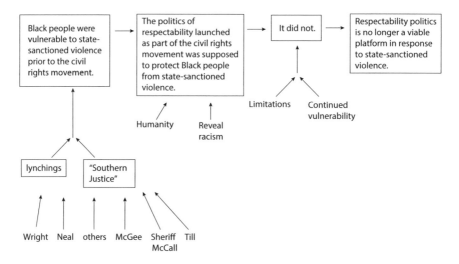

Conclusion

We make and encounter arguments all the time in our day-to-day lives, and often these are complex. Sometimes important parts of the argument are left unstated, sometimes the relationships among the different parts are not clear, and often context goes a long way. In Anderson's essay we have an example of a fully formed, explicit argument that nevertheless is highly complex in form and content and may challenge us as readers.

Anderson's essay is a good example of how choices of selection and arrangement work together to build a strong case. These choices of selection and arrangement are strategic responses to a particular controversy. When building your case, be strategic by molding your choices of selection and arrangement to your particular audience, making sure above all that you have met the standard of prima facie by addressing the issues relevant to the controversy you respond to. I hope you get a lot from this chapter—the essay alone is worth considerable analysis and discussion. Often, when I am working with students on revising their arguments, I find it most valuable to identify the type of argument they are making, and then double-check to be sure they are addressing the topoi, the issues common to that type of argument. This is a useful practice because it helps you meet the standard of prima facie. Also, while it isn't necessary to follow the order of the issues as outlined for each type of resolution, doing so can provide a useful arrangement pattern.

PROBE

Consider the following statement, known as a motion: Defund the police.

What kind of claim is this? How might you address each of the four topoi for this claim if you were in support of the motion? How about if you were arguing against the motion?

Chapter 6
Attack and Defense

Key Terms

counterargument

rebuttal

attack

defense

refutation

inference

complete attack

stasis

stasis of fact

stasis of definition

stasis of quality

stasis of place or procedure

clashing point

Key Points

- Attack and defense are ways of looking at argumentative dialogue as a highly strategic practice.
- When making an attack, you should consider a wide range of selection and arrangement choices.
- When responding with a defense, you should consider both selection and arrangement choices, though your options are more limited than with attack.
- Drawing on stasis theory for your defense is a highly effective way to not only determine how to respond, but also give you some control over the direction of the argument.

PRIME

As you read, consider how familiar Liptak's six arguments are. Underline any you've heard before. Are there any you yourself have found convincing at some point?

6 Arguments to Refute Your Climate-Denying Relatives This Holiday

Sam Liptak (2021)

We all seem to have that one relative who denies climate change (and loudly) at the dinner table—the one who points to snow on the ground in November to disprove global warming, calls climate change an international hoax or insists climate change is part of "the natural planetary cycles."

Sigh.

It may seem futile to argue with these family members—you could say anything to them, read them every landmark climate report backed by thousands of scientists, and they still won't change their minds.[1]

But engaging in this sort of respectful discourse with nay-saying climate deniers—even if your uncle blindly disputes every point you make—is a step in the right direction. Our job as environmental activists (or even just someone who cares about our collective future) is to squelch anti-science rhetoric as we encounter it. Not to do so could mean backpedaling on so much of the progress that scientific research has advanced.

. . . Or maybe you're just in the mood to argue. Whatever inspires you to myth-bust this holiday season, here are six ways to respond to your family's climate-denying comments. In the most respectful, loving way, of course:

1. **Uncle Frank says, "Climate change is natural and normal—we've seen fluctuations throughout history."**

You say: The earth has been through a lot in the last 4.5 billion years. And yes, high levels of carbon dioxide have been released naturally in the earth's history. Scientists have attributed mass extinctions to atmospheric carbon dioxide from 580 million years ago, long before humans were around to burn ridiculous amounts of fossil fuels.[2]

What we're experiencing with climate change today, however, is far different than any warming or cooling humanity has seen—in rate and in scale.

---

1. Emma Tobin and Ivana Kottasová, "11,000 Scientists Warn of 'Untold Suffering' Caused by Climate Change," CNN, November 6, 2019, https://www.cnn.com/2019/11/05/world/climate-emergency-scientists-warning-intl-trnd/index.html.

2. Andrew Glikson, "Another Link between CO2 and Mass Extinctions of Species," The Conversation, March 21, 2013, https://theconversation.com/another-link-between-co2-and-mass-extinctions-of-species-12906.

Our present climate change is occurring 20 to 50 times faster than the most rapid climate change events in earth's history.[3]

That some of the world's mass extinctions have been tied to CO_2 shouldn't be a relief, though; it should be a wakeup call. Unlike in the past, *we* are the ones doing the damage (through the out-of-control burning of fossil fuels), not the earth.

The good news is it's entirely within our control to phase out fossil fuels and avoid the most devastating impacts of unchecked climate change. We don't have to be dinosaurs, and we definitely should stop burning them.

2. **When your cousin Wilma says, "Scientists can't even agree that climate change is happening."**

You say: *Well, actually* . . . 99 percent of scientists agree that climate change is happening *and* that humans are the primary cause.[4]

Perhaps you're thinking of indecisive politicians, many of whom are backed by the fossil fuel industry. Maybe that's why leaders are still dragging their feet when it comes to climate action—or worse, vocally denying its existence in the face of rigorous scientific report, after report, after report.[5]

The truth is politicians have known about climate change since (at least) the 1980s.[6] But leaders in the highest-emitting countries are doing next to nothing to slow climate change, let alone stop it.

3. **Grandpa says, "It's so cold outside. Sure could use some of that global warming."**

---

3. Peter U. Clark, et al., "Consequences of Twenty-First-Century Policy for Multi-Millennial Climate and Sea-Level Change," *Nature Climate Change* 6 (2016).

4. Jonathan Watts, "'No Doubt Left' about Scientific Consensus on Global Warming, Say Experts," *The Guardian*, July 24, 2019, https://www.theguardian.com/science/2019/jul/24/scientific-consensus-on-humans-causing-global-warming-passes-99.

5. "Report Reveals Certain Amount of Global Warming Irreversible," EarthDay.org, August 11, 2021, https://www.earthday.org/report-reveals-certain-amount-of-global-warming-irreversible/; Intergovernmental Panel on Climate Change, "Special Report: Global Warming 1.5°C," October 6, 2018, https://www.ipcc.ch/sr15/; "The Ocean Is Taking Heat for Unchecked Climate Change, UN Report Warns," EarthDay.org, September 25, 2019, https://www.earthday.org/the-ocean-and-cryosphere-are-taking-the-heat-for-unchecked-climate-change-new-un-report-warns/.

6. Spencer Weart, "The Discovery of Global Warming," *Scientific American*, August 17, 2012, https://www.scientificamerican.com/article/discovery-of-global-warming/; Oliver Milman, "Ex-NASA Scientist: 30 Years on, World is Failing 'Miserably' to Address Climate Change," *The Guardian*, June 19, 2018, https://www.theguardian.com/environment/2018/jun/19/james-hansen-nasa-scientist-climate-change-warning.

You say: Weather and climate are two different things. Weather fluctuates from day to day, while climate is defined by long-term trends and weather averages.

So, just because it's cold right now doesn't mean global warming isn't happening. The last five years have been the hottest five years on record, and that's counting the bitter polar vortexes that have driven Arctic air down across North America during that period.[7]

The earth is on track to warm up to two degrees Celsius this century, but winter's not going to disappear altogether in many parts of the world. Record low temperatures will just become rarer.

The U.S. saw nearly as many record highs as record lows in the 1950s. By 2000, the number of record highs was double the record lows.[8] And, as the cold becomes rarer, it will feel more intense and hit unexpecting places.[9]

And while you might not lose your winter altogether, unchecked climate change will bring other major weather shifts, in the form of extreme weather events like drought, wildfire and hurricanes that will become more frequent and more intense in our warming world.

So, bundle up and brace yourself for the extreme weather climate change brings—including the intense cold.

    4. Your mom says, "Plants and animals will adapt to the changes."
    (*Mom, stop embarrassing me!*)

You say: Climate change is occurring too rapidly to allow for species to adapt. And this is about more than the pictures of starving polar bears you see on Facebook (sorry, Mom).

Climate change threatens over 40 percent of amphibians, nearly 33 percent of corals and more than a third of marine mammals. At this point, with climate change not even at its fullest force, more than one million species are at risk of extinction.[10]

---

7. "2020 Ties for Warmest Year on Record," EarthDay.org, January 15, 2021, https://www.earthday.org/2020-ties-for-warmest-year-on-record/.

8. Peter T. Doran and Maggie Kendall Zimmerman, "Examining the Scientific Consensus on Climate Change," *Eos* 90, no. 3 (2009).

9. Alejandra Borunda, "Snow in Texas and Ice in Alabama? Unusual Cold Weather Could Become More Common," *National Geographic*, November 13, 2019, https://www.nationalgeographic.com/science/article/arctic-blast-polar-vortex-cold-weather-climate.

10. Stephen Leahy, "One Million Species at Risk of Extinction, UN Report Warns," *National Geographic*, May 6, 2019, https://www.nationalgeographic.com/environment/article/ipbes-un-biodiversity-report-warns-one-million-species-at-risk.

This is because climate change is compounding the effects of other already-existing detrimental human activities like overfishing and deforestation.

A U.N. report published in May of [2019] ranked the top five direct drivers of the disappearance of species.[11] Climate change was third, behind changes in land and sea use and overexploitation of organisms (all human-caused).

Currently, species are going extinct at 1,000 times the natural rate of extinction. That means we could lose 30 to 50 percent of the total species found on earth by mid-century. Can you pass the cranberry sauce?

5. Uncle Frank is back at it: "Climate change is a good thing."

You say: Hold my eggnog.

For many reasons—economic, environmental, physiological—climate change will have a net negative impact on the world. New research even shows we've significantly underestimated the financial risks of climate change around the world.[12]

The United States stands to lose billions of dollars, second only to India in terms of the negative economic impact.[13] In our warming world, U.S. estimates currently sit at a loss of 10 percent of its $19 trillion GDP by 2100. If we start curbing climate change, this amount could fall to 1 percent.

But enough with the economic hypotheticals. We're already seeing how dangerous climate change is to plants and animals as well as humans.[14]

Higher temperatures have increased heat-related deaths.[15] Higher temperatures also worsen air quality, which scientists have connected to everything from more violent crimes to more cancers.[16]

11. "UN Report: Nature's Dangerous Decline 'Unprecedented'; Species Extinction Rates 'Accelerating,'" UN Sustainable Development Goals, May 6, 2019, https://www.un.org/sustainabledevelopment/blog/2019/05/nature-decline-unprecedented-report/.

12. Ruth DeFries et al., "The Missing Economic Risks in Assessments of Climate Change Impacts," September 20, 2019, https://www.lse.ac.uk/GranthamInstitute/publication/the-missing-economic-risks-in-assessments-of-climate-change-impacts/.

13. Katharine Ricke, et al., "Country-Level Social Cost of Carbon," *Nature Climate Change* 8 (2018).

14. "Addressing Climate Change Is One of the Best Ways to Improve Public Health," EarthDay.org, June 24, 2021, https://www.earthday.org/addressing-climate-change-is-one-of-the-best-ways-to-improve-public-health/.

15. Nick Watts, et al., "The 2018 Report of the *Lancet* Countdown on Health and Climate Change: Shaping the Health of Nations for Centuries to Come," *Lancet* 392, no. 10163 (2018).

16. "On Edge? It Might Be What's in the Air," EarthDay.org, October 11, 2019, https://www.earthday.org/air-pollution-and-violent-crime/.

But what's just as scary are the statistics on natural disasters: Hurricanes are reaching new extremes—with the number of categories 4 and 5 increasing over the last 30 years.[17] Wildfires, too, are claiming larger burn areas and increasing in intensity.

What's so great about that?

6. Your stepdad says, "It won't affect me or anyone I know."

You say: Climate impacts are already here and now, and they will only get worse if we continue to do nothing. Climate change affects individuals disproportionately, hurting the poorest and most vulnerable communities worse than others, so you may just be feeling a buffer from your comparative privilege.

Climate justice recognizes that climate change isn't just a physical problem—it's an ethical one, too.[18] The individuals and communities who will be most affected by climate change are the ones contributing the least to it.

But this is also a generational issue—you may not have to bear the brunt of our collective inaction on climate change, but let's try to have some empathy for future generations (even if you don't understand TikTok or selfies).

Your great-grandchildren—who are currently on track to inherit a world four degrees warmer than yours and feel its effects at every stage of their life— will have to clean up the mess your generation made in their fight for survival.[19]

They'll grow up in a world with more air pollution, more vector-borne diseases and more extreme weather events to deal with.[20]

The future of humanity is on the line.

In conclusion, you can't choose your family, but you can try to change their mindsets on climate change. Some of these arguments may stick; some may go in one ear and out the other.

These conversations aren't easy, but we should try to engage in them when we can. After all, the future of humanity is on the line.

---

17. "The Calm Before the Storm? Experts Predict Hurricane Season to Get Worse," EarthDay.org, October 8, 2019, https://www.earthday.org/the-calm-before-the-storm-experts-predict-hurricane-season-to-get-worse/.

18. "The People Behind the Plastic: How Plastic Production Affects Marginalized Communities," EarthDay.org, August 19, 2019, https://www.earthday.org/the-people-behind-the-plastic-how-plastic-production-affects-marginalized-communities/.

19. "The Kids Aren't All Right, Says New Study on Climate and Health," EarthDay.org, November 18, 2019, https://www.earthday.org/new-study-on-climate-and-children-health-risk/.

20. "Toxic Air Pollution Suffocates New Delhi, Northern India," EarthDay.org, November 5, 2019, https://www.earthday.org/toxic-air-pollution-suffocates-new-delhi-northern-india/.

Perhaps if you convince them, your newly informed, ex-climate-denying relatives will even head to the polls in [the next election] to vote for our future (or give their vote to someone who can't yet). That vote may end up putting us on a course to a greener, more sustainable future.

And if that happens, you'll definitely have something interesting to talk about next holiday.

PAUSE

When was the last time you engaged in an argument that made you feel uncomfortable? What was it about? What was the context? What made it uncomfortable?

Introduction

When I introduced argumentation in Chapter 1 and identified its basic building blocks in Chapter 3, I often used the metaphor of conversation. In a lot of ways, arguing works like a conversation or dialogue. As a metaphor, dialogue captures many elements of the argumentation process. Kenneth Burke famously describes argumentation in *The Philosophy of Literary Form* using what is now known as his parlor metaphor:

> Imagine that you enter a parlor. You come late. When you arrive, others have long preceded you, and they are engaged in a heated discussion, a discussion too heated for them to pause and tell you exactly what it is about. In fact, the discussion had already begun long before any of them got there, so that no one present is qualified to retrace for you all the steps that had gone before. You listen for a while, until you decide that you have caught the tenor of the argument; then you put in your oar. Someone answers; you answer her; another comes to your defense; another supports what you have to say; another disagrees. The discussion, however, is interminable. The hour grows late, you must depart. And you do depart, with the discussion still vigorously in progress.

Burke's emphasis on time is important: the conversation has started at some point long in the past, has grown over the countless years, and will continue to develop into the future. This parallels many aspects of argumentation: the importance of research to get a sense of what has been said about your topic in the past, to see where the controversy lies; the necessity of forming your own point of view as a way to participate in the conversation in the present; and the need to anticipate possible responses to your argument in the future.

Sometimes the dialogue is not a metaphor at all. In her article above, Liptak looks to prepare her readers to engage in real conversations. Taking hypothetical statements a family member might say questioning the science of climate change, Liptak provides concise, researched responses. In other words, she provides counterarguments to some common arguments a climate change denier might make. A **counterargument** is an argument made directly in response to a specific case. It is sometimes known as a **rebuttal** and is made up of both attack and defense.

Attack, in argumentation, is the process of pointing out limitations in your opponent's argument. **Defense** is the process of responding to your opponent's attacks. Attack and defense are central to argumentation. When people argue, they are making arguments and counterarguments: these are the central activities of argumentation. Sometimes—especially in the context of debate—this process is known as refutation. **Refutation** is planning and making arguments and counterarguments in response to an opposing case, or set of arguments and counterarguments.

> Counterargument and rebuttal are synonyms. They both mean an argument made in response to another specific argument.

Okay, that was a lot of terminology to throw at you all at once, so let's put some of this into context. Often, I'll ask my students before they leave campus for Thanksgiving break to tell me about their plans. Since my courses often involve analysis of current events, the subject of politics typically comes up, and while some of my students say they look forward to political discussions at the holiday table, many say their holiday get-togethers have been marked politics-free zones. Discussion of politics is explicitly forbidden, or else understood to be something that just isn't done.

We've all, I'm sure, experienced rancorous debate during family get-togethers or in other contexts where contentious issues come up. Perhaps you have felt that feeling of tension, or perhaps exhilaration, when someone makes a claim you happen to strongly disagree with. Perhaps you jumped at the chance to make your counterargument, or else maybe you waited, confidently making note of any missteps you could take advantage of later, anticipating sweet victory.

Experiences like these may make us believe that the purpose of arguing is to win any cost. This view of debate obscures the fact that the primary purpose of argumentation is not winning but decision-making. Argumentation continues to hold a valued place in democratic cultures because it has been shown over the millennia to be helpful in making good decisions. The purpose of refutation, engaging in attack and defense, is to test your own case and evaluate the cases of others. Of course, the fact that argumentation privileges evaluation over winning doesn't mean we shouldn't take argumentation so seriously. Just the opposite: by engaging in rigorous refutation, we create greater confidence in the outcome of the debate. This only works if it is a process of exchanging claims and evidence. A shouting match does nothing to aid decision-making.

> The purposes of refutation, engaging in attack and defense, are to test your own case, and evaluate the cases of others.

Of course, as I've noted throughout the book so far, we engage in argumentation all the time, so much so that it often feels natural. Because of that, much of what we will cover in this chapter may be familiar and what you already do in an argument. But there will be strategies that are new to you as well. Regardless of how familiar you are with the strategies and approaches presented here, by considering argumentation in a systematic way, you can build a foundation of strategies that you can practice going forward, to improve your ability to engage effectively in argumentation.

Attack

Like case construction, which was covered in Chapter 5, establishing an attack presents choices of selection and arrangement. You must decide which arguments you wish to attack, which parts of the argument you wish to attack, what type of attack to make, and how many attacks to make. You must also consider how best to arrange your attacks.

Which Arguments to Attack

It is typically not a good idea to attack every argument made in the case you are refuting. For one thing, doing so increases the likelihood that you will make counterarguments that are incompatible with one another. Let's say you are responding to Liptak's arguments above, and you say, climate change isn't really happening, and if it is it's really not so bad, and besides it's too cold outside anyway. Well, which is it? Is climate change not happening, or is it happening but that's a good thing because it will warm up cold regions of the world? Rather, you want to approach attack the same way you do case construction: by making effective decisions, taking into consideration the strength and relevance of the opposing arguments.

Generally, you'll want to attack the *strongest* and most *relevant* opposing arguments. If the case you're arguing against has made strong arguments that are not relevant, you may choose to ignore these, or you may choose to concede these while emphasizing that they are not relevant to the case. For example, the claim that we need not limit our consumption of fossil fuels because we continue to have access to an abundant supply of them is not particularly relevant in an argument about human contributions to climate change. In this situation, it may be a good idea to grant that argument and either show that it is not relevant or, in fact, that it hurts the opposing case.

Which Parts of the Argument to Attack

As we know, every argument is made up of an implicit or explicit claim, evidence, and an implicit or explicit relationship between claim and evidence. Below, I'll introduce this last element of an argument as the inference. You may choose to address any of these, as well as the underlying context. You may also choose to address a combination of these.

Claim

A claim can be addressed by offering a denial or providing a counterclaim. The example below denies the original claim.

> Claim: Scientists are not in agreement about the human causes of climate change.
>
> Denial: Actually, 99 percent of scientists do agree that human behavior is causing climate change.

This is a claim of fact that denies the original claim.

Alternatively, you could provide a counterclaim, which doesn't deny the original claim but instead reframes it.

> Claim: Climate change is really not as bad as it's made out to be.
>
> Counterclaim: Climate change has significant negative economic, ecological, and geopolitical impacts.

This is a claim of quality that gives a frame, a way of understanding, to the original claim.

Evidence

Your response could question the evidence used in your opponent's case, critiquing the selection choices, or questioning the legitimacy of the source.

For example, if your opponent supports their argument with statistics that show the earth is getting colder, not warmer, you might counter that those statistics come from a single specific patch of water in the North Atlantic and do not reflect the planet as a whole.

Or, if someone cites a scientist who claims the changes in global temperatures are not caused by human behavior, you might counter that the scientist is not a climate scientist, or that this scientist's research is paid for by groups hostile to climate change science. In other words, you could question whether or not the expert is qualified or biased.

Inference

Another option for responding to an argument you want to counter is to attack the pattern drawn from the evidence that supports the claim, the **inference**.

> *Inference refers to the pattern linking evidence to claim; common types of inference patterns, which are the subjects of later chapters, include example, comparison, cause to effect, sign, commonplace, and quasi-logic.*

Say, for example, you are arguing with someone at the Thanksgiving table about climate change, as Liptak suggests above, and they argue that increased global temperatures are actually due to increased solar energy. They may even pull up a graph of solar energy and global temperatures on their phone.

In reality, there are a number of possible responses here, not least of which is to critique the evidence as mentioned above, because in fact solar energy has been down relative to 1950, whereas global temperatures are sharply up.

But let's say hypothetically that they had a graph showing a correlation between energy emitted from the sun and global temperatures. In that case, you could point out that a correlation does not prove causation; that is, just because the two things are correlated does not mean they are causally related. The implied inference pattern is from cause to effect, but the actual inference pattern is sign, or correlation.

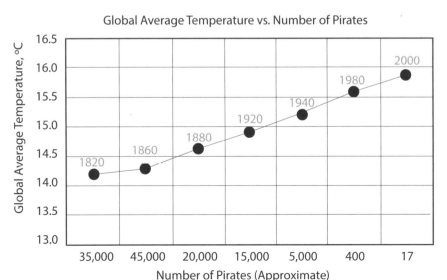

The fact that correlation is not causation has been the source of many comical graphs, linking things like cheese consumption and strangulation, or as in our graph (inset), increased global temperatures and decreased pirate population. The graph shows clearly that the two are correlated: as the pirate population goes down, global temperatures rise. But no one would seriously think the two are causally linked.

So it's not enough simply to show that two things are linked by correlation—that a change in one implies a change in the other. For the argument that one thing causes the other to work, you'd have to isolate other possible factors. We'll go over this in more detail in Chapter 11, but here it is enough to recognize that, in addition to responding to your opponent's claim or questioning the evidence, you can also attack the inference pattern, or the patterns being drawn out of the evidence.

Assuming causation when only correlation has been established is only one possibility here: whatever the inference pattern of the argument you're responding to, you can look for ways the evidence doesn't add up to the claims being made. In later chapters we'll cover several types of inference patterns in detail, including tests specific to each type of inference pattern.

Underlying Context

Sometimes the most effective response to a line of argument is to shift the conversation altogether by attacking the assumptions on which the argument is built. Let's say, for example, that you want to respond to an argument that, for the particular job this person is in, or the particular location, or for a set of circumstances unique to this person, climate change is a good thing. "Based on predictions for this area," this person might argue, "I'll be able to grow a greater variety of crops here in ten years than I can now, and with greater yields due to an increased growing season."

Let's say the evidence does support this person's argument, and you find it is a reasonable claim to make based on the evidence. "But," you might respond, "is it ethical to consider only your own well-being? Shouldn't you also consider the greater good?" In this response, you are not addressing the claim, or the evidence, or the inference. Rather, you are questioning the underlying context or assumptions on which the argument rests.

So how do you decide whether to attack the claim, the evidence, the inference pattern, or the underlying context? This is a strategic consideration—you have to ask yourself what has the greatest potential to affect the outcome of the debate, with the least investment of time and effort. Typically, this is where the opposing argument is weakest (again, in its claim, evidence, inference, or underlying context), but the claim itself has the greatest relevance.

The Type of Attack

Once you have chosen which part of the argument to attack, the next decision to make is what type of attack to make. Arguments typically lend themselves to multiple possible types of attack, some of which we will take a closer look at here.

Counterargument

As discussed above, countering your opponent's claim with one of your own can be an effective response, not only because it may undermine confidence in your opponent's claim but also because it gives your audience a competing claim, which they may find more acceptable.

Identify Inconsistencies

If inconsistencies exist in your opponent's argument, identifying these can be a very effective attack because doing so not only forces your opponent to respond to the inconsistency but also may cause your opponent to lose credibility with the audience.

For example, you may find that your opponent has made two arguments, each of which undermines the other. Let's say they argue that economic growth is more important than environmental protection, and also that the government should stop subsidizing green energy production like solar and wind. Well, these two arguments are at cross-purposes with one another, as green energy is a quickly growing economic industry.

Pointing out this inconsistency will force your opponent to concede one or the other, which may significantly undermine their argument as a whole. More than that, audiences typically feel less confident in both claims when their inconsistency with one another is pointed out, even though logically only one claim should be in doubt. On top of that, audiences may lose trust in the speaker or writer herself when her inconsistencies are pointed out.

Identify Shortcomings

One way to respond to an argument is to simply point out where the argument is weak. You may say, for example, "Those data are from over a century ago; they're not reliable." Or you could state, "That's a very weak analogy—Antarctica and Arizona do not have much in common."

Sometimes, simply identifying such shortcomings can be effective, particularly if the shortcomings appear in a part of the argument that is crucial for its success. If the shortcomings exist in elements of the argument that are not so important, however, this type of attack is limited.

Ask a Question

Rarely, a well-placed question can have a powerful impact on an opposing argument. Most of the time, however, asking a question of the opposing argument is not particularly effective. If the argument is taking place in real time, during a formal debate, or in an informal conversation, for example, then your opponent can simply respond by answering the question, which both stops your attack and gives your opponent the opportunity to strengthen their argument. The same goes for online arguments, which proceed more slowly than in real time but nevertheless typically offer multiple opportunities for case building.

> Asking a question is only a good idea when the question is important to your opponent's argument and you know that it is unanswerable.

Generally, then, asking a question is only a good idea when the question is important to your opponent's argument and you know that it is unanswerable. For example, if your opponent is claiming that climate change is a global conspiracy, a hoax, you can ask, "Where is the evidence?" Typically, such conspiracy theories falter when asked to provide real evidence for their claims. The evidence either will not exist beyond "Oh, so-and-so told me they saw . . ." or will be so weak that it is readily refuted.

Label the Strategy

When your opponent is using a strategy that may be effective with the audience because it is misleading, simply naming the strategy can reduce its effectiveness. Let's say, for example, that your opponent is arguing that we can either combat climate change or support our economy but not both. Combating climate change, they argue, is expensive and will raise taxes. Supporting our economy, on the other hand, will increase pollutants that contribute to climate change. You can label this strategy a false dilemma, which would give you the opportunity to make a case for combating climate change without devastating the economy. Other things you can point out in your opponent's strategy include loaded or biased language, or any fallacies as described in Chapter 14.

Recontextualize

Finally, as I mentioned above, you can make an argument for rethinking the assumptions of the argument, placing it into a broader context. Economic concerns are important, you might argue, but not as important as human lives. Or, you might argue, while practical concerns about how to mitigate climate change are worth discussing, the moral principle that demands we do something cannot be overlooked.

How Many Attacks to Make

As we discussed with case construction in Chapter 5, your strategy for deciding the number of attacks should find the right balance, presenting a strong case without leaving yourself vulnerable to attack from your opponent and allowing you to maintain credibility. Remember that, as with case construction, presenting too many attacks on a wider range of issues may weaken your credibility, create inconsistencies, and suggest to your audience that you lack confidence.

Arrangement

Your arrangement choices for your attack are the same as when building your case. It is not necessary to respond to the issues in your opponent's case in the same order they used. You can choose to respond to their weakest argument first, for example, even if they buried it in the middle of their case.

In formal debate, there is the notion of a **complete attack**. A complete attack

1. Restates your opponent's argument in a way that the audience will accept as faithful to the original, using the original language when possible;
2. States clearly the basis for the attack (e.g., evidence, inference pattern, underlying context, etc.);
3. Develops the attack and supports it with evidence rather than relying on assertion;
4. Makes the significance of what the attack has accomplished clear.

In everyday debate, complete attacks are the exception rather than the norm, for a number of reasons. One is that—in both everyday and formal debate—there are time constraints. We typically have a limited amount of time to make our case. But more than that, using a complete attack every time you respond to your opponent in conversation or formal debate can get pretty old, pretty quickly. Even if your attack is solid, you may find your audience getting annoyed with you.

In writing, a complete attack may be more advisable in some situations, depending on your audience. Typically when you write you have word limits, whether these are explicit (e.g., an op-ed in a newspaper, an assignment for a course) or implicit (e.g., a social media post, an email message to a busy reader). These constraints limit your ability to make all your attacks complete attacks.

> The more knowledgeable your audience is about the subject, and the more accepted the argument to which you are responding, the more they will expect your counterargument to use complete attacks.

However, there are some situations when your audience will accept, even expect, a complete attack—especially when these are central to your argument. Generally speaking, the more knowledgeable your audience is about the subject, and the more accepted the argument to which you are responding, the more they will expect your counterargument to use complete attacks.

Defense

Putting together a defense faces more limitations than an attack, because a defense must respond to the attack. In a debate setting, not responding to an attack can sometimes be equivalent to conceding that point. In written works, you want to be sure you are anticipating potential counterarguments, as Liptak does above.

Nevertheless, you do have some choices of selection and choices of arrangement available to you in your defense.

First, you have to decide how seriously to take an attack. If you believe an attack is misleading, is not relevant, does not meet the standard of prima facie, or will otherwise be ineffective, you do not have to spend much time responding to it. Simply pointing out its limitation(s) will be enough to defend against it to a reasonable audience.

In fact, when an attack is baseless, you are better off not spending much time responding to it. Responding in detail to a conspiracy theory, for example, not only uses up valuable time or space but also implicitly gives credence to that conspiracy theory. By taking it seriously, you are in effect arguing that it is worth taking seriously.

Second, you need to decide whether your defense should follow the arrangement pattern of your original argument or the arrangement pattern of the attack you're responding to.

Whatever you decide, you will need to do more than just repeat your original argument; rather you should

1. carefully consider the attack, where it suggests there may be shortcomings in your original argument, and
2. use the attack as an opportunity to strengthen your argument.

Ultimately, you want to return to your original argument, now strengthened by having responded to the attacks leveled against it.

Stasis

Stasis is a theory for deciding the best way to respond to an attack that goes back to ancient Greece and Rome, coming out of forensic rhetoric, that is, out of court cases. It answers the question: If someone accuses you of something, what is the best way to respond?

Stasis lays out four different categories of response, which may remind you of the four different types of claim but are a bit different. These are (1) fact, (2) definition, (3) quality or value, and (4) place or jurisdiction. The **stasis of fact** asks whether or not the act in question occurred or exists. The **stasis of definition** asks what the act should be called. The **stasis of quality** asks whether or not the act is justified. The **stasis of place or procedure** asks whether or not the discussion is taking place in the appropriate space.

> *Stasis* is a theory for defense, asking, if someone accuses you of something, what is the best way to respond?

Let's say, for example, your roommate accuses you of stealing their new coat.

You could respond with a stasis of fact: "No, I did not steal your coat."

You could respond with a stasis of definition: "No, I was just borrowing it."

You could respond with a stasis of quality: "I did take your coat, and it's a good thing I did, too. It turns out there was a recall on it, and if I hadn't taken it and given it to the brand representative who came by, you would be in serious danger."

Or, you could respond with a stasis of place: "Don't accuse me of stealing your coat here in front of all our friends. If you want to hash this out, let's go somewhere more private."

The thing to keep in mind when it comes to stasis is that it is not the original assertion that determines stasis but rather the response to it. In each of the above examples, the assertion was the same: that you stole your roommate's coat. It was how you responded to the assertion that determined the point of stasis.

Although originally developed for forensic rhetoric, stasis theory has been applied to the kinds of arguments we are talking about in this book: deliberative argument, or argument for making informed decisions. In the case of deliberative argument, you are not responding to accusations but rather defending attacks against your case.

Having a good understanding of stasis can be a powerful advantage in an argument, because it allows you to control the **clashing point**, or the substance of the disagreement. By responding with one point of stasis or another, you can have some control over what you and your opponent will debate—especially if they are not able to change the point of stasis in their response.

> It is not the attack but the defense that determines the point of stasis being taken.

So how can you know which point of stasis to take up in your response to any attack? The most important thing to remember here is that stasis is progressive: this means that if you respond with a stasis of definition (I didn't steal it, I borrowed it), you have conceded the stasis of fact. By taking up an argument about definition, you are in effect accepting that you did take the coat. Likewise, if you take up a stasis of quality, you are conceding both fact and definition. By arguing, "I did steal the coat, but it was a good thing," you are acknowledging that you both took the coat and that it was theft.

The exception here is the stasis of place or procedure, which concedes nothing but rather puts a hold on the argument until an appropriate place is found or procedure followed. Stasis of place is preemptive: you can defer the argument altogether. In the case of the coat, you put a hold on the questions of whether or not you took it, what it should be called, and whether or not it was a bad thing until you can find an appropriate place to have the discussion.

You should pursue the highest point of stasis you can support.

In deliberative argument, the stasis of procedure may instead address the underlying context, or the rules of the debate. You might argue that your opponent had not followed the proper rules, or that the rules of the debate were inequitable or biased.

Since stasis is progressive, you should pursue as high a point of stasis as you can support. So if you can support a stasis of fact, pursue that; if not, definition, and so on. Again, the exception here may be the stasis of place or procedure, depending on the circumstances. In the classical tradition, the stasis of place was considered the weakest, something to avoid if possible. These days, however, there are times when pursuing stasis of place is a good strategy.

Conclusion

The next time you're at your Thanksgiving table with family members who are skeptical about the human causes of climate change (or some other controversy), drawing on Liptak's counterarguments may be helpful. Sometimes people are simply misinformed, or uninformed, and providing them with claims and evidence that counter their beliefs is all they need to change their minds—especially if done in a supportive, noncombative way. Of course, this is not always the case—as you know, it's possible to win a debate without having changed any of your opponents' minds. We'll consider some of the reasons for this, and how it might be addressed, in later chapters.

For now, it's worth remembering that attack and defense are ways of looking at argumentative dialogue as a highly strategic practice. Attack, or pointing out the limitations of your opponent's case, and defense, responding to your opponent's attack, ask you to make a number of choices of selection and arrangement as you build and revise your written argument or engage in everyday arguments in real time.

Attack and defense have a military connotation that seems at odds with the cooperative foundation we have established for argumentation so far. It doesn't sound cooperative to attack your opponent's case, or to have to defend your argument against future attacks. Despite this connotation, these terms are most established in the field. Regardless of the terms we use, we still need to approach argumentation in a measured and cooperative way.

More importantly, attack and defense are cooperative even if the people involved in the argument don't view it that way. That is, if you are involved in an argument and all you care about is winning, you'll have to make the best arguments you can and do your best job to point out the limitations of the argument you are opposing. Your opponent will have to do the same. Taken all together, this effort helps assure both you and your opponent as well as the audience that the best possible arguments are being put forward, which makes everyone more confident in the results.

So, when looked at from the perspective of any one individual involved in an argument, attack and defense may seem self-motivated, driven by a desire to win. But looked at as a system, a process of argumentation, they are in fact working together to reveal the best possible outcomes with the highest possible degree of confidence in the results.

PROBE

Write a letter to someone you've had a discussion with, where you feel you still have something left to say. Include a summary of the points you each had already made, rebut any arguments you had not rebutted already, and make any new arguments that you did not get a chance to make in the previous discussion(s). Or, for a shorter variation, do this in a bulleted list.

Chapter 7
Providing and Considering Evidence

Key Terms

evaluating arguments

echo chamber

examples

instances

illustrations

statistics

mean

median

mode

social consensus

testimony

tangible object

Key Points

- Reasonable claims emerge from evidence.
- Participants in an argument must agree to the evidence—even if they disagree with the meaning of the evidence—for it to count.
- Several types of evidence exist, each with its own standards.
- Several general tests of evidence can be used to determine whether or not evidence should be trusted.

PRIME

How confident are you that you can identify good quality evidence? What are potential sources of quality evidence for arguments about political issues? What about academic settings?

In the Name of Love

Miya Tokumitsu (2014)

"Do what you love. Love what you do."

The commands are framed and perched in a living room that can only be described as "well-curated." A picture of this room appeared first on a popular design blog, but has been pinned, tumbl'd, and liked thousands of times by now.

Lovingly lit and photographed, this room is styled to inspire *Sehnsucht*, roughly translatable from German as a pleasurable yearning for some utopian thing or place. Despite the fact that it introduces exhortations to labor into a space of leisure, the "do what you love" living room—where artful tchotchkes abound and work is not drudgery but love—is precisely the place all those pinners and likers long to be. The diptych arrangement suggests a secular version of a medieval house altar.

There's little doubt that "do what you love" (DWYL) is now the unofficial work mantra for our time. The problem is that it leads not to salvation, but to the devaluation of actual work, including the very work it pretends to elevate—and more importantly, the dehumanization of the vast majority of laborers.

Superficially, DWYL is an uplifting piece of advice, urging us to ponder what it is we most enjoy doing and then turn that activity into a wage-generating enterprise. But why should our pleasure be for profit? Who is the audience for this dictum? Who is not?

By keeping us focused on ourselves and our individual happiness, DWYL distracts us from the working conditions of others while validating our own choices and relieving us from obligations to all who labor, whether or not they love it. It is the secret handshake of the privileged and a worldview that disguises its elitism as noble self-betterment. According to this way of thinking, labor is not something one does for compensation, but an act of self-love. If profit doesn't happen to follow, it is because the worker's passion and determination were insufficient. Its real achievement is making workers believe their labor serves the self and not the marketplace.

Aphorisms have numerous origins and reincarnations, but the generic and hackneyed nature of DWYL confounds precise attribution. Oxford Reference links the phrase and variants of it to Martina Navratilova and François Rabelais, among others. The internet frequently attributes it to Confucius, locating it in a misty, Orientalized past. Oprah Winfrey and other peddlers of positivity have included it in their repertoires for decades, but the most important recent evangelist of the DWYL creed is deceased Apple CEO Steve Jobs.

His graduation speech to the Stanford University class of 2005 provides as good an origin myth as any, especially since Jobs had already been beatified as the patron saint of aestheticized work well before his early death. In the speech, Jobs recounts the creation of Apple, and inserts this reflection:

> You've got to find what you love. And that is as true for your work as it is for your lovers. Your work is going to fill a large part of your life, and the only way to be truly satisfied is to do what you believe is great work. And the only way to do great work is to love what you do.

In these four sentences, the words "you" and "your" appear eight times. This focus on the individual is hardly surprising coming from Jobs, who cultivated a very specific image of himself as a worker: inspired, casual, passionate—all states agreeable with ideal romantic love. Jobs telegraphed the conflation of his besotted worker-self with his company so effectively that his black turtleneck and blue jeans became metonyms for all of Apple and the labor that maintains it.

But by portraying Apple as a labor of his individual love, Jobs elided the labor of untold thousands in Apple's factories, conveniently hidden from sight on the other side of the planet—the very labor that allowed Jobs to actualize his love.

The violence of this erasure needs to be exposed. While "do what you love" sounds harmless and precious, it is ultimately self-focused to the point of narcissism. Jobs' formulation of "do what you love" is the depressing antithesis to Henry David Thoreau's utopian vision of labor for all. In "Life without Principle," Thoreau wrote,

> . . . it would be good economy for a town to pay its laborers so well that they would not feel that they were working for low ends, as for a livelihood merely, but for scientific, even moral ends. Do not hire a man who does your work for money, but him who does it for the love of it.

Admittedly, Thoreau had little feel for the proletariat (it's hard to imagine someone washing diapers for "scientific, even moral ends," no matter how well-paid). But he nonetheless maintains that society has a stake in making work well-compensated and meaningful. By contrast, the twenty-first-century Jobsian view demands that we all turn inward. It absolves us of any obligation to or acknowledgment of the wider world, underscoring its fundamental betrayal of all workers, whether they consciously embrace it or not.

One consequence of this isolation is the division that DWYL creates among workers, largely along class lines. Work becomes divided into two opposing classes: that which is lovable (creative, intellectual, socially prestigious) and that which is not (repetitive, unintellectual, undistinguished). Those in the lovable work camp are vastly more privileged in terms of wealth, social status, education, society's racial biases, and political clout, while comprising a small minority of the workforce.

For those forced into unlovable work, it's a different story. Under the DWYL credo, labor that is done out of motives or needs other than love (which is, in fact, most labor) is not only demeaned but erased. As in Jobs' Stanford speech, unlovable but socially necessary work is banished from the spectrum of consciousness altogether.

Think of the great variety of work that allowed Jobs to spend even one day as CEO: his food harvested from fields, then transported across great distances. His company's goods assembled, packaged, shipped. Apple advertisements scripted, cast, filmed. Lawsuits processed. Office wastebaskets emptied and ink cartridges filled. Job creation goes both ways. Yet with the vast majority of workers effectively invisible to elites busy in their lovable occupations, how can it be surprising that the heavy strains faced by today's workers (abysmal wages, massive child care costs, et cetera) barely register as political issues even among the liberal faction of the ruling class?

In ignoring most work and reclassifying the rest as love, DWYL may be the most elegant anti-worker ideology around. Why should workers assemble and assert their class interests if there's no such thing as work?

***

"Do what you love" disguises the fact that being able to choose a career primarily for personal reward is an unmerited privilege, a sign of that person's socioeconomic class. Even if a self-employed graphic designer had parents who could pay for art school and cosign a lease for a slick Brooklyn apartment, she can self-righteously bestow DWYL as career advice to those covetous of her success.

If we believe that working as a Silicon Valley entrepreneur or a museum publicist or a think-tank acolyte is essential to being true to ourselves—in fact, to loving ourselves—what do we believe about the inner lives and hopes of those who clean hotel rooms and stock shelves at big-box stores? The answer is: nothing.

Yet arduous, low-wage work is what ever more Americans do and will be doing. According to the US Bureau of Labor Statistics, the two fastest-growing occupations projected until 2020 are "Personal Care Aide" and "Home Care Aide," with average salaries of $19,640 per year and $20,560 per year in 2010, respectively. Elevating certain types of professions to something worthy of love necessarily denigrates the labor of those who do unglamorous work that keeps society functioning, especially the crucial work of caregivers.

If DWYL denigrates or makes dangerously invisible vast swaths of labor that allow many of us to live in comfort and to do what we love, it has also caused great damage to the professions it portends to celebrate, especially those jobs existing within institutional structures. Nowhere has the DWYL mantra been more devastating to its adherents than in academia. The average PhD student of the mid-2000s forwent the easy money of finance and law (now slightly less easy) to live on a meager stipend in order to pursue their passion for Norse mythology or the history of Afro-Cuban music.

The reward for answering this higher calling is an academic employment marketplace in which around 41 percent of American faculty are adjunct professors—contract instructors who usually receive low pay, no benefits, no office, no job security, and no long-term stake in the schools where they work.

There are many factors that keep PhDs providing such high-skilled labor for such extremely low wages, including path dependency and the sunk costs of earning a PhD, but one of the strongest is how pervasively the DWYL doctrine is embedded in academia. Few other professions fuse the personal identity of their workers so intimately with the work output. This intense identification partly explains why so many proudly left-leaning faculty remain oddly silent about the working conditions of their peers. Because academic research should be done out of pure love, the actual conditions of and compensation for this labor become afterthoughts, if they are considered at all.

In "Academic Labor, the Aesthetics of Management, and the Promise of Autonomous Work," Sarah Brouillette writes of academic faculty,

> . . . our faith that our work offers non-material rewards, and is more integral to our identity than a "regular" job would be, makes us ideal employees when the goal of management is to extract our labor's maximum value at minimum cost.

Many academics like to think they have avoided a corporate work environment and its attendant values, but Marc Bousquet notes in his essay "We Work" that academia may actually provide a model for corporate management:

> How to emulate the academic workplace and get people to work at a high level of intellectual and emotional intensity for fifty or sixty hours a week for bartenders' wages or less? Is there any way we can get our employees to swoon over their desks, murmuring "I love what I do" in response to greater workloads and smaller paychecks? How can we get our workers to be like faculty and deny that they work at all? How can we adjust our corporate culture to resemble campus culture, so that our workforce will fall in love with their work too?

No one is arguing that enjoyable work should be less so. But emotionally satisfying work is still work, and acknowledging it as such doesn't undermine it in any way. Refusing to acknowledge it, on the other hand, opens the door to the most vicious exploitation and harms all workers.

Ironically, DWYL reinforces exploitation even within the so-called lovable professions where off-the-clock, underpaid, or unpaid labor is the new norm: reporters required to do the work of their laid-off photographers, publicists expected to Pin and Tweet on weekends, the 46 percent of the workforce expected to check their work email on sick days. Nothing makes exploitation go down easier than convincing workers that they are doing what they love.

Instead of crafting a nation of self-fulfilled, happy workers, our DWYL era has seen the rise of the adjunct professor and the unpaid intern—people persuaded to work for cheap or free, or even for a net loss of wealth. This has certainly been the case for all those interns working for college credit or those who actually purchase ultra-desirable fashion-house internships at auction. (Valentino and Balenciaga are among a handful of houses that auctioned off month-long internships. For charity, of course.) The latter is worker exploitation taken to its most extreme, and as an ongoing Pro Publica investigation reveals, the unpaid intern is an ever larger presence in the American workforce.

It should be no surprise that unpaid interns abound in fields that are highly socially desirable, including fashion, media, and the arts. These industries have long been accustomed to masses of employees willing to work for social currency instead of actual wages, all in the name of love. Excluded from these opportunities, of course, is the overwhelming majority of the population: those who need to work for wages. This exclusion not only calcifies economic and professional immobility, but insulates these industries from the full diversity of voices society has to offer.

And it's no coincidence that the industries that rely heavily on interns—fashion, media, and the arts—just happen to be the feminized ones, as Madeleine Schwartz wrote in *Dissent*. Yet another damaging consequence of DWYL is how ruthlessly it works to extract female labor for little or no compensation. Women comprise the majority of the low-wage or unpaid workforce; as care workers, adjunct faculty, and unpaid interns, they outnumber men. What unites all of this work, whether performed by GEDs or PhDs, is the belief that wages shouldn't be the primary motivation for doing it. Women are supposed to do work because they are natural nurturers and are eager to please; after all they've been doing uncompensated childcare, elder care, and housework since time immemorial. And talking money is unladylike anyway.

***

The DWYL dream is, true to its American mythology, superficially democratic. PhDs can do what they love, making careers that indulge their love of the Victorian novel and writing thoughtful essays in the *New York Review of Books*. High school grads can also do it, building prepared food empires out of their Aunt Pearl's jam recipe. The hallowed path of the entrepreneur always offers this way out of disadvantaged beginnings, excusing the rest of us for allowing those beginnings to be as miserable as they are. In America, everyone has the opportunity to do what he or she loves and get rich.

Do what you love and you'll never work a day in your life! Before succumbing to the intoxicating warmth of that promise, it's critical to ask, "Who, exactly, benefits from making work feel like non-work?" "Why *should* workers feel as if they aren't working when they are?" Historian Mario Liverani reminds us that "ideology has the function of presenting exploitation in a favorable light to the exploited, as advantageous to the disadvantaged."

In masking the very exploitative mechanisms of labor that it fuels, DWYL is, in fact, the most perfect ideological tool of capitalism. It shunts aside the labor of others and disguises our own labor to ourselves. It hides the fact that if we acknowledged all of our work as work, we could set appropriate limits for it, demanding fair compensation and humane schedules that allow for family and leisure time.

And if we did that, more of us could get around to doing what it is we *really* love.

PAUSE

Near the end of her piece, Tokumitsu argues that "all of our work [is] work." And yet, not all work is compensated equally. Make a list of three to five high-paying jobs, and a list of three to five low-paying jobs. Based on this list, what sorts of things does the labor market seem to value, and what does it seem to place little value on?

Introduction

Tokumitsu begins her piece with a description of a photo of what she calls the "'do what you love' living room," which opens her original piece. You can find the same photo and others like it by plugging some of those key terms into an Internet search engine. This photo is perhaps an unexpected choice to serve as evidence for the argument Tokumitsu is making, that the DWYL work culture serves to devalue human labor. Tokumitsu's accurate and insightful description of the photo works to support her argument very well. Though she draws on multiple forms of evidence, her description of the photo captures her argument so well that it almost makes her argument seem self-evident.

Understanding evidence is important, especially with the proliferation of so-called fake news. During the early days of the COVID-19 pandemic in the United States, a flurry of dubious advice circulated on social media. Many of the posts were alleged to be advice from doctors or prestigious universities but were in reality just unsubstantiated assertions. Even the office of the president, Donald Trump, pushed some medical remedies that had little to no evidence supporting their efficacy.

Providing evidence is the cornerstone of argumentation. Argumentation is giving an audience reasons to accept claims, and reasonable people will want evidence to do so. We've looked at evidence, as well as claims and warrants, in previous chapters, of course. In earlier chapters, however, we were focused on analyzing arguments: looking at their various parts and how they fit together. In this chapter we will move from analyzing arguments to **evaluating arguments**. That is, we will focus more on the relative strength of arguments—considering whether or not an audience should *accept* a particular argument—rather than how they are put together. We will also focus more on individual arguments rather than overall cases.

Evidence Is the Foundation for Claims

We begin by looking at evidence as the foundation for a claim: reasonable people make claims based on evidence. If the participants in a dispute accept the evidence, the evidence serves as the basis for the argument. They can be said to be standing on the shared ground of the evidence, even if they ultimately disagree about what that evidence suggests.

> Sometimes people can agree that some bit or body of evidence is acceptable, but still disagree on what the evidence means, or what it suggests should be done.

Several examples can illustrate this point. When the Omicron variant of COVID-19 first was discovered in South Africa, there was some debate about whether or not the variant produced a milder set of symptoms than previous variants of the virus did. Scientists agreed that there was lots of evidence to suggest the virus spread very quickly. And they agreed that symptoms appeared milder. So they agreed on the evidence. But some scientists believed the symptoms could be milder because the variant itself caused milder symptoms, while other scientists believed the population of South Africa—where many people had already gotten infected with an earlier variant of the virus—was more resistant. Despite agreeing on the evidence, then, there was still some ambiguity on what it meant.

Other times the evidence itself might be controversial or faulty. The 2016 election, in which Donald Trump was elected president, was notable among other things for the inability of most polls to predict the outcome. Hillary Clinton led Trump in every nationwide poll prior to the November election. Even in key battleground states, polling showed Clinton with a significant lead. So what happened? The evidence—polling data—supported a claim that Clinton would win the presidency, but that didn't happen. Was the evidence faulty? Many people thought so, leading many pundits afterward to wonder if polling no longer works. Even in early 2020, in the leadup to the next general election, many people doubted the accuracy of polls predicting a Biden victory.

This controversy shows the importance of evidence when it comes to evaluating arguments, and it shows that errors are possible even at the highest levels, with the greatest stakes. A careful approach to evaluating evidence is very important.

Evidence is the foundation of a claim. We make claims based on evidence. And so, the quality of our claims is dependent on the quality of our evidence.

If we continue to think about argumentation as a sort of conversation, a way of making decisions collectively based on reasons, then evidence is what we respond with to questions like "What makes you think so?" or "How do you know?"

In order for the evidence to be accepted as part of the exchange of arguments, it needs to be agreed upon by participants in the argument. As I state above, this does not mean all participants will always agree about the meaning of the evidence. Someone might respond to Tokumitsu by saying that Steve Jobs's graduation speech (which serves as evidence in the essay) actually presents a very different view of work than what Tokumitsu suggests.

In addition to disagreeing with the meaning of evidence, evidence is subject to dispute in other ways: someone you are debating or a member of your audience may reject your evidence or provide counterevidence. Nevertheless, when we argue about the meaning or evaluate the strength of a particular bit of evidence, we are—at least temporarily—agreeing to accept the evidence as potential grounds for the argument.

So evidence is one place an argument can begin. It serves to bring the participants to enough of an agreement that they can begin a genuine argument, a genuine exchange of claims and reasons. If we can agree that the evidence is strong and relevant to the controversy, then we can move to what it means, how it ought to be evaluated, and what actions or policies we should adopt because of it.

What happens if not everyone agrees about the strength or relevance of the evidence? Then the discussion of how to respond to the controversy pauses, because we have to first establish whether or not we can rely on the evidence. The evidence itself becomes the source of controversy.

Determining the Acceptability of Evidence

So what needs to happen for the participants in an argument to agree on the evidence? In some specialized cases, such as in courts of law, there are fixed rules about evidence. A judge may rule certain evidence inadmissible based on these rules. In scientific studies the evidence must be obtained by following valid, transparent, and reproducible methods.

But in everyday arguments the acceptability of evidence is—as with argumentation in general—subject to the willing acceptance of a reasoning audience. When we argue, we want the audience to accept our claims willingly, and without any force (other than the force of our logic). We believe we are aware of things that, if the audience were aware of them as well, would lead them to accepting our claims. We present this evidence to our audience, and if they accept it, accept also its relevance to our claims, and accept our interpretation of it, they are likely to accept the claims themselves.

There's a common idea that when people hold views different from your own, it is because they are uninformed. If people just had greater access to information, could educate themselves on the issues, they would adopt different positions—positions that happen to echo your own. Sometimes that is the case, but not always. The Internet is often hailed for its ability to provide everyone with almost unlimited information. With access to the Internet, someone could educate themselves about almost anything, right? And with more information, we might expect to see higher levels of agreement about controversies that currently divide us.

It does not always play out like this in reality, though. A recent study in the *American Journal of Political Science* did show a correlation between access to high-speed Internet and higher consumption of news. So that tracks—more access to the Internet, more consumption of information. The problem was that this higher consumption of news did not lead to more moderate views. On the contrary, the study showed that access to the Internet led participants to consume more politically extreme news.

This suggests that when people can freely access news from any source, they tend to favor news that supports points of view they already hold, rather than points of view that differ from their own. This phenomenon, sometimes called an **echo chamber**, has been identified in numerous contexts. Given the algorithms governing social media, for example, we are less likely to encounter points of view that differ from our own on social media than from a traditional news source—even when the social media post links to a traditional news source.

So it's not enough to have greater access to information, to evidence—we need to also know which evidence to trust in which contexts. When the argument being made aligns with points of view or values we already hold, we are much less likely to be critical of the evidence provided. Given how highly saturated our media lives are, and the relative infrequence with which we encounter oppositional points of view, it is more important now than ever to look at evidence critically.

Evaluating Evidence: Vaccines and Autism

Discussion of the evidence is common in argumentation and debate across contexts and media. It's particularly foregrounded in conspiracy theory arguments, precisely because the evidence is so often unreliable. Take, for example, the conspiracy theory that vaccines cause, rather than prevent, illnesses. The evidence for this notion comes in large part from a 1998 article by Andrew Wakefield in the *Lancet* medical journal. Many in the anti-vaccine community cite this article as the scientific basis for their views—even though the *Lancet* retracted the article after publication.

The journal retracted the article because they found fault with the evidence: they did not provide counterevidence, or make a counterclaim. In retracting the article the *Lancet* implicitly made the argument that the evidence provided in the article was faulty.

Structurally, when evidence is questioned, we begin a distinct argument in which the original evidence serves as a claim, and we begin to exchange claims that support or detract from the reliability of the original evidence.

So in the case of the *Lancet* retracting Wakefield's article, they made the argument that the selection methods of the children in the study did not ensure randomness within the population being studied but rather were carefully chosen to influence the results. They provided evidence also that the authors of the study had reason to be biased: lawyers representing parents suing vaccine manufacturers provided funding for the study.

This evidence was brought forward to support the claim "The evidence in the Wakefield study is faulty." This claim was made in response to the evidence first provided in the Wakefield study.

Because the participants involved in the argument did not agree to the evidence, the argument could not proceed until the acceptability of the evidence itself was established.

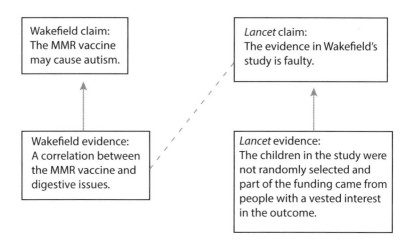

Common Types of Evidence

Here we'll take a closer look at five common types of evidence: examples, statistics, tangible objects, testimony, and social consensus.

Examples are a common type of evidence, covered in more detail in Chapter 9. They include both **instances**, which are brief references to something outside your immediate argument to support a claim, without any development, as well as **illustrations**, which are fully developed instances. If I say, for example, that a certain contemporary composer is great because she is doing for contemporary music theory what other great composers of the past—like Johann Sebastian Bach—had done, my reference to Bach is an instance. If pressed, I might fully flesh out the parallels and give more specific ways the two are similar. The fully developed example is an illustration.

The claim, that the contemporary composer is great, is my interpretation of the examples. Implicitly, I'm generalizing that (1) Bach and other great composers push developments in music theory, and (2) at least part of what it means to be a great composer is to push developments in music theory.

Both the evidence itself and the extent to which it supports the claim are open to argument. If someone does not accept the evidence, then arguments will have to be exchanged until we can come to some agreement about the evidence itself. Only then could we decide whether or not the evidence supports the particular claim.

Statistics are a form of numerical evidence that includes raw numbers, percentages, ratios, and index numbers. We'll cover statistical evidence in Chapter 9 as well, but basically, anytime you are using numbers to support a claim, you are drawing on statistics. Averages are a common form of statistics, and they include the **mean**, the **median**, and the **mode**. Rates of change, such as growth of population over time, are statistical measures. Probability statements, which express the likelihood of some occurrence, including the outcomes of controlled experiments, are also a form of statistics. Tokumitsu cites several statistics to support her arguments, including trends in the labor force. Like with examples, statistical evidence must be accepted as evidence before the argument can proceed.

Social consensus, or social norms, consists of widely held beliefs that function as if they were facts.

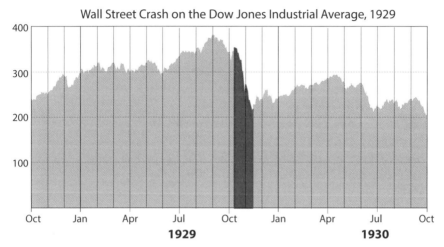

The Dow Jones Industrial Average, which is graphed above at the start of the Great Depression, is an example of an index. Indexes track changes in a set of figures over time.

Sometimes the beliefs are knowledge-based, such as common knowledge. For example, it is common knowledge that George Washington was the first president of the United States. This would likely be accepted by most U.S. audiences without question. Just because something is common knowledge, however, does not mean it *cannot* be contested. While most people readily accept 1776 as the founding date of the United States, others argue that it should be 1619, when the first enslaved Africans were brought to U.S. shores.

TYPES OF AVERAGES

You may remember from math class that there are three distinct ways of taking the average of a set of numbers.

- Mean: To find the mean, you add up all the numbers in a set, then divide the sum by how many numbers there are.
- Median: To find the median, you arrange all the numbers in a set from smallest to largest. The number that falls in the middle is the median.
- Mode: To find the mode, determine which number in a set comes up the most frequently.

Other times, social consensus is not based on knowledge but rather on the way historical events or figures are viewed. An example of this sort of shared historical understanding might be that the California missions were responsible for developing the western territories. Again, historical understanding, even when widely shared, may still be contested. Many argue, for example, that the California missions represent not development but rather the violent eradication of Native peoples.

Finally, social consensus might be neither about knowledge nor historical understanding but about shared value judgments. These may be as simple as fashion dos and don'ts, or more complex and deep-seated, like values that suggest certain careers should only be available to men and others only to women. DWYL, as it is presented in Tokumitsu's essay, is an example of social consensus about values. Obviously, these too may be contested.

Testimony, or statements of personal observation or professional opinion, often serve as evidence as well. This sort of evidence comes up frequently in court cases, when expert testimony can serve as evidence for some sort of technical issue, or witness testimony can serve as evidence for some event or series of events. Testimony is common outside of legal contexts also, like when people give product or film reviews, or vouch for someone you haven't met. Testimony can be contested by other experts or witnesses, or by questioning the credibility of the source.

A physical or **tangible object** can also serve as evidence in certain contexts. The weapon used to commit a crime, for example, would be an important piece of evidence in a relevant criminal case. Tangible objects might serve as important evidence in historical contexts as well. A set of prehistoric bones might serve as evidence for a newly discovered ancient creature, a drawing might serve as evidence for some aspect of daily life in an ancient civilization, or a historical document might serve as evidence for some important past debate. Tangible objects can be contested if they are deemed inauthentic or misidentified.

Tests of Evidence

Several tests of evidence exist to determine whether or not the evidence should convince us. Of course, this doesn't mean people are only convinced by evidence that passes these tests; on the contrary, people accept claims with insufficient or faulty evidence all the time. But if the evidence cannot pass these tests, then most of the time it should not convince us.

Accessibility

The first test of evidence is quite simple: Does the audience have access to the evidence for examination? Can the audience look at the evidence and make their own determinations about it?

In some cases an audience will justifiably accept a claim without directly being presented with the evidence. If the evidence is already well known to the audience, for example, they may not need to see it again. Or if the evidence is highly specialized, they may be willing to take the interpretation of experts rather than wanting to make their own assessment.

For example, a doctor may do a series of tests and tell a patient that they have a particular condition. The patient is not likely to ask to see the test results themselves unless they have training in their interpretation. More likely, should they want to question the results, they may show them to other experts.

But when the evidence is not well known and remains inaccessible even to experts, then any claims made on its basis are highly problematic. We should not accept claims based on evidence that is not made available to us. Sometimes people in positions of power may make claims based on evidence they argue must remain secret. A president may cite issues of national security in refusing to provide evidence, for example. A reasonable audience must make decisions about whether or not such claims are justified.

Credibility

Credibility comes from the classical concept of ethos, which has to do with the level of trust between speaker and audience. The credibility of a source depends on either its reputation or its credentials. You want the evidence to come from sources that have consistently provided accurate and reliable evidence, or from people who have the appropriate training to provide the evidence.

Reputation

Has the source been known to consistently provide reliable evidence in the past? There has always been controversy about the reputation of sources, and this has only intensified recently. Nevertheless, major newspapers such as the *New York Times* and major magazines such as *Newsweek* are widely recognized as having high standards for accuracy and reliability. In academic contexts, journals that publish peer-reviewed articles are considered more reliable. Your university library will have excellent resources for determining the credibility of both news and scholarly sources.

Credentials

If the evidence provided requires the interpretation of the expert, the expert should be appropriately credentialed: they should have the appropriate combination of education and experience. Groups opposing climate change policy, for example, will often draw on testimony from scientists whose expertise lies in a field other than climate science. In that case, the expert does not have the relevant credentials, no matter how impressive the credentials they have. A world-renowned tailor, after all, would be less appropriate than an unknown local surgeon when faced with a medical controversy.

When writing arguments, use the credibility of your sources to your advantage by pointing to the sources when appropriate.

If there is a chance the audience would not recognize the reputation or credentials of your source, you will need to qualify the source. That is, you will need to provide evidence to support the claim that this source is reputable and/or appropriately credentialed. You can justify a source's reputation by providing evidence about how long it has been around, what other well-respected and knowledgeable people are associated with it or have had positive things to say about it, or its connection with other institutions that are respected. You can justify a source's credentials by stating them and making their relevance to the issue at hand clear.

Generally speaking, it is a good idea to get in the habit of introducing sources in a way that lends them credibility:

> Unless conditions change unexpectedly, schools may have to stay closed in the fall.

> According to Dr. Anthony Fauci, director of the National Institute of Allergy and Infectious Diseases, schools may have to stay closed in the fall unless conditions change unexpectedly.

While both contain essentially the same information, the second example has more rhetorical force and is more transparent about its sources.

Internal Consistency

Sometimes evidence contradicts itself. When asked his take on the debunked theory that the coronavirus was originally manufactured in a Chinese lab, Secretary of State Mike Pompeo responded:

Effective evidence must be consistent: it must present compatible information throughout.

> "Look, the best experts so far seem to think [the coronavirus] was man-made. I have no reason to disbelieve that at this point."

> But when the reporter questioning him pointed out that both the scientific community and the U.S. intelligence community did not believe that to be true, Pompeo responded by undermining his previous position:

"That's right. I agree with that. Yes. I've seen their analysis. I've seen the summary that you saw that was released publicly. I have no reason to doubt that that is accurate at this point."

He claims to believe that the virus was man-made, but also that the virus was not man-made. Pompeo's testimony, then, would not make good evidence regardless of which claim you wanted to draw on. Either way, a reasonable audience could respond by pointing out that Pompeo had also stated he believed the opposite.

Effective evidence must be consistent: it must present compatible information throughout. The same source making inconsistent claims or providing contradictory information is bad evidence.

External Consistency

Different sources making inconsistent claims are natural to a controversy, but if a piece of evidence is radically at odds with the consensus, then it should not be convincing. This is one of the trickiest things to get a handle on when faced with everyday arguments. Scientists and experts disagree about things all the time. How can we know who we should believe? Some psychologists have argued that gaming addiction, compulsive or uncontrolled video game usage, is a mental disorder, while others disagree. Many economists argue that the minimum wage should be increased to help the most vulnerable, while some others suggest that doing so would have an overall negative impact.

When there is a lack of consensus around a given issue, the well-informed must continue to look at the evidence and provide their best interpretation. But it is important to remember to reference the majority opinion when consensus does exist. For example, the vast majority of scientists agree that climate change is occurring due to an increase in global greenhouse gases produced through human activity. A handful of scientists dispute this view, but the stronger evidence lies with the scientific consensus on the issue. People who choose to believe the minority view do so often because it supports beliefs they already hold, rather than coming to this conclusion after a careful review of the available evidence.

Relevance

Relevance is measured by the extent to which the evidence, if true, would influence a reasonable audience to accept the claim at hand. If I am arguing that there is a high probability of life on Mars, for example, and I present as evidence the abundant life in deep-sea thermal vents, a reasonable audience is not likely to accept my claim based on that evidence. There is too great a difference between the conditions on Mars and the conditions in deep-sea thermal vents. My evidence in that case would not be sufficiently relevant to my claim.

Adequacy

Adequacy is a test of the sufficiency of the evidence to support the claim in question: Is the evidence, taken together, enough to accept the claim with a high degree of probability? Tokumitsu links to a photo as evidence for her argument that the DWYL mantra erases the labor of work. The image does represent precisely what she is arguing: the photo shows a room benignly bringing work into a space of rest. But if Tokumitsu used the photo alone as evidence for her claim, it would probably be insufficient to convince all but the most believing audience.

Conclusion

Tokumitsu provides multiple types of evidence throughout her essay, including examples, tangible objects, and statistics. Some of these she draws on extensively, while others she touches on briefly, but all are important for supporting her argument. A reasonable audience may accept some of her evidence while rejecting other evidence. Depending on how relevant and adequate the evidence, an audience can discount some of her evidence while still accepting her overall claim. Or they may accept some evidence and reject other evidence, leading them to respond with a counterclaim, or with an additional argument that builds on Tokumitsu's.

Most of the time evidence does not speak for itself, and much of the time multiple interpretations of the same piece of evidence are possible. One could easily respond to Tokumitsu with their own interpretation of the DWYL mantra, or a different interpretation of the texts she draws on. Interpreting evidence is therefore often necessary, and another opportunity to present your case with a fair and appropriate interpretation of the evidence that best supports it.

PROBE

Not every audience will expect the standards of evidence identified in this chapter. What do you think you should do if you're making a speech to an audience you know would accept evidence that they really shouldn't?

Chapter 8
Visual and Multimodal Arguments

Key Terms

visual rhetoric

emotionally charged

framing

perspective

Key Points

- Visual rhetoric uses images to persuade an audience, but not all visual rhetoric makes an argument.
- Visual representations can be classified as arguments if they have truth value.
- Visual representations can be evaluated using a number of tests specific to them.
- Context is important in evaluating both whether or not an image is an argument and the strength and validity of the image.
- Emotional response to a visual image is neither necessarily true or false; it can be either depending on the circumstances.

PRIME
Make a short list of any famous photographs or images you can think of. What do you think makes them so powerful?

Speech to the Troops at Tilbury

Queen Elizabeth I (1588)

My loving people,

We have been persuaded by some that are careful of our safety, to take heed how we commit our selves to armed multitudes, for fear of treachery; but I assure you I do not desire to live to distrust my faithful and loving people. Let tyrants fear. I have always so behaved myself that, under God, I have placed my chiefest strength and safeguard in the loyal hearts and good-will of my subjects; and therefore I am come amongst you, as you see, at this time, not for my recreation and disport, but being resolved, in the midst and heat of the battle, to live and die amongst you all; to lay down for my God, and for my kingdom, and my people, my honour and my blood, even in the dust.

I know I have the body but of a weak and feeble woman; but I have the heart and stomach of a king, and of a king of England too, and think foul scorn that Parma or Spain, or any prince of Europe, should dare to invade the borders of my realm: to which rather than any dishonour shall grow by me, I myself will take up arms, I myself will be your general, judge, and rewarder of every one of your virtues in the field.

I know already, for your forwardness you have deserved rewards and crowns; and We do assure you in the word of a prince, they shall be duly paid you. In the mean time, my lieutenant general shall be in my stead, than whom never prince commanded a more noble or worthy subject; not doubting but by your obedience to my general, by your concord in the camp, and your valour in the field, we shall shortly have a famous victory over those enemies of my God, of my kingdom, and of my people.

PAUSE

Queen Elizabeth I relies on a series of contrasts or binary oppositions in this short text, such as the contrast she draws between "armed multitudes" and "faithful and loving people" in the opening sentence. What are some others? How do you think the way she looked added effect to any of these contrasts?

Introduction

This is perhaps a strange text to begin a chapter on **visual rhetoric**, or the use of elements beyond simply text for persuasion. For one—it's a text. There are no images that are part of the text, though you can see in the following figure an image of how one artist has imagined the event at which this speech was given.

But even leaving aside the speech's fit for this chapter, you may be wondering what the speech is doing in a book on argumentation at all. It's short, it makes some off-putting statements about the power of a woman's body, and it doesn't seem in general to subscribe to the tenets of argumentation that we have been learning so far. We learned at the beginning of this book that arguments must provide justification for claims, but this speech seems to be making assertions only, without providing evidence.

Elisabetta

You may be surprised to learn, then, that this speech played a historic role in magnifying the power and status of Queen Elizabeth I throughout England and Europe toward the end of the sixteenth century. Why this speech, you might ask, this insignificant thing?

Well, let's take a look at the context here. The speech was given in 1588, as the Spanish Armada, a massive fleet of warships, was threatening to ferry a vast army of Spanish and allied troops from Europe to invade England. The whole country feared this invasion, which threatened not only the stability of England but also the very existence of the Church of England.

Tilbury, where the speech was given, was a village roughly twenty-five miles east of London, overlooking the river Thames. There, England had gathered some four thousand troops, ready to defend against what promised to be a much larger Spanish force waiting across the English Channel. And there, on what everyone assembled anticipated was the eve of a great battle, entered Queen Elizabeth I's procession, featuring the queen herself, in armor, riding atop a white gelding.

Arguing with Visuals

In this context, let me first defend the speech itself a bit. It is short, but what soldier wants to stand in the August heat, anticipating a violent assault, and listen to a long speech? Today's reader may take issue with the queen's characterization of a woman's body as "weak and feeble," and it is true that such language may perpetuate negative stereotypes about the potential and role of women. But the words must be understood in their visual context. Elizabeth I says this atop a warhorse, covered in armor. She does not present the body of "a weak and feeble woman." On the contrary, her physical presence undermines these words, and thus she invites listeners to question the very stereotype she invokes.

The power of this speech, then, is not so much from the words alone but from the words she speaks in this particular context, and presented as they are by her striking physical figure. It is not just the words but also the visuals surrounding them that lend this argument its force.

Queen Elizabeth I's speech to the troops at Tilbury reminds us that persuasion can be achieved in multiple ways beyond argumentation strictly, including with visuals, music and sound, and appeals to emotion and trust. Persuasion, of course, is not the same as argumentation, and in fact there has been some debate as to whether or not visual representation can ever make arguments.

Is Queen Elizabeth I's presence, dressed as she was, an argument in and of itself? Let's remember that argumentation means providing audiences with reasons for claims. Can it be possible for Elizabeth I to use her body to provide both claims and reasons?

To answer this, it is helpful to go back to a term that was introduced in Chapter 3, *truth value*. If you recall from that chapter, for a statement to be considered a claim it must be able to be supported as either true or false, acceptable to a particular audience or not. Cashews are tasty, for example, does not have truth value. It's not in the realm of truth at all but rather in the realm of personal taste. Some might find cashews tasty while others may not. Coming to a definitive understanding of whether or not cashews are tasty is a futile endeavor, because it will always come down to personal taste. Therefore, most reasonable people wouldn't argue to try to persuade someone that cashews are or are not tasty.

The statement "U.S. cashew consumers must do more to ensure workers who process the nuts are fairly compensated," however, does have truth value. This is a claim of policy, and reasonable people could very well exchange claims and evidence debating it.

The question then is, can visual representations possibly make claims that have truth value? Obviously, visual representations like photographs or videos are often presented as evidence for claims. For example, if a tree blows over in a windstorm and falls on someone's house, an insurance company may take photos of the roof to assess the extent of the damage. On their own, the photos cannot make claims—they are too ambiguous. The owner of the house might look at the photos and see evidence that the damage is light. A roofing expert, on the other hand, might look at the same photos and conclude that repairs would be costly. The insurance company might consider the photos evidence that the damage was weather-related. The photos are not claims, then, but they did provide evidence for claims of damage.

In order for a photo to be an argument, it has to present a claim and provide justification for that claim. Can a photo or video do this? Can a photo be true or false? Aren't photographs supposed to just be representations of what is? Can an image, in other words, have truth value?

Truth Value in Visual Representations

Let's consider these questions in light of the following photo, an advertisement for the Indian clothing designer Venfield as part of the National Water Conservation Campaign.

Now, it is clear this photo has been manipulated to make something appear to be the case that is not the case. Most likely, this photo does not represent something that is—there was never a fish put in a fishbowl with a dripping spigot. Rather, sophisticated photo editing techniques were used to make it appear that a goldfish is looking worriedly at the steady drip of water from its home. So from that point of view this photo is not true.

But if we look at the photo in the context of an advertising campaign, which in turn exists in the context of concerns about water shortage, then we can see the photo say something beyond mere representation. In fact, we can see that this photo is indeed making a claim that may or may not be true, that is, that reasonable people may agree or disagree with: water is running low, and we need water to survive. The photo is in essence making an argument from analogy, that the bowl is analogous to the earth, the goldfish is analogous to life, and the dwindling amount of water is analogous to the relatively limited available freshwater on earth (for more on analogy, see Chapter 10). The argument, essentially, is that water is an important, finite, and rapidly depleting resource—it's an argument of quality.

One might raise the objection that there are words supplementing the image here: "Save water. Save life." If the photo needs the text to make its argument, then indeed the text is the claim and the photo is the evidence. But I think the argument would be clear with the photo alone. The photo does not really work as evidence, because it is clearly a manufactured image. It really only works as a claim. This photo, then, suggests that images can in fact make arguments. In fact, some of the most iconic images in history hold the power they do because of the argument they implicitly make: the earth seen as a whole from space suggesting a greater unity obscured by the factious politics and global affairs of the late 1960s, a vulture waiting near a starving child during the Sudanese famine of the early 1990s, mandated school integration after *Brown v. Board of Education.*

Emotional Appeals in Visual Arguments

Much of the time images are used to make arguments, as in the above examples, is in advertisements. Often, the evidence they provide is **emotionally charged**, which means that they may appeal to your emotions rather than formal logic. But as I've been making clear throughout this book, formal logic is not a good model for real, everyday arguments. In the fishbowl ad we know the fish is safe from harm, but we may still accept the claim that reducing water usage saves lives. In the past, emotions were treated with a mixture of skepticism and awe in argumentation theory and in textbooks about argumentation. Emotions are no longer viewed as inherently invalid—indeed, there is a growing body of research showing that emotions are vital to our ability to make good decisions. Rather, a particular emotional response is sometimes reasonable, and sometimes not, depending on the circumstances. In other words, like arguments in general, our emotions can be correct or incorrect. Anger, for example, might be justified in one situation and inappropriate in another. Emotions are valid when they appropriately respond to real-world phenomena. Just like with arguments, a simple test for validity in emotions is whether or not an audience exercising reason would accept the emotions as justified. Because emotions come loaded with historically accumulated stereotypes, particularly around gender, it is important to consider both the makeup of the audience and the values they hold in common when evaluating the reasonableness of an emotion. For example, dismissing an argument made by a woman as too emotional should be viewed with skepticism.

> Emotions are valid when they appropriately respond to real-world phenomena. Just like with arguments, a simple test for validity in emotions is whether or not an audience exercising reason would accept the emotions as justified.

Evaluating Visual Evidence

Images can make arguments and often also serve as powerful evidence. Because of this, they shouldn't be undervalued. We need look no further than the several recent events in which visual evidence—particularly video evidence—played important roles in either convicting or overturning criminal convictions.

Take, for example, the case of former Chicago police officer Jason Van Dyke, who was convicted of the second-degree murder of seventeen-year-old Laquan McDonald based largely on dashcam video evidence, or former Minneapolis police officer Derek Chauvin, who was likewise convicted of the murder of George Floyd based largely on video evidence. These cases are notable, in fact, because convictions of police officers accused of excessive force are exceedingly rare—according to the National Police Misconduct Project, police officers are rarely charged, and just over 10 percent of police officers charged are ever sentenced to prison.[1]

Most experts agree that what made Van Dyke's case different was the availability of police dashcam footage, which showed McDonald walking away when Van Dyke shot him sixteen times. In fact, Van Dyke was only charged with murder after the video footage was released. It's clear, then, that visual representation can serve as powerful evidence.

The tests for evaluating evidence described in the previous chapter are also useful for evaluating visual evidence. Asking questions about the photo's recency, for example, can help us determine whether or not it is appropriate evidence in the particular case at hand. Accessibility, likewise, is important.

Selection of the Image

We can ask further questions to evaluate visual evidence. You may remember some controversy surrounding the size of the crowd gathered to watch Donald Trump's inauguration. The newly inaugurated president claimed it was the largest crowd in history, with 1.5 million attendees, he estimated. Lots of photos like the two below circulated on social media and in the news, each presenting contrasting evidence for Trump's claim.

The first question to ask is whether or not the image is the most accurate image available in the context of the particular controversy. Things like **framing** (what the photo leaves in, what it excludes, and how it draws attention to particular elements within it) and **perspective** (the point of view, or the placement of the camera in relation to the subject matter), as well as timing and clarity, can all affect what an audience might reasonably take from a photograph. Thus, the principle of selection, the factors that determine what elements are and are not noticeable in any given image, needs to be accounted for.

---

1. Cato Institute, "2010 NPMRSP Police Misconduct Statistical Report Draft," April 5, 2011, http://web.archive.org/web/20150312220534/http://www.policemisconduct .net/2010-npmsrp-police-misconduct-statistical-report/.

Shortened view, Trump Inauguration, 2017   *Extended view, Trump Inauguration, 2017*

So, concerning these two examples, how do we determine which is better evidence of crowd size? To be good evidence, the photograph should present the most accurate representation possible. The first photo shows only the sections of the National Mall closest to the stage, where the crowd is tightly packed. But from that perspective it is hard to tell whether or not this is a good representation of the crowd as a whole. The second photo allows us to see that the crowd gets thinner as we get closer to the back of the National Mall and is thus the more accurate perspective.

Distortion and Manipulation

As we all are increasingly aware, images are easily manipulated and distorted. In fact, even video can be distorted, a capability made famous in comedian Jordan Peele's public service announcement impersonating President Obama. In the video Peele uses his impersonation of Obama and software that syncs mouth movements in video to audio voiceover to warn of the dangers of video manipulation. The sophistication of such manipulation makes determining fakes difficult. In some cases, it may be necessary to consult experts, especially if the video does not reflect external consistency.

External Consistency

We went over external consistency in Chapter 7 (you can go back quickly now to refresh your memory). Here I want to say a bit more on external consistency specifically in photographic and other visual arguments and evidence. While photos often provide strong, compelling evidence, it is always a good idea to see if other types of evidence corroborate it. In the case of Trump's inauguration, experts looked at other data, such as subway tickets purchased going into the area of the National Mall on the day of the inauguration, to see if Trump's claims of 1.5 million attendees held up. A reasonable audience should consider all the available evidence, including visual evidence, expert testimony, and statistics, to make a decision about which claims to accept or to make their own claims.

Conclusion

Queen Elizabeth I's appearance at her speech at Tilbury inspired some paintings that became iconic in her day. That alone doesn't suggest necessarily that her appearance was an argument in and of itself, but it does tell us that people in the audience noticed—they paid attention to what she looked like.

And it's clear that Elizabeth I paid careful attention to how she would appear as well. Sitting astride a warhorse in battle armor is not typical daywear for a queen, even in sixteenth-century England. She knew what she was doing. And it worked, because her physical presence made a large impact on the audience. Historians often cite that image of the queen, in full armor astride a white horse, as making the reputation of the new queen as a powerful and capable leader. More to the point, it was her giving her speech as a woman, her presence as a woman, that is in fact the most powerful aspect of her argument. Moreover, it implies that she is providing evidence for, and presenting, a claim just by being there.

If someone tells you not to do something because it isn't safe, and you go ahead and do it and are fine, didn't you in effect provide a rebuttal to their argument? That's what's going on in Elizabeth's speech as well. She is making an argument that she has nothing to fear from her people, armed or not. She could have written that in a speech and had it delivered by one of her representatives, but that would not have been nearly so powerful because it would be missing key evidence that she is not afraid—namely, her presence in front of her army.

There's another element to Elizabeth I's argument: gender identity. Elizabeth I acknowledges this when she says, "I know I have the body but of a weak and feeble woman; but I have the heart and stomach of a king." She knows that gender is not accidental to her argument but part and parcel of it. Elizabeth I is therefore making an argument not just about herself as a political leader but also about the role of a woman. Most importantly for this chapter, she does this not just through her words but through her representing herself visually, through the appearance of her body. It is clear, then, that in some cases it is possible to make arguments without words. The speech is short and, while a good speech, Elizabeth I knows that the main force of her argument is not in her words but in her physical appearance before her armed troops on the battlefield. Her body presents both a number of claims and evidence for these claims (I am not afraid, for here I am; I, as a woman leader, have a place on the battlefield, and here I am).

When considering whether a visual representation is a self-contained argument, on the one hand, or evidence for an argument only, on the other, we must decide whether or not the visual representation has truth value. In the case of Elizabeth I's presence on the field at Tilbury, we see that it does.

PROBE

The rise of images created by artificial intelligence (AI) presents a new challenge for argumentation, because it can create images that appear highly compelling but do not in fact represent an actual occurrence. Do an Internet search for an AI-generated image or a video known as a deep fake. How might you use the tests identified in this chapter to assess this image or video?

Chapter 9
Argument from Example

Key Terms

anecdotal example

statistical example

population

case

sample

sample size

confidence level

confidence interval

representative

sorting effect

classification

Key Points

- Argument from example involves reasoning from part to whole, or from whole to part.
- The warrant in argument from example is that what is true of the whole is true of the part.
- Anecdotal examples are effective for their use of storytelling.
- Statistical examples are compelling for their use of scientific methodology.

PRIME

Imagery is language that evokes the senses (touch, taste, smell, sight, sound). Cockburn uses imagery in a highly effective way throughout this essay. Choose a page from this essay and underline every example of imagery on that page.

21st Century Slaves

Andrew Cockburn (2003)

Sherwood Castle, headquarters to Milorad Milakovic, the former railway official who rose to become a notorious slave trafficker in Bosnia, looms beside
the main road just outside the northwest Bosnian town of Prijedor. Under
stucco battlements, the entrance is guarded by well-muscled, heavily tattooed
young men, while off to one side Milakovic's trio of pet Siberian tigers prowl
their caged compound.

I arrived there alone one gray spring morning—alone because no local
guide or translator dared accompany me—and found my burly 54-year-old
host waiting for me at a table set for lunch beside a glassed-in aquamarine
swimming pool.

The master of Sherwood has never been shy about his business. He once
asked a dauntless human rights activist who has publicly detailed his record
of buying women for his brothels in Prijedor: "Is it a crime to sell women?
They sell footballers, don't they?"

Milakovic threatened to kill the activist for her outspokenness, but to me
he sang a softer tune. Over a poolside luncheon of seafood salad and steak,
we discussed the stream of young women fleeing the shattered economies of
their home countries in the former Soviet bloc. Milakovic said he was eager
to promote his scheme to legalize prostitution in Bosnia—"to stop the selling
of people, because each of those girls is someone's child."

One such child is a nearsighted, chainsmoking blonde named Victoria,
at 20 a veteran of the international slave trade. For three years of her
life she was among the estimated 27 million men, women, and children
in the world who are enslaved—physically confined or restrained and
forced to work, or controlled through violence, or in some way treated
as property.

Victoria's odyssey began when she was 17, fresh out of school in Chisinau,
the decayed capital of the former Soviet republic of Moldova. "There was no
work, no money," she explained simply. So when a friend—"at least I thought
he was a friend"—suggested he could help her get a job in a factory in
Turkey, she jumped at the idea and took up his offer to drive her there,
through Romania. "But when I realized we had driven west, to the border
with Serbia, I knew something was wrong."

It was too late. At the border she was handed over to a group of Serb men,
who produced a new passport saying she was 18. They led her on foot into
Serbia and raped her, telling her that she would be killed if she resisted. Then

they sent her under guard to Bosnia, the Balkan republic being rebuilt under a torrent of international aid after its years of genocidal civil war.

Victoria was now a piece of property and, as such, was bought and sold by different brothel owners ten times over the next two years for an average price of $1,500. Finally, four months pregnant and fearful of a forced abortion, she escaped. I found her hiding in the Bosnian city of Mostar, sheltered by a group of Bosnian women.

In a soft monotone she recited the names of clubs and bars in various towns where she had to dance seminaked, look cheerful, and have sex with any customer who wanted her for the price of a few packs of cigarettes. "The clubs were all awful, although the Artemdia, in Banja Luka, was the worst—all the customers were cops," she recalled.

Victoria was a debt slave. Payment for her services went straight to her owner of the moment to cover her "debt"—the amount he had paid to buy her from her previous owner. She was held in servitude unless or until the money she owed to whomever controlled her had been recovered, at which point she would be sold again and would begin to work off the purchase price paid by her new owner. Although slavery in its traditional form survives in many parts of the world, debt slavery of this kind, with variations, is the most common form of servitude today.

According to Milorad Milakovic, such a system is perfectly aboveboard. "There is the problem of expense in bringing a girl here," he had explained to me. "The plane, transport, hotels along the way, as well as food. That girl must work to get that money back."

In November 2000 the UN-sponsored International Police Task Force (IPTF) raided Milakovic's nightclub-brothels in Prijedor, liberating 34 young women who told stories of servitude similar to Victoria's. "We had to dance, drink a lot, and go to our rooms with anyone," said one. "We were eating once a day and sleeping five to six hours. If we would not do what we were told, guards would beat us."

Following the IPTF raids, Milakovic complained to the press that the now liberated women had cost a lot of money to buy, that he would have to buy more, and that he wanted compensation. He also spoke openly about the cozy relations he had enjoyed with the IPTF peacekeepers, many of whom had been his customers.

But there were no influential friends to protect him in May this year, when local police finally raided Sherwood Castle and arrested Milakovic for trafficking in humans and possessing slaves.

We think of slavery as something that is over and done with, and our images of it tend to be grounded in the 19th century: black field hands in chains. "In those days slavery thrived on a shortage of person power," explains

Mike Dottridge, former director of Anti-Slavery International, founded in 1839 to carry on the campaign that had already abolished slavery in the British Empire. The average slave in 1850, according to the research of slavery expert Kevin Bales, sold for around $40,000 in today's money.

I visited Dottridge at the organization's headquarters in a small building in Stockwell, a nondescript district in south London. "Back then," said Dottridge, "black people were kidnapped and forced to work as slaves. Today vulnerable people are lured into debt slavery in the expectation of a better life. There are so many of them because there are so many desperate people in the world."

The offices are festooned with images of contemporary slavery—forced labor in West Africa, five- and six-year-old Pakistani children delivered to the Persian Gulf to serve as jockeys on racing camels, Thai child prostitutes. File cabinets bulge with reports: Brazilian slave gangs hacking at the Amazon rain forest to make charcoal for the steel industry, farm laborers in India bound to landlords by debt they have inherited from their parents and will pass on to their children.

The buying and selling of people is a profitable business because, while globalization has made it easier to move goods and money around the world, people who want to move to where jobs are face ever more stringent restrictions on legal migration.

Almost invariably those who cannot migrate legally or pay fees up front to be smuggled across borders end up in the hands of trafficking mafias. "Alien smuggling [bringing in illegal aliens who then find paying jobs] and human trafficking [where people end up enslaved or sold by the traffickers] operate exactly the same way, using the same routes," said a veteran field agent from the U.S. Immigration and Naturalization Service (INS). "The only difference is what happens to people at the other end." As the fees people must pay for transport rise in step with tightening border controls, illegal immigrants are ever more likely to end up in debt to the traffickers who have moved them— and are forced to work off their obligations as slaves.

It's dangerous for outsiders to show too close an interest in how these trafficking mafias work (a point that had occurred to me at Sherwood Castle), but in Athens I found a man who has made the study of slave trafficking his specialty and lives to tell the tale.

In 1990 Grigoris Lazos, a sociology professor at Panteion University, embarked on what he thought would be straightforward research on prostitution in Greece. Bright and intense, he resolved to go straight to the source, the prostitutes themselves. Through them he eventually made contact with the people who had enslaved them. Over the course of a decade—and in the face of intense disapproval from his professional colleagues—Lazos gained access to trafficking operations from the inside and was able to paint a clear picture of the interplay between prostitution and slavery in his country.

"You should note the difference between a small trafficking gang and a large network, which uses the Internet and bank accounts," he said. "Any bar owner or group of bar owners in Greece can send someone up to southern Bulgaria to buy women for cash. The cost of a girl in that area is $1,000, or, if you negotiate, you might be able to get two for $1,000. Best to try on a Monday for cheap prices, because most trafficking happens at the weekends. Mondays are slow, so you can get the leftovers."

"A network, on the other hand," he continued, "has the ability to bargain and complete financial transactions from a distance. Simply call Moscow, ask for women, and they will be sent to Romania and from there on through Bulgaria to Greece. The parties don't even have to know each other. The importer simply says, 'I want so-and-so many first quality women, so-and-so many second quality, so-and-so many third quality.'"

Flicking through his exhaustive files, the professor rattled off the cold data of human trade. "Between 1990 and 2000 the total amount earned in Greece from trafficked women, that is to say those who were forced into this kind of prostitution, was 5.5 billion dollars. Voluntary prostitutes, those who were working of their own accord and are mostly Greek women, earned 1.5 billion dollars."

The efficiency and scope of the Greek traffickers' operations studied by Lazos is by no means unique. In Trieste, the gateway from the Balkans into northern Italy, investigators from the local anti-mafia commission tracked the activities of Josip Loncaric, a former taxi driver from Zagreb, Croatia.

By the time Loncaric was finally arrested in 2000 he owned airlines in Albania and Macedonia and was involved in moving thousands of people destined for work not only in prostitution but in any menial task requiring cheap labor in the prosperous world of the European Union. His Chinese wife, who was also his business partner, provided a link to criminal Chinese triads with which Loncaric did profitable business smuggling Chinese as well as Kurds, Iraqis, Iranians, and any other afflicted people willing to mortgage themselves in hopes of a better future. Many of Loncaric's Chinese victims found themselves locked up and forced to work 18 hours a day in restaurants or in the famous Italian leather workshops.

Trafficking mafias and smugglers, in the last decade of the 20th century, brought 35,000 people a year into Western Europe through the Trieste area, guiding them at night through the rugged mountains and forests straddling the border with Slovenia. But this is only one of many funnels between poor worlds and rich ones. Thousands of miles away I found another flood of migrants fleeing Central America on their way to El Norte, the United States, where they could ultimately become slaves.

These migrants' homes were ravaged by the wars of the 1980s and '90s and reduced to further ruin by a succession of natural and man-made disasters. Hurricane Mitch pounded Honduras and Nicaragua in 1998; afterward the number of homeless street children in Central America jumped by 20 percent. El Salvador was hit by a 7.6 earthquake in 2001. Large parts of the region have been without rain for the past three years, and the world price of coffee has crashed, ruining the Central American coffee industry and leaving 600,000 workers unemployed. In Guatemala more than half a million coffee workers face starvation.

Many economists argue that the North American Free Trade Agreement has made its own contribution to the flood of people trying to move north, maintaining that cheap U.S. corn imported into Mexico has effectively driven millions of Mexican peasant corn farmers out of business and off the land. They suggest that for every ton of corn imported into Mexico, two Mexicans migrate to the U.S.

The tiny Guatemalan town of Tecún Umán lies on the bank of the Suchiate River. Here migrants from Central America gather to cross into Mexico on their way north. Those with valid travel documents for Mexico cross the bridge over the river; those without them pay a few cents to be ferried across on rafts made from tractor inner tubes.

No matter where they come from, a great majority of migrants arrive in Tecún Umán penniless, easy prey for the local hoteliers, bar owners, and people smugglers—known as coyotes—who live off the flow of humanity. It is a town where, in the words of one former resident, "everything and everyone is for sale."

Some of the luckier migrants find a temporary safe haven at Casa del Migrante, a walled compound just a few yards from the muddy riverbank. "Every day, morning and night, I give a speech here," says the Casa's director, Father Ademar Barilli, a Brazilian Jesuit who remains surprisingly buoyant despite the surrounding misery. "I talk about the dangers of the trip north and urge them to go back. It's a bad choice to go home, but a worse one to try to go on to the U.S."

Barilli warns migrants about the bosses in Mexico who may take their precious documents and force them into slavery on remote plantations. He tells them about the brothels in Tapachula, the Mexican town across the river, where girls are forced into prostitution. Most, remembering the misery they have left behind, disregard his warnings. As Adriana, a 14-year-old prostitute in a Tapachula bar, exclaimed when asked if she would consider going home to Honduras: "No, there you die of hunger!"

Despite Barilli and Casa del Migrante, Tecún Umán itself is hardly safe. The week before I arrived, a dead coyote had been dumped just outside the gates of the compound with a hundred bullets in his body. "People are killed here because of the traffic in people and babies. There are many mafias involved in the business of this town. Aquí uno no sale en la noche—Here you don't go out at night," Barilli said.

As I calculated the amount of daylight left, Barilli explained what local bar owners say to girls from the buses that roll in every day from the south. "They talk about a job working in a restaurant. But the job is in a bar. After the girl has worked for a while just serving drinks, the owner denounces her to the police and gets her arrested because she has no documents. She is jailed; he bails her out. Then he tells her she is in his debt and must work as a prostitute. The debt never ends, so the girl is a slave."

Barilli cited a recent case involving a bar named La Taverna on the highway out of town. The owner, a woman, had duped six girls in this fashion. "Some of them got pregnant, and she sold the babies," he said. Thanks partly to the efforts of a Casa del Migrante lay worker (who afterward went into hiding in response to a flood of very credible death threats), the bar owner was finally arrested and jailed.

Stepped-up security in the wake of 9/11 has made the major obstacle on the road from the south, the border between Mexico and the U.S., more difficult than ever to clear. With heightened control has come a commensurate increase in the price charged by smuggling gangs to take people across: up from an average of about $1,000 a person to $2,000. Survivors of the journey arrive deeply indebted and vulnerable to slavers.

In Immokalee, Florida, I sat in a room full of men and women with the same Maya features I had last seen on the faces of the people in Tecún Umán. Almost all of them were farm laborers, toiling on Florida's vast plantations to pick fruit and vegetables consumed all over the U.S. They were meeting at the headquarters of a farmworker organization, the Coalition of Immokalee Workers (CIW), to discuss ways of improving conditions in their ill-paid occupation. When the rapid-fire Spanish conversation died away, an elderly man picked up a guitar and began to sing about Juan Muñoz, who left Campeche, Mexico, "to seek his fortune in the U.S." but ended up in Lake Placid, Florida, working "as a slave" for a cruel boss who stole all his money.

Blues singers composed similar laments about the miseries of plantation life in the Old South, and we think of those songs as part of our heritage. But this song was not about the past. Juan Muñoz is a real person, a 32-year-old who left his small farm in Campeche because he couldn't earn enough money to feed his family. He made his way across the border to Marana, Arizona, where a coyote promised him a ride all the way to a job picking oranges in

Florida. The ride cost $1,000, which Muñoz was told he could pay off over time. On arrival he found he had in fact joined the modern slave economy.

Highway 27 runs through citrus country in the heart of Florida, which supplies 80 percent of U.S. orange juice. The pickers in the fields that line the highway are overwhelmingly immigrants, many undocumented and all poor. They earn an average $7,500 a year for work that is hard and unhealthy, toiling for bosses who contract with growers to supply crews to pick crops. The law generally leaves these people alone so long as they stick to low-paid but necessary work in the fields.

Sweatshop conditions in the fields are almost inevitable, since the corporations that buy the crops have the power to keep the prices they pay low, thus ensuring that wages paid by harvesting companies to pickers stay low too. These conditions lead to a high turnover in the workforce, since anyone with a prospect of alternative work swiftly moves on. Hence the appeal to crew bosses of debt-slave crews, whose stability and docility are assured. That is how Juan Muñoz found himself held captive along with at least 700 others in the well-guarded camps operated by the Ramos family in and around the little town of Lake Placid.

"They had almost all been picked up in Arizona by coyotes who offered to take them to Florida and then sold them to the crew bosses," says Romeo Ramirez, a 21-year-old Guatemalan who went undercover to investigate the Ramoses' operation on behalf of the CIW.

Captives in eight camps in and around Lake Placid were living "four to a room, which stank, sleeping on box springs." Not surprisingly, the workers were terrified of their bosses. "People knew they would be beaten for trying to get away," said Ramirez, citing the rumor about one would-be escapee who "had his knees busted with a hammer and then was thrown out of a car moving 60 miles an hour.

"The workers were paid by the growers every Friday," Ramirez continued, "but then they would all be herded to the Ramoses' stores in Lake Placid and forced to sign over their checks. By the time they had paid for rent and food, their debt was as high as ever." One such store, Natalie's Boutique, is a block from the police station.

In April 2001 a team from the CIW helped four of the captive laborers, including Muñoz, to make a break. Spurred to action by the unequivocal testimony of the escapees, the FBI and INS mounted a raid—although the prominent "INS Deportation Service" sign on the side of the bus accompanying the raiding party gave the crew bosses enough warning to send the workers out into the orange groves around Lake Placid to hide. Nevertheless, the brothers Ramiro and Juan Ramos, along with their cousin José Luis Ramos, were eventually charged with trafficking in slaves, extortion, and possession of firearms. In June 2002 the three Ramoses were convicted on all counts and received prison sentences totaling 34 years and 9 months.

This 21st-century slave operation may have been ignored by the Ramoses' corporate clients; and federal agencies may have been slow to react to prodding by the CIW. But the slave crews were hardly out of sight. The main camp in which the Ramoses confined their victims was just on the edge of town right beside a Ramada Inn. On the other side of the compound a gated community, Lakefront Estates, offered a restful environment for seniors.

"The slaves in Lake Placid were invisible, part of our economy that exists in a parallel universe," points out Laura Germino of the CIW. "People were playing golf at the retirement community, and right behind them was a slave camp. Two worlds, speaking different languages."

The Ramos case was in fact the fifth case of agricultural slavery exposed in Florida in the past six years. All came to light thanks to the CIW, which is currently promoting a boycott of fast-food giant Taco Bell on behalf of tomato pickers. The corporation boasts of its efforts to protect animal welfare in its suppliers' operations. Corporate officials also say they demand compliance with labor laws, but point out that since they cannot monitor suppliers' labor practices continually they rely on law enforcement to ensure compliance.

Slavery and slave trafficking in the U.S. today extend far beyond farm country into almost every area of the economy where cheap labor is at a premium. In 1995 more than 70 Thai women were rescued after laboring for years behind barbed wire in the Los Angeles suburb of El Monte, making clothes for major retailers while federal and state law enforcement repeatedly failed to obtain a proper warrant to search the premises. In June 2001 federal agents in Yakima, Washington, arrested the owners of an ice cream vending company and charged them with using Mexican slaves, working to pay off transportation debts, to sell ice cream on city streets. According to Kevin Bales, there are between 100,000 and 150,000 slaves in the U.S. today.

The Department of State puts the number of people trafficked into the U.S. every year at close to 20,000. Many end up as prostitutes or farm laborers. Some work in nursing homes. Others suffer their servitude alone, domestic slaves confined to private homes.

The passage by Congress in 2000 of the Victims of Trafficking and Violence Protection Act, which protects such slaves against deportation if they testify against their former owners, perhaps has helped dispel some fearfulness. The growth of organizations ready to give help, like the CIW or the Coalition to Abolish Slavery and Trafficking, a southern California group that has assisted more than 200 trafficked people, means that victims are not alone. Public scrutiny in general is rising.

Still, such captives the world over are mostly helpless. They are threatened; they live in fear of deportation; they are cut off from any source of advice or support because they cannot communicate with the outside world. And the harsh fact remains that this parallel universe, as Laura Germino called it, can be a very profitable place to do business. Before sentencing the Ramoses, U.S. District Court Judge K. Michael Moore ordered the confiscation of three million dollars the brothers had earned from their operation, as well as extensive real estate and other property.

Moore also pointed a finger at the agribusiness corporations that hired the Ramoses' picking crews. "It seems," he said, "that there are others at another level in this system of fruit picking—at a higher level—that to some extent are complicit in one way or another in how these activities occur."

A former slave named Julia Gabriel, now a landscape gardener in Florida and a member of CIW, remembers her arrival in the U.S. from Guatemala at the age of 19. She picked cucumbers under armed guard in South Carolina for 12 to 14 hours a day; she saw fellow captives pistol-whipped into unconsciousness. "Maybe this is normal in the U.S.," she thought. Then a friend told her, "no, this is not normal here," so Gabriel found the courage to escape.

"This is meant to be the country to which people come fleeing servitude, not to be cast into servitude when they are here," says Attorney General John Ashcroft. But some historians argue that the infamous trans-Atlantic slave trade that shipped millions of Africans to the New World was abolished only when it had outlived its economic usefulness. Now slave traders from Sherwood Castle to sunny Florida—and at hundreds of points in between—have rediscovered the profitability of buying and selling human beings. Which means that, in the 21st century, slavery is far from gone.

In a dim, airless room in northern India, a dozen children bend over gas burners making bracelets that sell for 40 cents a dozen. These children, between 9 and 14 years old, work ten hours a day, every day—traded by their parents to the workshop owner for cash. The average sum that enslaves an Indian child? $35.

Unlike drugs, a woman's body can be sold over and over. Owners of Israeli brothels [. . .] can buy young women from Moldova or Ukraine for around $4,000 each. With ten prostitutes to service customers, even a small operation can make a million dollars a year. Traffickers posing as employment agents find victims in poor Eastern European towns and lure them abroad with promises of good jobs. When the women arrive—in Israel, Germany, Switzerland, Japan, the U.S.—they're delivered to buyers who typically beat, rape, or terrorize them into compliance.

Debt traps entire families in bondage for generations. Mothers and daughters haul handmade bricks at a southeast India kiln while fathers and sons stoke the fires. Kiln owners acquire workers by loaning poor families money for expenses far beyond their means: medical care or a funeral. Despite years of work to pay these loans, exorbitant interest and dishonest accounting perpetuate the debts, and parents pass the burdens on to their children. Roughly two-thirds of the world's captive laborers—15 to 20 million people—are debt slaves in India, Pakistan, Bangladesh, and Nepal.

Each woman's home is a 4-by-6-foot *pinjara*—Hindi for cage. Brothels line Falkland Road in Mumbai, with the youngest, prettiest women displayed in street-level cages to attract customers day and night. Many women are delivered into these ramshackle hives by traffickers; many others are sold outright by parents or husbands. Some 50,000 women—nearly half shipped a thousand miles across India from Nepal—work as prostitutes in this city. Violence, disease, malnutrition, and lack of medical care reduce their life expectancy to less than 40 years.

One U.S. shelter has rescued 10,000 child prostitutes. Sociologist Lois Lee [. . .] has spent 24 years working with children from 11 to 17 years old who've been trafficked by pimps. One young resident [. . .] at her Children of the Night shelter in southern California was forced to work as a prostitute in Oregon, Washington, Idaho, and Nevada before escaping her captor. "The sexual exploitation of American children cuts across every economic, ethnic, and social line," Lee says. "This is not just a Third World problem."

"I have to believe that this can change." So says social worker Marisa Ugarte. She speaks quietly of three boys living in a Mexico shelter, one 12 years old, the other two no more than 15. All had been shuttled between Tijuana and San Diego, California, and prostituted to pedophiles. Ugarte directs the Bilateral Safety Corridor Coalition, a network of 62 U.S. and Mexican organizations fighting trafficking. "People are beginning to see," Ugarte says, "that slavery is still real."

PAUSE

Make a list of the examples from Cockburn's piece that you found most effective. What do they have in common?

Introduction

Cockburn's article is rhetorically powerful—most people reading it, especially those who believed slavery ended with the U.S. Civil War, find a moving, effective argument.

The strength of Cockburn's piece comes in large part from its selection of stories about specific people and places, which serve as examples to support the argument that slavery continues as a global phenomenon driven by consumerism.

Examples are an excellent strategy for making arguments because they leave us with these stories, narratives that are both memorable and representative of some larger point. We see this playing out powerfully in Cockburn's piece, which, by virtue of its examples, provides both a glimpse into a hidden world and a powerful argument about the relationship between consumption in wealthy nations and labor conditions in nations with greater income inequality.

Cockburn could have chosen any one of the number of women in a similar position as Victoria, the young woman from Moldova with whom he opens his piece. That's important: he chooses Victoria because she is so similar to the other women he is writing about—she is representative. At the same time, a good example has unique qualities, a way with words, for example, or a particularly compelling narrative. Not all women enslaved in the global sex trade were kidnapped by a friend and transported across eastern Europe, for example, and the injustice of Victoria's enslavement is representative of the injustice of the global sex trade.

The examples he chooses are compelling, and the implied inference is that they are representative: the wide-ranging piece takes us from eastern Europe to Greece and Italy, from the border of Guatemala and Mexico to Florida and California in the United States. By using such a broad range of examples, Cockburn suggests that this is a widespread phenomenon. There is a clear implication here that these are not isolated cases; rather, they represent a pattern of such incidents. The inference here, then, is that what is characteristic of the part—the individual person or place—is characteristic of the global slave trade as a whole (for a refresher on inferences, see Chapter 6).

Argument from Example

Argument from example is the first of a series of patterns of inference that we will examine carefully over the next five chapters. Our first, argument from example, or argument from part to whole, is one of the more common patterns of inference in everyday argumentation.

There are two basic types of arguments from example, anecdotal and statistical.

Anecdotal Examples

While Cockburn does draw on statistical examples, the majority of his examples are anecdotal. **Anecdotal examples** describe specific objects, places, people, or occurrences to make an argument about larger patterns. When Cockburn describes Victoria's situation, women enslaved in El Monte, California, or ice cream vendors in Yakima, Washington, he is providing anecdotal examples.

The warrant in an argument from example is that the examples provided are actually representative of the whole—they are not special cases. Cockburn goes to some length in this piece to make the case that the examples he uses are in fact representative cases: the testimony of victims pointing to others in similar circumstances, estimates of the sex trafficking industry in Greece in the billions of dollars, and evidence from experts on the vastness of the global slave trade all support Cockburn's warrant that the examples he provides are not special cases but are rather typical of the global slave economy as a whole.

Arguing from example involves generalization. That is, the alternative to argument from example is to describe every single case. Of course, that's not possible. We can't list every possible example, every possible part of the whole, because we don't have the time and we don't typically have knowledge of every single case. This means that when we make arguments from example we have a level of uncertainty. Uncertainty is one of the underlying assumptions of argumentation, as you know, so this is nothing new. However, it does open arguments from example to certain vulnerabilities.

In the case of Cockburn's piece, it may very well be the case that not every case of slavery is as bad as those Cockburn describes. How much of a difference this makes depends on the argument Cockburn is making. If Cockburn is making the argument simply that while most people tend to think of slavery as an economic system that existed in the past but has since been abolished, then he needs only a few cases to make his point. Once he has established that these are not isolated cases but reflect a system—however small—his case would be made.

> Arguing from example involves making generalizations, or abstractions, from single, concrete cases.

But Cockburn may be making an argument beyond this, not simply that slavery still exists as a system but that it may in fact, in terms of sheer numbers, eclipse the system of slavery that existed in the Americas up to the late nineteenth century. If that is indeed his argument, he needs to go beyond a minimum standard of proving that a pattern of cases exists to show that it is a widespread problem on a large enough scale. Examples alone may be insufficient to make this case—which is why Cockburn also brings in statistical evidence, such as the market value of the industry, or the price paid for an enslaved person today and in the transatlantic slave trade.

Arguing from example, then, involves making generalizations, or abstractions, from single, concrete cases. The inference is that what is characteristic of the individual case is characteristic of the larger category that case is made to represent. The warrant is that the cases are indeed representative.

Tests

Anecdotal examples should meet certain tests to be compelling. These tests are

Number and range: Are there a sufficient number of examples given to make it likely that these do indeed represent the whole? Is the range of examples broad enough, or does it appear that the examples were cherry-picked? How many places is sufficient for Cockburn to have observed to make his case? How widespread should their locations be?

Presence or absence of significant counterexamples: Counterexamples would not be particularly effective against Cockburn's article, as showing that slavery does not exist in a given city does not do much to undermine Cockburn's argument that slavery is a widespread current problem, so long as we accept Cockburn's examples. In other cases, however, significant counterexamples are highly effective.

Representativeness: To what extent do the examples represent all stakeholders? There are practical as well as ethical aspects to the test of representativeness. Who, for example, is it practical for Cockburn to interview for this piece? Some human smugglers may not be willing to be interviewed, and attempting to do so may put Cockburn in danger. Who is it ethical for Cockburn to interview? Is it ethical to interview very young victims of trafficking for this piece? Under what circumstances?

Statistical Examples

A **statistical example** uses data collection and analysis to reason from part to whole, inferring that members of a particular group likely share similarities. Statistical examples are common when you want to make generalizations about a **population** but cannot describe every single **case** in that population. Let's say, for example, you are working for a nonprofit organization aimed at increasing voter turnout among eligible voters from ages eighteen to twenty-four. You have been tasked with determining a communications strategy to connect with this population, so you decide to conduct a survey to find out which communications platforms are used most frequently by this group. You quickly learn that there are roughly thirty million people in this age range in the United States—it is not practical to ask each individual case what platforms they prefer! Rather than take on the impossible task of asking every case in the population, you decide to ask a **sample** (sometimes represented by the letter *n*) of individuals. This sample will serve as your example case when making arguments about which communications platforms Americans between eighteen and twenty-four prefer.

> **Population:** in statistics, the group of things, people, or events being studied.
>
> **Case:** the individual things, people, or events that make up the population.
>
> **Sample:** the cases selected, using some predetermined criteria, to represent the population.

Your warrant in arguments using statistical examples is that what is true of the sample is true of the population as a whole.

Tests

There are a number of tests to check if an argument from statistical example is reasonable. We will review some of the most common—and least technical—below.

Sample Size

First, the **sample size**, the number of cases selected from the population, must be sufficient to establish a pattern. A sufficient sample size depends on the size of the overall population you are trying to make generalizations about. If you want to get an idea of how many gummy bears will be red out of a thousand gummy bears, a sample size of a hundred should be enough; but if you want to know how many people are likely to vote for a particular candidate in an upcoming election, out of a population of fifty thousand, you would need to poll many more than a hundred people.

Just how large a sample size you need depends on a variety of factors. Generally speaking, the larger your sample size with respect to your population, the more confident you can be in the results. The level of confidence is described using two terms: *confidence level* and *confidence interval*. **Confidence level** is the degree of probability that the pattern established in the sample is descriptive of the population as a whole, and is presented as a percentage. So if you are counting gummy bears and you have a confidence level of 95 percent, it means that you are 95 percent certain that the proportion of red gummy bears in your sample will match the proportion of red gummy bears in the total population of a thousand gummy bears.

Confidence interval is also known as the margin of error. It is the degree of uncertainty in your confidence level. So if you are counting red gummy bears and you have a confidence level of 95 percent and a confidence interval of 4, then you are 95 percent certain that the proportion of red gummy bears in your sample will match that in the overall population, +/– 4 percent. You first add, and then subtract, the confidence interval from the confidence level to get the range of accuracy in the statistical example. In this case, the statistical example may be as high as 99 percent accurate or as low as 91 percent accurate.

When conducting your own statistical research, there are complicated formulas for determining confidence level, confidence interval, and appropriate sample size. It is best to work with a statistician, or at least to have taken several classes in statistics, when setting up a statistical study. When considering statistical evidence provided in arguments you come across, make sure to look into these factors so that you can know whether or not the statistical example can reasonably be generalized.

> When evaluating statistical evidence, be sure to consider factors such as confidence level, confidence interval, and sample size to determine how persuasive the evidence should be.

As the 2016 and 2020 presidential elections in the United States made quite clear, and to the frustration of many people whose job it is to predict elections, statistical examples are not actually predictive. They are simply a snapshot of any particular population—whether that be likely voters or gummy bears.

Representativeness

Second, the sample chosen from among the population should also be appropriately **representative**. This means that the population must be accurately determined, and the makeup of the sample should match the makeup of the population as a whole. Consider again the example of polling ahead of an election. Let's say we have an election for mayor of a town with a population of 100,000 people. Is the population, for the purposes of polling, 100,000?

No, because we're only interested in those members of the population who are likely to have a bearing on the election—in other words, those who may, and who are likely to, vote. Out of that 100,000, maybe only 75,000 will be eighteen or older on election day, the minimum age to vote in the election. So the population for our purposes drops to 75,000. But now, maybe many of the people who are eligible to vote in the election do not typically vote. Because they are unlikely to vote in the upcoming election, polling them on their opinions would not give us a good idea of the outcome of the election. So let's say only 40 percent of eligible voters typically vote in mayoral elections. That would bring our population down to 30,000, or 40 percent of 75,000 eligible voters. There may be other factors as well that affect who is a likely voter in the upcoming election and thus the population from which the sample should be taken.

The sample must, then, not only be appropriately sized but also appropriately chosen based on those factors that make them representative of the population we are interested in. In the case of the mayoral election, we must be sure that our sample consists of eligible voters who are likely to vote in the upcoming election. The sample size must be chosen at random to avoid selection bias, after the population has been appropriately narrowed. In the case of our election polling, we would want to randomly select only from among those people who are both eligible and likely to vote in the upcoming election. Beyond those necessary limiting factors, which lead to greater accuracy, however, we must be sure no factors affect our sampling that would lead to decreased accuracy. For example, if there is a neighborhood in town that is mostly one political party or another, sampling too much in that neighborhood would likely provide inaccurate results.

In other words, we need to also be aware of a phenomenon called sorting effect. You know the saying opposites attract? Not here. **Sorting effect** is the tendency that certain underlying conditions will end up grouping people according to shared traits. This is a pretty complicated way of saying that birds of a feather flock together. The fact that neighborhoods often have a political bent, as in the above example, may be the result of sorting effect. If a town was roughly 50 percent Whig and 50 percent Tory, you might expect these to be distributed randomly. In reality, however, neighborhoods with particular characteristics attract particular types of people.

> The sample in a statistical example must not only be appropriately sized but also appropriately chosen based on those factors that make them representative of the population in which we are interested.

Another example may be seen on a shopping trip to the mall. As you head down the corridor, you may notice that one store may be filled with mostly teenagers, while another store tends to have mostly young adults, and another middle-aged people. Why is this? Surely the stores don't have age restrictions. Rather, people are sorting themselves based on their perception of which stores are appropriate for their age group.

In our example in which we are polling likely voters, we would need to consider who is more likely to answer our poll and who is less likely. If we are calling only landlines, who is more likely to own a home phone? Who is more likely to answer? How might we get different results if we were to text message mobile phones instead? What about an email poll? Each of these methods will have a sorting effect, which we need to consider both when designing our poll and when analyzing our results.

Cockburn draws on statistical examples when he provides estimates of the size and value of the slave trade, or statistics about the increase in the homeless population in a given city. These statistical examples not only provide context for his anecdotal examples but also evidence that his argument is not limited simply to the relatively few examples he provides.

Over the last several decades, America has become increasingly geographically polarized, with people with conservative views moving to conservative zip codes and people with liberal views moving to more liberal zip codes. Not only does this make it less likely that the average person will know people with significantly different political opinions, it also might make polling more complicated.

Classification

Classification is a special type of argument from example that is the inverse of generalization. Typically, as I point out above, with examples we move from the specific to the more general—that's generalization. Cockburn sees several cases of modern-day slavery and makes the generalization that slavery is widespread and operates in certain ways based on these individual cases.

In classification, on the other hand, you take something abstract, and make it concrete; it is reasoning from the more general to the specific, or from whole to part. Take the claim "Brexit is an example of democracy at work." Well, democracy is an abstract concept, not easy to pin down. So we're more likely to ask "What is democracy?" rather than "What is Brexit an example of?" Someone might respond with the claim that Brexit is an example of democracy at work. This claim seeks to link the specific case of Brexit with the abstract concept of democracy.

Brexit does not enjoy nearly the same level of popularity as democracy does, so by linking Brexit with democracy, the claim implicitly asks the audience to accept Brexit according to the virtues of democracy. The inference is that what is true of the whole is probably true of the part, and the warrant, the same as with generalization, is that the part is indeed representative of the whole.

Tests

A few tests exist to determine whether or not an argument from classification should be accepted.

Does the particular member really belong to the class? The claim that Brexit is an example of democracy at work is a claim of definition; it asks its audience for a particular interpretation of Brexit. To address the common topics of a claim of definition, the argument would have to lay out the criteria for democracy and how Brexit fits those criteria. The test here, then, is whether or not the criteria are properly identified, and whether or not Brexit fits those criteria.

Is there reason to think that the particular member is an exceptional case, so that the general principle might not apply? Perhaps, generally speaking, we agree that populist movements like Brexit are examples of democracy at work. However, it may be that in the case of Brexit particularly, some conditions exist that make it an exception.

Fallacy of division: Assuming that what is true of the whole is automatically true of its parts. Consider, for example, if you are in charge of hiring someone, and you see they are coming from a highly reputable organization. Well, you might think, if they are coming from this organization, then they must be good. But, of course, even exceptional organizations may have plenty of unsatisfactory employees.

Conclusion

Cockburn's argument about modern-day slavery is both powerful and memorable thanks to his use of compelling examples. Even months from now, you may find yourself remembering the stories of Victoria, or Juan Muñoz, or the enslaved in India or here in the United States. The stories stay with you.

Because of this, argument from example is among the most common and most effective patterns of inference, involving both generalization, in which you make a case going from part to whole, and classification, in which you make a case going from whole to part. In either case the inference is the same: that the part is representative of the whole. In both cases, as well, the warrant makes the same point: that the part is indeed representative of the whole.

Argument from example is an extremely versatile inference pattern, spanning anecdotal examples that can provide rich details and compelling narratives, like those we see in Cockburn's piece above, as well as statistical examples that can provide very compelling data. Both statistical examples and anecdotal examples carry their own advantages and disadvantages and should be approached according to their distinct strengths. The strength of anecdotal examples lies in their capacity for rich narrative and emotional power, while the strength of statistical examples lies in their observation of scientific methodology.

PROBE

Cockburn's essay underscores the interconnectedness of our globalized world and highlights the exploitative practices that span continents. Consider the ethical implications of your own choices and actions as a consumer, traveler, or advocate. How might you leverage your agency and knowledge to promote more sustainable and equitable practices within your spheres of influence?

Chapter 10
Arguing from Comparison

Key Terms

analogy
literal analogy
evidence case
conclusion case
connective
judicial analogy

a fortiori
legal precedent
justice
figurative analogy
evidence relationship
conclusion relationship

Key Points

- Analogy is among the strongest inference patterns in informal argumentation.
- Literal analogies compare things, events, or situations that are in the same category.
- Two special types of literal analogy are the judicial analogy and the analogy a fortiori (the greater and the lesser).
- Figurative analogies compare the relationship between two things, events, or situations.
- Several tests of both literal and figurative analogies exist.

PRIME

What comes to mind when you hear the word *analogy*? Can you think of any analogies you've come across recently?

Lecture Delivered at Franklin Hall

Maria W. Miller Stewart (1832)

[1] Why sit ye here and die? If we say we will go to a foreign land, the famine and the pestilence are there, and there we shall die. If we sit here, we shall die. Come let us plead our cause before the whites: if they save us alive, we shall live—and if they kill us, we shall but die.

[2] Methinks I heard a spiritual interrogation—"Who shall go forward, and take off the reproach that is cast upon the people of color? Shall it be a woman?" And my heart made this reply—"If it is thy will, be it even so, Lord Jesus!"

[3] I have heard much respecting the horrors of slavery; but may Heaven forbid that the generality of my color throughout these United States should experience any more of its horrors than to be a servant of servants, or hewers of wood and drawers of water! Tell us no more of southern slavery; for with few exceptions, although I may be very erroneous in my opinion, yet I consider our condition but little better than that. Yet, after all, methinks there are no chains so galling as the chains of ignorance—no fetters so binding as those that bind the soul, and exclude it from the vast field of useful and scientific knowledge. O, had I received the advantages of early education, my ideas would, ere now, have expanded far and wide; but, alas! I possess nothing but moral capability—no teachings but the teachings of the Holy Spirit.

[4] I have asked several individuals of my sex, who transact business for themselves, if providing our girls were to give them the most satisfactory references, they would not be willing to grant them an equal opportunity with others? Their reply has been—for their own part, they had no objection; but as it was not the custom, were they to take them into their employ, they would be in danger of losing the public patronage.

[5] And such is the powerful force of prejudice. Let our girls possess what amiable qualities of soul they may; let their characters be fair and spotless as innocence itself; let their natural taste and ingenuity be what they may; it is impossible for scarce an individual of them to rise above the condition of servants. Ah! why is this cruel and unfeeling distinction? Is it merely because God has made our complexion to vary? If it be, O shame to soft, relenting humanity! "Tell it not in Gath! publish it not in the streets of Askelon!" Yet, after all, methinks were the American free people of color to turn their attention more assiduously to moral worth and intellectual improvement, this would be the result: prejudice would gradually diminish, and the whites would be compelled to say, unloose those fetters!

Though black their skins as shades of night,
Their hearts are pure, their souls are white.

[6] Few white persons of either sex, who are calculated for any thing else, are willing to spend their lives and bury their talents in performing mean, servile labor. And such is the horrible idea that I entertain respecting a life of servitude, that if I conceived of there being no possibility of my rising above the condition of a servant, I would gladly hail death as a welcome messenger. O, horrible idea, indeed! to possess noble souls aspiring after high and honorable acquirements, yet confined by the chains of ignorance and poverty to lives of continual drudgery and toil. Neither do I know of any who have enriched themselves by spending their lives as house-domestics, washing windows, shaking carpets, brushing boots, or tending upon gentlemen's tables. I can but die for expressing my sentiments; and I am as willing to die by the sword as the pestilence; for I am a true born American; your blood flows in my veins, and your spirit fires my breast.

[7] I observed a piece in the *Liberator* a few months since, stating that the colonizationists had published a work respecting us, asserting that we were lazy and idle. I confute them on that point. Take us generally as a people, we are neither lazy nor idle; and considering how little we have to excite or stimulate us, I am almost astonished that there are so many industrious and ambitious ones to be found; although I acknowledge, with extreme sorrow, that there are some who never were and never will be serviceable to society. And have you not a similar class among yourselves?

[8] Again. It was asserted that we were "a ragged set, crying for liberty." I reply to it, the whites have so long and so loudly proclaimed the theme of equal rights and privileges, that our souls have caught the flame also, ragged as we are. As far as our merit deserves, we feel a common desire to rise above the condition of servants and drudges. I have learnt, by bitter experience, that continual hard labor deadens the energies of the soul, and benumbs the faculties of the mind; the ideas become confined, the mind barren, and, like the scorching sands of Arabia, produces nothing; or, like the uncultivated soil, brings forth thorns and thistles.

[9] Again, continual hard labor irritates our tempers and sours our dispositions; the whole system becomes worn out with toil and fatigue; nature herself becomes almost exhausted, and we care but little whether we live or die. It is true, that the free people of color throughout these United States are neither bought nor sold, nor under the lash of the cruel driver; many obtain a comfortable support; but few, if any, have an opportunity of becoming rich and independent; and the employments we most pursue are as unprofitable to us as the spider's web or the floating bubbles that vanish into air. As servants, we are respected; but let us presume to aspire any higher, our employer

regards us no longer. And were it not that the King eternal has declared that Ethiopia shall stretch forth her hands unto God, I should indeed despair.

[10] I do not consider it derogatory, my friends, for persons to live out to service. There are many whose inclination leads them to aspire no higher; and I would highly commend the performance of almost any thing for an honest livelihood; but where constitutional strength is wanting, labor of this kind, in its mildest form, is painful. And doubtless many are the prayers that have ascended to Heaven from Afric's daughters for strength to perform their work. Oh, many are the tears that have been shed for the want of that strength! Most of our color have dragged out a miserable existence of servitude from the cradle to the grave. And what literary acquirements can be made, or useful knowledge derived, from either maps, books or charts, by those who continually drudge from Monday morning until Sunday noon? O, ye fairer sisters, whose hands are never soiled, whose nerves and muscles are never strained, go learn by experience! Had we had the opportunity that you have had, to improve our moral and mental faculties, what would have hindered our intellects from being as bright, and our manners from being as dignified as yours? Had it been our lot to have been nursed in the lap of affluence and ease, and to have basked beneath the smiles and sunshine of fortune, should we not have naturally supposed that we were never made to toil? And why are not our forms as delicate, and our constitutions as slender, as yours? Is not the workmanship as curious and complete? Have pity upon us, have pity upon us, O ye who have hearts to feel for other's woes; for the hand of God has touched us. Owing to the disadvantages under which we labor, there are many flowers among us that are

"—born to bloom unseen,
And waste their fragrance on the desert air."

[11] My beloved brethren, as Christ has died in vain for those who will not accept of offered mercy, so will it be vain for the advocates of freedom to spend their breath in our behalf, unless with united hearts and souls you make some mighty efforts to raise your sons and daughters from the horrible state of servitude and degradation in which they are placed. It is upon you that woman depends; she can do but little besides using her influence; and it is for her sake and yours that I have come forward and made myself a hissing and a reproach among the people; for I am also one of the wretched and miserable daughters of the descendants of fallen Africa. Do you ask, why are you wretched and miserable? I reply, look at many of the most worthy and interesting of us doomed to spend our lives in gentlemen's kitchens. Look at our young men, smart, active and energetic, with souls filled with ambitious fire; if they look forward, alas! what are their prospects? They can be nothing but the humblest laborers, on account of their dark complexions; hence many

of them lose their ambition, and become worthless. Look at our middle-aged men, clad in their rusty plaids and coats; in winter, every cent they earn goes to buy their wood and pay their rents; their poor wives also toil beyond their strength, to help support their families. Look at our aged sires, whose heads are whitened with the frosts of seventy winters, with their old wood-saws on their backs. Alas, what keeps us so? Prejudice, ignorance and poverty. But ah! methinks our oppression is soon to come to an end; yea, before the Majesty of heaven, our groans and cries have reached the ears of the Lord of Sabaoth. As the prayers and tears of Christians will avail the finally impenitent nothing; neither will the prayers and tears of the friends of humanity avail us any thing, unless we possess a spirit of virtuous emulation within our breasts. Did the pilgrims, when they first landed on these shores, quietly compose themselves, and say, "the Britons have all the money and all the power, and we must continue their servants forever"? Did they sluggishly sigh and say, "our lot is hard, the Indians own the soil, and we cannot cultivate it"? No; they first made powerful efforts to raise themselves, and then God raised up those illustrious patriots, WASHINGTON and LAFAYETTE, to assist and defend them. And, my brethren, have you made a powerful effort? Have you prayed the Legislature for mercy's sake to grant you all the rights and privileges of free citizens, that your daughters may rise to that degree of respectability which true merit deserves, and your sons above the servile situations which most of them fill?

PAUSE

Identify an analogy used by Maria Stewart in her speech. How does she use this analogy to convey her message and make her argument more persuasive?

Introduction

You may have learned about analogies in your English courses, or while studying for a standardized test like the SATs. As with many of the terms I've introduced so far, analogy has a specialized meaning in argumentation that differs from both of those contexts. **Analogy** in argumentation is simply argument from comparison. It is a common and useful pattern of inference, especially when moving from the more familiar to the less familiar. While analogy is identified as the weakest pattern of formal reasoning, it is one of the strongest inference patterns you can make in informal reasoning.

The reason analogy is weak in formal reasoning is because—remember back to Chapter 4—formal reasoning operates on certainty. If there is any wiggle room, any space for probability rather than certainty, then formal reasoning falls apart. So analogy in formal reasoning must compare two things that are identical. For absolute certainty it must always be oranges and oranges.

But in the real world things are never identical. Rather, they exhibit varying degrees of similarity. Even two oranges, after all, will show some limited differences in size, shape, color, blemish, taste, and so on. In informal reasoning we're working not with certainty but rather with probability, and therefore we gain new information (this orange is riper, and likely to be tastier, than that orange) at the expense of absolute certainty.

And given that argument from analogy provides new information based on something we already know, it is likely to be highly persuasive. This is why the argument from analogy is one of the most commonly used inference patterns in contemporary argumentation.

> **Analogy is among the strongest inference patterns in informal argumentation.**

We make analogies to compare different things all the time, from the sarcastic ("Lunch was *literally* like eating cardboard today") to the statistical ("Michael Jordan won more championships and averaged more points per game than LeBron James"). When we make these comparisons to justify a particular relationship between a claim and evidence, we are making an argument from analogy.

The warrant in an argument from analogy is that things that are basically alike will probably be alike in the respect under discussion. In essence, we are arguing that because our two cases are similar in some respects, they will be similar in some other related respect as well.

Let's take a closer look at Stewart's speech, above, for an example.

I'm not sure a more powerful first line has ever been uttered: "Why sit ye here and die?" Who were "ye" and why are they dying? Stewart was a Black American woman born in Connecticut in the early nineteenth century. After white lawyers prevented her from inheriting her husband's estate, Stewart turned to writing and speechmaking to earn money. The speech reprinted above was her second public speech.

In it she calls on Black people in the North, and Black women especially, to consider the state of their freedom. Stewart was an abolitionist, to be sure, but she argued here that the freedom granted northern Blacks was only a modest improvement over the conditions of their counterparts enslaved in the South. In that respect her arguments were a precursor to some of those that would gain influence during the American civil rights movement of the mid-twentieth century.

By the end of the speech we see how radical it is, with Stewart, drawing on analogy, calling for northern Blacks to rise up in the same way that the American heroes of the Revolutionary War did.

It may make sense to begin at the end, then, with this powerful analogy. She rests her argument here on the premise that the conditions European settlers faced in North America are similar to the conditions free Blacks face in the informal apartheid of the antebellum North. Both, Stewart suggests, were impoverished and lacked power compared with the dominant culture under which they found themselves (Great Britain for the settlers, the white establishment for free Blacks). Both, she claims, faced barriers to ownership of capital (namely, land for the settlers; land in addition to other forms of capital for free Blacks). Based on these similarities, Stewart claims that since the settlers were able to rise in power, so too should free Blacks by following their example.

The claim is that, given these essential similarities, the difference with respect to the particular situation can be overcome. The warrant is that, since early settlers and free Blacks are basically alike, they will probably be alike when it comes to their ability to gain access to financial and social improvement.

She argues, in essence, that free northern Blacks should claim what they need to thrive from their white counterparts in the same way European colonists claimed what they needed to thrive from Great Britain—by demand, negotiation, and, implicitly, by force.

Literal Analogy

This is a powerful argument, radical even, and it is an example of a **literal analogy**. The literal analogy involves comparison of two things, events, places, situations, and so on that are essentially similar. They are in the same sphere of reality. We might think of them as being in the same category: two cities, two trees, two religions, or two literary styles, for example.

A political campaign might compare the demographics, economics, and social infrastructure of Iowa—where their candidate won the caucus—with New Hampshire, to predict how their candidate might do in that state. They might find that, given essential similarities between the two states, their candidate is expected to do as well in New Hampshire as she did in Iowa. Or they might find the opposite, that given essential differences between the two states, their candidate is not likely to win the New Hampshire primary.

These are arguments from analogy. If we take the first claim, for example, that because the candidate did well in Iowa, she is likely to do well in New

Hampshire, our warrant is that because Iowa and New Hampshire are alike in certain aspects that are relevant to this particular candidate—percentage of households in the state that consist of married couples, say—the candidate is likely to perform similarly in both states.

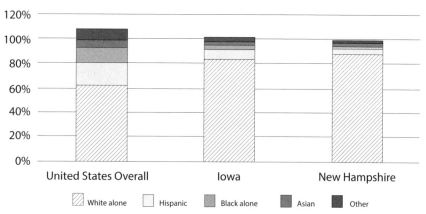

Iowa and New Hampshire Don't Reflect National Demographics

Source: Census.gov

Or we could make another argument from analogy, but one that rests on essential differences. For example, only 2 percent of the New Hampshire population is Black. This is well below the national average of 12 percent. We might expect a candidate who polls well with Black voters but not white to struggle in New Hampshire but fare better nationally. The inference is that these two populations are dissimilar. The warrant is that, given this dissimilarity, they will likewise be dissimilar in the respect central to the argument.

The two things being compared in a literal analogy have technical names. The **evidence case** is the part of the analogy that is expected to already be familiar to the audience, the part that establishes the basis of the analogy. Let's say you owned a successful business in Boston, Massachusetts, and you wanted to open up another branch in a different city. You'd want the business to do as well in the new city as it is doing in Boston, obviously, so you decide to look for other cities in the United States that are most similar to Boston. Boston, since it is a city you already know well, serves as the evidence case in an argument from analogy you're making (to yourself, to investors, etc.) about opening a second branch of your business. You're beginning with the warrant that another city similar to the one in which your business is thriving will support another thriving branch of your business.

Doing some research, you decide on Philadelphia. Like Boston, you reason, Philadelphia is a port city, highly educated, and known for its colonial history. Both cities have similar climates, and both have significant higher education industries. Philadelphia serves as what is called the **conclusion case**: the part of a literal analogy that serves as the subject of the claim. The similarities between Boston and Philadelphia, what you know about Boston that is also the case in Philadelphia, are known as the **connective**. You're using what you already know about Boston to make a claim about Philadelphia, based on similarities between the two cities.

In a literal analogy it is not important for the similarities between the evidence case and the conclusion case to be well known ahead of time. Often you'll have to do research about the evidence case to know what you're looking for in a conclusion case.

Literal analogies are used often when making historical arguments. Michelle Alexander's acclaimed book *The New Jim Crow* famously compares the modern legal system that leads to mass incarceration of the U.S. Black population with the Jim Crow laws of the first half of the twentieth century. Likewise, calls for southern secession leading up to the Civil War often drew on comparisons to colonial rebellion against Great Britain.

And, of course, Stewart makes a historical argument using a literal analogy to compare northern Blacks with European colonists.

Judicial Analogy

There are two specialized types of literal analogy: the **judicial analogy** and the analogy **a fortiori**.

The judicial analogy, as the name implies, is most often, though not exclusively, invoked in law courts. Often the judicial analogy is raised in court with reference to **legal precedent**, or a court's decision in a previous case that establishes a principle having bearing on the current case. For example, in the well-known case *Roe v. Wade*, which until it was overturned protected a woman's right to undergo medical procedures to terminate a pregnancy, the plaintiffs (represented by the pseudonym Roe) argued that another similar case on the constitutionality of laws barring contraception (*Griswold v. Connecticut*) established an implied right to privacy that bears on the current case. *Griswold v. Connecticut* was argued to have established legal precedent for *Roe v. Wade*.

The judicial analogy is not limited to law courts by any means. In fact, it is widely used to establish behavioral norms and forms the basis of many of our everyday arguments about justice. The rhetorician Chaïm Perelman defined **justice** as the belief that essentially similar cases should be treated in similar ways. This is essentially a judicial analogy. We see this definition of justice operating in

Although common in law courts, judicial analogies are often used to support values and norms outside of the courtroom too.

the common aphorism "What's good for the goose is good for the gander." It is this notion of justice that is breached when, for example, we see a wealthy person avoid prosecution for a crime that sends a poor person to prison, or evidenced by the unequal sentencing guidelines for drugs more commonly used by people of color compared to drugs more commonly used by white people.

Analogy a Fortiori

The analogy a fortiori is another specialized type of literal analogy, going back to some of the earliest treatises on rhetoric and argumentation. You may remember Gorgias stating, in his *Encomium of Helen*, that "it is the nature of things, not for the strong to be hindered by the weak, but for the weaker to be ruled and drawn by the stronger, and for the stronger to lead and the weaker to follow." This comparison between weaker and stronger, greater and lesser, is the basis of a fortiori.

A fortiori holds that what is true of or for the lesser is especially true of or for the greater, or vice versa: if we cannot expect something of the greater, even less so may we expect it of the lesser. Gorgias, as we read in Chapter 2, implies that if we do not hold the gods to blame for Helen's actions, then we have far less grounds to hold Helen to blame. We cannot, in this case, blame the lesser and not the greater.

For a more contemporary example, say a new employee asks his boss for a larger account. "How can I give you a larger account," his boss says, "when you have done so poorly with a small account?" Implicitly, the boss is arguing that if the employee did not perform well with a small account, it is even less likely that he will perform well with a larger account.

The converse of this is also an analogy a fortiori. For example, if a cell phone carrier is pressuring you to buy a warranty for your phone, you might respond, "I was offered an extended warranty on my car and didn't buy one, so I'm certainly not going to buy the warranty on my phone." The implied argument is that what is not true for the more expensive car is even less likely to be true for the less expensive cell phone.

Testing Literal Analogies

You can ask yourself a series of questions to determine whether or not a literal analogy holds up. These tests are useful both for assessing literal analogies and for developing counterarguments.

First, are the cases being compared dissimilar in some important respect? Let's say your successful business in Boston sells Harvard University–branded clothing. In that case, the business may not do so well in Philadelphia. Despite the many similarities, the two cities are dissimilar when it comes to the extent to which they value Harvard University, located near Boston. Judicial analogies likewise may be tested with this question. If a case is significantly dissimilar, it cannot serve as precedent for another case.

Second, you can ask yourself whether or not the two cases are being presented accurately. Information distorted or left out can greatly affect the apparent similarity between an evidence case and its conclusion case.

Third, consider whether or not a better analogy is available. Perhaps you may think that Stewart's comparison of pilgrims and northern Blacks is not appropriate because it makes you uncomfortable. But does a better analogy exist? Is there a more effective or powerful analogy out there that can make her case? If not, then the analogy used is appropriate.

TESTS OF LITERAL ANALOGIES

1. Are the cases being compared dissimilar in some important respect?
2. Are the two cases are being presented accurately?
3. Is a more appropriate analogy available?

Figurative Analogy

There is a second type of analogy, fundamentally distinct from the literal analogy. Whereas the literal analogy compares two concrete things that are widely seen as in the same category, the **figurative analogy** compares the relationship between things, rather than the things themselves. Some experts in argumentation call this a *comparison of ratios*, others a *resemblance of structures*. There are highly technical discussions aimed at defining the specific thing being compared in a figurative analogy.

For our purposes, however, it is enough to look at common everyday usage. Commonly, this is called a metaphor. If I say to my child, "You are my sunshine," I'm comparing my relationship to my child with the common relationship of people to sunshine. A person and sunshine do not belong in the same category. Rather, it is the relationship between people and sunshine and me and my child that I am comparing in that metaphor.

A figurative analogy describes the relationship between things, rather than the things themselves.

Likewise, a figurative analogy compares the relationship between things that belong in different categories. The structure of a figurative analogy likens the evidence relationship to the conclusion relationship, often using *like* or *as*.

Some proponents of public education reform, for example, argue that teachers in low-performing districts are unfairly protected by tenure, which makes it difficult to fire teachers who don't meet performance standards. These reformers argue that the achievement gap can be closed by removing tenure protections for teachers. Diane Ravitch argues in her book *Reign of Error* that this is completely wrongheaded. Tenure protections play no visible role in the achievement gap: teachers in both high- and low-achieving districts are protected by tenure. Rather, she writes, "The reformers want to get rid of a few rats by burning down the whole barn."

This is an example of a figurative analogy. Teachers (good or bad) are not in the same category as rats, and tenure protections are not in the same category as barns. In fact, in a figurative analogy only one element is similar among the two pairs. Here it is the observation that it is unwise to remove protections from all just to expose a few who are unwanted. This principle applies to both situations: the rats in the barn and teachers with tenure. Thus, Ravitch argues, the relationship between the rats and the barn is similar to the relationship between teachers and tenure protections, particularly with respect to the proposed reforms.

Similar to literal analogies, the pairs in figurative analogies have technical terms. The pair [barn: rats] that most people in the audience will already be familiar with or they can readily grasp, and which serves as the premise for the argument, is called the **evidence relationship**.

The pair [tenure: teachers] that is less familiar to the audience, or else more difficult for them to grasp, and which is the subject of the argument being made is called the **conclusion relationship**.

For a figurative analogy to work, it is important for the evidence relationship to be familiar enough to the audience so as to appear obvious to them. Because a figurative analogy hinges on only one similarity, spending a lot of time explaining the evidence relationship may undermine your ability to show its relevance to your conclusion relationship and thereby make your case. Saying, "Of course you should get french fries with your cheeseburger; they go together like Hákarl and brennivin" is probably not going to be an effective analogy.

Testing Figurative Analogies

As with literal analogies, there are a number of ways to test figurative analogies for logical consistency.

First, we can ask whether the analogy is meant to illustrate a complex structure or is meant as an argument in and of itself. For example, is the comparison of barns and tenure being used simply to illustrate what tenure is like, or is it used to make an argument against the removal of tenure? In the case of Ravitch's metaphor above, the analogy is used to make an argument against removing tenure in the context of educational reform, and so it would pass our first test in this particular case.

We can imagine other cases, however, in which the analogy is advanced only to illustrate what something is like. For example, in making the argument that we ought to let experts set economic policy because the economy is so complex as to be a Gordian knot, I'm using the figurative analogy of the Gordian knot only to illustrate the complexity of the economy. The argument itself would have to be advanced another way, whether with a different figurative analogy or, more likely, with a different analogy or inference pattern altogether.

The second test of figurative analogies is to ask if there are other arguments to support the argument made by the figurative analogy, or if the figurative analogy is relied on alone to make the argument. It is rare for an audience to accept a figurative analogy as the sole justification for an argument. More commonly, the figurative analogy is used to introduce the argument, and other arguments are called upon to bolster it.

The final test of figurative analogies is to ask if the two pairs really are similar as we're being asked to accept. In the example above, what we're being asked to accept, again, is not that there are many similarities between tenure and barns or bad teachers and rats, but rather that in both cases it is not a good idea to remove protections from all to expose a small number. But maybe that rule doesn't apply in one or the other cases. Someone could respond to such an argument by claiming that in fact removing protections for all teachers is a good idea because it will allow for better systems to be established.

TESTS OF FIGURATIVE ANALOGIES

1. Is the analogy being used to make an argument, or to illustrate a complex concept?
2. Is the analogy doing all the work of arguing on its own, or does it have help from other arguments?
3. Does the relationship being made hold up to scrutiny?

Conclusion

Analogies are common inference patterns, probably the most common after examples. We tend to use analogies especially when we want our audience to draw on what they already know to make an inferential leap to what we want them to accept. The two major types of analogies are literal, which compare things that are in the same conceptual category, and figurative, which compare the relationship between two things that are not in the same conceptual category. When making arguments using this inference pattern, you'll want to choose evidence cases that are likely to be highly familiar to your audience, and part of your argument will have to be about showing relevant similarities. The two cases cannot just be similar; they have to be similar where it matters to the argument. If I say, "Well, if you love dogs, you should get a chair for your next pet. After all, they both have four legs," I'm not making a very good analogy. The two cases, while similar in some respects, are not similar in the ways that matter (they are not, in fact, in the same category).

Figurative analogies are trickier than literal analogies most of the time, though a really good figurative analogy has power beyond the similarities themselves. Once you get an audience to accept a figurative analogy, all the connotations of the evidence relationship can potentially transfer to the conclusion relationship. Alexander's *The New Jim Crow*, for example, doesn't make a neutral comparison between slavery and the modern-day prison system. On the contrary, because the evidence relationship of slavery carries with it so many negative connotations, some of those negative connotations may carry over to the conclusion relationship, even when they are not directly linked.

Because analogies are such powerful strategies for making arguments, it is important to know when they are being made incorrectly or in a misleading way. If the relationship between the two cases is misleading or spurious, then the analogy should be rejected.

PROBE

Think of a contemporary social or political issue that resonates with the themes Stewart discusses. Create an analogy that connects this present-day issue to a historical event or circumstance. Explain how this analogy helps shed light on the current situation and its implications for societal progress.

Chapter 11
Arguing from Cause to Effect

Key Terms

necessary condition

sufficient condition

contributing factor

pragmatic argument

data

hypothesis

common thread

Key Points

- Arguments about cause and effect attempt to explain how two things are interrelated in such a way that they predict that the existence of one leads to the existence of another.
- The warrant in an argument from cause to effect is that the thing in question is caused by something else.
- Arguments about causes can move from cause to effect, or from effect to cause.
- The inference in an argument from cause to effect is that the existence or performance of one thing or phenomenon will lead to some other.
- Specialized types of arguments from cause to effect exist in different contexts.

PRIME

Turker seems to present several reasons for his patient being in the difficult situation she's in when he meets her. Identify each of these reasons as you read.

Hippocratic Hypocrisy

Ron Turker, M.D. (2017)

Recently, Congressman Raul Labrador (R- Idaho) proclaimed that "nobody dies because they don't have access to health care."[1] My experience has been different.

When I heard his words I thought of a sweet young woman whose body and community both turned against her. Somehow, I was supposed to be her last hope.

Fifteen years before I met her, I stood at my graduation wondering what lay ahead. On a hot June day in 1987, together with a hundred of my medical school classmates, draped in caps, gowns and sweat, we took an oath. Looking back it's a bit ironic that the ceremony to recognize my professional coming of age was marked by dressing up in centuries-old Catholic church regalia and reciting ancient Greek words. The Hippocratic words, an oath to Apollo, Asclepius and company were lost even as they passed my lips, but the gist seemed clear. We trained to help, teach, and heal, to treat our patients with respect and dignity no matter their circumstances.

While medical school and my surgical residency taught me about complex body systems and how they interact, it left the dizzying complexity of the U.S. health system to the school of hard knocks. "You'll figure it out," said one of my professors. "Sink or swim."

Medical students and residents train in the insulated bubbles of universities or "indigent" hospitals. In those years my imagination conjured up an umbrella of U.S. healthcare that was blind to the patient's ability to pay. Reality tells us that in every life there will come a passing rain shower of illness or injury and sometimes a devastating storm. In the quarter of a century since I left my training behind, I have found that U.S. health coverage isn't really an umbrella but more of a hodgepodge quilt. Much of it is compassionate, honest care, but there are the ugly swatches of greedy cash-only "boutiques" and huge threadbare holes and gaps defined by a "good luck out there" philosophy. We tell ourselves that we have the best healthcare system in the world but there is nothing systematic about it.

---

1. Saphora Smith, "Idaho Republican Labrador Booed over 'Nobody Dies' Comment on Health Care," NBC News, May 7, 2017, https://www.nbcnews.com/news/us-news/idaho-republican-labrador-booed-over-nobody-dies-comment-health-care-n755976.

The wildly diverse and competing incentives of hospital dollars, doctor dollars and all the ancillary industries that come to feed at the healthcare trough have whipsawed me through my career. I trained to be a doctor but somehow found myself in meetings with a marketing agency to discuss my "service line product," "market share analysis" and "robust practice profiles." All euphemisms for how to avoid the uninsured patient.

For many years I worked at a publicly funded hospital, the classic landing zone for the uninsured. It wasn't a salaried position. I made my income the same way private practice doctors do, in a fee-for-service model, or as it's more commonly known in the hospital corridors, "eat what you kill." A hell of a metaphor for those of us who took the oath. My paycheck and our frustrated office manager reflected my inability to say no to those without insurance.

I was frustrated and disappointed too, mostly by a medical landscape that set up a push and pull between me and my colleagues, where "high productivity" doctors took home more income by doing more *to* people rather than *for* people. But my worries were insignificant compared to those of the young woman whom I'd yet to meet. I'll call her Emma. She lived in a small town in Washington, just north of the Columbia Gorge.

Emma had a common complaint, back pain that was slowly getting worse. In her late twenties, married with three children, her situation was both similar to and very different than mine. I was also married with kids of my own, and even though I was the lowest-paid doctor in my group because of my "choice" to take all patients, I was a surgeon. That meant that I could live comfortably and support my family.

Her concerns were more basic. Emma and her husband both worked at low-paying jobs to support their kids. Her concern was one that I never had to think about: whether to visit a doctor to address the increasing pain in her back or hold on a bit longer until she or her husband found a job with health coverage. She had to weigh buying shoes for her kids and putting food on the table against a possible expensive battery of tests and scans. With no insurance they could quickly have been looking at thousands of dollars of debt, a very common path to bankruptcy in the U.S. Her strategy was as good as any. She decided to wait.

The pain grew by the week but she managed to deal with it. She pushed aside any suspicions that this might be something other than a misplaced disc or the "toddleritis" of a young mom. She didn't entertain the possibility of something worse. She literally couldn't afford to.

As I lived my life a world away from hers, a nest of normal body cells, preprogrammed to live, grow and die became inexplicably immortal and the world silently welcomed another statistic. The cancer quietly multiplied cell by cell and began to grow. Slowly at first but then at a logarithmic pace, it invaded the back of her abdomen. The Affordable Care Act was still a few years into the future and would have no impact on either the woman or her family.

Emma was delighted when her husband eventually found a job with benefits and it would only be three short months before they were eligible for health insurance. The news alone temporarily blunted the pain. But the cancer followed no calendar as it slowly choked off the two major blood vessels to her lower body. Her spinal cord was insidiously crushed. By the time the pain had become unbearable she was just two weeks shy of the date when her health coverage would begin.

Since World War II, when wage freezes made the addition of health insurance an enticing perk to attract good workers, we have permanently locked employment status to healthcare access and we have never looked back. Why we stuck with such an arbitrary system is anybody's guess. It would make as much sense to say that those who drive a Ford get a basic form of healthcare and those who drive a BMW get premium care. Good luck to all those who use mass transit. Inertia and dollars most likely kept the status quo. The result for many Americans is, no job, no doctor, simple as that.

The day that this young mom stopped walking was the day that she was rushed to a local Emergency Department. It's the classic portal of entry into a medical system that doesn't willingly throw open its doors to the uninsured. The common sentiment is that people without insurance can get help in the E.D. which has a mandate to stabilize those who are acutely sick or injured, but offers no guarantee beyond that. She was just a little lady with a very big problem, one way beyond the capacity of emergency care.

I'll be honest. When I answered the evening phone call from a doctor in another town I was annoyed. I thought it was going to be the typical Friday night dump, a simple problem at an inconvenient hour in a patient whose wallet biopsy came back negative. But when he told me the story of the young woman with back pain and how she waited for nine months until she couldn't walk anymore I was ready to listen. He told me about the tumor, her paralysis and the scans that looked awful.

"No one here will touch her," he said, candidly. "It is too big and she has no insurance." He asked if we could take her at our tertiary hospital.

Disarmed by his honesty I just said, "Sure, send her up."

Each day as the tumor had grown it had choked off a bit more of the blood supply to her legs and pelvis. Her body's natural reaction was to open up more and more blood vessels to bypass the blockage. These rapidly expanding veins and arteries, thin-walled and flimsy, are what fed her lower body. They also created a surgical minefield.

By the time that she and I met this tumor had consumed most of the back of her abdomen and left her spinal cord with less than ten percent of the normal space it once had. Our first trip to the operating room for a biopsy was a near disaster. The hemorrhaging started almost immediately. Packing off the abdomen bought us a short respite in which she and I had a tough conversation. I explained the situation to her. It was unlikely that we could remove the tumor without killing her. The biopsy showed a type of cancer that would not be responsive to chemotherapy or radiation. A complete surgical removal was the only real option for survival but given how invasive the cancer was, the chance of that was slim. Faced with the reality of a painful, paralyzed death or the significant possibility of dying on the operating table, she considered her children. She wanted to be a mother to them and not a fading burden, so she asked us to try and remove it no matter the consequences.

Five experienced surgeons, three anesthesiologists, and an interventional radiologist spent fourteen hours trying to pry the tumor from her belly, unsuccessfully. The hemorrhage was audible. In the end the cancer had won. The best we could do was debulk it and even that was nearly fatal.

She told me before the surgery that if the cancer couldn't be removed, then she preferred to die on the table. My training and my conscience wouldn't let that happen. I was weak, not heroic. When she woke up I had to explain to her that I had failed her on both accounts. I don't think I've ever had a harder conversation.

It is very likely that an earlier presentation to the medical system would have made it possible to remove the tumor in its entirety or to at least avoid the outcome as it was. The mathematics of biology and doubling cell growth dictates that her chances would have been far better. But she avoided us because we are financially intimidating and we avoid people like her, the uninsured, because they don't help us pay our bills.

Emma spent the last two months with her family before dying in pain. It was a financial nightmare to arrange for her to have even the simple dignity of dying at home, again, due to her under-funded status. The only way to make her comfortable enough to leave the hospital was to drip nerve-numbing anesthetics into her spine through a small catheter. No one wanted to pay. The state finally stepped up and helped her with home hospice care.

Years after her death, the nascent Affordable Care Act felt like it held some promise. Even if imperfect it signaled a change in our communal thinking from every man for himself, to one of concern for the health of our neighbors and friends. I'm incredibly saddened that our political winds now push us backward. In the interest of making America "great again" we set our compass from whence we came, to a time when healthcare was just a crap shoot between those who deserve, and those who, arbitrarily, do not.

Mr. Labrador was correct. Emma, like countless others had "access" to healthcare just as readily as she had access to a brand-new Lexus. The argument is both specious and cruel.

When I took my oath in 1987, healthcare spending in the U.S. represented 10 percent of our gross domestic product; now it's nearly 18 percent. Despite the recent rhetoric, this growth didn't start with the Affordable Care Act nor did it accelerate during its implementation.[2] As doctors, like me, and the healthcare we provide become more expensive, *access* shrinks like Alice's door. The essence of our oath shrinks with it.

It's agonizing to watch our elected representatives vote to overturn the Affordable Care Act and then gloat over "the win," while they further tear down the already dysfunctional machinery of our medical care. They held up "Obamacare" as a political piñata to swing at, but once broken, they had no idea what to do with what fell out.

Now, thirty years past my graduation, the pageantry, the costume and the words of the Hippocratic oath have faded in my mind. But I still clearly see and hear Emma who died a difficult death due to our communal lack of compassion. We are the richest nation in the world and yet we withhold medical care from each other in a short-sighted attempt to keep more for ourselves. We hand out bootstraps to those who don't own boots and tell them to pull themselves up. Many of us spend our weekends on hard-back benches professing our love of God and neighbor, we promise to "Do unto others . . ." but come Monday we do for ourselves.

PAUSE

After reading Turker's piece, what questions do you have? What do you find yourself wondering about?

Introduction

I have to be honest: this essay brought me to tears the first time I read it. For me, a father of three, the story of Emma is heart-wrenching. Emma's story makes a

---

2. Data from the Organization and Cooperative Development and Centers for Medicare and Medicaid Services.

powerful anecdotal response to the claim that starts this piece, from Congressman Raul Labrador, that "nobody dies because they don't have access to health care." Labrador is making a claim about causes. He is arguing, implicitly, that while there may be problems associated with lack of health care, these don't rise to the level that necessitates drastic changes to the system.

Turker, in this essay, is responding to Labrador, arguing that in his experience people do die precisely due to lack of health care. He and Labrador are arguing about causes.

As Turker's essay shows, arguments about causes can have major implications. In this chapter we will consider how arguments from cause to effect work, and how to test them for validity.

We see arguments from cause to effect frequently in medical contexts because medicine is often about finding the precise cause of a change in health. For example, if someone is presenting with several symptoms, it is important for doctors to know exactly what is causing those symptoms. Especially when several illnesses present with similar symptoms, it is important for doctors to know for sure the underlying cause.

Similarly, when medical researchers are investigating new medicines and vaccines, it is important for them to know whether or not it is the medicine or vaccine specifically that is having an impact. Randomized control trials, which give certain participants a dosage of the drug being tested and certain participants a placebo (a substance that looks like the drug being tested, but which has no active ingredients), are designed to isolate the specific effect(s) of the drug, if any.

However, we often see arguments about cause and effect in other contexts as well. When we talk about changing political policies, for example, we often debate the effects such policies might have. Will raising the minimum wage lead to more economic growth because it gives people more money to spend and lifts them out of poverty, or will it lead to less economic growth because it will result in fewer available jobs? What about raising or lowering taxes? What might be the effects of those changes?

The Structure of Arguments from Cause to Effect

Arguments about cause and effect attempt to explain how two things are interrelated in such a way that they predict that the existence of one leads to the existence of another. When you make an argument from cause to effect, you are asking your audience to accept that if X occurs, Y will follow; or conversely, if Y has occurred, X must have preceded it. Of course, lots of things follow one another without necessarily being causally related. You'll read more about this in the following chapter, but a simple example is leaves changing colors in the fall and the onset of cooler weather. In northern climates, if you see the leaves on most trees changing all at once (or close to all at once), you can be sure that cooler weather will soon follow. But of course the changing leaves do not cause the cooler weather.

So an argument from cause goes further than simply saying Y follows X, to say that Y follows *from* X, or that X is the cause of Y. In the example of the leaves changing colors, we can hypothetically remove the changing leaves and still have cold weather. But in a causal argument, if we remove X, we don't get Y.

In his essay above, Turker argues that in his experience people do indeed die because they lack health insurance. He argues that this lack of health insurance is the cause of death. This is different than arguing, for instance, that lack of health insurance is correlated with a higher incidence of death, which could be pretty easily established by looking at statistical data. Rather, he is arguing that the lack of health insurance contributes to people dying. It is the cause.

The inference in an argument from cause to effect is that the existence or performance of one thing or phenomenon will lead to some other. The warrant in an argument from cause to effect is that the thing in question is caused by something else. The cause can also be a combination of factors, as it is in Turker's example of Emma.

Arguments about causes can move from cause to effect, or from effect to cause. Anxious about a test the next day, a friend may say to you, "I'm not going to sleep well tonight, because I'm so nervous about the test tomorrow." This is a prediction about the future, and essentially an argument moving from cause (nerves about tomorrow's test) to effect (poor sleep that night). But it could also be that, upon a test being returned to a friend with a grade lower than she had hoped, she says, "I knew I wasn't going to do as well as I had wanted on this test, because I didn't sleep at all the night before." This is an argument from effect (doing poorly on the exam) to cause (not enough sleep the night before).

We can be making an argument from cause even when we don't use the word *cause*. Alternate phrases include *led to*, *contributed to*, and *brought on*, as well as the converse, *prevent*. Often we imply causal arguments contextually. I recently made the commitment to avoid my cell phone for at least an hour prior to bed because I found I was having trouble falling asleep. I'm basically making the argument to myself that interacting with my cell phone was keeping me awake.

Turker's resolution also makes an argument from cause to effect. It is a direct rebuttal to Labrador, who argues that lack of health insurance is not a cause of death for anyone. He gives the example of Emma, whom he argues died because the lack of widespread or universal health insurance created a health-care system that systematically denies care to Emma and people like her. Others unfamiliar with Emma's case may argue that the cause of death was complications from cancer, but Turker is arguing that this is not the whole story. His argument is that while the direct cause of death was complications from cancer, had Emma had access to health care earlier, the cancer could have been caught and she could have survived. Another doctor could look at the same evidence and disagree with Turker, arguing that the cancer was such that death was inevitable, even if it had been caught earlier. A policymaker like Labrador may argue that it was a lack of education that caused Emma's death, because had she known how serious her case was, she would have entered the health-care system sooner. So despite arguments from cause making direct connections between cause and effect, these connections are more or less likely, not certain. Like arguments generally, then, causal inferences follow with some degree of probability, not certainty.

Cause and Effect in Public Discourse

Issues of concern to the general public, as well as political issues, frequently involve arguments from cause to effect. We frequently talk about the causes of things because we want to either avoid repeating negative effects or reproduce positive effects. Economic downturns and their responses are often compared to earlier recessions, like the Great Depression, to see if the causes are similar, or to see if the responses are sufficiently different to avoid another such economic disaster. After World War I, leaders from every major European nation worked together to analyze the causes of that war to put policies in place to prevent another war of such proportions. Presidential candidates have teams trying to explain why a previous candidate did or did not do well in a particular state. A friend may tell you, for example, that Hillary Clinton lost the 2016 election because Donald Trump was able to inflame long-standing anti-immigrant and anti-Black sentiment to motivate white working-class and suburban voters. This is an explanation for behavior, moving from effect (the election of Donald Trump) to cause (racist and xenophobic sentiment).

A causal inference both identifies a relationship by linking two things or phenomena and explains that relationship by stipulating that one is the cause of the other. Rarely in politics, but more commonly in medicine and the sciences, all other possible causes could be controlled for. In these cases the argument is deductive because the claim follows with certainty. When causal inferences are extended through informal argument, they rely on a warrant that one phenomenon has influence on another. We are asking our audience to make an inferential leap, accepting the influential relationship, even though it cannot be observed directly.

Arguing from cause to effect in political contexts often involves two stages. Stage one is to identify a possible cause or causes for the phenomenon in question. Possible causes are identified by studying research, or considering previous arguments on the same controversy. Once you isolate the most probable cause or set of causes, the second step is to provide evidence that this cause or set of causes should be considered the cause or causes for the phenomenon. In court cases prosecutors often use the first step to establish means and opportunity, and the second step to establish motive.

Types of Causes

Claims about cause can take a variety of forms, and we can imply cause even when we do not use the word *cause*. The term *cause* can have a range of meanings, from necessary condition to contributing factor.

Cause as Necessary Condition

To say that "*x* causes *y*" could mean that *x* is a necessary condition for *y*. A **necessary condition**, as the name implies, must be present for something to occur, but it does not guarantee that it will occur. For example, a seed may be a necessary condition for a particular plant. You have to have the seed for that plant to grow the plant, but on the other hand simply having the seed does not guarantee the plant will grow. You may leave the seed on the table, and nothing will happen. When scientists look for other planets that may support life, they are looking for a set of necessary conditions. However, even if a planet with the necessary conditions is found, that does not guarantee that there will be life on this planet.

Cause as Sufficient Condition

Related to necessary condition is the term *sufficient condition*. A **sufficient condition** is a factor or set of factors that, if present, will cause something to occur. So when we say "*x* causes *y*," we might be saying that *x* is a sufficient condition for *y*. This goes a bit further than necessary condition, because if you have all the sufficient conditions, you will get the outcome they lead to. For example, for fire you need to have oxygen, fuel, and sufficient heat. These are sufficient conditions for fire: if you put oxygen, fuel, and a spark together, you will get fire.

Cause as Contributing Factor

Often when we make an argument from cause to effect we mean neither necessary condition nor sufficient condition, but rather that something contributed to the occurrence of something else. Lifestyle habits like regular smoking and drinking, eating fatty and high-cholesterol foods, and consuming excessive sodium all have been linked to heart disease. None of these is a necessary condition, because we've all heard stories of the uncle who smoked a pack a day until he died peacefully in his sleep at the age of ninety-six. Neither is any of these a sufficient condition for similar reasons. But each of these is a **contributing factor**, a cause or set of causes that increases the likelihood that something will occur.

Argument from Cause to Effect in Turker

How about in Turker's essay? Is Turker making the case that lack of health insurance is a necessary or sufficient condition for the death of his patient, Emma? Is he arguing that lack of health insurance was a contributing factor? We know that not everyone who lacks health insurance dies, something that Labrador relies on in his argument and Turker would readily acknowledge. So lack of health insurance is not a sufficient condition for death. That leaves necessary condition and contributing factor. On the one hand, when Turker argues that his patient, Emma, died for lack of health insurance, he could be seen as essentially arguing that her not having health insurance was a necessary condition for death. Had she had access to health insurance, she would not have died. On the other hand, there is room to interpret Turker's argument as "Emma's lack of health insurance was a contributing factor to her death." After all, not everyone who gets cancer without having health insurance dies, and the converse is also true: some people who get cancer and have health insurance do die.

But we have to remember that Turker isn't necessarily making an argument about people in general, but rather about Emma specifically. If he is arguing that lack of health insurance is a contributing factor, then Turker might be arguing that Emma would probably have died from cancer either way, but lack of health insurance influenced the outcome, making her suffering more severe, for example. So let's take a closer look.

Turker writes: "It is very likely that an earlier presentation to the medical system would have made it possible to remove the tumor in its entirety or to at least avoid the outcome as it was." As we know, we don't deal with certainties in argumentation, only likelihoods. In this case it is clear Turker is arguing that had Emma been covered by health insurance, she would have had access to medical intervention when the tumor was still small and removable. Thus he is arguing that if Emma had health insurance, she would have been able to screen for and find the cancer earlier. Had the cancer been found earlier, Turker argues, Emma would have survived. Turker is essentially making the case that lack of health insurance was a necessary condition in her early death from cancer.

Uses of the Argument from Cause to Effect

Arguing from cause to effect can be used in a variety of different ways, depending on the meaning of cause at play in the particular case.

To predict events. People may rely on arguments from cause to predict what will happen in the future, based on current or past events. Every year everyone in our family gets a flu shot because it helps prevent getting sick from the flu and lowers the severity of symptoms if we do get it. We are relying on the argument that an effect of the flu vaccine is that it lowers the risk of getting the flu, or that the flu vaccine is a contributing factor to not getting the flu.

One of the tricky things about arguments about vaccines, however, and one of the reasons perhaps that something so central to modern health has recently been a point of controversy, is that arguments about vaccines ask audiences to believe that if they take the vaccine, something will NOT occur. This resembles a conditional syllogism: if you take a vaccine, you will not get the flu. You did not get the flu, so this is the result of the vaccine at work. However, recalling back to Chapter 2, accepting the consequent does not make a conditional syllogism valid. You don't know if you did not get the flu because of the vaccine or because you were not exposed to the virus or because of some other reason.

However, an argument about vaccines does not rely on formal logic but rather on a very large set of evidence about outcomes related specifically to vaccines: the randomized control trials described above, and user data accumulated in the general population since then. So, though these arguments may appear to be conditional arguments, they are in reality informal arguments about cause, supported by a large body of evidence.

To identify causes of events. People may rely on arguments from cause to explain why certain events occurred. A couple of years ago we rented a small cabin by a lake. Our middle child was just at the age where he was learning to swim, but he couldn't swim without a flotation device. By the end of the week, though, he was able to swim without any help. "See what a week at the lake did?" we said when we saw this. We were implicitly making the claim that spending a week swimming at the lake was the cause of his learning to swim. Many policymakers similarly have argued that extreme heat events have become more numerous due to global climate change. The effect is the increased number of extreme heat events. The cause is global climate change.

To justify certain actions based on their outcomes. Someone may argue that certain actions are justified if they lead to desirable results. This is the line of argument behind the common phrase "The ends justify the means." A runner, for example, may motivate herself in the last stretch of a race by telling herself that she could get her best time. Policymakers may argue that while lowering social welfare for the unemployed seems cruel, in the end it will be good because it will put pressure on the unemployed to return to work. When the Trump administration proposed dramatic tax cuts for corporations and the wealthiest Americans, they argued that these would be justified by a more robust economy overall. Arguments like these are called **pragmatic arguments** because they lead to desirable goals, even if they are not desirable in and of themselves.

To assign responsibility. Argument from cause to effect is often used to assign responsibility. In the deadly Camp fire in California in 2018, identifying the cause of the fire led to the indictment, prosecution, and guilty plea of the utility company PG&E for eighty-four counts of manslaughter. Identifying the cause allowed prosecutors to assign responsibility.

Cause and Effect in Scientific Experiments

From 1817 to 1896, over thirty million people died from cholera, a disease caused by the bacteria *Vibrio cholerae.* Cholera was then one of the most concerning health issues in the world. In fact, in the nineteenth century there were fewer years without a cholera pandemic than there were with a cholera pandemic. A persistent type of bacteria, *Vibrio cholerae* still infects people today, with cases found all over the world, including the United States.

In 1854 John Snow, a London physician, linked a cholera outbreak to contaminated water by plotting all the cases on a map and noticing they were densely distributed around a single well (an effective use of visual evidence; see Chapter 8).

But if Snow had discovered the cause of cholera in 1854, why did severe cholera outbreaks continue for another fifty years?

The answer is that despite Snow's discovery, people continued to argue about causes of cholera until the late nineteenth century. Misinformation persisted for decades.

For a long time after Snow published his findings, Europe's health experts and policymakers continued to believe that the cause of cholera (as well as other diseases like the plague) was breathing in bad air. Information did not travel as quickly then as it does now. On top of that, the theory of bad air as a cause of disease was an old one, and deeply entrenched, so it was difficult for doctors to change their minds—even when faced with contradictory evidence. Policymakers, too, resisted Snow's explanation because it meant modernizing the water system—at great expense.

Scientific arguments call for analysis of **data**, a specialized type of evidence gathered through systematic observation. By identifying patterns in these data, scientists make interpretations about what the data suggest. These observations are called hypotheses.

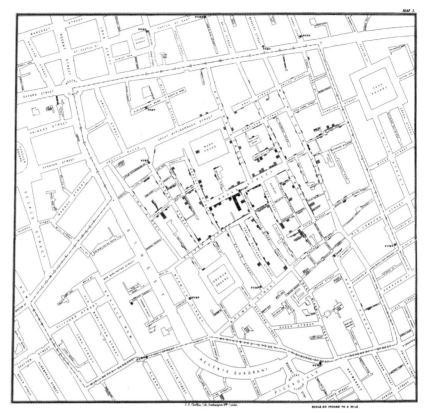

John Snow, Public domain, via Wikimedia Commons

A **hypothesis** is a testable explanation for a phenomenon or set of phenomena, based on analysis of data. While scientific arguments about cause and effect share a lot in common with arguments from cause to effect generally, there are some features of these arguments specific to scientific discourse.

People tend to think of hypotheses as predictions or educated guesses about some problem that are then tested through scientific observation. While this may be how it is done in some scientific disciplines, it doesn't really describe how much—I would say most—scientific reasoning proceeds. Most of the time, scientists are not driven by guesses they want to test but rather problems or questions they want to answer.

Consider, for example, COVID-19, the illness caused by the novel coronavirus at the center of a global pandemic starting in 2019. The spread of this virus among humans presented a whole bunch of problems and questions that scientists then set about solving. These questions range from the very general (Where did the virus come from? How did it pass to humans?) to the very specific (How effective are masks at preventing transmission? Why is loss of smell a symptom of COVID-19?). Scientists gather data relevant to these questions using a variety of methods and make hypotheses in response to these questions based on the data.

Stuart Firestein, professor of biology at Columbia University, puts it this way:

> Questions are more relevant than answers. Questions are bigger than answers. One good question can give rise to several layers of answers, can inspire decades-long searches for solutions, can generate whole new fields of inquiry, and can prompt changes in entrenched thinking.

The questions Firestein is lauding here are often opportunities to identify causes.

Testing for Possible Causes in Scientific Studies

When faced with a question in science that asks for identifying the cause, scientists develop studies to identify and test possible causes. On the simplest level, scientists can identify a specific event and look for underlying causes. Snow, for example, interviewed several people (those Snow interviewed were his sample) who lived in the area affected by cholera and found that while many in the area did become infected with cholera, some others did not. What might account for this? In the course of his interviews, he looked for some **common thread**, or a potential factor shared among all the individuals in a common population (in this case either the group that did get cholera, or conversely the group that did not). He found that many of those who did not get sick were brewers and drank beer rather than water. So here was an (atypical) case where it seems drinking beer was healthier than drinking water.

Sometimes scientists are looking not for what a single population has in common but rather a difference between two populations. Snow, in the course of his investigations, found that three water companies supplied water to the area where people were getting sick with cholera. Two water companies drew their water from a highly populated part of the river Thames, while another company drew its water from a cleaner area upriver. He analyzed this data and came up with his hypothesis that contaminated water was the cause of cholera infections. Snow essentially was identifying the difference between those in the sample who did become infected with cholera and those who did not. In this case the difference was where they received their water.

Conclusion

Arguments from cause to effect are one of the most varied and complex among all the common inference patterns. There is a pretty wide range from arguments like

"Gas + oxygen + spark causes fire" to "Climate change causes wildfires." Both are about causes, but *cause* is used in different ways—as a sufficient condition in our first example, and as a contributing factor in our second. We also use arguments from cause to effect for a variety of reasons. We might use argument from cause to effect to predict events, to identify causes of events, to justify certain actions based on their outcomes, or to assign responsibility.

Because of this ambiguity, arguments about causes are sometimes difficult to resolve. Nevertheless, arguments from cause to effect are both important and potentially powerful. We need to make arguments about the causes of geopolitical problems like armed conflict, social problems like persistent inequalities, and economic problems like inflation, even when we can't be certain about the outcomes of these arguments.

Arguments from cause to effect in scientific contexts have their own criteria, which are attempts to isolate actual causes (whether these are necessary, sufficient, or contributing factors) from potential causes. These criteria allow scientific arguments about cause to both have a high degree of probability and be highly effective to an audience exercising reasonable judgment.

PROBE

Write about a time you were sure of the cause of something but turned out to be wrong.

Chapter 12
Arguing from Sign

Key Terms

correlation

argument from sign

infallible sign

fallible sign

severance

Key Points

- Sign arguments involve correlation.
- They are often used to make claims about the nature of unknowable concepts such as human character, economic health, or an organizational culture.
- They are sometimes confused with arguments about the causes of things.
- Several tests of arguments from sign exist.

PRIME

How confident are you that you can define the term *correlation*? Make a list of any words or ideas that come to mind when you hear the word *correlation*.

Untitled (One Day This Kid . . .)

David Wojnarowicz (1990-1991)

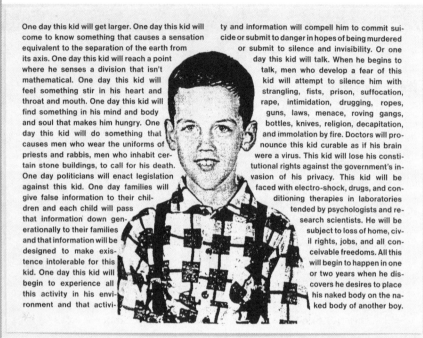

One day this kid will get larger. One day this kid will come to know something that causes a sensation equivalent to the separation of the earth from its axis. One day this kid will reach a point where he senses a division that isn't mathematical. One day this kid will feel something stir in his heart and throat and mouth. One day this kid will find something in his mind and body and soul that makes him hungry. One day this kid will do something that causes men who wear the uniforms of priests and rabbis, men who inhabit certain stone buildings, to call for his death. One day politicians will enact legislation against this kid. One day families will give false information to their children and each child will pass that information down generationally to their families and that information will be designed to make existence intolerable for this kid. One day this kid will begin to experience all this activity in his environment and that activity and information will compel him to commit suicide or submit to danger in hopes of being murdered or submit to silence and invisibility. Or one day this kid will talk. When he begins to talk, men who develop a fear of this kid will attempt to silence him with strangling, fists, prison, suffocation, rape, intimidation, drugging, ropes, guns, laws, menace, roving gangs, bottles, knives, religion, decapitation, and immolation by fire. Doctors will pronounce this kid curable as if his brain were a virus. This kid will lose his constitutional rights against the government's invasion of his privacy. This kid will be faced with electro-shock, drugs, and conditioning therapies in laboratories tended by psychologists and research scientists. He will be subject to loss of home, civil rights, jobs, and all conceivable freedoms. All this will begin to happen in one or two years when he discovers he desires to place his naked body on the naked body of another boy.

PAUSE

Untitled (One Day This Kid . . .) is a work of visual art. How do image and text work together in this piece to have an impact on the viewer?

Introduction

Patterns of inference are the basic structures of arguments, providing writers with both a way to arrange their argument and also a "quasi-logic," a momentum to the argument that pairs claim and evidence in a way that often feels like logic (even when it, strictly speaking, isn't logical).

It's easy to see such a quasi-logic operating in Wojnarowicz's piece above. The momentum of the piece suggests a relationship between sexual identity and violence.

But is that really what's going on? Is it all that's going on? In other words, is Wojnarowicz making the argument that "this kid's" sexual identity is the cause of his being abused and repressed? That immediately doesn't strike us as reasonable, doesn't meet the test of prima facie.

At the same time, the relationship between homosexuality and the appearance of violence seems inescapable here. Wojnarowicz's examples seem to suggest that violence—from that first "division that isn't mathematical" to the "loss of home, civil rights, jobs, and all conceivable freedoms"—appears as the response to homosexuality.

And in fact, many arguments against homosexuality do claim that violent repression is a reasonable response. Proponents of conversion therapy and other groups committed to the suppression of gay rights sometimes contend that homosexuality is the cause of violence, arguing that gay men have increased suicide rates and are more likely to engage in other self-destructive behavior.[1]

But is Wojnarowicz making a similar argument? Is he arguing that the kid's being gay is the cause of the various forms of violence to which he will be subjected? This is a type of victim blaming, and we wouldn't expect Wojnarowicz, openly gay himself and a prominent gay rights and AIDS activist, to make such an argument. So let's analyze the argument to make an informed assessment.

If Wojnarowicz's argument is indeed that homosexuality causes violence against homosexuals, then it is an argument from cause to effect. So let's review the tests of the argument from cause to effect to find out. As was presented in the previous chapter, the first test is to determine whether or not a correlation has been confused for a cause.

In a **correlation**, two things often appear together, but neither causes the other. Stop signs, for example, are correlated with cars coming to a halt at intersections (for that matter, they are correlated with intersections). They are not, however, the cause of the cars' stopping (that would be the braking mechanism in conjunction with the action of the driver).

The distinction may appear minor here, but as we shall see as we return to Wojnarowicz, it is a crucial one.

Wojnarowicz writes, "All this will begin to happen in one or two years when he discovers he desires to place his naked body on the naked body of another boy." The first thing to notice is that Wojnarowicz does not use the word *because* but rather *when*, a choice that in avoiding cause points to correlation and not causation. Moreover, the implication is that

> *Correlation* is a pattern of relationship in which two or more things commonly occur together.

---

1. Of course, many dispute those claims.

the sexual contact is consensual, and so the act itself cannot be said to be the cause of violence, having been the expression of a mutual desire. Rather, like the stop sign, the act sets things in motion that are already there in our society.

We can see, therefore, that Wojnarowicz is not suggesting that the boy's being gay is causing violence to occur but rather that violence is a common method society uses to repress this boy's sexual identity. Thus, Wojnarowicz argues the nonconforming sexual identity is not the cause of the violence, but in a heteronormative society violence and nonconforming sexual identity are correlated.

This difference may appear subtle, but it is really important because it shows that Wojnarowicz is making an argument not against homosexuality but, on the contrary, against society's violent response to homosexuality.

Argument from Sign

Upon closer examination, then, we can see that Wojnarowicz is making a different kind of argument, not one of cause and effect but a pattern of inference called the argument from sign.

In making an argument from sign, Wojnarowicz turns the argument from cause to effect on its head, suggesting that gay men are more likely to be the victims of violence not because they are gay but because of society's violent response to their sexuality. This puts the blame squarely where it should be, on the perpetrators, not the victims, of violence.

Causation	Correlation
If A then B, because of A.	If A then likely B.

The **argument from sign** is a common pattern of inference that deals not with cause and effect but with the relative level of predictability. A sign inference asks an audience to make a leap of judgment from the known to the unknown, based on evidence that two things commonly appear together, or are correlated.

In northern climates the return of the red-winged blackbird is a sign of the coming spring. The red-winged blackbird doesn't cause winter to end, but its return signals that winter is nearing its end. The blackbird therefore predicts that spring is near.

The underlying warrant is that you can predict the occurrence of one thing from the preceding occurrence of another thing.

Because arguments from sign frequently deal with uncertainty about the future, they're common when people deliberate about the likelihood of future developments or outcomes, such as economic gains and losses, sporting contests, long-term weather patterns (think Groundhog Day), and elections.

In election seasons, stories about random phenomena that have historically predicted U.S. presidential elections abound, from mock elections in elementary schools to a Chinese clairvoyant monkey.[2]

Many of the pundits and pollsters got the outcome of the 2016 U.S. election wrong, but Spirit Halloween didn't. The costume chain predicted that Donald Trump would win the presidency, based on sales of his masks relative to Hillary Clinton's. Essentially, the prediction was an argument from sign that the higher sales figures for Trump masks meant that Trump would win the election.

TRY IT

(Hint: there is more than one right answer.)

Which of the following make an argument from sign?

    a. That guy is so shady; he never makes eye contact. I'm sure he's the one who took your phone.

    b. Bigmart's stock is going to go up. I had to wait for someone to pull out before I got a parking space.

    c. No one picked up at the doctor's office, so I guess they're closed.

    d. I don't expect the attorney general to do much to fight against discriminatory voting laws. He voted for such laws three times as a senator.

    e. I'm sure I won't get the flu this year. I got vaccinated against it.

Infallible and Fallible Signs

There are two types of sign, the infallible sign and the fallible sign.

Something can be called an **infallible sign** when the correlative follows the sign each and every time, without fail, as the name implies. The example of the red-winged blackbird, above, is an infallible sign. Every time the blackbird returns, sustained warmer weather is sure to follow.

---

2. Jennifer Earl, "This Elementary School Has Correctly Predicted Every Presidential Election since 1968," CBS News, November 4, 2016, http://www.cbsnews.com/news/benjamin-franklin-elementary-school-has-correctly-predicted-every-presidential-election-for-48-years/; Neal Baker, "Seal of Ape-oval: China's 'Monkey King' Predicts Donald Trump WILL WIN the US Presidential Election," *Sun*, November 4, 2016, https://www.thesun.co.uk/news/2118303/donald-trump-us-election-2016-china-monkey-king/.

Infallible signs are typically not at the centers of controversy; usually there is a high level of agreement or quick acceptance of an infallible sign. Someone says to you, "They're going to open the city pool soon." "How do you know?" "Because I saw them filling it up this morning."

Chances are, this is where the question ends, with both parties agreeing that the pool will be open soon. "Great, I'll get my bathing suit out of storage," you might say.

The **fallible sign**, on the other hand, predicts only with some degree of probability, not the certainty the infallible sign provides. Fallible sign inferences, therefore, are inductive arguments that make a case for something based on its correlation to something else.

Wojnarowicz is making this kind of an inference, a fallible sign inference linking sexuality to violence in order to make the argument that society violently suppresses nonconforming sexual identity. This is a significantly different argument than the argument from cause to effect that we considered earlier, which suggested that it was nonconforming sexuality that caused the violent reaction to it, blaming the victim for the violence perpetrated against him.

Surface and Essence

The argument from sign can be especially effective when asking an audience to leap to the unknown, making it a common inference for arguments about future or unknown past events, as well as things that are mysterious or hidden from observation, such as the human psyche, an organization's culture, or the nature of a political regime. The argument from sign is common in economics news, for example, which seeks to provide readers some certainty about a future that is fundamentally unknowable:

> "Five signs the economy is improving"
>
> "Seven signs we're headed for economic collapse"

It's also a common line of argument in the courtroom, as in the example of O. J. Simpson and the bloody gloves found at the crime scene. Prosecutor Christopher Darden asked Simpson to try the gloves on—and they didn't fit! Many interpreted this as evidence that the gloves did not belong to Simpson, and therefore Simpson wasn't the killer. The gloves' not fitting was understood to be a sign that the killer was someone with smaller hands, and that Simpson was innocent.

A powerful example of the use of sign in public address appears in Martin Luther King Jr.'s 1963 "I Have a Dream" speech at the Lincoln Memorial. Here King is making the case that racism persists, despite some historical progress, by pointing to its signs.

There are those who are asking the devotees of civil rights, "When will you be satisfied?" We can never be satisfied as long as the Negro is the victim of the unspeakable horrors of police brutality. We can never be satisfied as long as our bodies, heavy with the fatigue of travel, cannot gain lodging in the motels of the highways and the hotels of the cities. We cannot be satisfied as long as the Negro's basic mobility is from a smaller ghetto to a larger one. We can never be satisfied as long as our children are stripped of their self-hood and robbed of their dignity by signs stating: "For Whites Only." We cannot be satisfied as long as a Negro in Mississippi cannot vote and a Negro in New York believes he has nothing for which to vote. No, no, we are not satisfied, and we will not be satisfied until "justice rolls down like waters, and righteousness like a mighty stream."

Like Wojnarowicz, King is making a connection between the surface or exterior of something and what lies beneath. He posits a relationship between symptoms of discrimination, like police brutality and voter suppression, and the underlying essence of systemic racism. Taken together, King is arguing, these are signs that African Americans are systematically being denied their civil rights.

Because racism, like the human psyche or the future, is impossible to observe directly and without ambiguity (you can't point to racism, even if you can point to a racist act), King employs the argument from sign to indicate its existence. Again, the warrant depends on correlation, that the existence of the sign (e.g., police brutality against African Americans) predicts the existence of the underlying essence (e.g., racism).

The important thing to keep in mind when it comes to arguments from sign is that, unlike in the argument from cause, it is not necessary to show cause in a sign argument. Correlation is sufficient to carry the claim. This is clear in arguments that link smoking to lung cancer, for example. Scientists do not need to argue that smoking causes cancer (if they did, they would have to show that smoking leads to cancer every time, or at least most of the time). Rather, scientists may argue that smoking is correlated with a higher risk for developing lung cancer. This correlation is sufficient to link smoking and lung cancer.

Sign Arguments as a Method of Establishing a Person's Character

One of the most common uses of the argument from sign is to establish a person's character. The rhetorician Chaïm Perelman writes about the argument from sign as a method of establishing a speaker's or writer's character, and the ways the establishment of character can be used in making an argument. Perelman's analysis takes our now-familiar definition of the argument from sign, that the exterior or surface of something is representative of an underlying structure, and applies it to people. Simply put, Perelman argues that a person's acts are a sign of that person's character.

The relationship between the person making the argument and the argument itself has an interesting and complex place in argumentation. On the one hand, the person making an argument is often considered irrelevant. Especially in our liberal modern culture, it is commonplace to believe that who is making an argument should not bear on whether or not an argument is valid or convincing.

> *Ad hominem* refers to a rebuttal directed at the character of a person rather than the argument they made. For example, "She's a liar!"
>
> *Ad personem* is an argument that appeals to an audience to question the character of a speaker. For example, "You can't trust any of what she's said, because she's a liar!"
>
> *Ad hominem* and *ad personem* claims are highly related, with ad hominem claims often implying ad personem claims.

If a thief, as he is leaving your house loaded to the chin with your valuables, tells you that it's time to change your smoke alarm batteries, his maligned character as a thief doesn't affect whether or not you should believe him.

Accordingly, it is uncommon to openly appeal to character or authority in contemporary argument. Even the most widely celebrated scientist in the world would not present an argument without evidence, and we expect even our president to make the case for their economic policies, for example.

On the other hand, it is difficult to overestimate the power of character in argumentation. Aristotle called this the appeal to ethos and suggested it may be "the most effective means of persuasion [the rhetor] possesses." Ultimately, establishing ethos is about presenting yourself as someone the audience should trust. Perhaps ironically, this typically means avoiding directly appealing to your own authority, which might actually separate you from your audience.

Many have argued that ethos is in fact the precondition for effective argumentation. Until you have established ethos, shown yourself to be "the right kind of person," your argument will fall on deaf ears.

The Unity and Stability of the Subject

Using an argument from sign to establish a person's, organization's, or political regime's character necessarily depends on the extent to which your audience will accept the relative unity or stability of an individual across contexts and time. A belief in a high level of unity holds that a person changes none or little depending on the context in which she is placed, as in the proverbs "You can't change a leopard's spots" and "Once a crook, always a crook." A belief in a low level of stability, on the other hand, holds that people change according to their circumstances.

So how willing your audience is to accept arguments based on someone's essential character depends on how much of a role they see time and context playing. What if your neighbor were to ask you to borrow your rental car after wrecking your car last week, claiming "That was last week—I've changed"? Chances are, you wouldn't accept that claim. But if it were a space of ten accident-free years since the last time your neighbor had borrowed your car, you might be more willing to lend the car.

When Senator Jefferson Beauregard Sessions III came before the Senate for confirmation to be the United States' eighty-fourth attorney general, many questioned his competence based on his past record, which included allegations of racial bias and voter intimidation (allegations that were enough to block his earlier nomination to a federal judgeship in the Alabama Southern District). Several senators read from a 1986 letter from Coretta Scott King, arguing that Sessions was actively involved in racially motivated voter suppression and intimidation.

The relevance of the earlier letter depends on the extent to which the audience is ready to believe that Sessions has or has not changed over time. Senator John Cornyn, for example, argued that Sessions's earlier actions "[do] not characterize [Sessions's] entire record of twenty years in the United States Senate or how [he] conducted [himself] as a prosecutor."

Part of Cornyn's argument, then, was that over the course of Sessions's Senate career he had changed. Cornyn countered the argument that we can judge Sessions's character by his prior actions by attempting to separate Sessions from these earlier actions.

Profiles as Arguments from Sign

Profile pieces in newspapers and magazines, as well as essays that seek to depict someone's character, are essentially definition arguments that use sign inference to portray an individual's unique character.

Consider the following examples, first from John McPhee's *The Pine Barrens*, and then Gloria Steinem's "Patricia Nixon Flying."

> I walked through a vestibule that had a dirt floor, stepped up into a kitchen, and went into another room that had several overstuffed chairs in it and a porcelain-topped table, where Fred Brown was seated, eating a pork chop. He was dressed in a white sleeveless shirt, ankle-top shoes, and undershorts. He gave me a

cheerful greeting and, without asking why I had come or what I wanted, picked up a pair of khaki trousers that had been tossed onto one of the overstuffed chairs and asked me to sit down. He set the trousers on another chair, and he apologized for being in the middle of his breakfast, explaining that he seldom drank much but the night before he had had a few drinks and this had caused his day to start slowly. "I don't know what's the matter with me, but there's got to be something the matter with me, because drink don't agree with me anymore," he said. He had a raw onion in one hand, and while he talked he shaved slices from the onion and ate them between bites of the chop. . . .

—*The Pine Barrens*, John McPhee

McPhee isn't just describing everything he noticed when he met Fred Brown. This isn't an exhaustive description. Instead, McPhee focuses on those specific details that, when taken together, become signs of Brown's character, who he is, what makes him simultaneously distinct and typical. Why, for example, does McPhee mention that Brown didn't ask him what he was doing there? Why does he specify the pants, emphasize the slices of raw onions? Is this just what McPhee noticed when he was there? Possibly. But more likely, McPhee took note of myriad details and chose these to give a particular impression of Fred Brown (who incidentally is himself a sign argument for the character of a place, the Pine Barrens of New Jersey).

She had shared all the vilification and praise without ever emerging in public as an individual. I was eager to meet her, but all her other interviewers said Mrs. Nixon had put them straight to sleep.

She was sitting in the front of the plane, freckled hands neatly folded, ankles neatly crossed, and smiling a public smile as a sleek young staff man sat me next to her. I didn't want to ask the questions she had answered so blandly and often about her husband ("I just think he'd make a wonderful president") or politics ("You'll have to ask Dick about that"), but to ask about herself.

—"Patricia Nixon Flying," Gloria Steinem

Like McPhee, Steinem goes beyond mere description. Unlike McPhee, who seems to have been swimming in potential noteworthy details about his subject, Steinem is attempting to reveal what's of interest about someone who has not presented an interesting subject to her previous interviewers but has rather been presented only in relation to her husband. This makes her choice of details all the more vital, as they must simultaneously show the subdued, reverent image previous journalists have found (after all, Steinem isn't trying to argue that they got it wrong, really) while at the same time revealing glimpses of something more (implying that, maybe, previous journalists did not get her completely right, either). Ultimately, Steinem is proposing that certain details about Patricia Nixon ("hands neatly folded, ankles neatly crossed") suggest an underlying character. Moreover, like McPhee, Steinem builds on these details to present Nixon herself as a sign of a larger political and cultural zeitgeist.

Countering an Argument from Sign

As evidenced by Cornyn's argument, one can counter a sign argument by delinking the sign from what it allegedly points to. This counterargument, by which one argues against a perceived relationship between a sign and its referent, is called **severance**.

Severance can be accomplished in a number of ways. One way is that discussed above in relation to Attorney General Sessions, to claim that intervening time has changed the individual's character.

Another is to point to extenuating circumstances, arguing that the characteristics in question do not point to an underlying essence but rather are caused by something else. For example, many of Martin Luther King's critics at the time argued that what King had identified as signs of systemic racism—police brutality and voter suppression—were actually caused by the protests themselves. Such figures, opposing the civil rights movement, maintained that King and others like him either invented or instigated examples of problems and injustices suffered by African American citizens.

Governor S. Ernest Vandiver of Georgia, for example, called King a "racial agitator," and FBI director J. Edgar Hoover said King was "the most notorious liar in the country." Both lines of counterargument attempted to separate in listeners' or readers' minds the acts of violence against African Americans (surface) from systemic racism (essence) in an effort to deny that anything like systemic racism existed. Basically, the argument was that violence against African Americans was not a sign of racism, but was caused by civil rights activism itself.

> Most people are other people. Their thoughts are someone else's opinions, their lives a mimicry, their passions a quotation. —Oscar Wilde, De Profundis

This line of counterargument may not have been successful (or justified) in the previous example, but it can be extremely effective under the right circumstances. Consider the case of Ethan Anthony Couch, who in 2013 was convicted of intoxication manslaughter for killing four people when he drove his pickup truck into two other vehicles. The lawyers for Couch effectively argued during the sentencing hearing that he suffered from "affluenza" and was therefore not a criminal but a victim of his socioeconomic conditions. The judge agreed, sentencing Couch to two years' probation instead of the twenty years in prison the prosecution sought.

In addition to pointing to context and suggesting change over time, other avenues for severing the sign from its referent include arguing the action being debated is an anomaly, indicating it is the result of education or a lack thereof, or suggesting the actor was influenced by bad company.

TESTS OF SIGN INFERENCES

As with any type of inference, there are several patterns of unreasonable uses of sign inferences. It is important to understand the tests of sign inferences, therefore, to recognize whether or not the inference is justified in a particular case.

You can ask yourself these five questions in relation to a sign inference, as a way to ascertain its reasonableness. These questions need not be taken together. That is, if a sign inference fails in regard to even one of the questions, then it is likely unreasonable.

1. Typically, do the sign and what it signifies appear together?

    Reasonable: "Dad's gonna buy jelly." "How do you know?" "He just bought peanut butter."

    Unreasonable: "Dad's gonna buy jelly." "How do you know?" "He just bought new tires."

2. Are there any coevident signs that point to something else (countersigns)?

    Reasonable: "The economy is improving." "What makes you say that?" "Unemployment is down, and hiring is up."

    Unreasonable: "The economy is improving." "What makes you say that?" "Unemployment is down." "Yes, but hiring is down, too."

3. Is it possible the sign points to something else?

    Reasonable: "The House will pass the new health care bill." "Oh yeah? Why do you think so?" "Vitanza the moderate backs it."

    Unreasonable: "The House will pass the new health care bill." "Oh yeah? Why do you think so?" "Vitanza the moderate backs it." "Yes, but Vitanza is backing it only so that his party appears willing to compromise. The majority will vote against it."

4. Are we justified in assuming this isn't just a coincidence?

Reasonable: "Jones is going to have a good game tonight." "How do you know?" "He's starting at shooting guard, and every time he starts in that position he scores at least twenty-five points."

Unreasonable: "Jones is going to have a good game tonight." "How do you know?" "I'm wearing my lucky socks, and every time I wear them he scores at least twenty-five points."

5. Is causation being confused with correlation?

Reasonable: "Vaccines don't cause autism." "Yes, they do." "No, they don't. Research shows that rates of autism among unvaccinated children are similar to those who have been vaccinated. This shows that there's no link between vaccination and autism."

Unreasonable: "Vaccines cause autism." "No, they don't." "Yes, they do. Research shows that autism is diagnosed within six months of vaccinations in 80 percent of cases. This shows that there is a link between vaccination and autism."

Conclusion

Sign inferences, as we see above in our example from Wojnarowicz, are some of the most common in literary argument. Because arguments from sign make claims by suggesting a surface feature represents an underlying essence, they are highly flexible: they can make claims about people's character, about cultural values, or about future outcomes, among other things. Regardless of the argument being made, in arguments from sign the warrant is that the presence of one thing can predict the existence of something else.

Sign inferences involve correlations. They point to patterns or changes that vary in relation to one another. Most sign inferences deal with fallible signs, which depend on probability, rather than certainty, and are therefore claims.

Correlation is often confused with causation, but the distinction is important. Arguments from sign do not ascribe cause, and they don't need to. They are effective when correlation is enough.

Untitled (One Day This Kid . . .), by David Wojnarowicz, illustrates a sign argument. Wojnarowicz identifies several surface manifestations of homophobia, which he links to an underlying societal intolerance toward gay Americans.

Sign arguments often seek to establish a link between the known and the unknown, suggesting that we can make the leap from the known to the unknown. This is particularly useful when making arguments about things that are not fully knowable, such as human character, economic health, and organizational culture.

When making arguments from sign, we claim that the way something or someone acts in one situation suggests an underlying character that reliably predicts how that thing or person will act in another situation. The success of the prediction is dependent on the extent to which the audience believes in an essential nature that does not change across time and context.

Severance is the technique of countering an argument from sign by delinking the connection between the sign and what it is suggested to correlate with.

To test inferences from sign, we can ask a series of questions. Typically, do the sign and what it signifies appear together? Are there any signs that point to something else (countersigns)? Is it possible the sign points to something else? Are we justified in assuming this isn't just a coincidence? Is causation being confused with correlation?

PROBE

Make a list of signs that reflect the character of a loved one.

Chapter 13
Commonplaces and Argument from Form

Key Terms

commonplaces
enthymeme
pragmatism
principle
quantity
quality

argument from form
dilemma
hypothesis
comparison
quasi-logical

Key Points

- Arguments from commonplaces rely on beliefs that are so widely accepted that they appear to be common sense.
- People often hold multiple, apparently contradictory, beliefs.
- Arguments from form, sometimes referred to as quasi-logical arguments, follow the patterns of deductive logic but are informal arguments.
- Arguments from form are often used to make claims about things that cannot be readily tested in other ways.

PRIME

Take a moment to do an Internet search for a recording of this speech by Malcolm X. How does listening to the speech impact you differently than reading it?

The Ballot or the Bullet

Malcolm X (1964)

Mr. Moderator, Brother Lomax, brothers and sisters, friends and enemies: I just can't believe everyone in here is a friend and I don't want to leave anybody out. The question tonight, as I understand it, is "The Negro Revolt, and Where Do We Go from Here?" or "What Next?" In my little humble way of understanding it, it points toward either the ballot or the bullet.

Before we try and explain what is meant by the ballot or the bullet, I would like to clarify something concerning myself. I'm still a Muslim, my religion is still Islam. That's my personal belief. Just as Adam Clayton Powell is a Christian minister who heads the Abyssinian Baptist Church in New York, but at the same time takes part in the political struggles to try and bring about rights to the black people in this country; and Dr. Martin Luther King is a Christian minister down in Atlanta, Georgia, who heads another organization fighting for the civil rights of black people in this country; and Rev. Galamison, I guess you've heard of him, is another Christian minister in New York who has been deeply involved in the school boycotts to eliminate segregated education; well, I myself am a minister; and I believe in action on all fronts by whatever means necessary.

Although I'm still a Muslim, I'm not here tonight to discuss my religion. I'm not here to argue or discuss anything that we differ about, because it's time for us to submerge our differences and realize that it is best for us to first see that we have the same problem, a common problem—a problem that will make you catch hell whether you're a Baptist, or a Methodist, or a Muslim, or a nationalist. Whether you're educated or illiterate, whether you live on the boulevard or in the alley, you're going to catch hell just like I am. We're all in the same boat and we all are going to catch the same hell from the same man. He just happens to be a white man. All of us have suffered here, in this country, political oppression at the hands of the white man, economic exploitation at the hands of the white man, and social degradation at the hands of the white man.

Now in speaking like this, it doesn't mean that we're anti-white, but it does mean we're anti-exploitation, we're anti-degradation, we're anti-oppression. And if the white man doesn't want us to be anti-him, let him stop oppressing and exploiting and degrading us. Whether we are Christians or Muslims or nationalists or agnostics or atheists, we must first learn to forget our differences. If we have differences, let us differ in the closet; when we come out in front, let us not have anything to argue about until we get finished arguing with the man. If the late President Kennedy could get together with Khrushchev and exchange some wheat, we certainly have more in common with each other than Kennedy and Khrushchev had with each other.

If we don't do something real soon, I think you'll have to agree that we're going to be forced either to use the ballot or the bullet. It's one or the other in 1964. It isn't that time is running out—time has run out! 1964 threatens to be the most explosive year America has ever witnessed. The most explosive year. Why? It's also a political year. It's the year when all of the white politicians will be back in the so-called Negro community jiving you and me for some votes. The year when all of the white political crooks will be right back in your and my community with their false promises, building up our hopes for a letdown, with their trickery and their treachery, with their false promises which they don't intend to keep. As they nourish these dissatisfactions, it can only lead to one thing, an explosion. And now we have the type of black man on the scene in America today—I'm sorry, Brother Lomax—who just doesn't intend to turn the other cheek any longer.

Don't let anybody tell you anything about the odds are against you. If they draft you, they send you to Korea and make you face 800 million Chinese. If you can be brave over there, you can be brave right here. These odds aren't as great as those odds. And if you fight here, you will at least know what you're fighting for.

I'm not a politician, not even a student of politics; in fact, I'm not a Democrat, I'm not a Republican, and I don't even consider myself an American. If you and I were Americans, there'd be no problem. Those Honkies that just got off the boat, they're already Americans; Polacks are already Americans; the Italian refugees are already Americans. Everything that came out of Europe, every blue-eyed thing, is already an American.

And as long as you and I have been over here, we aren't Americans yet.

Well, I am one who doesn't believe in deluding myself. I'm not going to sit at your table and watch you eat, with nothing on my plate, and call myself a diner. Sitting at the table doesn't make you a diner, unless you eat some of what's on that plate. Being here in America doesn't make you an American. Being born here in America doesn't make you an American. Why, if birth made you American, you wouldn't need any legislation, you wouldn't need any amendments to the Constitution, you wouldn't be faced with civil rights filibustering in Washington, D.C., right now. They don't have to pass civil rights legislation to make a Polack an American.

No, I'm not an American. I'm one of the 22 million black people who are the victims of Americanism. One of the 22 million black people who are the victims of democracy, nothing but disguised hypocrisy. So, I'm not standing here speaking to you as an American, or a patriot, or a flag-saluter, or a flag-waver—no, not I. I'm speaking as a victim of this American system. And I see America through the eyes of the victim. I don't see any American dream; I see an American nightmare.

These 22 million victims are waking up. Their eyes are coming open. They're beginning to see what they used to only look at. They're becoming politically mature. They are realizing that there are new political trends from coast to coast. As they see these new political trends, it's possible for them to see that they have to have a recount. They had to recount in Massachusetts to see who was going to be governor, it was so close. It was the same way in Rhode Island, in Minnesota, and in many other parts of the country. And the same with Kennedy and Nixon when they ran for president. It was so close they had to count all over again. Well, what does this mean? It means that when white people are evenly divided, and black people have a bloc of votes of their own, it is left up to them to determine who's going to sit in the White House and who's going to be in the dog house.

It was the black man's vote that put the present administration in Washington, D.C. Your vote, your dumb vote, your ignorant vote, your wasted vote put in an administration in Washington, D.C., that has seen fit to pass every kind of legislation imaginable, saving you until last, then filibustering on top of that. And your and my leaders have the audacity to run around clapping their hands and talk about how much progress we're making. And what a good president we have. If he wasn't good in Texas, he sure can't be good in Washington, D.C. Because Texas is a lynch state. It is in the same breath as Mississippi, no different; only they lynch you in Texas with a Texas accent and lynch you in Mississippi with a Mississippi accent. And these Negro leaders have the audacity to go and have some coffee in the White House with a Texan, a Southern cracker—that's all he is—and then come out and tell you and me that he's going to be better for us because, since he's from the South, he knows how to deal with the Southerners. What kind of logic is that? Let Eastland be president, he's from the South too. He should be better able to deal with them than Johnson.

In this present administration they have in the House of Representatives 257 Democrats to only 177 Republicans. They control two-thirds of the House vote. Why can't they pass something that will help you and me? In the Senate, there are 67 senators who are of the Democratic Party. Only 33 of them are Republicans. Why, the Democrats have got the government sewed up, and you're the one who sewed it up for them. And what have they given you for it? Four years in office, and just now getting around to some civil rights legislation. Just now, after everything else is gone, out of the way, they're going to sit down now and play with you all summer long—the same old giant con game that they call filibuster. All those are in cahoots together.

Don't you ever think they're not in cahoots together, for the man that is heading the civil rights filibuster is a man from Georgia named Richard Russell. When Johnson became president, the first man he asked for when he got back to Washington, D.C., was "Dicky"—that's how tight they are. That's his boy, that's his pal, that's his buddy. But they're playing that old con game. One of them makes believe he's for you, and he's got it fixed where the other one is so tight against you, he never has to keep his promise.

So it's time in 1964 to wake up. And when you see them coming up with that kind of conspiracy, let them know your eyes are open. And let them know you got something else that's wide open too. It's got to be the ballot or the bullet. The ballot or the bullet. If you're afraid to use an expression like that, you should get on out of the country, you should get back in the cotton patch, you should get back in the alley. They get all the Negro vote, and after they get it, the Negro gets nothing in return. All they did when they got to Washington was give a few big Negroes big jobs. Those big Negroes didn't need big jobs, they already had jobs. That's camouflage, that's trickery, that's treachery, window-dressing. I'm not trying to knock out the Democrats for the Republicans, we'll get to them in a minute. But it is true—you put the Democrats first and the Democrats put you last.

Look at it the way it is. What alibis do they use, since they control Congress and the Senate? What alibi do they use when you and I ask, "Well, when are you going to keep your promise?" They blame the Dixiecrats. What is a Dixiecrat? A Democrat. A Dixiecrat is nothing but a Democrat in disguise. The titular head of the Democrats is also the head of the Dixiecrats, because the Dixiecrats are a part of the Democratic Party. The Democrats have never kicked the Dixiecrats out of the party. The Dixiecrats bolted themselves once, but the Democrats didn't put them out. Imagine, these lowdown Southern Segregationists put the Northern Democrats down. But the Northern Democrats have never put the Dixiecrats down. No, look at that thing the way it is. They have got a con game going on, a political con game, and you and I are in the middle. It's time for you and me to wake up and start looking at it like it is, and trying to understand it like it is; and then we can deal with it like it is.

The Dixiecrats in Washington, D.C., control the key committees that run the government. The reason the Dixiecrats control these committees is because they have seniority. The only reason they have seniority is because they come from states where Negroes can't vote. This is not even a government that's based on democracy. It is not a government that is made up of representatives of the people. Half of the people in the South can't even vote. Eastland is not even supposed to be in Washington. Half of the senators and congressmen who occupy these key positions in Washington, D.C., are there illegally, are there unconstitutionally.

I was in Washington, D.C., a week ago Thursday, when they were debating whether or not they should let the bill come onto the floor. And in the back of the room where the Senate meets, there's a huge map of the United States, and on that map it shows the location of Negroes throughout the country. And it shows that the Southern section of the country, the states that are most heavily concentrated with Negroes, are the ones that have Senators and Congressmen standing up filibustering and doing all other kinds of trickery to keep the Negro from being able to vote. This is pitiful. But it's not pitiful for us any longer; it's actually pitiful for the white man, because soon now, as the Negro awakens a little more and sees the vise that he's in, sees the bag that he's in, sees the real game that he's in, then the Negro's going to develop a new tactic.

These Senators and Congressmen actually violate the constitutional amendments that guarantee the people of that particular state or county the right to vote. And the Constitution itself has within it the machinery to expel any representative from a state where the voting rights of the people are violated. You don't even need new legislation. Any person in Congress right now, who is there from a state or a district where the voting rights of the people are violated, that particular person should be expelled from Congress. And when you expel him, you've removed one of the obstacles in the path of any real meaningful legislation in this country. In fact, when you expel them, you don't need new legislation, because they will be replaced by black representatives from counties and districts where the black man is in the majority, not in the minority.

If the black man in these Southern states had his full voting rights, the key Dixiecrats in Washington, D.C., which means the key Democrats in Washington, D.C., would lose their seats. The Democratic Party itself would lose its power. It would cease to be powerful as a party. When you see the amount of power that would be lost by the Democratic Party if it were to lose the Dixiecrat wing, or branch, or element, you can see where it's against the interests of the Democrats to give voting rights to Negroes in states where the Democrats have been in complete power and authority ever since the Civil War. You just can't belong to that party without analyzing it.

I say again, I'm not anti-Democrat, I'm not anti-Republican, I'm not anti-anything. I'm just questioning their sincerity, and some of the strategy that they've been using on our people by promising them promises that they don't intend to keep. When you keep the Democrats in power, you're keeping the Dixiecrats in power. I doubt that my good Brother Lomax will deny that. A vote for a Democrat is a vote for a Dixiecrat. That's why, in 1964, it's time now for you and me to become more politically mature and realize what the ballot is for; what we're supposed to get when we cast a ballot; and that if we don't cast a ballot, it's going to end up in a situation where we're going to have to cast a bullet. It's either a ballot or a bullet.

In the North, they do it a different way. They have a system that's known as gerrymandering, whatever that means. It means when Negroes become too heavily concentrated in a certain area, and begin to gain too much political power, the white man comes along and changes the district lines. You may say, "Why do you keep saying white man?" Because it's the white man who does it. I haven't ever seen any Negro changing any lines. They don't let him get near the line. It's the white man who does this. And usually, it's the white man who grins at you the most, and pats you on the back, and is supposed to be your friend. He may be friendly, but he's not your friend.

So, what I'm trying to impress upon you, in essence, is this: You and I in America are faced with a government conspiracy. Everyone who's filibustering is a Senator—that's the government. Everyone who's finagling in Washington, D.C., is a Congressman—that's the government. You don't have anybody putting blocks in your path but people who are a part of the government. The same government that you go abroad to fight for and die for is the government that is in a conspiracy to deprive you of your voting rights, deprive you of your economic opportunities, deprive you of decent housing, deprive you of decent education. You don't need to go to the employer alone, it is the government itself, the government of America, that is responsible for the oppression and exploitation and degradation of black people in this country. And you should drop it in their lap. This government has failed the Negro. This so-called democracy has failed the Negro. And all these white liberals have definitely failed the Negro.

So, where do we go from here? First, we need some friends. We need some new allies. The entire civil rights struggle needs a new interpretation, a broader interpretation. We need to look at this civil rights thing from another angle—from the inside as well as from the outside. To those of us whose philosophy is black nationalism, the only way you can get involved in the civil rights struggle is give it a new interpretation. That old interpretation excluded us. It kept us out. So, we're giving a new interpretation to the civil rights struggle, an interpretation that will enable us to come into it, take part in it. And these handkerchief-heads who have been dillydallying and pussyfooting and compromising—we don't intend to let them pussyfoot and dillydally and compromise any longer.

How can you thank a man for giving you what's already yours? How then can you thank him for giving you only part of what's already yours? You haven't even made progress, if what's being given to you, you should have had already. That's not progress. And I love my Brother Lomax, the way he pointed out we're right back where we were in 1954. We're not even as far up as we were in 1954. We're behind where we were in 1954. There's more segregation now than there were in 1954. There's more racial animosity, more racial hatred, more racial violence today in 1964, than there was in 1954. Where is the progress?

And now you're facing a situation where the young Negro's coming up. They don't want to hear that "turn-the-other-cheek" stuff, no. In Jacksonville, those were teenagers, they were throwing Molotov cocktails. Negroes have never done that before. But it shows you there's a new deal coming in. There's new thinking coming in. There's new strategy coming in. It'll be Molotov cocktails this month, hand grenades next month, and something else next month. It'll be ballots, or it'll be bullets. It'll be liberty, or it will be death. The only difference about this kind of death—it'll be reciprocal. You know what is meant by "reciprocal"? That's one of Brother Lomax's words, I stole it from him. I don't usually deal with those big words because I don't usually deal with big people. I deal with small people. I find you can get a whole lot of small people and whip hell out of a whole lot of big people. They haven't got anything to lose, and they've got everything to gain. And they'll let you know in a minute: "It takes two to tango; when I go, you go."

The black nationalists, those whose philosophy is black nationalism, in bringing about this new interpretation of the entire meaning of civil rights, look upon it as meaning, as Brother Lomax has pointed out, equality of opportunity. Well, we're justified in seeking civil rights, if it means equality of opportunity, because all we're doing there is trying to collect for our investment. Our mothers and fathers invested sweat and blood. Three hundred and ten years we worked in this country without a dime in return—I mean without a dime in return. You let the white man walk around here talking about how rich this country is, but you never stop to think how it got rich so quick. It got rich because you made it rich.

You take the people who are in this audience right now. They're poor, we're all poor as individuals. Our weekly salary individually amounts to hardly anything. But if you take the salary of everyone in here collectively it'll fill up a whole lot of baskets. It's a lot of wealth. If you can collect the wages of just these people right here for a year, you'll be rich—richer than rich. When you look at it like that, think how rich Uncle Sam had to become, not with this handful, but millions of black people. Your and my mother and father, who didn't work an eight-hour shift, but worked from "can't see" in the morning until "can't see" at night, and worked for nothing, making the white man rich, making Uncle Sam rich.

This is our investment. This is our contribution—our blood. Not only did we give of our free labor, we gave of our blood. Every time he had a call to arms, we were the first ones in uniform. We died on every battlefield the white man had. We have made a greater sacrifice than anybody who's standing up in America today. We have made a greater contribution and have collected less. Civil rights, for those of us whose philosophy is black nationalism, means: "Give it to us now. Don't wait for next year. Give it to us yesterday, and that's not fast enough."

I might stop right here to point out one thing. Whenever you're going after something that belongs to you, anyone who's depriving you of the right to have it is a criminal. Understand that. Whenever you are going after something that is yours, you are within your legal rights to lay claim to it. And anyone who puts forth any effort to deprive you of that which is yours, is breaking the law, is a criminal. And this was pointed out by the Supreme Court decision. It outlawed segregation. Which means segregation is against the law. Which means a segregationist is breaking the law. A segregationist is a criminal. You can't label him as anything other than that. And when you demonstrate against segregation, the law is on your side. The Supreme Court is on your side.

Now, who is it that opposes you in carrying out the law? The police department itself. With police dogs and clubs. Whenever you demonstrate against segregation, whether it is segregated education, segregated housing, or anything else, the law is on your side, and anyone who stands in the way is not the law any longer. They are breaking the law, they are not representatives of the law. Any time you demonstrate against segregation and a man has the audacity to put a police dog on you, kill that dog, kill him, I'm telling you, kill that dog. I say it, if they put me in jail tomorrow, kill—that—dog. Then you'll put a stop to it. Now, if these white people in here don't want to see that kind of action, get down and tell the mayor to tell the police department to pull the dogs in. That's all you have to do. If you don't do it, someone else will.

If you don't take this kind of stand, your little children will grow up and look at you and think "shame." If you don't take an uncompromising stand—I don't mean go out and get violent; but at the same time you should never be nonviolent unless you run into some nonviolence. I'm nonviolent with those who are nonviolent with me. But when you drop that violence on me, then you've made me go insane, and I'm not responsible for what I do. And that's the way every Negro should get. Any time you know you're within the law, within your legal rights, within your moral rights, in accord with justice, then die for what you believe in. But don't die alone. Let your dying be reciprocal. This is what is meant by equality. What's good for the goose is good for the gander.

When we begin to get in this area, we need new friends, we need new allies. We need to expand the civil rights struggle to a higher level—to the level of human rights. Whenever you are in a civil rights struggle, whether you know it or not, you are confining yourself to the jurisdiction of Uncle Sam. No one from the outside world can speak out in your behalf as long as your struggle is a civil rights struggle. Civil rights comes within the domestic affairs of this country. All of our African brothers and our Asian brothers and our Latin-American brothers cannot open their mouths and interfere in the domestic affairs of the United States. And as long as it's civil rights, this comes under the jurisdiction of Uncle Sam.

But the United Nations has what's known as the charter of human rights, it has a committee that deals in human rights. You may wonder why all of the atrocities that have been committed in Africa and in Hungary and in Asia and in Latin America are brought before the UN, and the Negro problem is never brought before the UN. This is part of the conspiracy. This old, tricky, blue-eyed liberal who is supposed to be your and my friend, supposed to be in our corner, supposed to be subsidizing our struggle, and supposed to be acting in the capacity of an adviser, never tells you anything about human rights. They keep you wrapped up in civil rights. And you spend so much time barking up the civil rights tree, you don't even know there's a human rights tree on the same floor.

When you expand the civil rights struggle to the level of human rights, you can then take the case of the black man in this country before the nations in the UN. You can take it before the General Assembly. You can take Uncle Sam before a world court. But the only level you can do it on is the level of human rights. Civil rights keeps you under his restrictions, under his jurisdiction. Civil rights keeps you in his pocket. Civil rights means you're asking Uncle Sam to treat you right. Human rights are something you were born with. Human rights are your God-given rights. Human rights are the rights that are recognized by all nations of this earth. And any time any one violates your human rights, you can take them to the world court. Uncle Sam's hands are dripping with blood, dripping with the blood of the black man in this country. He's the earth's number one hypocrite. He has the audacity— yes, he has—imagine him posing as the leader of the free world. The free world!—and you over here singing "We Shall Overcome." Expand the civil rights struggle to the level of human rights, take it into the United Nations, where our African brothers can throw their weight on our side, where our Latin-American brothers can throw their weight on our side, and where 800 million Chinamen are sitting there waiting to throw their weight on our side.

Let the world know how bloody his hands are. Let the world know the hypocrisy that's practiced over here. Let it be the ballot or the bullet. Let him know that it must be the ballot or the bullet.

When you take your case to Washington, D.C., you're taking it to the criminal who's responsible; it's like running from the wolf to the fox. They're all in cahoots together. They all work political chicanery and make you look like a chump before the eyes of the world. Here you are walking around in America, getting ready to be drafted and sent abroad, like a tin soldier, and when you get over there, people ask you what are you fighting for, and you have to stick your tongue in your cheek. No, take Uncle Sam to court, take him before the world.

By ballot I only mean freedom. Don't you know—I disagree with Lomax on this issue—that the ballot is more important than the dollar? Can I prove it? Yes. Look in the UN. There are poor nations in the UN; yet those poor nations can get together with their voting power and keep the rich nations from making a move. They have one nation—one vote, everyone has an equal vote. And when those brothers from Asia, and Africa and the darker parts of this earth get together, their voting power is sufficient to hold Sam in check. Or Russia in check. Or some other section of the earth in check. So, the ballot is most important.

Right now, in this country, if you and I, 22 million African-Americans— that's what we are—Africans who are in America. You're nothing but Africans. Nothing but Africans. In fact, you'd get farther calling yourself African instead of Negro. Africans don't catch hell. You're the only one catching hell. They don't have to pass civil rights bills for Africans. An African can go anywhere he wants right now. All you've got to do is tie your head up. That's right, anywhere you want. Just stop being a Negro. Change your name to Hoogagagooba. That'll show you how silly the white man is. You're dealing with a silly man. A friend of mine who's very dark put a turban on his head and went into a restaurant in Atlanta before they called themselves desegregated. He went into a white restaurant, he sat down, they served him, and he said, what would happen if a Negro came in here?" And there he's sitting, black as night, but because he had his head wrapped up the waitress looked back at him and says, "Why, there wouldn't no nigger dare come in here."

So, you're dealing with a man whose bias and prejudice are making him lose his mind, his intelligence, every day. He's frightened. He looks around and sees what's taking place on this earth, and he sees that the pendulum of time is swinging in your direction. The dark people are waking up. They're losing their fear of the white man. No place where he's fighting right now is he winning. Everywhere he's fighting, he's fighting someone of your and my complexion. And they're beating him. He can't win any more. He's won his last battle. He failed to win the Korean War. He couldn't win it. He had to sign a truce. That's a loss. Any time Uncle Sam, with all his machinery for warfare, is held to a draw by some rice-eaters, he's lost the battle. He had to sign a truce. America's not supposed to sign a truce. She's supposed to be bad. But she's not bad any more. She's bad as long as she can use her hydrogen bomb, but she can't use hers for fear Russia might use hers. Russia can't use hers, for fear that Sam might use his. So, both of them are weaponless. They can't use the weapon because each's weapon nullifies the other's. So the only place where action can take place is on the ground. And the white man can't win another war fighting on the ground. Those days are over. The black man knows it, the brown man knows it, the red man knows it, and the yellow man knows it. So they engage him in guerrilla warfare. That's not his style. You've got to have heart to be a guerrilla warrior, and he hasn't got any heart. I'm telling you now.

I just want to give you a little briefing on guerrilla warfare because, before you know it, before you know it—it takes heart to be a guerrilla warrior because you're on your own. In conventional warfare you have tanks and a whole lot of other people with you to back you up, planes over your head and all that kind of stuff. But a guerrilla is on his own. All you have is a rifle, some sneakers and a bowl of rice, and that's all you need—and a lot of heart. The Japanese on some of those islands in the Pacific, when the American soldiers landed, one Japanese sometimes could hold the whole army off. He'd just wait until the sun went down, and when the sun went down they were all equal. He would take his little blade and slip from bush to bush, and from American to American. The white soldiers couldn't cope with that. Whenever you see a white soldier that fought in the Pacific, he has the shakes, he has a nervous condition, because they scared him to death.

The same thing happened to the French up in French Indochina. People who just a few years previously were rice farmers got together and ran the heavily-mechanized French army out of Indochina. You don't need it—modern warfare today won't work. This is the day of the guerrilla. They did the same thing in Algeria. Algerians, who were nothing but Bedouins, took a rifle and sneaked off to the hills, and de Gaulle and all of his highfalutin' war machinery couldn't defeat those guerrillas. Nowhere on this earth does the white man win in a guerrilla warfare. It's not his speed. Just as guerrilla warfare is prevailing in Asia and in parts of Africa and in parts of Latin America, you've got to be mighty naive, or you've got to play the black man cheap, if you don't think some day he's going to wake up and find that it's got to be the ballot or the bullet.

I would like to say, in closing, a few things concerning the Muslim Mosque, Inc., which we established recently in New York City. It's true we're Muslims and our religion is Islam, but we don't mix our religion with our politics and our economics and our social and civil activities—not any more. We keep our religion in our mosque. After our religious services are over, then as Muslims we become involved in political action, economic action and social and civic action. We become involved with anybody, anywhere, any time and in any manner that's designed to eliminate the evils, the political, economic and social evils that are afflicting the people of our community. The political philosophy of black nationalism means that the black man should control the politics and the politicians in his own community; no more. The black man in the black community has to be re-educated into the science of politics so he will know what politics is supposed to bring him in return. Don't be throwing out any ballots. A ballot is like a bullet. You don't throw your ballots until you see a target, and if that target is not within your reach, keep your ballot in your pocket. The political philosophy of black nationalism is being taught in the Christian church. It's being taught in the NAACP. It's being taught in CORE meetings. It's being taught in SNCC meetings. It's being taught in Muslim meetings. It's being taught where nothing but atheists and agnostics come together. It's being taught everywhere. Black people are fed up with the dillydallying, pussyfooting, compromising approach that we've been using toward getting our freedom. We want freedom now, but we're not going to get it saying "We Shall Overcome." We've got to fight until we overcome.

The economic philosophy of black nationalism is pure and simple. It only means that we should control the economy of our community. Why should white people be running all the stores in our community? Why should white people be running the banks of our community? Why should the economy of our community be in the hands of the white man? Why? If a black man can't move his store into a white community, you tell me why a white man should move his store into a black community. The philosophy of black nationalism involves a re-education program in the black community in regards to economics. Our people have to be made to see that any time you take your dollar out of your community and spend it in a community where you don't live, the community where you live will get poorer and poorer, and the community where you spend your money will get richer and richer. Then you wonder why where you live is always a ghetto or a slum area. And where you and I are concerned, not only do we lose it when we spend it out of the community, but the white man has got all our stores in the community tied up; so that though we spend it in the community, at sundown the man who runs the store takes it over across town somewhere. He's got us in a vise.

So the economic philosophy of black nationalism means in every church, in every civic organization, in every fraternal order, it's time now for our people to become conscious of the importance of controlling the economy of our community. If we own the stores, if we operate the businesses, if we try and establish some industry in our own community, then we're developing to the position where we are creating employment for our own kind. Once you gain control of the economy of your own community, then you don't have to picket and boycott and beg some cracker downtown for a job in his business. The social philosophy of black nationalism only means that we have to get together and remove the evils, the vices, alcoholism, drug addiction, and other evils that are destroying the moral fiber of our community. We ourselves have to lift the level of our community, the standard of our community to a higher level, make our own society beautiful so that we will be satisfied in our own social circles and won't be running around here trying to knock our way into a social circle where we're not wanted.

So I say, in spreading a gospel such as black nationalism, it is not designed to make the black man re-evaluate the white man—you know him already—but to make the black man re-evaluate himself. Don't change the white man's mind—you can't change his mind, and that whole thing about appealing to the moral conscience of America—America's conscience is bankrupt. She lost all conscience a long time ago. Uncle Sam has no conscience. They don't know what morals are. They don't try and eliminate an evil because it's evil, or because it's illegal, or because it's immoral; they eliminate it only when it threatens their existence. So you're wasting your time appealing to the moral conscience of a bankrupt man like Uncle Sam. If he had a conscience, he'd straighten this thing out with no more pressure being put upon him. So it is not necessary to change the white man's mind. We have to change our own mind. You can't change his mind about us. We've got to change our own minds about each other. We have to see each other with new eyes. We have to see each other as brothers and sisters. We have to come together with warmth so we can develop unity and harmony that's necessary to get this problem solved ourselves. How can we do this? How can we avoid jealousy? How can we avoid suspicion and the divisions that exist in the community? I'll tell you how.

I have watched how Billy Graham comes into a city, spreading what he calls the gospel of Christ, which is only white nationalism. That's what he is. Billy Graham is a white nationalist; I'm a black nationalist. But since it's the natural tendency for leaders to be jealous and look upon a powerful figure like Graham with suspicion and envy, how is it possible for him to come into a city and get all the cooperation of the church leaders? Don't think because they're church leaders that they don't have weaknesses that make them envious and jealous—no, everybody's got it. It's not an accident that when they want to choose a cardinal [as Pope] over there in Rome, they get in a closet so you can't hear them cussing and fighting and carrying on.

Billy Graham comes in preaching the gospel of Christ, he evangelizes the gospel, he stirs everybody up, but he never tries to start a church. If he came in trying to start a church, all the churches would be against him. So, he just comes in talking about Christ and tells everybody who gets Christ to go to any church where Christ is; and in this way the church cooperates with him. So we're going to take a page from his book.

Our gospel is black nationalism. We're not trying to threaten the existence of any organization, but we're spreading the gospel of black nationalism. Anywhere there's a church that is also preaching and practicing the gospel of black nationalism, join that church. If the NAACP is preaching and practicing the gospel of black nationalism, join the NAACP. If CORE is spreading and practicing the gospel of black nationalism, join CORE. Join any organization that has a gospel that's for the uplift of the black man. And when you get into it and see them pussyfooting or compromising, pull out of it because that's not black nationalism. We'll find another one.

And in this manner, the organizations will increase in number and in quantity and in quality, and by August, it is then our intention to have a black nationalist convention which will consist of delegates from all over the country who are interested in the political, economic and social philosophy of black nationalism. After these delegates convene, we will hold a seminar, we will hold discussions, we will listen to everyone. We want to hear new ideas and new solutions and new answers. And at that time, if we see fit then to form a black nationalist party, we'll form a black nationalist party. If it's necessary to form a black nationalist army, we'll form a black nationalist army. It'll be the ballot or the bullet. It'll be liberty or it'll be death.

It's time for you and me to stop sitting in this country, letting some cracker senators, Northern crackers and Southern crackers, sit there in Washington, D.C., and come to a conclusion in their mind that you and I are supposed to have civil rights. There's no white man going to tell me anything about my rights. Brothers and sisters, always remember, if it doesn't take senators and congressmen and presidential proclamations to give freedom to the white man, it is not necessary for legislation or proclamation or Supreme Court decisions to give freedom to the black man. You let that white man know, if this is a country of freedom, let it be a country of freedom; and if it's not a country of freedom, change it.

We will work with anybody, anywhere, at any time, who is genuinely interested in tackling the problem head-on, nonviolently as long as the enemy is nonviolent, but violent when the enemy gets violent. We'll work with you on the voter-registration drive, we'll work with you on rent strikes, we'll work with you on school boycotts. I don't believe in any kind of integration; I'm not even worried about it because I know you're not going to get it anyway; you're not going to get it because you're afraid to die; you've got to be ready to die if you try and force yourself on the white man, because he'll get just as violent as those crackers in Mississippi, right here in Cleveland. But we will still work with you on the school boycotts because we're against a segregated school system. A segregated school system produces children who, when they graduate, graduate with crippled minds. But this does not mean that a school is segregated because it's all black. A segregated school means a school that is controlled by people who have no real interest in it whatsoever.

Let me explain what I mean. A segregated district or community is a community in which people live, but outsiders control the politics and the economy of that community. They never refer to the white section as a segregated community. It's the all-Negro section that's a segregated community. Why? The white man controls his own school, his own bank, his own economy, his own politics, his own everything, his own community—but he also controls yours. When you're under someone else's control, you're segregated. They'll always give you the lowest or the worst that there is to offer, but it doesn't mean you're segregated just because you have your own. You've got to control your own. Just like the white man has control of his, you need to control yours.

You know the best way to get rid of segregation? The white man is more afraid of separation than he is of integration. Segregation means that he puts you away from him, but not far enough for you to be out of his jurisdiction; separation means you're gone. And the white man will integrate faster than he'll let you separate. So we will work with you against the segregated school system because it's criminal, because it is absolutely destructive, in every way imaginable, to the minds of the children who have to be exposed to that type of crippling education.

Last but not least, I must say this concerning the great controversy over rifles and shotguns. The only thing that I've ever said is that in areas where the government has proven itself either unwilling or unable to defend the lives and the property of Negroes, it's time for Negroes to defend themselves. Article number two of the constitutional amendments provides you and me the right to own a rifle or a shotgun. It is constitutionally legal to own a shotgun or a rifle. This doesn't mean you're going to get a rifle and form battalions and go out looking for white folks, although you'd be within your rights—I mean, you'd be justified; but that would be illegal and we don't do anything illegal. If the white man doesn't want the black man buying rifles and shotguns, then let the government do its job. That's all. And don't let the white man come to you and ask you what you think about what Malcolm says—why, you old Uncle Tom. He would never ask you if he thought you were going to say, "Amen!" No, he is making a Tom out of you.

So, this doesn't mean forming rifle clubs and going out looking for people, but it is time, in 1964, if you are a man, to let that man know. If he's not going to do his job in running the government and providing you and me with the protection that our taxes are supposed to be for, since he spends all those billions for his defense budget, he certainly can't begrudge you and me spending $12 or $15 for a single shot, or double-action. I hope you understand. Don't go out shooting people, but any time, brothers and sisters, and especially the men in this audience—some of you wearing Congressional Medals of Honor, with shoulders this wide, chests this big, muscles that big—any time you and I sit around and read where they bomb a church and murder in cold blood, not some grown-ups, but four little girls while they were praying to the same god the white man taught them to pray to, and you and I see the government go down and can't find who did it.

Why, this man—he can find Eichmann hiding down in Argentina somewhere. Let two or three American soldiers, who are minding somebody else's business way over in South Vietnam, get killed, and he'll send battleships, sticking his nose in their business. He wanted to send troops down to Cuba and make them have what he calls free elections—this old cracker who doesn't have free elections in his own country. No, if you never see me another time in your life, if I die in the morning, I'll die saying one thing: the ballot or the bullet, the ballot or the bullet.

If a Negro in 1964 has to sit around and wait for some cracker Senator to filibuster when it comes to the rights of black people, why, you and I should hang our heads in shame. You talk about a march on Washington in 1963, you haven't seen anything. There's some more going down in '64. And this time, they're not going like they went last year. They're not going singing "We Shall Overcome." They're not going with white friends. They're not going with placards already painted for them. They're not going with round-trip tickets. They're going with one-way tickets.

And if they don't want that non-violent army going down there, tell them to bring the filibuster to a halt. The black nationalists are going to wait. Lyndon B. Johnson is the head of the Democratic Party. If he's for civil rights, let him go into the Senate next week and declare himself. Let him go in there right now and declare himself. Let him go in there and denounce the Southern branch of his party. Let him go in there right now and take a moral stand—right now, not later. Tell him, don't wait until election time. If he waits too long, brothers and sisters, he will be responsible for letting a condition develop in this country which will create a climate that will bring seeds up out of the ground with vegetation on the end of them looking like something these people never dreamt of. In 1964, it's the ballot or the bullet. Thank you.

PAUSE

What do you find striking about Malcolm X's speech? Where do you find yourself agreeing? Where do you find yourself resisting his argument?

Introduction

Malcolm X is making a powerful argument that, unfortunately, remains highly relevant today. Though the argument is long and touches on several topics related to the particular context for the speech, Malcolm X boils it down to the single memorable line that gives the speech its name: the ballot or the bullet.

Unlike some of the arguments we examine in this book, Malcolm X does not spend much time in this speech presenting detailed evidence or extended examples. This is not to say Malcolm X relies on assertions without evidence, or that his examples are insufficient, but rather that he chooses to develop only those arguments he expects need elucidation—either because the audience may not be familiar with the issue, or because they may be resistant to the argument. Much of the time, however, Malcolm X seems to anticipate that the audience will be willing to assent to his premises, without persuasion. Why is this?

Sometimes we don't need to spend as much time providing reasons for our claims when we know we are engaging a friendly audience, one that we know is likely to accept our claims on their face. This is what is meant by preaching to the choir. But is Malcolm X preaching to the choir here? Is he making an argument that is likely to be accepted, immediately, without reasons?

The argument Malcolm X is making—that if white Americans refuse to accept the voting rights of Black Americans, Black Americans will have no choice but to take up arms to win these rights by force—is an argument not likely to be taken lightly. It was a pretty provocative argument then, as it would be now. It's clear too that Malcolm X doesn't see his audience as completely friendly to his argument, as he suggests in his opening line "friends and enemies . . ." So it probably isn't the case that Malcolm X assumes his argument doesn't need much support. In fact, if we look closely we will see that he does provide support for his arguments, relying often on two distinct inference patterns: commonplaces and arguments from form.

Commonplaces

Commonplaces are widely held beliefs or culturally embedded assumptions that an audience will generally accept as true. They are typically so widespread, or so central to an audience's values, that they go without saying. Aristotle called them "storehouses of the mind." As social knowledge, sometimes commonplaces reveal blind spots or prejudices in an audience's views that ought to be examined and revealed for their limitations.

Recently, for example, I was browsing social media and saw a neighbor's post about how a particular politician was a crook. The neighbor didn't provide any evidence of criminal activity at all, but the post got plenty of likes and comments. Now, okay, I'm not so naive that I think social media represents the kind of public forum that accepts only well-reasoned arguments, but at the same time, claims that this family has criminal ties have actually become fairly widespread—despite a complete lack of evidence being called on to support that view. And I'm reminded of the 2016 presidential election, where the idea that Hillary Clinton was involved in criminal activity became so popular it gave rise to a rally chant—again, despite there being no evidence of her criminal activity. What gives? Why are people so willing to believe that this or that political figure is a criminal without any evidence?

Well, politicians are all crooks, aren't they?

That is to say, of course there are plenty of good politicians, civil servants who genuinely want to implement policies for the benefit of all. Despite this, however, deservedly so or not, many people in the United States are ready to accept the idea that politicians are self-motivated and dishonest. In fact, if you type "honest politician" into an Internet search, many of the top hits are parodies. Some suggest the term is an oxymoron.

The idea that all politicians are crooks (except for those I support), because it is generally accepted, is a commonplace. When we make arguments from commonplaces, we typically do not need to support them but can assume that our audience will accept them without evidence. The commonplaces play a role parallel to evidence—they stand in for it.

Just because commonplaces are not evidence per se does not mean they cannot be effective and justified beginnings. While any commonplace can be examined and potentially undermined, often, as is the case with Malcolm X's argument here, commonplaces represent reasonable starting points for arguments. Recall from Chapter 1 that one of the foundations of argumentation is some level of agreement: at the very least, participants in an argument must have agreement about what the controversy is and a mutual willingness to resolve their differences by providing reasons for their claims. I also suggested that there is always a level of uncertainty to argumentation because, in informal logic, we are rarely dealing with objectively established truths. Rather, we are almost always working with the beliefs of a particular audience at our starting point. Aristotle had a term to describe this audience-centered model of argumentation: the *enthymeme*.

An **enthymeme** is a logical statement used in informal argumentation, resembling the syllogism, but in which at least one of the premises is a commonplace, a socially accepted belief, and not an objective truth. As I've said in previous chapters, we rarely argue about things that are objective truths, at least not seriously. I've had students point to examples like arguments that the earth is flat, not spherical, or that the moon doesn't exist. But these are, at most, idle entertainment, not arguments most people take seriously. Most of the time when we argue, then, we begin with socially accepted beliefs like that a democratic government has certain commitments to its citizens, or that argumentation is an alternative to physical force, to point to two commonplaces Malcolm X relies on in his speech above. Most people will accept these premises without skepticism because they are widely accepted values, despite not being objective truths.

Because they are beliefs, commonplaces are not certain—they can be argued against. You might think, how could anyone argue against something that is so widely accepted that it is common sense, that it goes without saying? Well, the truth is that we humans are not entirely logical beings; we're not computers that begin with a set of rules and follow them regardless of the outcomes. Instead, we tend to hold multiple, often contradictory beliefs, and we are ready to exchange one set of values for another when it seems right to do so. For example, democratic societies like ours tend to value both unity and individual choice.

Historians point to many times when, boosted by a rhetoric of national unity, we came together to complete large projects or respond to large perceived threats. Some of you reading this book may remember the feelings of national unity that seemed to permeate U.S. culture after the 9/11 terrorist attacks, for example. At the same time, we can confidently call the United States a liberal country that values individual freedoms. We saw these two values put against each other in debates about how the United States should respond to the COVID-19 pandemic, as well. Because both of these sets of values exist simultaneously, we can make arguments drawing on either one. For example, we can make arguments drawing on the rhetoric of unity to limit individual freedoms, as was done following 9/11, in support of laws like those contained in the Patriot Act. At the same time, we can make arguments rooted in the value of individual freedoms, even if it means a decreased sense of unity. We can see examples of this with the Black Lives Matter movement, which argues for better recognition of the rights and freedoms of Black Americans, and which some opponents have tried to dismiss as divisive.

> Although commonplaces may appear unassailable, the truth is that humans often simultaneously hold multiple contradictory beliefs.

Other such pairs of contradictory values in the United States include coordination and decentralization: we want our president, for example, to function in ordered, efficient ways, but we don't want too much power concentrated in the executive branch. Egalitarianism and expertise is another such pairing. Equality of opportunity is central to the United States' self-image, but that doesn't mean we would choose our doctor for an upcoming surgery by picking a random name from among our social media contacts.

What this means is not that we humans are nonsensical and illogical, but rather that when we are faced with contradictory values, we must make choices about which set of values to privilege in a given case. It means we must make arguments. The warrant in such arguments is that the particular value is represented in the particular case.

Pragmatism vs. Principle

Commonplaces often come up in such pairs, wherein one value is pitted against the other. In the case of pragmatism vs. principle, we are forced to choose between the commonplace of **pragmatism**, which emphasizes the outcomes or consequences of our actions, and **principle**, which emphasizes standing by our ideals or beliefs, regardless of the consequences. Both of these values are common in everyday culture.

A recent court case illustrates how such commonplaces can serve as the basis for very important arguments. *Sharp v. Murphy* (2020), argued before the U.S. Supreme Court, asked the court to decide between these two commonplaces. The case involved a murder that occurred in Oklahoma. Much of the eastern half of Oklahoma was historically a Native American reservation that was never dissolved. At issue in the case was whether or not the state of Oklahoma had standing to prosecute the murder, or whether the case should be handled by the tribal courts. On the one hand, lawyers representing the convicted murderer and member of the Muscogee-Creek tribe argued that, as the crime took place on tribal land and was committed by a member of the tribe, the case ought to be decided by a federal court. On the other hand, lawyers representing Sharp and the state of Oklahoma argued that if the Supreme Court decided in favor of Murphy, it would leave Oklahoma without jurisdiction to prosecute crimes in nearly all of the eastern part of the state, which includes Tulsa, the state's second-largest city. The stasis here is not (1) fact: whether or not Murphy is guilty of the murder, nor (2) definition: whether or not it is rightfully called a murder, nor (3) quality: whether or not the murder was justified, but rather (4) place: what is the appropriate place for the case to be decided?

The line of argument advanced by Murphy is rooted in principle: if the federal government, and not the state of Oklahoma, has jurisdiction over all such crimes occurring on tribal lands, and if Congress never dissolved the reservation covering most of eastern Oklahoma, then on principle the federal government has jurisdiction here. The principle here is that the sovereignty of tribal lands with respect to the states must be upheld.

The line of argument advanced by Sharp is rooted in pragmatism: if the state of Oklahoma is found not to have jurisdiction in this particular case, then they by extension would not have jurisdiction in any future case taking place on nearly three million acres of the state, including most of Tulsa. The practical implications here, they argued, could be disastrous for the state, as it would prevent them from exercising judicial authority in much of the state. Further, it would give rise to a number of other practical concerns. If the state loses jurisdiction in this area, then who would be responsible for collecting taxes? for law enforcement? for issuing permits, licenses, and so on?

Malcolm X frequently appeals to principle throughout his speech, such as the principle represented in the aphorism "What's good for the goose is good for the gander." Here Malcolm X raises the principle of justice or fairness, that people who are essentially alike should be treated alike. At other points he takes a more pragmatic view, such as when he argues that, practically, Black people in America are not Americans, or that it may be more expedient to pursue the rights of Black people in America under the aegis of human rights, rather than civil rights. Implicit in each of these arguments—whether from principle on the one hand or pragmatism on the other—is the converse of that commonplace, even if the speech does not make that tension explicit.

Quantity vs. Quality

Another common pair of commonplaces is that of quantity vs. quality. The commonplace of **quantity** values achieving the greatest good, for the greatest number, at the least cost. The commonplace of **quality** values that which is unique, unusual, or irreplaceable.

An example of a controversy that pits quantity against quality might be to what extent we should develop a particular marsh. The argument from quantity might be that we need to develop this marsh to provide jobs to an economically depressed area. The argument from quality might be that we cannot develop this marsh because it is home to a particularly rare species of bird.

Other pairs of commonplaces include egalitarianism vs. expertise or authority, care for others vs. loyalty to one's own group, and unity vs. individual choice.

Arguments from Form

While commonplaces play a noticeable role in Malcolm X's argument, his central inference involves presenting two options, with seemingly no alternative: the ballot or the bullet. "If we don't do something real soon, I think you'll have to agree that we're going to be forced either to use the ballot or the bullet," he writes. His argument is that if Black people in America do not achieve the freedoms guaranteed them by the Constitution—including but not limited to the right to a representative government selected and certified through a free vote—then violence may be the only alternative.

Malcolm X repeats this pair of alternatives frequently throughout the piece—the ballot or the bullet—which also provides the title to the piece. Well, what does this argument pattern remind you of, "either this or that"? It looks very similar to a disjunctive syllogism, doesn't it? The disjunctive syllogism, you'll recall from Chapter 2, is a type of formal reasoning that presents two alternatives, and then either denies or accepts one alternative or the other. So, for example, either we'll take the highway to the lake, or else we'll take the winding lane. We also learned that, in a valid disjunctive syllogism, accepting one alternative typically means rejecting the other. We took the highway; therefore, we did not take the winding lane. Or we took the winding lane; therefore, we did not take the highway.

The type of reasoning Malcolm X is using here is not formal reasoning but rather a type of informal inference pattern known as the argument from form. An **argument from form** is an inference pattern that resembles a deductive or formal argument but is actually informal. What makes Malcolm X's argument informal rather than formal? The key distinction between formal and informal arguments, you'll recall, is that formal arguments involve conclusions that contain no new information and follow with certainty from the premises, whereas informal arguments involve conclusions that contain new information and follow their premises only with some degree of probability. Malcolm X's conclusion here, that the right to vote needs to not only be free and unencumbered but also lead to real, visible change for the voters, and that this right is very, very important, follows not with certainty but only with a degree of probability from the premises.

> Arguments from form appear to follow the patterns—and thus the necessity—of formal logic, but in reality they are claims that require acceptance of an audience for their validity.

Dilemma

Malcom X's argument is an example of a dilemma, which looks like a disjunctive syllogism. In a **dilemma** the audience is presented with alternatives, each of which leads to negative outcomes. In this case, we have either the status quo, which leads to the continued disenfranchisement of Black Americans, or violence, which could lead to the destruction of human lives. Neither of those being particularly attractive alternatives, Malcolm X argues for significant, real, and immediate political changes—including the repeal of laws and the change of policies that keep Black Americans from voting, especially in the South.

The inference in a dilemma is that the options presented are exhaustive—they represent the entire range of possible options. In a disjunctive syllogism this is indeed the case, but in the dilemma, because we are dealing with real life, messy and unpredictable, there are always potentially other options. We must question whether or not there are reasonable alternatives. If no reasonable alternatives exist, then we ought to accept the conclusion. However, if we can identify preferable alternatives, then we can make an argument for these. In the case of Malcolm X's argument, perhaps there are other options in addition to doing nothing and engaging in violent resistance. Nonviolent resistance, for example, is one alternative many were arguing for around the same time as Malcolm X was making this argument. For an audience to accept the conclusion in an argument from dilemma, then, they must accept the inference that there are no alternatives beyond those presented.

> Dilemmas work by suggesting that there are a limited number of alternatives, each of which leads to negative outcomes. In reality, though, there are always other possibilities.

Hypothesis

A hypothesis is an argument from form that resembles a conditional syllogism. You'll recall from Chapter 2 that a conditional or if/then syllogism presents two statements followed by a conclusion. You'll recall also that in a valid conditional syllogism one must either accept the antecedent (the "if" part) or deny the consequent (the "then" part). So in the conditional syllogism "If Bob comes over for dinner tonight, he won't come over tomorrow," we can either accept the antecedent (Bob comes over for dinner tonight) or deny (in this case doubling the negative) the consequent (Bob does come over tomorrow).

> A *hypothesis* is a statement resembling a conditional syllogism that seeks to explain something, and which serves as a basis for scientific inquiry.

In an argument drawing on hypothesis, similarly, we make some sort of statement that seeks to explain some phenomenon/a, test that statement, and either confirm or deny the hypothesis based on the results. A **hypothesis**, then, is a statement that seeks to explain something, and which serves as a basis for scientific inquiry. Arguments relying on hypothesis are sometimes known as scientific arguments, although you can also look at argumentation in the personal and public spheres as a kind of hypothesis testing. After all, when you engage in argumentation, you work collaboratively with your audience and fellow debaters to test a range of arguments possible in response to a given controversy, to determine which has the most explanatory power, and which will lead to the best decisions.

Scientific Arguments

Scientific arguments, like arguments in general, begin not with the hypothesis but rather with a question or controversy: some unknown that matters to the participants and which they want to see resolved. The hypothesis responds to the inquiry and is tested using a method appropriate to both the inquiry and the field. For example, in 1801 the physicist Thomas Young wondered if light was made up of waves or particles. His hypothesis was that if light were made up of waves, it would behave like waves in a pond, extending outward in concentric rings. To test his hypothesis, he set up his now famous "double slit" experiment, and based on his observations he concluded that light does indeed behave like a wave.

Not all scientific inquiry proceeds as cleanly as this (and my example of Young's experiment is simplified). Often, the hypothesis does not precede the observations but is rather a response to the observations. Sometimes, in highly technical sciences, the controversy or inquiry may not be readily apparent—perhaps not even to those involved in the project.

Nevertheless, when we use the hypothesis as an inference pattern in argumentation, we make a prediction about what might happen under certain conditions and compare that prediction with observed outcomes:

Prediction: If Fido came in from the rain, we will see his muddy footprints on the floor.

Observation: There are a dog's muddy footprints on the floor.

Conclusion: Fido did come in from the rain.

While this appears like a conditional syllogism, it is important to remember that the argument from hypothesis is an example of informal argumentation and is therefore only some degree of probable, not certain.

We have to be careful, then, of a number of potential pitfalls in hypothesis arguments. First, consider the possibility that the outcomes predicted by the hypothesis may have come about anyway. In that case, the argument would not be valid. Consider, for example, the hypothesis that childhood vaccines are responsible for causing autism in children, which we looked at in Chapter 7. Wakefield showed that children in his study developed autism-like symptoms shortly after

> When we use a hypothesis as an inference pattern in argumentation, we make a prediction about what might happen under certain conditions and compare that prediction with observed outcomes.

receiving the measles, mumps, and rubella (MMR) vaccine. The problem with the line of argument here is that the vast majority of children in the UK (where the study took place) receive the MMR vaccine as toddlers, so finding that some children diagnosed with autism had received the MMR vaccine shortly prior is to be expected. But the converse is also true: many children not diagnosed with autism also received the MMR vaccine. It is not reasonable, then, to argue that the vaccine caused autism, because it is highly likely that the children in the study would have been diagnosed with autism regardless of whether or not they had received the MMR vaccine. In fact, coming to this wrong conclusion is parallel to affirming the consequent in formal logic.

Comparisons

Comparisons are arguments that present similarities and/or differences among a set of objects, situations, ideas, places, people, or phenomena. Arguments from comparison appear to be mathematical because often the comparison appears quantifiable. Comparison arguments ask us to make determinations about more or less.

Take, for example, the phrase you hear anytime a president is up for reelection: Are you better off today than you were four years ago? Well, how precisely do you measure better off? Perhaps you personally are better off, but the country is worse off. Someone who owns a debt collection business, for example, may be financially better off as the country as a whole is financially worse off.

Another common argument from comparison includes lists of the best cities to retire in, or the best colleges and universities. Often these are arguments made with lots of numerical data, and each city or college gets a numerical score. Together, this may make it seem like these are objective valuations. But of course they're not. These are value judgments, arguments made with numerical data as evidence. They may be good arguments, with a high probability of being accurate, but they are informal arguments nevertheless, lacking the certainty of formal reasoning.

Quasi-logical

Arguments from form such as those discussed above gain their power from appearing deductive. It is the form of the argument that gives them their power. Because they follow patterns that look a whole lot like common patterns of deductive logic, they can persuade audiences that the conclusions they arrive at are certain. The appearance of certainty can be very effective for an audience. However, it is important to remember that while arguments from form appear to have the certainty of formal logic, they are in fact informal arguments that have some degree of probability.

A technical term to describe these types of argument is **quasi-logical**: an argument that relies on the inference that the form justifies the conclusion in the specific case at hand. This can be a completely reasonable inference pattern, but it is important to consider whether or not the conclusion is in fact justified in the particular case. Quasi-logical arguments are similar to mathematical patterns of reasoning, such as the disjunctive or conditional syllogism or comparisons of more or less. They do not, however, meet the strict definitions of deductive logic and are therefore considered informal arguments.

Conclusion

"The Ballot or the Bullet" remains one of the most powerful speeches in American rhetoric, notable not only for its important contributions to justice for Black Americans but also for reasons personal to Malcolm X, serving as a sort of turning point in his relationship to the civil rights movement as a whole. Malcolm X uses his opening, in fact, to show his willingness to work in a large tent. Our interest in the speech here is for its effective use of the quasi-logical argument. Much of the rhetorical force of the speech comes from those arguments that closely resemble deductive arguments. While deductive arguments, when valid, make conclusions that follow from their premises with certainty, quasi-logical arguments such as those Malcolm X uses follow only with a degree of probability.

As evidence, quasi-logical arguments, such as the argument from hypothesis, are particularly effective when dealing with matters that are difficult to test in other ways.

PROBE

What is an example of a commonplace that you nevertheless disagree with? Write a paragraph that gives reasons for why you disagree.

Chapter 14
Validity and Fallacies

Key Terms

normative function
argument appraisal
hasty generalization
fallacy of composition
fallacy of division
countersign
deficiencies of clarity
equivocation
ambiguity
vagueness
fallacy of the heap
slippery slope
vacuity
circular reasoning

begging the question
digression
non sequitur
straw man
self-sealing argument
deficiencies of relevance
ad hominem
appeal to authority
appeal to popularity
appeal to tradition
appeal to ignorance
appeal to inappropriate emotion
appeal to threat
tu quoque

Key Points

- The study of argumentation involves evaluating whether or not a particular argument should convince a reasonable audience.
- Informal arguments have a set of criteria, distinct from those of formal logic, for determining whether or not an argument should be considered valid.
- Each inference pattern has its own standards of reasonableness specific to it.
- Two types of fallacy, deficiencies of clarity and deficiencies of relevance, may occur in any type of argument, regardless of the inference pattern.

PRIME

What are some fallacies you've heard already? Make a list.

Supremacy Crimes

Gloria Steinem (1999)

You've seen the ocean of television coverage, you've read the headlines: "How to Spot a Troubled Kid," "Twisted Teens," "When Teens Fall Apart."

After the slaughter in Colorado that inspired those phrases, dozens of copycat threats were reported in the same generalized way: "Junior high students charged with conspiracy to kill students and teachers" (in Texas); "Five honor students overheard planning a June graduation bombing" (in New York); "More than 100 minor threats reported statewide" (in Pennsylvania). In response, the White House held an emergency strategy session titled "Children, Violence, and Responsibility." Nonetheless, another attack was soon reported: "Youth with 2 Guns Shoots 6 at Georgia School."

I don't know about you, but I've been talking back to the television set, waiting for someone to tell us the obvious: it's not "youth," "our children," or "our teens." It's our sons—and "our" can usually be read as "white," "middle class," and "heterosexual."

We know that hate crimes, violent and otherwise, are overwhelmingly committed by white men who are apparently straight. The same is true for an even higher percentage of impersonal, resentment-driven, mass killings like those in Colorado; the sort committed for no economic or rational gain except the need to say, "I'm superior because I can kill." Think of Charles Starkweather, who reported feeling powerful and serene after murdering ten women and men in the 1950s; or the shooter who climbed the University of Texas Tower in 1966, raining down death to gain celebrity. Think of the engineering student at the University of Montreal who resented females' ability to study that subject, and so shot to death 14 women students in 1989, while saying, "I'm against feminism." Think of nearly all those who have killed impersonally in the workplace, the post office, McDonald's.

White males—usually intelligent, middle class, and heterosexual, or trying desperately to appear so—also account for virtually all the serial, sexually motivated, sadistic killings, those characterized by stalking, imprisoning, torturing, and "owning" victims in death. Think of Edmund Kemper, who began by killing animals, then murdered his grandparents, yet was released to sexually torture and dismember college students and other young women until he himself decided he "didn't want to kill *all* the coeds in the world." Or David Berkowitz, the Son of Sam, who murdered *some* women in order to feel in control of *all* women. Or consider Ted Bundy, the charming, snobbish young would-be lawyer who tortured and murdered as many as 40 women, usually beautiful students who were symbols of the economic class he longed to join. As for John Wayne Gacy, he was obsessed with maintaining the public mask of masculinity, and so hid his homosexuality by killing and burying men and boys with whom he had had sex.

These "senseless" killings begin to seem less mysterious when you consider that they were committed disproportionately by white, non-poor males, the group most likely to become hooked on the drug of superiority. It's a drug pushed by a male-dominant culture that presents dominance as a natural right; a racist hierarchy that falsely elevates whiteness; a materialist society that equates superiority with possessions, and a homophobic one that empowers only one form of sexuality.

As Elliott Leyton reports in *Hunting Humans: The Rise of the Modern Multiple Murderer*, these killers see their behavior as "an appropriate—even 'manly'—response to the frustrations and disappointments that are a normal part of life." In other words, it's not their life experiences that are the problem, it's the impossible expectation of dominance to which they've become addicted.

This is not about blame. This is about causation. If anything, ending the massive cultural cover-up of supremacy crimes should make heroes out of boys and men who reject violence, especially those who reject the notion of superiority altogether. Even if one believes in a biogenetic component of male aggression, the very existence of gentle men proves that socialization can override it.

Nor is this about attributing such crimes to a single cause. Addiction to the drug of supremacy is not their only root, just the deepest and most ignored one. Additional reasons why this country has such a high rate of violence include the plentiful guns that make killing seem as unreal as a video game; male violence in the media that desensitizes viewers in much the same way that combat killers are desensitized in training; affluence that allows maximum access to violence-as-entertainment; a national history of genocide and slavery; the romanticizing of frontier violence and organized crime; not to mention extremes of wealth and poverty and the illusion that both are deserved.

But it is truly remarkable, given the relative reasons for anger at injustice in this country, that white, non-poor men have a near-monopoly on multiple killings of strangers, whether serial and sadistic or mass and random. How can we ignore this obvious fact? Others may kill to improve their own condition—in self-defense, or for money or drugs; to eliminate enemies; to declare turf in drive-by shootings; even for a jacket or a pair of sneakers—but white males addicted to supremacy kill even when it worsens their condition or ends in suicide.

Men of color and females are capable of serial and mass killings, and commit just enough to prove it. Think of Colin Ferguson, the crazed black man on the Long Island Railroad, or Wayne Williams, the young black man in Atlanta who kidnapped and killed black boys, apparently to conceal his homosexuality. Think of Aileen Carol Wuornos, the white prostitute in Florida who killed abusive johns "in self-defense," or Waneta Hoyt, the upstate New York woman who strangled her five infant children between 1965 and 1971, disguising their cause of death as sudden infant death syndrome. Such crimes are rare enough to leave a haunting refrain of belief as evoked in Pat Parker's poem "jonestown": "Black folks do not / Black folks do not / Black folks do not commit suicide." And yet they did.

Nonetheless, the proportion of serial killings that are not committed by white males is about the same as the proportion of anorexics who are not female. Yet we discuss the gender, race, and class components of anorexia, but not the role of the same factors in producing epidemics among the powerful.

The reasons are buried deep in the culture, so invisible that only by reversing our assumptions can we reveal them.

Suppose, for instance, that young black males—or any other men of color—had carried out the slaughter in Colorado. Would the media reports be so willing to describe the murderers as "our children"? Would there be so little discussion about the boys' race? Would experts be calling the motive a mystery, or condemning the high school cliques for making those young men feel like "outsiders"? Would there be the same empathy for parents who gave the murderers luxurious homes, expensive cars, even rescued them from brushes with the law? Would there be as much attention to generalized causes, such as the dangers of violent video games and recipes for bombs on the Internet?

As for the victims, if racial identities had been reversed, would racism remain so little discussed? In fact, the killers themselves said they were targeting blacks and athletes. They used a racial epithet, shot a black male student in the head, and then laughed over the fact that they could see his brain. What if *that* had been reversed?

What if these two young murderers, who were called "fags" by some of the jocks at Columbine High School, actually had been gay? Would they have got the same sympathy for being gay-baited? What if they had been lovers?

Would we hear as little about their sexuality as we now do, even though only their own homophobia could have given the word "fag" such power to humiliate them?

Take one more leap of imagination: suppose these killings had been planned and executed by young women—of any race, sexuality, or class. Would the media still be so uninterested in the role played by gender-conditioning? Would journalists assume that female murderers had suffered from being shut out of access to power in high school, so much so that they were pushed beyond their limits? What if dozens, even hundreds of young women around the country had made imitative threats—as young men have done—expressing admiration for a well-planned massacre and promising to do the same? Would we be discussing their youth more than their gender, as is the case so far with these male killers?

I think we begin to see that our national self-examination is ignoring something fundamental, precisely because it's like the air we breathe: the white male factor, the middle-class and heterosexual one, and the promise of superiority it carries. Yet this denial is self-defeating—to say the least. We will never reduce the number of violent Americans, from bullies to killers, without challenging the assumptions on which masculinity is based: that males are superior to females, that they must find a place in a male hierarchy, and that the ability to dominate *someone* is so important that even a mere insult can justify lethal revenge. There are plenty of studies to support this view. As Dr. James Gilligan concluded in *Violence: Reflections on a National Epidemic*, "If humanity is to evolve beyond the propensity toward violence . . . then it can only do so by recognizing the extent to which the patriarchal code of honor and shame generates and obligates male violence."

I think the way out can only be found through a deeper reversal: just as we as a society have begun to raise our daughters more like sons—more like whole people—we must begin to raise our sons more like our daughters—that is, to value empathy as well as hierarchy; to measure success by other people's welfare as well as their own.

But first, we have to admit and name the truth about supremacy crimes.

PAUSE

Imagine an argument that would be considered a fallacy to one audience or in one context but would be a valid argument to another audience or in another context. Explain.

Introduction

Much of this book has been about helping you learn to analyze arguments, to understand what's going on in the arguments we come into contact with. We can break the arguments down into parts, see how the parts fit together, and in doing so have a better sense of how we might respond to these arguments, or how we can put similar arguments together ourselves. Of course, we don't have to know how an argument is put together to decide whether or not we are convinced by it, nor do we have to know how an argument is put together to make arguments ourselves.

Arguments convince us or do not convince us all the time, whether or not we know how they are structured. And, as I have maintained throughout this book, we make arguments all the time—again whether or not we know exactly how we are putting them together. So you evaluated arguments and made arguments prior to reading this book or taking the class for which this book was assigned. My guess (my hope!), however, is that what you look for in a convincing argument has, or will have, changed by your having read this book, and that the types of arguments you make have likewise changed. You may not find the same types of arguments convincing, and you may have a different process and set of standards for making your own arguments.

Argument Appraisal

All this points to another element of studying argument, which is that as we study argumentation, we develop a set of standards for what arguments should look like. This aspect of argumentation is known as the **normative function** of the study of arguments, the way that by analyzing and comparing arguments we understand not only what arguments do and do not convince people but what arguments should and should not convince people. When we make judgments about what arguments would convince people if they were being reasonable— that is, exercising reason—we are engaging in **argument appraisal**. We are, in other words, deciding not just how arguments are made but what makes a good argument.

As we saw in Chapter 2, when we appraise formal arguments we make a binary decision: formal arguments are either valid or invalid. They are valid when the conclusion follows with certainty from the premises, and they are invalid when the conclusion does not follow with certainty from the premises. With informal arguments, validity is, strictly speaking, dependent on the audience. One audience may find an argument unconvincing, whereas another audience may find the same argument convincing. When the audience consists of multiple members, some of the audience will find a given argument more convincing than others.

So how do we determine whether or not an informal argument is good? There are a number of criteria, including the truth of the evidence presented and several standards of reasonableness, many of which we see operating in Steinem's piece.

Truth of the Evidence

The first criterion—and this is particularly important today, with misleading claims and "fake news" playing such a prominent role in public debate—is that the evidence presented and upon which the argument is built is true. Knowingly using false or misleading evidence is unethical, but any argument that draws on false or misleading evidence is a bad argument—whether or not the writer is aware that the evidence is false. This is why, as discussed in Chapter 7, it is so important to make sure you are drawing on reliable sources of information for your arguments.

Validity

The second criterion has to do with validity. As discussed in Chapter 3, an informal argument is valid when the relationship between the claim and the evidence is warranted. In Chapter 2 we learned that validity in formal arguments is about the form the argument takes, the relationship of claim to evidence, rather than the truth of the statements themselves. A formal argument is valid if, when the evidence is true, the claim must be true. Validity in formal arguments follows the rules relevant to that pattern of inference. In formal argumentation, fallacy means lack of validity.

Often people try to apply the rules of validity for formal argumentation to informal arguments, but as we've seen, this is not so simple. Informal argumentation is messier than formal argumentation and depends on the audience for its validity, and in informal argumentation the truth of the statements matters very much. So the definition of fallacy in the context of formal arguments does not work in the context of informal arguments. Instead, we need a definition of validity and fallacy that is not as reductive as formal logic, but which, at the same time, does not lead to the standard that any argument that will convince someone is a good argument.

Take some of the arguments Steinem is arguing against, for example. Steinem argues that the assumption that many white men have of their inherent superiority is an underlying cause of mass shootings and serial murders—crimes that have no apparent benefit to the perpetrators and are committed to give them a sense of power over others. As Steinem readily points out, there are several potential counterarguments to her resolution. One could argue, for example, that "men of color and females are capable of serial and mass killings." Steinem accepts this but argues these are the exceptions that prove the rule. Raising these exceptional cases to argue against Steinem's generalizations regarding the vast majority of cases is formally valid but not sufficiently relevant. It does not actually help us decide whether or not a sense of entitlement among white men is an underlying cause of these sorts of crimes. So there is no formal fallacy here: the structure of the counterargument is just fine. But it is not a helpful argument to consider if we accept the evidence that the vast majority of perpetrators of crimes like mass shootings and serial murders—those Steinem characterizes as "supremacy crimes"—are white men.

So the standards for informal argumentation do not come from the form they take but rather from the extent to which they support the purpose of argumentation, which is to make the best decisions possible with the knowledge we have available. Of course, this is exactly what the process of argumentation is meant to accomplish: when we debate, whether orally in front of an audience or in the pages of an Internet forum or in the opinion section of a newspaper or around the dinner table, we seek to make the best decision possible under the circumstances. Knowledge of fallacies is a shortcut here, because over centuries of argumentation we have come to recognize certain types of arguments as less likely to lead to these outcomes than others. In informal argumentation it is experience, not form, that serves as the basis for argument standards, and these are standards not of validity but of reasonableness.

REVIEW

A categorical syllogism asks us to draw circles containing each category in the syllogism to determine validity. If we know for sure where to put each part, then the argument is valid.

A conditional syllogism is valid only when it affirms the antecedent or denies the consequent.

A disjunctive syllogism is valid when it accepts one statement and rejects the other. It is invalid when it accepts both, if accepting both is not possible.

Standards of Reasonableness

Each pattern of inference has its own set of standards and deficiencies. Many of these were covered in the chapters specific to the inference pattern, so some of these will be repeated here. Others are being introduced here for the first time.

Fallacies Common to the Argument from Example

For more on the argument from example, as well as tests of this inference pattern that will help flesh out the fallacies below, take another look at Chapter 9.

Hasty Generalization

The inference in the argument from example is that the specific examples given are representative of the whole. When we make the leap from the example to the whole without sufficient evidence, when the conclusion is unwarranted based on the evidence, we are making a **hasty generalization**. In statistical examples, hasty generalizations occur when the sample size is too small given the population. As we saw in Chapter 9, there are a variety of factors that go into determining just how big a sample size you need given a population. If the sample size doesn't meet the standards discussed there, then an argument based on that statistical pattern may be making a hasty generalization.

In anecdotal examples, a hasty generalization occurs when the individual example does not actually represent the whole. My grandmother, for example, loved salt and salty foods. She loved pickled foods (which are high in salt), and salt herring, cooked with plenty of salt, and sprinkled salt liberally on her dishes—and she lived to be ninety-four! Now, while this is an accurate description of my grandmother, if I were to use her example to make the argument that a diet high in salt is not unhealthy, or—in the extreme—that a diet high in salt may prolong your life, I would be making a hasty generalization. The truth is that most people who eat diets high in salt are at risk for certain health problems. Arguing otherwise, based on the example of my grandmother, would be making a hasty generalization.

Unrepresentative Samples

Statistical examples that rely on polling may fall into the fallacy of unrepresentative samples. If you want to know what the outcome of an election might be, you should be polling likely voters, not just everyone in a given voting district or everyone of voting age. Otherwise, your sample will not represent the population in question. A sample may also be biased based on factors that have nothing to do with what you are trying to measure. If you want to determine whether most people think the Chicago Bulls or the Los Angeles Lakers are going to win an upcoming match, you will probably get very different results if you poll exclusively in Chicago than if you poll exclusively in Los Angeles. Your sample needs to be taken in such a way that it represents the population you want to measure—in this case, most people familiar with professional basketball.

Fallacy of Composition

The **fallacy of composition** is the faulty assumption that what is true of the part is automatically true of the whole. It's easy to see where this assumption falls flat with some basic chemistry. A water molecule is made up of two hydrogen atoms (H_2) and one oxygen atom (O). H_2, the part, is a highly flammable gas at room temperature, but H_2O, the whole, is of course a nonflammable liquid. What is true of the part (H_2: flammable, gas) is not true of the whole (H_2O: nonflammable, liquid). Here's an example more parallel to what you might find in everyday arguments: in economics, one household can improve its financial position by spending less, thereby increasing how much it saves. However, if all households were to spend substantially less all at once, it may actually have a negative impact on most people's financial position, because decreased spending would lead to a worse economy, which would in turn affect all households.

Fallacy of Division

The **fallacy of division** is the faulty assumption that what is true of the whole is automatically true of the part. This is the converse of the fallacy of composition, above. We could of course take the same example of water and run it backward: H_2O is a nonflammable liquid, but it would be wrong to assume that H_2 is likewise a nonflammable liquid. Another example from economics may be more useful, though. We know that, on average, women in the United States earn significantly less than men. This does not mean, however, that my mother necessarily makes less than my father. What is true of the whole (women as wage earners in the United States) is not necessarily true of the part (any given woman wage earner).

Fallacies Common to the Argument from Comparison

This is covered in detail in Chapter 10, which describes the argument from comparison and provides a method for testing such arguments. I'll just review this briefly here. An argument from comparison is considered to be faulty when the similarities at issue do not outweigh the differences. This is nearly always going to be highly contextual. Let's say, to go back to the example used in Chapter 10, that you own a successful business in Boston, and you want to open up another branch in Philadelphia. Again, you reason that the cities are highly alike: both are port cities with a highly educated populace and a rich history. You decide that, given these similarities, your business that is doing well in Boston will likewise do well in Philadelphia. Is that a reasonable conclusion, or is it fallacious? The answer depends on the context. What kind of business is it? Are you going to try to sell lobster bisque in Philadelphia? That may not work, which means the analogy was fallacious. Higher education consulting, on the other hand, may work just fine. Timing may also be an issue. Does your business in Boston do well because it has a long tradition and excellent reputation locally? Well, how can you be sure that can be replicated in Philadelphia?

Again, as with all fallacies, it's clear here that whether or not a particular line of reasoning is fallacious depends on the context and audience, rather than any kind of litmus test.

Fallacies Common to the Argument from Cause to Effect

Sign Is Confused with Cause

This is covered in detail in Chapter 11. One of the most common pitfalls in arguments from cause to effect is mistaking a sign for a cause. A sign predicts some event or phenomenon with some degree of probability, but not because it is responsible for that event or phenomenon. A clear example is the one provided in Chapter 11: leaves falling from the trees mark the onset of colder weather, but they don't of course cause the colder weather to happen. That's easy to see. It may be more challenging to distinguish between sign and cause in arguments using statistics. Let's say a study finds that, as cell phone use has gone up, so too has the incidence of certain types of cancer. The authors of the study conclude that cell phone use is correlated with an increased risk of developing these cancers. Your friend reads the article and then texts it to you saying, "See?! Cell phones cause cancer!" The mistake here is assuming that, because the two things are correlated—increased cell phone use is, hypothetically, a sign that one is at greater risk of these cancers—one is the cause of the other. In fact, more research of a different sort would have to be done to show a cause/effect relationship.

Failing to Identify a Common Cause for Both Cause and Effect

In some cases, what is thought to be a cause of some other event is in fact itself the effect of something else, which is causing both things to happen. So, event 1 is thought to be the cause of event 2, but in reality both are the effects of event 3. Let's say you develop a runny nose on Monday, which turns into both a runny nose and a sore throat on Tuesday. You decide that the runny nose is the cause of the sore throat, but in reality both might be caused by the same underlying condition: strep throat, for example.

Post hoc, ergo propter hoc

Literally, this means "after, therefore because of" in Latin. It's the common tendency to attribute something that follows something else as its effect. So if you have been studying but getting Cs on your math tests all semester, then decide not to study the night before your next test but get some rest instead and get a B, you may come to the conclusion that resting rather than studying the night before a test is a better approach. This may or may not be true—there simply isn't enough evidence in this case to decide whether or not the extra sleep (or, indeed, the lack of studying) was the cause of improvement. It might be that the test was easier, or that you began studying in a new way, or that the format of the test was different. Just because the improved grade came after the night of extra sleep is not enough to conclude that it caused you to perform better.

Confusing Cause with Effect

When two things repeatedly occur together, it's easy to get the impression that there is a causal relationship between them. As mentioned already, sometimes what appears as a cause-effect relationship is not one at all but rather correspondence or coincidence. Other times the relationship is one of cause and effect, but we may mistake the effect as the cause. If your friend Sarah is upset every time she loses a basketball game, you might say to her, "You know, maybe the reason you're losing these games is because you're so upset." This, of course, overlooks the reality that Sarah is upset because her team lost the game; she didn't lose the game because she was upset.

One place where we commonly see this lack of clarity about the relationship between cause and effect is in controversies about the purported link between video games and violence: Do violent video games cause violent behaviors among teens? Or is violence in video games simply a representation of violent values (such as notions of white male supremacy, which Steinem points out) in our culture? Again, just showing that these two things (violent behavior and violent video games) occur together is not sufficient to prove that one is the cause of the other.

Fallacies Common to the Argument from Sign

Correlation

The first test of an argument from sign is that the sign and what it purportedly signifies generally occur together. So, in temperate climates, falling leaves are a sign of impending cold weather because cold weather generally follows. Accumulated experience allows us to accept this sign. An economic slowdown, however, is typically not a sign that consumer spending will increase.

No Obvious Countersigns

Sometimes a sign does point to the occurrence of something else, but a countersign points to a different outcome. A **countersign** is an occurrence or phenomenon that suggests a correlation different from some other specified sign. If you live in a temperate climate, and you see a tree with no leaves, you may not come to the conclusion that cold weather is approaching if there are any countersigns. For example, the trees around it are still green. Green trees nearby are a countersign: they suggest that cold weather is not approaching. You may take a closer look at the tree and realize that it is losing its leaves for some other reason.

The Same Sign Doesn't Point to Opposite Things

A sign can sometimes point to opposing outcomes. Rising credit card debt, for example, can sometimes point to a drop in the stock market, because it may be an indication that personal finances are in trouble. On the other hand, credit card debt can also be a sign of increased spending, which would suggest the market may go up. Credit card debt alone, then, is insufficient evidence to make an argument about the future of the stock market one way or another.

The Relationship Is Not Coincidence

The most obvious examples here are superstitions. Yes, your favorite team won when you wore those green and yellow socks, but wearing the socks actually has no relationship to how well your team is likely to do. It was just a coincidence.

Common General Fallacies

Two types of fallacy, deficiencies of clarity and deficiencies of relevance, may occur in any type of argument, regardless of the inference pattern.

Deficiencies of Clarity

Deficiencies of clarity arise when the language used in an argument is not sufficiently precise and leads to confusion. Several types of deficiencies of clarity are listed below.

Equivocation

In an **equivocation** the meaning of a single word or phrase changes from one part of the argument to another.

> Ex. Those who violate the law must be punished. People who fly are trying to violate the law of gravity and should therefore be punished.

The meaning of *law* changes from the first sentence to the second, referring first to a code of conduct and second to a principle of physics.

Ambiguity

Ambiguity occurs when a word or phrase has more than one meaning, and it is not clear enough which meaning is meant. The meaning of the word or phrase doesn't necessarily change, as in equivocation, but it is not clear which meaning the arguer wants us to understand.

> Ex. It says on the jar that this peanut butter is all-natural, but how can it be natural when it doesn't occur like this in nature?

Vagueness

The lack of clarity in a **vagueness** is not so much to do with multiple possible meanings available in the word or phrase, as in ambiguity, but rather that the language is simply imprecise. A term is vague when it is not clear what is meant by it.

Ex. She comes from a middle-class family.

Often, the go-to definition of middle class comes from the Pew Research Center, which defines middle class as earning anywhere from two-thirds to double the median household income. But people earning less than two-thirds of the median and people earning well over double the median income regularly consider themselves middle class. Others define middle class not according to income at all but by education level. So "She comes from a middle-class family" relies on a vague term.

Fallacy of the Heap

The **fallacy of the heap** happens when someone makes the argument that, because it is impossible to know when precisely a series of small changes add up to something completely different, we can't ever reclassify it. Say you have a small pile of sand, and you add a grain of sand to it, one at a time. Well, at which grain of sand precisely does the small pile become a big pile? The fallacy occurs when one makes the argument that because you can't say which grain of sand brought the pile from a small one to a large one, you can't ever call the pile large. The fallacy stems from the lack of clarity about how the pile ought to be classified as it is now, small or large. Conversely, the lack of clarity about the precise moment when it goes from being a small pile to a large pile should not keep us from classifying the pile at any given point.

Ex. U.S. involvement in Vietnam went from playing an advisory role assisting the French to a war with a half million U.S. combat troops by adding troops little by little.

At which level of troops did U.S. involvement become a war? The lack of clarity may keep the argument from moving forward. The fallacy of the heap occurs, then, when an inability to determine when a difference in degree becomes a difference in kind keeps the argument from moving forward in clear terms.

Slippery Slope

This is something like the converse of the fallacy of the heap. In the fallacy of the heap, one does not know precisely when a difference in degree becomes a difference in kind. The **slippery slope** fallacy suggests that any difference in degree is a difference in kind. The lack of clarity about how to make appropriate distinctions may prevent the argument from effectively continuing.

Ex. We must send troops to stop the military aggression in Ukraine, because if we don't, fighting will expand throughout the region and eventually lead to a world war. We don't want to fight a world war, so we need to put an end to the military aggression now.

The fallacy here is that once something is started there is no way to stop it or reverse its effects, an assumption that makes it more difficult to put forward clear and reasoned arguments about whether or not the conditions in the case at hand may lead to a larger conflict.

Vacuity

A **vacuity** is another word for a hole or an empty space. In argumentation it means failing to provide evidence for your claims. Sometimes an audience will accept certain claims without evidence, as happens when claims are taken from commonplaces (see Chapter 13). That's not a vacuity. A vacuity occurs when evidence is missing that the audience needs to make a fair and reasoned conclusion.

Ex. Apply for a credit card from us today! You'll earn ten points for every $100 you spend.

What about the interest rate, penalties for missed payments, or other potential pitfalls? Failing to provide this necessary information is a type of vacuity.

Circular Reasoning

Circular reasoning is restating a claim in such a way as to make it seem like it's based on evidence, but really it is just using different language to say the same thing. An argument based on circular reasoning has no inference, no leap it is asking its audience to make, no relationship between claim and evidence, because the claim is in fact just a restating of the evidence.

Ex. Gun rights are for the common good because everyone benefits from the unrestrained possession of firearms.

Begging the Question

People in everyday conversation often use the phrase "begs the question" to mean something like "raises the question." In argumentation, however, the fallacy of **begging the question** means something quite different. In begging the question, you make a claim that assumes other claims but does not actually establish them. Someone might hide a claim within a question, for example, so that there is no possible answer to the question without implicitly accepting the claim. Otherwise, someone might make a claim that takes something as given when it has not been established.

Ex. Do you still watch American Idol?

If you answer no, it implies that you used to. If you answer yes, it implies that you continue to watch it. The question begs the question, "Did you ever watch American Idol?" That would need to be answered first.

> Ex. State-sponsored murder only doubles the evil of the original crime.

This begs the question, "Is capital punishment state-sponsored murder?"

Digression (Red Herring)

This is possibly the most common fallacy used in contemporary political discourse. In a **digression**, you ignore the question or controversy at hand and pivot instead to something that is an easier win for you. If you're asked about a controversial bit of your history, you misdirect, talk about something else more likely to gain the approval of your audience.

> Ex. The growing federal budget deficit keeps us from meeting important priorities.
>
> A tax cut gives people more control over their own money.

Well, the initial claim doesn't really have anything to do with the relative amount of control people will have over their money. Rather, the initial claim has to do with problems created by a rising budget deficit. Talking about an advantage of a proposal that doesn't address the actual controversy in this way shifts the conversation to something that may be more "winnable," but it doesn't actually respond to the issue at hand. It is a fallacy to the extent that it does not help us make a reasoned decision.

Non Sequitur

In a **non sequitur** there is no logical connection between the claim and the evidence; no inference exists. "There is no way she is faster than me. Her favorite color is blue." It's nonsensical. Sometimes, however, a non sequitur can have the appearance of being reasonable when it isn't.

> Ex. I think we should hire Emily for the accounting position. She's had a long career in military intelligence.

The positive connotation of Emily's military career presents her candidacy for the accounting position in a good light, but there really isn't much of a relationship between military intelligence and accounting, so it's a non sequitur.

Straw Man

A **straw man** argument responds to a typically easy-to-refute claim that was not actually made, rather than the claim that actually has been made. In a sense, you build a counterargument and respond to that, rather than the argument you are actually trying to refute.

> Ex. I am opposed to athletes kneeling for our national anthem; I am a patriot.

"I am a patriot" is a straw man, because no one is questioning the speaker's patriotism here. Rather, the question at hand is whether or not it is acceptable to kneel during the national anthem in protest of government policies. The speaker's own patriotism, or lack thereof, is not at issue, but possibly easier to make a case for.

Self-Sealing Argument

A **self-sealing argument** makes a case that seems to hold no matter what the outcome is; it encompasses opposite results.

> Ex. We need to hold firm and be strong in our dealings with North Korea.
>
> It worked: See, I was right.
>
> It didn't work: We were not firm and strong enough.

Either outcome is made to support the claim, which means we are never in the position where we can test the claim with evidence.

Deficiencies of Relevance

Deficiencies of relevance decrease the likelihood that an argument will lead toward the best possible outcome because they shift attention away from the issues at hand. As you recall from Chapter 5, relevance is a measure of how likely it is that a reason will lead you to accept a resolution if you accept the reason. If accepting the reason means you are highly likely to accept the resolution, then it has relevance. If accepting the reason has little bearing on whether or not you accept the resolution, it does not have relevance. The fallacies below fall short in relevance. They may distract audiences from more relevant arguments, or they may appear relevant when they are not actually so.

Ad Hominem

An **ad hominem** argument substitutes an attack on the person presenting an argument for an actual counterargument.

> Ex. Dr. Lopez's fiscal policies are terrible. She is highly disliked by all her colleagues.

Appeal to Authority

The **appeal to authority** presents an authority's acceptance of a claim as support for that claim. This is only a deficiency of relevance when it substitutes for an argument.

> Ex. These sneakers are the best for running, because an Olympic runner endorsed them.

Appeal to Popularity (Bandwagon Effect)

The **appeal to popularity** presents popular acceptance of a claim as support for that claim. Again, this is only a deficiency of relevance when it substitutes for an argument.

> Ex. Brand X toothpaste is the most popular toothpaste in the country, so it must be the best.

Appeal to Tradition

The **appeal to tradition** presents the long-standing acceptance of a claim as support for that claim, instead of making an argument.

> Ex. This statue has stood in our town square for almost a hundred years. It cannot be taken down now.

Appeal to Ignorance

The **appeal to ignorance** argues that because we don't know the opposite to be true, a claim must be true.

> Ex. No one has ever proven that aliens do not exist; therefore, aliens must exist.

Appeal to Inappropriate Emotion

Emotions are not in and of themselves bad evidence for a claim. Anger arising from injustice, for example, can be powerful evidence. But when someone makes an **appeal to inappropriate emotion**, they are substituting emotion for evidence when the emotion is not relevant to the situation.

> Ex. White people have enjoyed systemic privilege in the United States for centuries. I find that statement offensive, so it must not be true.

Appeal to Threat

The **appeal to threat** is not a fallacy so much as an unwillingness to engage in argumentation. As I argue in Chapter 1, one of the basic assumptions of argumentation is that all parties involved want to come to the best possible outcome by giving reasons for their claims. Argumentation is a cooperative enterprise. A threat is coercive, meaning that it uses force rather than reason-giving.

Tu Quoque

Pronounced "tyu kwoh kwey," **tu quoque** is Latin for "you also." Tu quoque arises as a fallacy when one makes the argument that someone else is doing the same thing of which you are being accused. So if Jasmine accuses you of taking her slice of cake from the shared refrigerator, you respond by saying, "I saw you take Muriel's cookies from the pantry last week!" you are engaging the fallacy of tu quoque. As always, the extent to which tu quoque is a fallacy depends on how much an audience is willing to accept it as relevant to the case at hand. If the controversy is "What policies should be put in place to prevent us from taking one another's food?" then having a sense of who is taking the food matters. But if the question is whether you owe Jasmine an apology (and a slice of cake), then the fact that Jasmine took Muriel's cookies is not really that relevant. In that case, it is a fallacy.

So, when considering if an instance of tu quoque rises to the level of fallacy, you have to ask yourself how relevant the claim is in that particular situation.

Conclusion

Whether or not many of the fallacies listed above are actually fallacies will depend on the specifics of the argument. The idea of a fallacy in argumentation is borrowed from its roots in formal logic. In formal logic, the conclusion must follow with certainty from the premises. Any relationship between premises and conclusion that is not one of complete certainty, then, is a fallacy.

But in informal logic we are never dealing with certainty. Rather, we are dealing only with some degree of probability, or reasonableness, which is dependent on an audience (even if the audience is unclear, or is the speaker themself). In informal logic, then, a fallacy is only a fallacy if an audience agrees that it is.

In fact, even pointing out that someone's argument is based on a fallacy is itself an argument, a rebuttal that must be advanced with evidence, and which the audience must accept. Consider the fallacy of ad hominem. This is widely known as a fallacy and is often presented as unacceptable. But there are instances when an ad hominem argument may be perfectly reasonable. Let's say, for example, you are deciding

> In informal logic, a fallacy is only a fallacy when an audience decides that it is one, which is why being able to recognize one is so important.

between two candidates for a position. Each candidate is similar in terms of their qualifications: similar education, experience, and skills. But both are internal candidates and so you happen to know that one candidate is more of a team player who works well with others in her department, while the other is known to be a bit of a lone wolf who only puts effort into projects when he can get the credit. In this case, the argument "Let's not hire Roger because he's a selfish jerk" may not be an ad hominem fallacy because his character is in fact relevant to the particular controversy.

Whether or not an argument relies on fallacious reasoning often is as much an ethical question as it is one of logic. While some fallacies are deficiencies in form, such as non sequitur, and some are fallacies based on accumulated experience, such as knowing that arguments from sign and cause are easily mistaken for one another, many fallacies are lapses in argumentation as a procedure.

The most obvious of these, of course, is the appeal to threat, which relies on force and/or coercion to achieve its position rather than argumentation. Other fallacies listed above may also threaten to move the decision-making process away from the exchange of claims and evidence. Ad hominem or tu quoque, for example, may easily lead to name-calling rather than dialogue. The question—for all participants in an argument, including the audience—is what will allow the argument to continue according to the underlying principles of argumentation, including cooperation, justification for claims, uncertainty, and risk. When any of these principles of argumentation are abandoned, we move further away from the set of norms that help ensure that the process of argumentation will indeed lead us to the best possible outcome(s) for any given controversy.

PROBE

Imagine a hypothetical counterargument to one of Steinem's key claims in the essay. Consider how she might counter that response.

Chapter 15
Argumentation and Dialogue

Key Terms

spheres of argumentation

personal sphere

critical discussion

principle of nonviolence

principle of freedom of speech

principle of intellectual pluralism

agonistic argumentation

coalescent argumentation

Key Points

- Argumentation takes place according to the expectations of different spheres, depending on the goals of the discussion and the participants involved.
- Argumentation in the personal sphere is a way to decide outcomes for people directly involved in the argument, often friends, acquaintances, or family.
- By adhering to a set of expectations, known as critical discussion, participants in personal arguments can give themselves the best chance to come to decisions that are acceptable to everyone involved.

PRIME

As you read, consider the multiple roles or identities Mairs occupies in this letter to her son. How might these various positions influence her writing?

A Letter to Matthew

Nancy Mairs (July 1983)

My Dear Child—

Last night Daddy and I watched, on William F. Buckley Jr.'s *Firing Line*, a debate whether women "have it as good as men," and I have been talking to you in my head ever since. Odd not to be able to talk with you in person—I'm not yet used to your absences—but I thought I would put onto paper some of the things I would say to you if you were here.

They are not the sort of things I would say to Mr. Buckley if ever I met him. Mr. Buckley is an elderly man, fixed by his circumstances within a range of experiences so narrow that new ideas and new behaviors cannot squeeze through the boundaries. He is complete as he is. But you are just emerging into young manhood, still fluid, still making the choices that will determine the shape that manhood will take. I, as your mother and as a feminist, hope that the choices you make—you individually and your generation as a whole—will be transformative, that the manhood you develop will be so radically new that the question in Mr. Buckley's debate, smacking as it does of competition for goods and goodness, will no longer have any more meaning than questions like "do pigs have it as good as fiddlehead ferns?" or, more aptly, "do pigs have it as good as pigs?"

In many ways, of course, you've dashed my hopes already. You have, after all, lived for fourteen years in a dangerously patriarchal society, and you have put on much of the purple that Mr. Buckley wears with such aplomb. When I find myself disliking you—and I find myself disliking you with about the same regularity, I imagine, as you find yourself disliking me—I can usually tell that I'm responding to some behavior that I identify as peculiarly "masculine." I dislike your cockiness, for instance. When you first began to work with computers, I remember, you immediately assumed the attitude that you knew all that was worth knowing about computers; when you took up racquetball, right away you set yourself up as a champion. This kind of swaggering strikes me as a very old pattern of masculine behavior (I think of Beowulf and Unferth at Heorot), the boast designed to establish superiority and domination, which trigger challenge and thus conflict. Related to your cockiness is your quickness to generalize and, from your generalizations, to pronounce judgments: Calculus is a waste of time; Christians are stupidly superstitious; classical music is boring; Jerry Falwell and the Moral Majority are idiots. This is just the kind of uninformed thinking that empowers Jerry Falwell and the Moral Majority in the first place, of course, this refusal to experience and explore the ambiguities of whatever one is quick to condemn. More seriously, such a pattern of response enables men to create the distinctions between Us and Them—the good guys and the bad guys, the left wing and the right, the Americans and the Russians—that lead to suspicion, fear, hatred, and finally the casting of stones.

Well then, have you shattered all my hopes? By no means. For you are not merely arrogant and opinionated. These qualities are overshadowed by another, one I have seldom seen in men: your extraordinary empathic capacity, your willingness to listen for and try to fulfill the needs of others. When Sean was threatening suicide, you were genuinely engaged in his pain. When Katherine needed a male model to encourage her creepy little fifth-grade boys to dance, you leaped in with psychological (if not physical!) grace. When Anne left us for good, I felt your presence supporting and soothing me despite your relief at being an only child at last. Women have long been schooled in this sensitivity to others; but men have been trained to hold themselves aloof, to leave the emotional business of life to their mothers and sisters and wives. I think you are learning to conduct some of that business on your own. Clearly I believe that the ability to do so is a benefit and not the curse our patriarchal culture has made it out to be. In fact in an ironic way the answer to Mr. Buckley's question might be that women have it better than men, and it is the fear of such an answer that keeps men nervously posing the question in the first place. You'll remember that Freud ascribed to women a problem he called "penis envy"; a later psychoanalyst, Lacan, called it a "lack." If I've learned anything during the years I've spent in psychotherapy, I've learned that the feelings and motives I ascribe to others tell me little about them but much about myself, for I am projecting my own feelings and motives onto them. Freud ascribed to women penis envy; ascription = projection; therefore Freud was really suffering from womb envy. QED. A man, lacking the womb and yearning to return to his early identity with the mother, tries to hide his pain by denigrating everything associated with the womb: the blood, the babies, the intuitive and nurturing behaviors of childrearing. The very condition of having a womb in the first place he labels a pathology: hysteria. If I haven't got it, he tells himself, it can't be worth having. (But maybe, he whispers so softly that even he can't hear, maybe it is.)

I'm more than half serious, you know, amid this high-flown silliness. But I don't seriously believe, despite some psychological advantages, that in the "real world" women have it as good as men. In some highly visible ways they have it very bad indeed: They are raped, battered, prostituted, abandoned to raise their children in poverty. Less visibly but no less ruinously, they are brainwashed (often by their mothers and sisters as well as their fathers, brothers, lovers, and husbands) into believing that whatever they get is what they deserve, being only women. Imagine this, Matthew, if you can—and maybe you can, since you are just emerging from childhood, and children are often treated like women in our society. Imagine thinking yourself lucky to get any job, no matter how servile or poorly paid, any partner, no matter how brutal or dull, any roof over your head, no matter how costly the psychic mortgage payment. Imagine believing that's what you deserve. Imagine feeling guilty if you fail to feel grateful.

If you have trouble imagining such conditions, I'm not surprised. I have trouble too; and for many years I held back from calling myself a feminist because I couldn't conceive problems I hadn't experienced. The men in our family do not smack their women and children around. They seldom raise their voices, let alone their palms. They are gentle, courteous, witty, companionable, solicitous. And yet, of late, I've begun to recognize in them certain behaviors and attitudes which suggest that they, too, share a set of cultural assumptions about male power and rights which devalue women's lives. But our men worship their women, you may say; they put them right up on what one of my students once called a "pedastool." True enough, but tell me, how much actual living could you get done confined to a tiny platform several feet above the ground, especially if you had acrophobia?

Look, now that you're staying with them, at Aunt Helen and Uncle Ted, for instance. For forty-eight years they have sustained a relationship founded on domination and submission if ever there was one. Daddy has often insisted that their relationship is fine as long as it works for them. For a long time I tried to accept it too, because I believed that he must be right. I tend, as you know, to believe that Daddy is always right: I'm the product of a patriarchal society too, after all. But now I believe that he's wrong. Although I admire much about their marriage, especially its durability and friendliness, I balk at its basis in a kind of human sacrifice. Trying, I suppose, to compensate for not having graduated from high school, Uncle Ted kept Aunt Helen, a college graduate, confined in a life containing only himself, their one son, and the housework to maintain them. She could have worked, of course—she had the education, and they always needed the money, but Uncle Ted's manly pride insisted on his being the breadwinner, and her job became to stretch the crusts and crumbs from one meager meal to the next. So little had she to occupy her that she grieved for years after her child left for college, and clung to her housework to give her days meaning. Once, in the late sixties, I asked her why she didn't replace her old-fashioned washing machine with an automatic (my mother had had one since 1952), and she replied, "But then what would I do on Mondays?" Worse than the deprivation of stimulating activity has been the undermining of her self-confidence. Even her statements sound like questions, and she repeatedly turns to her husband: "Isn't that right, Ted?" She tiptoes through space as through conversation like our Lionel Tigress, cautious, timorous, whiskers twitching, ready to dash under the bed at a strange voice or a heavy footfall. I like to watch her bake a cake. There in her kitchen she plants her feet firmly and even, sometimes, rattles the pans.

Is Uncle Ted then a monster, some Bluebeard glowering and dangling the incriminating key that represents some independent act that will cost Aunt Helen her head? Hardly. He is a man of sincerity and rectitude, who has lived scrupulously, at considerable cost to himself, according to the code by which he was raised, a code that Rudyard Kipling, whom he admires, described as the "white man's burden." In it, women (among others, such as our "darker brethren") require the kind of protection and control they are unable, being more "natural" creatures, to provide themselves. He adores Aunt Helen, I do believe, and wants to do only what's best for her. But he assumes that he knows what's best for her, and so does she. In the name of manhood, he has taken from her the only authentic power a human being can hold: that of knowing and choosing the good. Such theft of power results in mastery. There is no mistressy.

I've been uneasy, as you know, about your spending this summer with them, largely, I suppose, because I don't want Uncle Ted to make a "man" of you. And I've encouraged you to subvert their patterns of interaction in a small way, by helping Aunt Helen with her chores just as you help Uncle Ted with his, even when he tries to divert you and she tells you to run along with him, not so that you can change those patterns (you can't) but so that you'll remain aware of them. You may well be tempted to fall into them because what Uncle Ted construes as "men's work" is infinitely more interesting than "women's work." You already know what a drag it is to set the table knowing that within an hour the dishes will be streaked and gummy, to wash those dishes knowing that they'll go right back on the table for breakfast, to fold a whole line of clothes that will crawl straight back into the hamper, muddy and limp, to be washed and hung out again. How much more pleasant and heartening to tramp through the woods checking the line from the brook, to ride the lawnmower round and round on the sweet falling grass, to plot traps for porcupines and saw down trees and paddle the canoe across the pond spreading algicide and possibly falling in. If everyone washed the dishes together, of course, everyone could go for a walk in the woods. How one would tell the men from the women though, I'm not sure.

But then, so what if you do fall into the patterns? Surely the world won't end if you and Uncle Ted take the fishing rods down to the Battenkill to catch a few trout for breakfast, leaving Aunt Helen to make the beds? Well yes, I think in a way it will, and that's why I'm writing you this letter. For Aunt Helen und Uncle Ted's marriage is not in the least extraordinary. On the contrary, the interactions between them, despite some idiosyncrasies, are being played out in millions of relationships throughout the world, including, in its own way, Daddy's and mine, within which you have lived your whole life. One partner is telling the other (though seldom in words) that she is weaker physically and intellectually, that her concerns are less meaningful to the world at large, that she is better suited (or even formed by God) to serve his needs in the privacy of his home than to confront the tangled problems of the public sphere. And instead of ignoring his transparent tactics for enhancing his uncertain self-image and increasing his own comfort, she is subordinating her needs to his, accepting the limits he decrees, and thereby bolstering the artificial pride that enables him to believe himself a "superior" creature. As soon as he feels superiority, he is capable of dividing his fellow creatures into Us and Them and of trying to dominate Them. That is, he is ready to make war.

This connection—between the private male who rules his roost and keeps his woman, however lovingly, in her place and the public male who imposes his will by keeping blacks poor and pacifying Vietnamese villages and shipping arms and men to Central America—is far from new. Virginia Woolf made it in *Three Guineas* nearly fifty years ago. "The public and the private worlds are inseparably connected," she wrote; "the tyrannies and servilities of the one are the tyrannies and servilities of the other." But *Three Guineas* has been largely ignored or denigrated: One male critic called it "neurotic," "morbid"; another, "cantankerous." (You know, I am sure, that when a man speaks out, he is assertive, forthright; when a woman speaks her "mind," she is sick or bitchy.) Moreover, its feminism has been labeled "old-fashioned," as though already in 1938 the problems Woolf named had been solved. If so, why do we stand today in the same spot she stood then, looking at the same photographs of dead bodies and burned villages? No, her feminism isn't out of date, though such a label shows a desperate attempt to set it aside. Rather, it says something, valid today, that men still do not want to hear: that if humanity—men and women—is to have it any good at all, men must give up their pleasure in domination, their belief in their superiority, the adulation of their fellow creatures, at the personal and private level of their lives. Now. They must stop believing that whoever they love will perish without their "protection," for the act of protecting leads to a sense of possession, and it necessitates enemies to protect from. They must completely and radically revise their relationships with themselves, their wives and children, their business associates, the men and women in the next block, the next city, the next country. They must learn to say to every other who enters their lives not, "You're over there, and you're bad," but, "You're over there, and you're me." Can they do it? Some feminists think not. They say that we should simply kill men off (except perhaps for the babies) and start fresh. I understand the anger that fuels such a proposal and the desire to sweep the rubbishy world clean. But I reject it because it perpetuates the violence that distinguishes masculine solutions to conflict. Our cultural heritage would still be based on killing, our mythology rooted in massacre.

No, I think that I will let you live. Will you let me live? If so, the terms of your existence must be transformed. What's been good enough for Aunt Helen and Uncle Ted, for Mr. Buckley, for Ronald Reagan and the other men who govern us and every other nation, for the Catholic Church, for the medical and legal professions, for the universities, for all the patriarchy, cannot be good enough for you. (And I address you personally, though obviously I mean all young men everywhere, because moral choice is always a lonely matter. You may all encourage one another—in fact, if the transformation is working, you will—but each will have to choose his way of being for himself.) You must learn to develop your identity through exploring the ways you are like, not different from or better than, others. You must learn to experience power through your connections with people, your ability to support their growth, not through weakening them by ridicule or patronage or deprivation. If this means dancing with the little boys, then dance your heart out; they'll dance on into the future with more assurance because of you. And who can shoot straight while he's dancing? I am demanding something of you that takes more courage than entering a battle: not to enter the battle. I am asking you to say no to the values that have defined manhood through the ages—prowess, competition, victory—and to grow into a manhood that has not existed before. If you do, some men and women will ridicule and even despise you. They may call you spineless, possibly even (harshest of curses) womanish. But your life depends on it. My life depends on it. I wish you well.

Now go help Aunt Helen with the dishes.

I love you,
    Mother

PAUSE

Reflect on a disagreement you've had in the past with family or friends. What were some of its characteristics? Did you come to a mutual understanding?

Introduction

There are many ways in which this is a typical letter from a mother to a son. Nancy's son Matthew is staying with relatives for a while, and it's clear Nancy both misses him and is entertaining some anxieties about what kind of person Matthew is growing to be. Perhaps you've sensed some of these anxieties from your own parents or caregivers, or perhaps you've experienced these anxieties as a parent or caregiver yourself. They're pretty typical. And as a pretty typical letter, there are many ways in which this follows the conventions of a letter from one family member to another. It begins with a story about a recent evening at home, it reveals insights into some of the other family members, it catches Matthew up and tells him a little about his family's past, and reminds him to be helpful around his aunt and uncle's house while he is a guest.

In other ways, though, this letter is not so typical. Parents don't typically provide literary analyses or summaries of feminist history in letters to their kids. They don't typically relate their actions, histories, and dispositions to gender politics. And they don't typically give such thorough rationales for what they are asking their kids to do.

These important differences suggest that, though it is made in a letter from a mother to her son, Mairs's "A Letter to Matthew" is a policy argument. "And I address you personally," she writes, "though obviously I mean all young men everywhere, because moral choice is always a lonely matter." She is essentially saying to her son, "I'd like you to act this way," or "You should change your actions in these ways." The word "should," as you'll recall from Chapter 3, lets us know that this is an argument of policy.

We tend to think of policy arguments as belonging to great forums like the pages of newspapers, presidential debates, and parliamentary halls, not in private letters from mothers to sons, but, as Mairs suggests, quoting Woolf, "The public and the private worlds are inseparably connected." We see policy arguments in the private world all the time, some weighty and well argued, like Mairs's, others more inconsequential, like "We should go see the new Marvel movie this week." Though in practice arguments in the personal sphere vary widely, in principle they still subscribe to the same assumptions and ideals of argumentation that are operating in the public sphere. In this chapter we consider how arguments work in the personal sphere.

Arguments between friends and family are often seen as something to avoid, or evidence that the relationship is suffering. But having the tools to engage in productive discussion is actually one way to avoid the kind of awful mudslinging or tense silences that can happen when people use words to fight instead of to come to mutual understanding.

We hear more and more that we are in a highly polarized age. Much of the time, this is exacerbated by the way we consume information on social media, which tends to surround us with only those opinions we want to hear and with which we already agree. The algorithms on social media are like a mirror that only shows you what you want to see; pretty soon, you'll get a very distorted image. In this context, as Liptak points out in Chapter 6, when you and your uncle Joe get together at the Thanksgiving table, you may have difficulty finding common ground, one of the basic conditions of productive argumentation. This leads to the sorts of situations I often hear from my students, where talk of politics is banned from family get-togethers, even if this isn't stated explicitly.

But when things are so polarized, and we only hear from those we agree with, that's when we need argumentation most. As I mention in Chapter 7, since argumentation is based on audience, expectations about evidence vary depending on how sympathetic your audience is to the argument being made. When you're preaching to the choir, you don't need much evidence. If you agree with the position being argued for, you may not be as critical an audience as you ought to be. You may believe assertions even when they are not supported by any evidence.

AUDIENCE

Who, in your analysis, is the audience for Mairs's letter? Is it

a. Her son, Matthew?
b. A public audience?
c. Both her son and a public audience?

As you think about your answer, consider the context of the letter (including the fact that it was published), as well as the content.

Spheres of Argumentation

We live in a diverse society, with numerous cultures—each with divergent values and expectations—coexisting and overlapping. We know that argumentation depends on the audience, so this diversity of values and expectations is going to condition the arguments we make as well. You most likely know this implicitly already: you wouldn't make the same argument to your parents about which movie to see this weekend that you would make to your friends. Your parents and friends each have different values, different points of view, and different ideas about what counts as an argument. The same is true, of course, across the spectrum of contexts in which you might find yourself making an argument: in school, at work, as part of an organization or social club, and so on.

Because there is not one way of making an argument, not a single formula for what makes a claim effective or what counts as evidence, we do better to think of argumentation as taking place in these different contexts, which in technical terms are called **spheres of argumentation**. A sphere of argumentation is a set of expectations that have developed over time in particular contexts. They are just another way of saying, when you look back at the history of argumentation in biology, for example, or among family or friends, or political debate, certain things have worked in these contexts while others have not. By organizing the different arguments into spheres, we can be more specific about what audience expectations are driving these different arguments. The three spheres of argumentation are personal, technical, and public. We'll take a look at each one in the following chapters, starting here with the personal sphere.

Argumentation in Public vs. Personal Spheres

Most of the arguments we've looked at closely throughout this book have been situated in the public sphere. They've been directed at gathering audiences around issues that affect people in general, addressing not private concerns but public ones. Sometimes the public sphere is described in terms of citizenship: we act in the public sphere as citizens, doing work that affects people as a whole. But citizenship may be too limited a scope for talking about the public sphere, because often policies debated and implemented in the public sphere affect non-citizens as well, and often noncitizens play central roles in advocating for certain public policies. In addition, many have argued that thinking of things in terms of citizenship, which is so closely tied with belonging to a particular country, is inadequate when it comes to controversies that affect us on a global level, like climate change and global economics. So it might be best to think about the public sphere as the spaces where arguments deal with the concerns of the many, citizens or not, rather than one or a few individuals. We'll look closer at the public sphere in Chapter 17.

Argumentation in the **personal sphere**, on the other hand, is typically just concerned with the people directly involved in the argument. The outcome of these arguments may have repercussions for people not involved in the discussion, but the argument itself is driven by interests limited to the group. For example, you may have an argument with a group of friends about where to go to dinner that night. One of you wants to go to a Mexican restaurant, while another advocates for Italian. The outcome of the discussion will potentially affect several people outside the group—the owners of the restaurants in question, the serving staff, and so on—but your argument focuses on these only to the extent that they are personal interests. That is, a member of your group who wants to spend their money in the community may bring up that the Mexican restaurant is locally owned while the Italian restaurant is a chain. Spending money locally has significance for people outside of your group of friends, but it only becomes a concern to the extent that a member of your group has an interest in it.

The sphere to which an argument belongs does not depend so much on the content of the argument but on how that content is being addressed. Often arguments begin in the personal sphere and migrate to the public sphere, or begin in the public sphere and migrate to the personal sphere. In the example above, when one of the friends brings up the issue of shopping locally, they are bringing an argument from the public sphere into the personal sphere. On the other hand, concerns that may have been silenced in the past as deeply personal, such as sexual assault or gender identity, have moved solidly into the public sphere. Mairs's letter to her son is an example of an argument moving from the public sphere to the personal sphere: she is concerned that her son not adopt the dominant gender roles he sees in popular culture and in his own extended family. Arguments about gender roles are common in the public sphere, and Mairs is bringing these concerns into her conversations with her son. At the same time, by publishing this letter as an essay in a collection of hers, she is also bringing personal concerns into the public sphere. Her family serves as an example of the ways gender norms are taken up in ordinary families, and her argument is implicitly that dominant gender roles can be revised if families have the same sorts of conversations with one another that she is having with her son.

> The sphere to which an argument belongs depends on who it means to influence.

Sometimes the controversy that fuels an argument is where a particular argument belongs. Someone might respond to Mairs's argument that the relationship between a man and his wife is private, up to them, and not to be debated in the public sphere.

Argumentation in the Personal Sphere

Argumentation in the personal sphere has a number of dominant characteristics that distinguish it from argumentation in the public or other spheres.

Arguments in the personal sphere are concerned mostly with the participants on an individual level. As I mention above, the primary characteristic of argumentation in the personal sphere is that the arguments concern the participants on a personal level. They don't rise to the level of public interest. Just because the concerns are personal, however, doesn't mean they are not important, or that they focus on trivial things like which movie to see or where to go to dinner. Mairs's letter to her son is a clear example of a personal argument that is nevertheless very important, dealing with questions of gender roles and gender dynamics, and asking her son, how will you act ethically in the world?

Arguments in the personal sphere are typically spoken. Arguments in the personal sphere typically proceed through conversation or dialogue. Even when written, such as Mairs's argument above, the arguments are typically informal and tend to sound like they could be spoken. That is, even written arguments in the personal sphere typically use a conversational style.

Arguments in the personal sphere typically arise when two or more people hold what they see as incompatible positions. In an argument in the personal sphere, each participant typically is trying to convince the other to see things from their perspective, to accept their arguments. They may use many different strategies to convince each other, some more or less effective than others, and more or less ethical than others. Most of the time, the approaches we take and the strategies we use when we argue in the personal sphere are not based on any overt teaching. We tend to learn how to argue in the personal sphere by engaging in these exchanges of points of view from an early age. Should we play hide-and-seek or tag? have pizza or hot dogs? go to the beach or for a hike? These sorts of situations in which different people have different preferences happen all the time, and we learn what works and what doesn't work by engaging in them. We also watch other people argue about the same sorts of things in similar ways. Ideally, we learn not to impose our preference by force or coercion, we learn to take turns, to hear one another out. These are all important conventions of argumentation in the personal sphere, which we tend to follow to the extent they are reflected in the cultures that influence us.

Arguments in the personal sphere are typically highly contextual and ephemeral. The relationship between the people involved in the argument will influence the argument. Depending on what the people know about each other, and given their history with one another, some things may not need to be said in the conversation at all, or can be established just by hinting at some shared experience or memory. Typically, arguments in the personal sphere, when spoken only, are not preserved in any way other than in the participants' memories. And, generally speaking, we don't prepare for these sorts of conversations. We don't study or prepare notes. Rather, we use whatever evidence occurs to us in that given moment, for better or worse. I know I am not alone in thinking of the perfect line of argument, example, or joke an hour or a day after the conversation is over. Unfortunately, there is nothing to be done but accept that the moment has passed.

Critical Discussion: The Ideal for Argumentation in the Personal Sphere

Much of the time, argumentation in the personal sphere takes place with just those procedures and standards that are implicit in conversation. Without a standard procedure or values, the extent to which argumentation in the personal sphere will lead to the desired outcome will depend on the shared values of the participants. If the participants both value cooperation and reason-giving, and are willing to accept the outcome of the discussion, then the argument should proceed very well. But if they do not share these values, then the argument may not go anywhere and may not lead to the best decision.

While argumentation in the personal sphere is much more informal than argumentation in the public sphere, we can still identify both a procedure and a set of values that, if agreed to by all participants, will lead to better outcomes. This procedure and set of values are known as **critical discussion**, which serves as the ideal model for argumentation in the personal sphere.

Critical discussion tends to follow these stages:

1. The participants identify the specific disagreement(s).
2. The participants agree to use discussion to resolve the disagreements.
3. The participants make the cases for each competing point of view in as much detail as the discussion requires.
4. Either the participants agree that some point of view or combination of points of view is the best outcome to the disagreement, or they agree that the disagreement can't be resolved.

Now, I don't make a habit of eavesdropping on people's arguments, but I would expect that most people, when they argue, do not explicitly state that they will follow these steps, or announce that they are moving from one stage to another. It would be odd, I'm sure you'll agree, for your roommate to say, "Now that we have identified specifically that we are disagreeing about the procedure for washing the dishes, let us agree that we will settle this through discussion, and not some other means." Not likely.

Though the participants won't likely say so explicitly, when we do observe people having arguments that have positive outcomes for both parties—even when the discussions are difficult—these observations tend to amount to something like these four stages. The purpose of studying arguments, again, is to use argumentation to achieve the best possible outcomes. Following these stages tends to lead to better outcomes for those involved.

We can see most of these stages quite clearly in Mairs's letter, in fact. Matthew is not directly disagreeing with his mother Nancy in the letter—we don't hear from Matthew at all. But Nancy is nevertheless describing a common disagreement in families: What roles should each partner take in relation to the other? And she is drawing on specific family relationships to show that the controversy is there in the family dynamics, even if it doesn't normally rise to an explicit disagreement.

The fact that Nancy is raising these issues shows that she is interested in talking about them, and there are several times in the letter itself when she seems open to dialogue. She also provides full and detailed examples to support her point of view. We don't ever get to see Matthew's response, so we don't know whether or not the disagreement will be resolved at the personal level (resolving it on the public level is much more challenging). Still, resolving the disagreement is at least set up by the tone and orientation of the letter itself.

CRITICAL DISCUSSION IN "A LETTER TO MATTHEW"

Go back through Mairs's essay and find direct textual evidence of each of the stages of a critical discussion. What evidence do you find? Do any stages appear to be better developed than others? Are any stages missing?

Expectations of a Critical Discussion

Not all arguments occurring in the personal sphere are going to reflect the normative standards of a critical discussion. We've all witnessed, or perhaps been involved in, arguments that do not rise to the level of argumentation as described throughout this book—arguments where coercion or fallacies win, or where the arguments just bubble under the surface, creating tension in the relationship that isn't fully resolved.

Critical discussion exists as a model precisely to avoid these sorts of negative outcomes. It is an ethical value, as much as a practical guide, and as such has a number of expectations.

The participants aren't just trying to make the argument go away. We've all had conversations we wish would just end. Maybe they make us uncomfortable, maybe we don't see a way to get to any positive outcomes, or maybe we're just not that interested. Whatever the reason, if we view our participation in the discussion as saying whatever we think will make the conversation end more quickly, we're not engaging in critical discussion. In a critical discussion, all the participants are working toward resolving the disagreement, which means they all agree that they have achieved the best possible outcome—even if the decision is simply that no resolution is possible.

Every participant has an equal opportunity to make their case, and everyone agrees that they will accept only reason-giving, rather than force or coercion, to decide the matter. This should be familiar to you by now, as it is one of the foundations of argumentation we've covered throughout this book. In an argument in the personal sphere, participants have to be especially aware of and account for the power dynamics inherent in individual roles and histories.

The merits of the case, rather than some external consideration, determine the resolution. Imagine two parents are having an argument about whether or not to get a dog. After both provide several reasons why getting a dog right now is a bad idea (the dog would have to be left for long periods alone, they live in a small apartment, allergies, etc.), they decide to get the dog anyway because, while they know it is a bad idea, they don't have the heart to tell their kid that they can't have a dog. Despite the fact that the parents engaged in thoughtful and reasoned discussion, this doesn't reflect a critical discussion because they didn't allow the merits of the case to drive their decision. Rather, they looked to an external factor, their unwillingness to break the news to their kid, to base their decision on.

There are no artificially constructed limitations to the argument. What if I am having an argument and I say, "Fine, I'm fully willing to have you convince me that cereal is a cold soup, but you only have the next five minutes to do it"? Does that allow us to arrive at the best possible outcome? Probably not, which is why having such arbitrary limits does not meet the standards of critical discussion. What if we're really close to getting to a resolution but need another five minutes? Because these artificial limitations do not serve the purpose of argumentation—to achieve the best possible outcome—they are not part of a critical discussion.

Participants share the value of cooperation. When two people cooperate in an argument, it doesn't mean they don't have different points of view or that they are not committed to making their best case. Cooperation doesn't mean you "let the other person win." Rather, it means that you don't see the argument in terms of winning and losing to begin with but as an opportunity to come to the best decision under the circumstances. When you cooperate in an argument, then, you are sincere, only providing claims and evidence you genuinely believe, you avoid arguments that you know are not relevant to the case, and you don't try to be purposely unclear.

The participants are guided by the principles of nonviolence, freedom of speech, and intellectual pluralism. The **principle of nonviolence** in this context means that you will avoid physical or verbal force to support your point of view. The **principle of freedom of speech** means that all speech is acceptable so long as it doesn't violate the principle of nonviolence. The **principle of intellectual pluralism** means that differences of opinion, different perspectives, and critical analyses are welcome producers of truth. Just because an opinion is unpopular doesn't mean it cannot be true, so long as there is substantial evidence to support it. Sometimes people use intellectual pluralism as a shield to protect ideas that are hateful or baseless conspiracy theories. One of the movements against teaching evolution in public schools called for "teaching the controversies," claiming intellectual pluralism when there isn't a real basis for their argument. Intellectual pluralism welcomes controversies when they arise as genuine differences of opinion among people who are similarly knowledgeable on the subject. But in the case of these arguments against evolution, there were no real controversies among scientists like the kind being advocated.

Coalescent Argumentation

Often I ask my classes to work through two different argumentation scenarios. In the first scenario, imagine that I present the controversy "Which is the best flavor of ice cream?" Some in the class prefer chocolate, others vanilla or strawberry. Still others prefer more decadent flavors like rocky road, mint chocolate chip, or chocolate peanut butter cup. Regardless of which flavors tend to get more love, I've never had a class unanimously agree that one particular flavor of ice cream is best.

In the second scenario, I tell my class to imagine I will order ice cream for them, but I can only order ice cream in one flavor. I ask them to work together to decide which ice cream flavor to order for the class. In this scenario some students will suggest chocolate, others vanilla or strawberry. If anyone suggests a flavor like rocky road or mint chocolate chip, they are prepared to make a compelling case for it. In the end the class almost always comes to a consensus and picks a single flavor for me to order.

The types of arguments my students make in these two different scenarios vary in interesting ways. In the first scenario students tend to make impassioned cases for one flavor or another, extolling its many virtues. They will also attack flavors they don't support, often in creative, if heated, ways. This type of argument falls under what is called **agonistic argumentation**, which means that it emphasizes conflict as a way to solve problems. When we debate the resolution "The United States should use military intervention to further its interests globally," we are engaging in agonistic argumentation. One side will argue for the motion (pro), the other will argue against the motion (con), and with both sides making their best arguments, we have some level of assurance that all the relevant issues will be discussed, and we will come to the best possible outcome under the circumstances. Agonistic argumentation is the most common model in books on argument, and this one is no exception. Although in agonistic argumentation the positive outcomes of conflict are emphasized, cooperation is still an underlying principle of agonistic argumentation, for all the reasons listed in

Chapter 1, including the agreement that the participants will attempt to resolve the controversy by exchanging reasons.

The second scenario is informed by a different model of argumentation altogether. Rather than emphasize conflict, the second scenario asks for a greater degree of cooperation. When I ask my class to work together to choose a single flavor of ice cream for me to order, there are no sides, really, though there are differences of opinion, and so there are no winners or losers. Rather, each of the students in the class recognizes that they are working for the benefit of all.

Coalescent argumentation proceeds according to the following three steps:

1. Participants identify the various positions, points of view, or goals represented.
2. Participants identify shared positions, points of view, or goals and decide not to argue about them.
3. Participants work to find ways of satisfying as many individual goals as do not significantly interfere with their satisfying the shared goals.

The model reflected in the second scenario is called coalescent argumentation. **Coalescent argumentation** is a strategy of argumentation that emphasizes consensus-building to solve disputes rather than conflict. It is the model of argumentation that informs critical discussion.

In the second scenario students often used the techniques of coalescent argumentation, even though they had not yet been taught them. Often they start by suggesting different flavors, some saying vanilla, others chocolate, and so on, just as they did in the first scenario. But they move quickly and often implicitly to identifying the shared goal: free ice cream. The majority of their time, then, they use to identify a flavor that will satisfy as many of them as possible. Sometimes this means taking a poll, with majority rule, but often special circumstances are taken into consideration, and they end up choosing a flavor that is not the most popular. Two students may have a milk allergy, for example, and so the class decides on lemon sorbet; or they might ask everyone to rank the top three flavors, for example, and decide that while the majority of the class prefers chocolate, vanilla is the least offensive to the most, so they go with that.

A critical discussion typically draws on coalescent rather than agonistic argumentation. While conflict in the personal sphere, among friends or family, for example, can be productive, it can also be harmful to the relationship. And generally speaking, people try to avoid conflict if possible, even when they disagree. More often than not, people tend to shy away from conflict by avoiding conversations that highlight disagreements altogether. So we ban or politely pivot away from controversial conversations at the holiday table, for example. Engaging in coalescent argumentation, in which we emphasize common goals that may underlie our differing opinions, often helps facilitate controversial conversations without making things so uncomfortable.

The Shortfalls of Argumentation in the Personal Sphere

Although critical discussion is a great model for argumentation in the personal sphere, you may have been reflecting on your own conversations with friends and family and wondering, "Do I typically engage in critical discussion?" It's not easy to do. When people studying everyday arguments observe conversations in real life or look over transcripts of these conversations, they find that these conversations often fall short of critical discussion in several ways.

For one, and I hinted at this above, people tend to look for ways to end an argument as quickly as possible, even if it means not really resolving anything. This is probably because arguments can be uncomfortable, especially if we associate them with conflict. So in everyday conversations people may avoid sharing their opinions if they differ or agree quickly without hearing reasons, never moving toward critical discussions, and so leaving disagreements unresolved.

On the other hand, sometimes people are heavily invested in one particular outcome. Imagine an argument between a parent and their high-school-age child about curfew. The child may be heavily invested in staying out later, until the same time as their friends, for example. They may not be willing to have a critical discussion about the matter because they are only really willing to accept one outcome. To have a critical discussion, all the parties have to accept that the actual resolution may not be the one they prefer.

Related to this, we sometimes see certain beliefs as so personal that they should not be argued about or even discussed. That varies from group to group and family to family. Some people may enjoy talking about religion, for example, even if their religious views differ, while others may consider religion too personal. Some families don't like to talk about sex, or sexuality, or gender expression. When certain beliefs are seen to be absolutely fundamental to who you are, so much so that they cannot be challenged, they cannot be subject to critical discussion.

Another common shortfall in arguments seen in everyday contexts is that power dynamics, skill, and resources often interfere with critical discussion. Your boss may voice opinions that you don't agree with, but you may fear reprisal if you say anything. You may be much more skilled at argumentation than your little sister and find yourself convincing her of your position on nearly every subject (though, after reading this book, you will undoubtedly look for ways to engage her more ethically). Your friend may always get to choose where you go on Friday nights because they have a car and you don't.

Finally, it is rare to have arguments that are fully developed, with clear claims and evidence and warrants, in everyday conversations. Often, especially when the person with whom you are arguing is someone you have a history with, much of the argument is implicit, and heavy with connotation. Sometimes spouses or old friends find they've really just been having the same argument for the last several years without ever coming to a resolution, so it keeps surfacing in new forms. When the terms of the argument are not clear, when all the participants are not really sure what they are arguing about, having a critical discussion becomes difficult.

We can address these shortfalls by drawing on critical discussion as a model. Next time you are having an argument with someone, see if you can use some of these to achieve a better outcome.

1. Reconstruct their argument more fully, and generously. If the person with whom you are arguing is relying a lot on connotation and implicit claims, see if you can verbalize these into a full argument, complete with claim, evidence, and warrant. Be careful not to appear combative when doing so. Phrases like, "So if I understand you correctly" and "What I'm hearing is" may help.

2. State your own position(s) as fully as possible, according to the standards you've learned throughout this book, and this chapter particularly.

3. Work together to determine specifically what is at issue, separating those issues that all parties are willing to concede from those that are disputed.

4. Identify any aspects of the debate that do not follow the conventions of critical discussion or coalescent argumentation and see if you can work together to address them.

Conclusion

Arguments are a part of everyday life, because people don't always agree on things. People have different experiences, different perspectives, and different values, all of which contribute to their having different preferences in decision-making. These differences are not a problem but rather a potential source for building knowledge. Really, sharing differences in productive ways is the only source for building knowledge. Personal relationships like those among family members and friends are not always rooted in agreement. Disagreement, though, is not in and of itself a problem. Argumentation in the personal sphere works best when it proceeds along some of the same assumptions of argumentation we've been learning throughout this book, especially transparency and cooperation. When we have a critical discussion, we are really just asking all participants to be transparent about their arguments and to cooperate to achieve the best possible outcome. Being transparent about what exactly everyone's argument is, what evidence each participant is basing their argument on, and what exactly is at issue helps the discussion move toward a resolution that will work for everyone.

PROBE

Think of an argument you may have had with a friend or family member. Were you engaging in agonistic or coalescent argumentation? How might the argument have turned out differently if you had engaged in one or the other?

Chapter 16
Academic Argument

Key Terms

technical sphere

conventions

field

data

observation

theory

metaknowledge

Key Points

- Academic arguments belong to the technical sphere, which requires a threshold level of specialized knowledge for participation.
- Academic arguments often involve analysis of data, or systematically gathered evidence.
- Analysis of data involves identifying relevant patterns.

PRIME

How confident are you that you can identify some of the "rules" of argument in academic settings?

Yer Own Motha Wouldna Reckanized Ya
Surviving an Apprenticeship in the "Knowledge Factory"

Suzanne Sowinska (1993)

*And I? I will do everything and anything until the end of my days to stop any-
one ever talking to me like that woman talked to my mother. It is in this place,
this bare, curtainless bedroom that lies my secret and shameful defiance. I read
a woman's book, meet such a woman at a party (a woman now, like me) and
think quite deliberately as we talk: we are divided: a hundred years ago I'd have
been cleaning your shoes. I know this and you don't.*

Carolyn Kay Steedman, *Landscape for a Good Woman*

Everyone knows that a "woman of letters," which is what it seems as a graduate student in an English department I am in training to become, it's not
someone who grew up in "the projects," a trailer court, a split-level exactly like
all the rest on the block, in subsidized housing, or otherwise on the "wrong
side of the tracks." Rather, the image of the female scholar, whose "job" is to
pass her cultural knowledge of literary texts from one generation of students
to the next, is one of refinement: she exudes an elegance of manners and
intellect particular to that class of well-educated women to which she belongs.
She is Virginia Woolf, arguing passionately for "a room of one's own"; she
is Gertrude Stein, reinventing languages; she is not Emma Goldman who,
among her more newsworthy activities, lectured and wrote extensively about
literature, nor is she Anzia Yezierska, who imagined a way to "authentically"
represent the Russian and Jewish immigrant culture which was part of her
verbal landscape as a child.

Although many English departments have become relatively comfortable
with a critical agenda that asserts that the writers we studied come from a multitude of race, class, and gender positions, the backgrounds of those of us who
study those writers is not generally given much thought at all. The actual life
experience of a female scholar is rarely discussed and generally her ascension
through the ranks of academia is assumed to be an unproblematic acquisition
of the written, verbal, and cultural skills needed to perform well in a university
setting. The participation of most poor and working-class women in academia,
however, is frequently not easy or comfortable and is often attended by chronic
interruptions while we seek outside avenues of cultural validation, financial
support, or whatever else is necessary in order for us to continue. Yet there are
many of us who are successful in obtaining jobs inside academic institutions.
We often stick out because we do not choose to adopt the largely middle-class

(and, of course, white) discourse in which most academic institutions conduct their business. We rankle the various ranks of academia to which we belong. We demand texts that describe our concerns when we study, speak to a different audience when we teach, prescribe different critical agendas when we argue, and write about different subjects when we write.

We also write theory and find ourselves resisting theoretical models that refuse to include descriptions of the reality of working-class life. We participate in the activity of theory making even though theory can represent the very sort of abstract thought that has traditionally marked unfamiliar ground in our socially constructed experiences of working-class culture. If we are to accept, for example, the theoretical trends, which posit a notion of the "subject" secured by its "position" within "discourse" (and not by reference to some sort of transcendent essentialism), we except both a limiting paradigm and a way of saying what we mean that linguistically alienates most of those "subjects" we intend to describe. In short, discourse theory with its formulation of passive subjects tends to overlook the ways that any symbolic system is subject to notions of "experience," the realm where class relations are understood, felt, and actually lived. The experiences of working-class women within the specific forms of knowledge gained from those experiences are never simply coded in one discourse but woven in between, through, and around a multitude of discourses. Forms of knowledge are ultimately discovered in what the fabric created by these often disparate discourses says or shows.

To begin to describe ways in which working-class "subjects" might be construed as active agents rather than as passive subjects necessitates a discussion of the role of experience in social relationships which is often missing from theories that focus on a concept of subjectivity as merely a function of the structure of discourse. To describe experience allows an opportunity to see how social relations can be appropriated, resisted, and undermined; it can also provide the basis for action.[1] I will accordingly try to focus my comments here on experiences, beginning with my own and later discussing some of those related to me by other poor and working-class women who have struggled with their apprenticeships as academics. What is the role of women working-class intellectuals (if that's what our training in academia makes us) in reproducing class society? How do our experiences of being working class shape our relationships to academia?

---

1. See Paul Willis and Philip Corrigan, "Orders of Experience: The Differences of Working-Class Cultural Forms" in *Social Text* 7 (Spring-Summer 1983) for an extensive discussion of the positioning of working-class "subjects" within discourse theory and the importance of "experience" in formations of meaning and knowledge.

When I was about twelve, a girl from one of my classes invited me to her house. Her mother wished to encourage a friendship between the two of us because we had the highest scores on that year's academic achievement tests. Her father was a neurosurgeon and her mother a part-time nurse. My father worked in a factory and my mother worked part time in a department store. The Murphys had a house in the country, about two miles outside of the town where school was. My family's house was about one mile on the other side of town in what we referred to as "the developments." My friendship with the daughter didn't last too long. I was allowed to visit at her house but there was always an excuse as to why she couldn't come to mine. But her mother and I became mutually fascinated with one another. Mrs. Murphy (Audrey, she insisted but I never felt quite entitled to say) seemed to want to know everything about me and about my family. How long had my father been in this country? What about my mother? How was it that I had such a large vocabulary and could use such sophisticated phrases? Why did I think it was that the rest of my family wasn't as smart as me? No adult had ever had time to take such an interest in me before, and I wanted very much to be listened to.

In my best twelve-year-old reasoning I explained to my friend's mother that my sophistication had come from reading, that my mother read between four and six books a week, and that I had picked up "reading" from her. She told me that it was an admirable thing that my mother kept herself up through reading, especially with all my brothers and sisters, and became embarrassed when I attempted a defense by asking her how many books a week she read. With her response and a trip to the room that housed their family library, I acquired my first definition of what literature was: what Audrey read were called novels, my mother read paperbacks. From that day on my reading practices changed. I became determined to know whatever it was that Audrey got from reading novels that my mother didn't get from reading what she read. Along with coveting the books she owned, I coveted Audrey's confidence, graciousness, and apparent wisdom and I tried desperately to find it at our town's tiny branch of the public library. And, although I occasionally slipped back into reading a gothic novel or two, after that most of my time was spent reading what my sister and I (and most university English departments) referred to as "classics."

What I was unable to understand until many years later was exactly how much the barely discernible note of disdain in Audrey's voice, as she differentiated my mother's reading habits from her own, was able to change totally the arrangement of one small part of my world and cause me to negotiate an adjustment to what I privately began to think of as more accepted or normal. I was, of course, making similar negotiations in other parts of my life. The older I grew the more familiar it became to keep making adjustments on many different levels. Without understanding what I was doing or why I was doing it, I began to feel ashamed of who I was, who my family was, what they thought about, where they came from, and I began to alter myself and my appearance in an attempt to escape association with what they seemed to represent to others.

By providing me with a range of choices and an advanced vocabulary, the novels I read began to help me satisfy my desire to get free from what I then perceived as the constraints of the social class in which I was being raised. The seemingly better worlds and richer landscapes each individual narrative offered provided me with a fantasy of escape and helped me to see how it was possible to make up for whatever social sophistication I lacked through language. More and more I began to live in two very separate worlds, the one that I was born into and the one I was constructing out of various fictions of what I thought normal, intelligent, educated people were really like. Today, I've learned to label these self-limiting activities as attempting to "pass" for middle class, but for a long time, including all of my undergraduate years, I lived in a confused state of preconsciousness where I often, although not always, felt an urgent need to mask my working-class origins. Nowhere did I feel a greater need for disguise than inside academic institutions where the heightened level of discourse both fascinated and intimidated me and put me in situations where I most feared that someone would discover that I was only pretending to be "educated" and force me to leave. Although I felt a great deal of tension, confusion, and discomfort, I was not able to articulate these feelings as linked to class oppression. The mechanisms of a dominant discourse were fully in operation: I internalized my feelings as somehow related to something out of place or missing in me rather than as indicative of a system of oppression carefully masked by myths of equal access and opportunity.

A deep passion for reading, which is intricately connected to notions of escape, survival, and passing, is part of the reality of almost all the poor and working-class women in academia that I know. To pass means to attempt to disguise working-class origins by outwardly adopting codes of behavior that come from outside working-class experience. Academic institutions present ideal situations for successful passing as they ostensibly operate under the premise that intelligence rather than background determines ability. Yet passing should also be seen positively as a skill that women from working-class backgrounds have developed in order to survive in academic environments. When used consciously, the ability to pass can become a valuable tool, capable of causing internal disruptions and potential manipulations of the institutions it operates within. But I'm jumping ahead of my argument here. Before I talk about how such experiences can be used for political ends, I must first describe their origins in class oppression.

For me, to be at college and to be able to read and interpret texts meant a freedom to experience words and worlds way beyond the grasp of what I had once considered to be available to me, but it also meant leaving behind the familiar validations of experience and community offered by my family and friends. My own passing included, among its other manifestations, altering my speech, changing the way I dressed, remaining silent during conversations about family, pretending to have enough money when I didn't, claiming I wasn't hungry when I was. I also developed a tendency toward automatic lying, filling in what I perceived as gaps in my background, telling people what I thought they wanted to hear, inventing, creating, making up stories. At that time in my life, these parts of me that I was giving up seemed unimportant, and I felt them as necessary sacrifices in order for me to be seen as legitimate. Nor did I think too much about the extra energy I was expending in my attempts to fit in: the trade-off was to become "educated," which would bring liberation.

Before I had developed any sense of class consciousness or a way to articulate class-based experience, I had learned to successfully negotiate my behavior away from the working-class culture I had been raised in to match that of the middle-class culture I had become immersed in. From this notion that there was a different set of cultural codes to adjust to eventually would come the recognition that the frames of reference for both sets of codes were illusory. At that time I was not concerned in any conscious or intentional way with identifying the nature of class relations as they operate within academic institutions. Nevertheless, through my experiences of difference eventually came the knowledge that exposed the central fallacy under which all educational systems operate: that success is determined by effort or ability rather than by class background. This was not an outside knowledge brought to me through a theory of class relations but something that arose out of my experience of class-based oppression.

Just as passing presents an aspect of experience that is unique to poor and working-class women in training to become academics, there are other social and intellectual survival strategies we use in attempts to continue to gain access to the cultural expertise offered by a university education. Where there are no family resources to provide us with the necessary financial or cultural prerequisites for our educations, we learn to do just about anything to be able to keep reading books. Economic survival is often the most basic of our concerns, and I will accordingly recount here some of the strategies other working-class women in academia have used in order to remain in school. I have one friend, for example, who described a period of about six weeks where she would take three or four books per night to sell at a used-book store on her way to the supermarket so she could have money to buy food. She was a Victorianist and, after being unable to part with Jane Austen, was alphabetically up to Dickens before her student-loan check finally arrived. This was after having sold off her classics, seventeenth-, eighteenth-, and twentieth-century texts and her copy of the abridged OED (which she was overjoyed to get thirty dollars for, describing the money as almost enough to feed her for two weeks).

Another friend had developed techniques for reading books without breaking their spines so she could return them a few days later claiming she was no longer enrolled in the course. Another shoplifted books but kept a record of every time she did, hoping to pay the money back in some future time when she had more cash. She knew that if she were caught she would have to agree never to "shop" at the university bookstore again, but she was hoping to make it through all her course work before that happened. She later acquired a stamp marked "used book" and began to change prices.

Another friend found a way to successfully hide her enrollment at a local university from the state so she could receive food stamps, which she then traded with others for money so she could buy books. Another worked every Monday night, the "single women and children" shift, at a local food bank. She told others that it was her way to help homeless women but privately confessed to me that it not only guaranteed her a meal but usually provided her with extra food she could take home. Another woman forged her father's name on a new income tax return when he refused to stop declaring her as his dependent.

One particularly desperate friend described how she frequently signed herself up as a paid participant for psychological and medical experiments conducted at the medical school of the university she was attending. She particularly liked the ones that involved only a few hours of her active participation but included two or three weeks of isolation and felt that she got some of her best studying done in hospital rooms. She stopped participating, however, after having agreed (for $460) to be part of an experiment comparing the spinal fluid of anorexics with that of "normal volunteers." Something went wrong with the spinal tap that her doctor-in-training performed on her; she spent two weeks in bed recovering from the botched procedure.

Another strategy common to women students from working-class backgrounds when faced with a lack of funding to continue their education is to seek employment within universities as clerical workers. There are a large number of working-class women in academia who have worked as secretaries, receptionists, filing clerks, word processors, or administrative assistants in universities, often in the very departments that will eventually grant them their degrees. In the English department where I am currently enrolled as an advanced graduate student, there has been a steady stream of fellow graduate students who also work as secretaries in our department. Many of them are relieved to find employment in such a familiar environment even though their jobs frequently put them in uncomfortable situations with both their professors and other students.

Of course, all students at one time or another find themselves in financially difficult situations. What makes the situation of poor and working-class women so unique is the way in which economic survival strategies are intimately connected to our self-esteem and collective notions of fear, shame, and defiance that make up our individual family or neighborhood landscapes. For the women I described above to have to "go on welfare" in order to stay in school meant she had to carry around a great deal of shame and a sense of having betrayed her familial and cultural values. In addition, her eventual employment as a secretary in a university left her feeling as though that was where she belonged: her proper place in the overall scheme of things was as a worker rather than as a thinker.

Much of what students from middle- or upper-class backgrounds take for granted and expect to be a part of college life is quite outside the experience of those of us who were the first in our families to attend college. I can imagine that most students from middle-class backgrounds have not had the experience of enjoying dining hall food (because it is like "eating out" every night) nor do they delight in the privacy offered by a dormitory room shared with only one other person. Furthermore, they probably don't feel as though their delight and excitement at their new surroundings needs to be hidden. These feelings were all part of my first few days at college.

If I had remained only within university environments, I may never have discovered that I was raised working class. Although three generations on my mother's side and two generations on my father's side of my family had been laborers, they all thought of themselves as equal players in a mainly middle-class America, the land of opportunity for all. The members of the Polish side of my family, my grandmother, aunts, uncles, and cousins, had a concept of themselves as culturally distinct, but there were no class distinctions made even though a general mood of inferiority and lack of a sense of entitlement pervaded almost all their interactions outside their immediate neighborhood. Their struggle was so entirely defined as an attempt to rid themselves of the markers of their status as immigrants that the fact that some of those markers were class based did not occur to them as that important. It must have seemed to them that to stop sounding, acting, and looking Polish would unquestionably mean one had obtained the status of sounding, acting, and looking like middle-class Americans.

Having been "born and raised in America," both my parents had achieved their parents' goals of cultural proficiency, but the class-based markers remained. In terms of their dealings with the world, these translated into very little confidence, pride, or conviction in their own right to exist, and what I learned from them was that in most cases it was best to submit to those in positions of greater authority, power, and knowledge. Clichéd messages like "Don't rock the boat"; "It's best to just let a sleeping dog lie"; and "It doesn't do any good to try and buck the system," which had been passed to them from their parents, informed their personal vocabularies of self-debasement and shame, which they then passed on to me. This discourse of subjugation and deference to others had become so naturalized in them that they were unable to imagine any other, let alone begin to touch on the causes or reasons for the differences they must have felt.

Education was devalued in the white working-class culture in which I was raised.[2] My parents actively tried to discourage me from attending college. Prophesies of failure from my mother abounded; she was sure that I wouldn't finish my first year, let alone graduate. Although they could afford to, they provided no financial support; they did not want to participate in my separation from them. They did not want me to go outside their world, to become unfamiliar, to become a part of any of the institutions that they vaguely sensed were responsible for their manipulation and oppression. They were, it seems, at least somewhat correct in their fears: my college education made me no longer completely one of them. Not only did my vocabulary change by the time I had finished college, but I also had begun to dress differently, was eating different foods, and, among countless other small changes, insisted on fresh ground rather than instant coffee. I also began to notice a change in my family's responses to me. My mother occasionally now used the tone of humility and deference with me that she usually reserved for authority figures like police, bank officials, and bureaucrats while privately asserting her dismay to my brothers and sisters at how much better than the rest of the family I thought I had become.

My understanding of feminism, which had become much more grounded in the four years of relatively uninterrupted "reading" that college had provided, also helped to alienate me from my family and cultural roots. I had become an activist, organizing demonstrations, participating in acts of civil disobedience, attending conferences, and helping to publish a feminist newspaper. The feminist agenda to which I had committed myself, however, failed to include a class analysis. Nevertheless, my participation in feminist and

---

2. My experience may be more typical of white working-class culture. In many experiences of working-class culture, education is valued as a tool for upward mobility. For example, in a workshop on classism I attended at the 1989 NWSA Conference, many of the black and Jewish working-class women reported having had a great deal of pressure from their families to attend college. In cases where family resources were limited, however, preference was given to support the education of male members of the family.

radical communities did provide me with the tools of self-discovery that I needed to begin to analyze the sense of difference of which I had always been acutely aware.

Coming out as a lesbian was the main event that prepared me for the much more difficult ordeal of coming out as working class. As part of the powerful discourse of positive self-esteem and discovery present in most lesbian and gay communities, the experience of coming out taught me to turn shame and fear into anger and action. For me, a critique of power relations first came from the oppression I felt as a member of a sexual minority. The process of growing to understand myself as working class was very similar to the process of growing to understand myself as lesbian. Because of my early proclivities for "reading," I went to the library. When I began to think of myself as a lesbian, I took out every lesbian novel I could find. A whole new world and language was opened to me. When I began to think of myself as working class, I searched the library again. I wanted retellings of experience, not theory, yet this time I had a harder time knowing quite what headings in the card catalog to look under to find novels told from the perspective of working-class women.

My discoveries in the library gave me the beginnings of a class analysis, a reason to begin graduate school, and a subject to study once I got there. Talking with other women graduate students who also identified as being from poor or working-class backgrounds became the only way to ensure my sanity in graduate school and to validate my own class-based experience. Once I began to share the strategies I had used for survival with these women and began to listen to their experiences, my own no longer seemed so strange or even so extreme. Together we began to unravel the layers of shame, fear, and insecurity that represented our legacies as working-class scholars. We also began to imagine the beginnings of an analysis of class and gender relations that would not only describe our experience but also help us develop peda-gogical approaches to use with other women students.

The lived experience of class-based oppression is what forces many working-class women academics from a cultural understanding of the operation of difference to a political recognition of the way in which social relations are ordered. We eventually learn to create rearticulations of our experience in order to discover a sense of identity. Leaving behind what is familiar to us in exchange for unfamiliar intellectual and economic survival strategies often provides a catalyst for critique and a desire to understand new terms in the subject/subjugated argument, allowing for the possibility of agency and real movement. The way that we exist as working class forms an identity not auto-matically written into the internal power relations of any particular context or discourse. What began as survival strategies have changed, for many of us, into powerful instruments we use to manipulate our environment. We have learned to reclaim the weapons of fear and shame once used against us, appropriating them for acts of defiance and creative undermining.[3]

There are, after all, advantages to our position. One fellow scholar argues that women from working-class backgrounds have nothing at stake in the middle-class ideologies that often pass for knowledge in academic institutions. She feels that her lack of complicity with the cultural values advanced by universities has put her in a better position than others to ask questions: "for bourgeois scholars, deconstruction is the latest critical theory; for working-class scholars it has always been a way of life."[4] The ability to see from at least two viewpoints at once, which the experience of passing provides, often makes it easier for working-class women to form alliances with members of other oppressed groups who experience similar disjunctions. We are also usually very adept at translating between individuals and institutions, exposing and demystifying self-perpetuating systems of authority. We tend to place the emphasis on individuals rather than on a set of invisible rules of conduct, trying to recognize and validate those students who seem to have a hard time adjusting to academic life.

The experience of feeling like an outsider in academic environments allows many of us access to a better understanding of the ideological function of the institutions we work within. One friend described to me how her position as working class gave her a clear understanding that the role of the state college she attended was to churn out teachers and low-level managers. She subsequently felt more knowledgeable and less pressured than those around her to adopt the facade of success that was being proffered by the institution. Another woman described how she used her ability to pass to gain access to classrooms. She knew what cultural knowledge she was supposed to be passing on to her students but instead chose to use her role as teacher differently. Common assignments for her included initiating discussions that, among other goals, would help students begin to deconstruct their experiences of difference and their complicity with the power relations at work within their immediate surroundings.

In general, we women graduate students from working-class backgrounds have an understanding of the nature of "work" that differs from those around us. On the one hand, our experience of work as physically difficult and labor intensive makes academic work seem easy, hardly like work at all. On the other hand, it is easy for us to see how institutions often disguise work as

---

3. I am especially indebted to my conversations with Helen Boscoe, Pamela Fox, Beth Hutchison, Barbara Schulman, and Rachel Stevens for their thoughts on both the subjugation and the resistances of working-class women in academia.

4. From a conversation with Rachel Stevens, November 1989.

something other than work: where being nominated to serve on an undergraduate curriculum committee, for example, is presented as a helpful addition to a curriculum vitae instead of as the additional two hours per week work time that it is. Many working-class women academics also have more of a notion of work as separate from life: being an academic is what you do for a living as opposed to who you are the rest of the time.[5]

Working-class women academics who have also worked as secretaries in educational settings are quick to understand exactly where decision-making power lies within their departments. One friend describes using her sense of camaraderie with other secretaries to cut through much of the bureaucratic red tape experienced by her fellow graduate students. She was able to secure office and classroom assignments, keys to rooms, parking permits, and other everyday survival needs through her ability to interact with secretaries as peers. There is also no better way that I can think of for deconstructing the intellectual and cultural mystique of the ivory tower than being "on staff," where it becomes very clear that undergraduate acceptances, graduate appointments, faculty appointments, and tenure decisions are based on politics rather than merit.

Through the experience of living within the particular social relation of being both female and a working-class scholar comes the knowledge of how both articulations of dominant forms of discourse and resources against them are carried in permanent conflict. This recognition punctures and deflates the persistent myth of both working-class and female passivity just as our position as "educated" destroys the fiction of working-class ignorance and subordination. Although these comments should not be seen as an attempt to valorize the survival strategies used by working-class women in academia, they do recognize those strategies as forms of resistance being cultivated within the very system that has produced our subordination. It is equally important to note that the danger of our potential incorporation into the middle class is great and that we must learn new ways to resist the temptation to abandon our cultures and families of origin for the promised land of middle-class respectability. "The master's tools will never dismantle the master's house," but perhaps we apprentices will begin to see ways that the internal form of a particular discourse can be used to control the master.[6]

---

5. For an in-depth study of the ideological role of the academic institution as workplace, see Evan Watkins, *Work Time: English Departments and the Circulation of Cultural Values* (Stanford UP, 1989).

6. Audre Lorde, "The Master's Tools Will Never Dismantle the Master's House," in *This Bridge Called My Back*, ed. Cherrie Moraga and Gloria Anzaldúa (Watertown, Mass.: Persephone, 1981).

Even today I am sometimes haunted by echoes of the shame I once felt but had no words for. I feel a great deal of sadness for the young scholar who carried that shame around and at the same time I am embarrassed by the "simple beliefs" I once had. My newly gained sense of entitlement often seems too fragile to sustain me, and if I'm not careful I can still become too paralyzed to use the privilege of my education to speak. But at last, after a long struggle, I have not needed to discard my family or cultural values. I live instead in a strangely ambiguous middle ground, insisting on the validity of my working-class roots and experiences yet also feeling outside of them, transported by means of education and political awareness to another place I can't quite call home.

My mother occasionally sends me what she calls "survival packages" to help me get by at school. They contain food, never money. In fact it always amazes me that she spends more money mailing the package to me than it would cost to send me a check and let me buy the food myself. But I'm glad she doesn't. Along with the canned beef stew that I no longer eat and always end up giving to a food bank, she inevitably includes a package or two of "International Coffees." These instant coffee drinks have pretentious packaging and names: Orange Cappuccino, Irish Creme, Suisse Mocha, Double Dutch Chocolate, and Cafe Vienna. She never drinks what the box proclaims are "elegant drinks" herself; she only buys them because they match her perception of what I like now that I live and work in such a "classy" environment. Her gifts never fail to bring a smile. Her attempts to understand me almost seem an ironic recognition of the in-between space in which I am always finding myself. I guess these are the coffee spoons with which I get to measure out my life.

PAUSE

Sowinska focuses on the position of working-class women in academia. Make a list of the identity positions you occupy. Which of these seem more welcome in academia, and which seem less welcome?

Introduction

In the previous chapter we looked at argumentation in the personal sphere, between people who engage with one another primarily as individuals. I mentioned in that chapter that there are three spheres of argumentation, with the second and third (after the personal sphere) being the technical sphere and public sphere, respectively.

So in this chapter I want to look at the second sphere, the technical sphere. The **technical sphere** is the space where arguments most relevant to experts take place. Arguments in the technical sphere have a broader appeal than in the personal sphere. They matter not only to those involved in the argument but also to the larger professional communities they belong to. Unlike the public sphere, though, which we'll cover in Chapter 17, participation in the technical sphere is not open to all but requires a threshold level of specialized knowledge.

As students you probably encounter the technical sphere most commonly in academic settings. When you read scholarly articles for your classes, when you have conversations with classmates and professors about scholarly issues, when you talk to your biology professor about a new experiment that you read about, or your English professor about a particularly interesting interpretation of *King Lear*, you are engaging in conversation in the technical sphere. In addition to academic arguments, arguments in the professions, such as law or accounting, are also arguments in the technical sphere.

In Sowinska's essay she makes it clear that she's not doing the traditional academic argument. In fact much of what she's arguing in this piece is that traditional academic argument has excluded personal experience—especially of those who do not reflect the dominant culture—as knowledge. You may find Sowinska's argument resonating with your own experiences as you think about yourself in relation to the academic work you do as a student. Maybe you've been asked to avoid using "I" in your writing, or maybe you've been told that your personal experience doesn't really count for evidence in this particular context. It's this tradition of excluding or not trusting the personal point of view that Sowinska is taking issue with in this essay.

At the same time, when we look specifically at the arguments Sowinska is making central in her essay, it's clear that she really is making a very academic argument. In fact, her argument follows the conventions of argumentation in the technical sphere very clearly.

Though there are elements of argumentation in the technical sphere that seem more or less common regardless of the field or discipline or profession, there are also numerous, sometimes subtle, differences from subject to subject or field to field. Recognizing these differences can be quite tricky, especially for people who are new to the field. You may have noticed that the writing you've been asked to do in your sociology class, for example, is quite different than the writing you've been asked to do in your chemistry class. And both of those, in turn, differ from the kind of writing you've been asked to do in this course. What may be particularly confusing is that often people use the same words to mean different things, or different words to mean quite similar things. This is because argumentation in the technical sphere is governed by lots of rules that operate at the level of the specific field.

So let's take a closer look at what argumentation in the technical sphere looks like.

Arguments in the Technical Sphere Are Governed by Special Rules

In the technical sphere, arguments have to follow specific rules, known as **conventions**. These conventions depend on the specific field in which the argument is taking place. While certain conventions may be shared across fields in the technical sphere, many of the conventions are actually dependent on the particular field. A **field** is an area of acute interest within the technical sphere. Fields include academic subjects like biology and communications, as well as theoretical orientations or worldviews, like modernism or pragmatism. Professions, such as law or architecture, can also constitute fields.

We're going to look most closely at arguments in the academic field in this chapter because those are the types of arguments you're most likely to encounter as students. We're going to look at arguments in academic fields generally, rather than any particular field, so it's important to emphasize that arguments in academic fields can vary significantly from field to field. What this chapter provides is a general overview with the understanding that certain fields may not conform to some of these conventions, and they may also introduce conventions not covered in this chapter.

Generally speaking, however, academic arguments begin with some interpretation of some data. What counts as data is going to vary significantly from discipline to discipline. For example, in an English literature class a novel can count as data. In that case you are making an interpretation of the novel, which is serving as your data. In psychology, however, a novel generally would not count as data. Data in psychology tends to come from observation of human subjects.

The interpretation of data and academic fields tends to be based on identification of patterns. So, for example, let's say you're reading a poem in an English class and you find that the color red is coming up a lot. Red forms a pattern for you, which you have observed. In a biology class, while you're going to be looking at very different data, you're still going to be looking for any emerging patterns in that data.

The third element in most academic arguments is a claim based on your interpretation of the patterns you've observed. Depending on the field you're writing in, this might be called a claim or a thesis or an argument. Some academic fields accept the raising of new questions, or the call for more research, as the centering point of an argument.

UNDERLYING ASSUMPTIONS OF ARGUMENTS IN ACADEMICS

1. Arguments begin with the interpretation of some data or accessible evidence.
2. Analysis of data involves identifying relevant patterns.
3. Claims evolve out of the analysis and are highly contextualized interpretations of the data patterns.

Evidence or Data

In academic arguments evidence is often referred to as **data**. Generally speaking, data serves the same role in academic arguments as evidence does in argumentation in general. Data is gathered through observation. **Observation** is the systematic and transparent recording of information. All three of these features are important when it comes to gathering evidence: systematic, transparent, and recording.

Observation must be systematic. There are more complicated definitions out there for what it means to have systematic observation, but for our purposes it's enough simply to say that there must be a set procedure that you're following when you gather your data, and from which you do not deviate, even when it may be convenient to do so. The types of systems that are appropriate for gathering data will differ from field to field. Sowinska argues that, because knowledge can be made from the experiences of working-class women, narrative of personal experience should be accepted as evidence. Implicitly, Sowinska is arguing for a new method or a new system for collecting data by narrating personal experience. Although it may seem like personal narrative is not a systematic way of gathering data, Sowinska argues persuasively for its value.

In other fields, observation will follow different rules. In some highly technical scientific fields, for example, instruments rather than humans are performing the observations. In fields that are centered around texts like English or philosophy, observation is done by reading books, articles or essays, or other texts. In fields such as art history or architecture, data is gathered by observing images or structures. In other fields data may be gathered by interviewing people or distributing surveys. Each of these different systems for gathering data will have its own specific rules that you must follow.

SUBJECTIVITY IN SCIENTIFIC OBSERVATION

Regardless of the method you're using to gather data, it's important to remember that there's always going to be a subjective element. In other words, you are never just making pure observations. You will notice some things and not notice other things. Two observers can look at the same object and notice very different things, meaning these two observers will end up gathering very different data. Consider again our example from Birk and Birk, introduced in Chapter 5: an artist, a lumberjack, and a tree scientist all looking at the same tree. Each one will notice very different things about that tree, because they have different priorities and different purposes for looking at that tree. The artist, for example, might notice the tree's relative symmetry, or the combination of colors that make up the foliage, while the lumberjack might notice how thick the tree trunk is. Some of these differences will be reflected in the different methods each of these people uses when observing the tree. But some differences will be down to the individual. In other words, even three lumberjacks looking at the same tree might each notice something different.

The same is true for situations in which scientific tools or computers are making the observations, because these tools must be designed, calibrated, and used by people, who always bring their experiences, training, and perspectives with them. On top of that, even if computers or tools are gathering the data, most of the time in the end it will be humans who make interpretations of that data. The human element is both a strength and a limitation of academic observation. It is a strength only to the extent that we can be systematic and transparent about gathering the data.

Observation must be transparent. In other words, it's very important that the observer is precise and clear about what system or what method they are using to make their observations, and they must communicate this method when describing their observations. If you've ever read a scientific article, you will have noticed that a significant portion of it is dedicated to what's called the methods section. This section describes in detail the system the researcher(s) used to gather their data. The methods section is almost like a recipe: it gives the precise tools and specific steps for recreating the same research project. Its purpose is, similarly to a recipe, to give future researchers interested in the same problem or similar ones all the information they will need to gather the same data in the same way, or to see if there's something about the system the researchers used to make their observations that may affect the data in a negative way.

Academic fields that don't typically rely on a methods section still must be clear and transparent about how they're making their observations. Often this is done by referencing previous studies and theoretical perspectives on similar issues. A critical analysis of a Shakespearean drama, for example, may make it clear that it's using a new historicist perspective, while an analysis of a new architectural space will state that it's drawing on a postmodern perspective in order to be clear about the way it's making its observations. Fields like these that draw heavily on text-based sources tend also to be systematic about pointing to specific passages they're using to make their analyses. That's why you'll notice the citation practices in these fields include in-text citations, which point to the page or paragraph numbers of source texts. With the rise of digital texts, page numbers are not always available, so subsequent researchers use the search function to identify the exact passages. Just like the methods section in a scientific article, these references to passages and page numbers allow future researchers to do similar work, either to build on the work that's already been done or to argue for a different interpretation.

Finally, *observations must be recorded*. This may be done in a notebook, using a computer program, or through voice or video recording. Again, different fields will have different methods for recording their data. Unless it is recorded, however, it is not data; it becomes data only once it is recorded.

FINDING AND INTERPRETING PATTERNS IN QUALITATIVE DATA

The types of patterns that may be valuable in a given set of data will depend on a lot of things, such as the purpose of the study, the field or specialization, the tools used to review the data, and the type of data (quantitative or qualitative; see Chapter 7).

Generally it is a good idea to look for four types of patterns in qualitative data. These patterns may be valuable to research in several fields, including those in social and natural sciences, humanities, and several professional fields. When you find these patterns in your data, the first step is to record them.

Exact Repetitions

An exact repetition is a pattern of the same word or thing coming up a significant number of times. If you are reading a poem and the word "red" comes up several times, that is an exact repetition. What counts as significant will depend on the data you are reviewing, your field, and your purposes. It should be enough times that you can make a compelling case to your audience that it is a meaningful repetition. Though basic and often the most obvious, exact repetition can nevertheless be very valuable. If you are a market researcher interviewing several people about their buying preferences for a particular product, for example, and one brand keeps coming up, that exact repetition may be very important to your research.

Similar Repetitions

Sometimes what you find repeated in data is not the exact same thing but rather a series of similar things or ideas. For example, if you are reading a poem and words like "sugar," "honey," "candy," and "sweet" keep coming up, that would be a repetition of the similar. Again, the repetition must happen enough times that you could make a compelling case to your audience that it is a significant repetition. Like with exact repetitions, repetitions of the similar can be a valuable pattern. Consider a usability researcher who notices people characterizing a product as "difficult to use," "confusing," "unwieldy," and "clunky." These could be an important repetition of the similar.

Binary Oppositions

A binary opposition is a pair of concepts that gain meaning through their difference from one another. Often these are abstract ideas that only gain coherence by making it clear that they do not belong to the other category. This doesn't mean you can't define each concept on its own, just that they are concepts that often come in pairs and are often defined against each other. Perhaps you are reading a poem that references equality. Think about how you might define something like equality. A reasonable definition might be the absence of inequality. So equality and inequality are binary oppositions, because one is often defined against the other. Or perhaps a market researcher finds that many people in a focus group continually reference their competitor brand when talking about their products (think Coke/Pepsi). This would be an important binary opposition in the data. Other common binary oppositions are masculine/feminine, liberal/conservative, developed/underdeveloped, upper class/lower class, and legal/illegal.

Anomalies

An anomaly is something that stands out for its difference. You may have heard the childhood song "One of These Things Is Not Like the Other." A blue balloon in a crowd of red balloons is an anomaly. Perhaps you notice that the imagery in a poem mostly reflects sweet things, but a particular character or experience is presented with bitter imagery. That bitter imagery might be an anomaly. A market researcher might find that, while a focus group responds positively to most of the products to which it is introduced, a particular product was unpopular.

List in Order of Importance

The next step, after recording exact repetitions, similar repetitions, binary oppositions, and anomalies, is to list them in order of importance. How do you know which patterns are important and which are not? This is where your knowledge of the discipline comes in. What disciplinary question or controversy are you responding to? The relevance of any particular pattern to the question or controversy you are responding to determines which patterns are more important than others, such that the more relevant a pattern is to your particular question or controversy, the more important it is.

For example, let's say you are researching the way women are portrayed in nineteenth-century British literature. As you read a novel relevant to your study, you notice that women are often portrayed as either mentally unstable or wildly immoral. You take note of these instances and decide they are important, because they deal directly with how women are portrayed. This repetition of the similar makes it to the top of your list of important patterns. Perhaps you also note that men in the novel, on the other hand, are portrayed very differently, even when they act in similar ways to the women. You decide that the binary women/men is also important. Were your research responding to a different question or controversy, you might find a different set of patterns to be important, even in the same novel.

Or say you are a market researcher trying to decide which products to introduce to a new market. Perhaps you find that the responses often compare your product with a similar product already available in that market. That binary opposition might make the top of your list of important patterns.

Make an interpretation of the data in relation to the text as a whole. This interpretation of your data will form the basis for your claim, discussed in the next section.

Claims

Like data, claims differ in nature from one academic field to another. The same statement may count as a claim in one field but not be accepted as a claim in another field. This causes making arguments in different disciplines to be particularly difficult for students because the rules that determine whether or not something counts as a claim are often complicated and implicit. On top of that, because faculty members don't often have opportunities to talk about the differences between their field and others, they often use the same language to mean different things without knowing it.

Generally speaking, a claim in an academic argument interprets the data with respect to existing theory in that discipline. **Theory** in academic fields is specialized knowledge that structures ways of thinking in that particular field. Sometimes theory functions as a kind of **metaknowledge**, knowledge about knowledge, or ways of knowing in that discipline. We learn the theories of a field by reading about them and by listening to experts in that field describe the theories. Experts in the field in turn modify and add to theory by making claims about it. Typically claims make interpretations of patterns evident in the data by relating those patterns to theory. A claim might reflect an attempt to apply existing theory to new data, it might reflect an attempt to apply new theory to existing data, or it might reflect an attempt to show the limitations of existing theories in the face of new data. Though the form a claim might take in academic arguments varies, the basic principles of claims described throughout this book apply. An academic claim must:

1. Be a statement: a sentence that clearly expresses a fact, an opinion, or a point of view;
2. Have truth value, meaning that it can be shown to be either true or false; and
3. Respond to a controversy.

Warrants

Warrants in academic arguments do the work of connecting the argument to the relevant field. They implicitly respond to the question "Why is this argument important to the field? Why does it matter?"

As we learned in Chapter 3, in argumentation generally the warrant is the contextual assumption or set of assumptions that links the evidence to the claim. In academic arguments, these assumptions are often made up of highly specialized knowledge. The warrant helps sort information, deciding what might function as a claim, what counts as evidence, and even what counts as a controversy.

So in the traditional argument model, you might have:

Claim: The cat was on my bed.

Evidence: There are little orange and white hairs on my blanket.

Warrant: Cats are animals that often shed small hairs.

In an academic argument the work of the warrant is similarly to ground the claim and evidence. So you might have:

Claim: When silicon nanowires are fabricated using chemical vapor deposition (CVP), they scatter and absorb more light than similarly sized wires fabricated using other methods, because of their relatively high density.

Evidence: A series of measurements performed under controlled conditions.

Well, what is the warrant here? Here the warrant will be rooted in information that shows why this claim is a claim. It will show what controversy it is responding to.

At first glance, to a nonexpert, the claim above seems like an observation parallel to the statement "The table is 60 inches long." This is where the warrant comes into play in academic arguments: it makes clear to its audience why the claim is a claim, why as reasonable experts they ought to take note of it. The warrant in academic arguments explicitly or implicitly situates the claim in the context of a specific controversy in the field. Potential warrants are described with a somewhat complex form known as the CARS model (see box).

THE CARS MODEL

One way to think about warrants in academic arguments is that they create spaces in which new research may exist. The Create a Research Space (CARS) model, developed from the work of John Swales, describes several potential warrants for academic arguments, which Swales describes as moves.

Move 1: Establishing Centrality

In academic arguments the controversy often begins with questions like "Why is the scholarship in which you are engaged important in the field? To whom in the field is it important, specifically?" The first move, then, is to show how the current topic is something that continues to be of interest to the field.

Step 1: Claiming centrality

Semiconducting nanowires have recently been of great interest to the scientific and technical communities because of several promising properties.

and/or

Step 2: Making a topic generalization

Semiconducting nanowires generally have been shown to have great efficiency due to their ability to trap light within their structures.

and/or

Step 3: Reviewing previous research

Scholars such as Bruno Latour, Charles Bazerman, and Christina Haas have analyzed the rhetorical operations through which scientific facts have come to be seen as universal natural truths, rather than knowledge claims in the technical sphere. Their work has shown scientific knowledge to be highly and self-consciously rhetorical.

Move 2: Establishing a Niche

Having shown that the topic is of general interest to the scholarly community, writers of academic arguments next specify with greater detail what controversy their research responds to.

Step 1A: Counterclaiming

Theories of social capital in economics, such as that presented in Putnam's analysis, fail to present a sufficiently clear formulation of measurement, which in turn clouds the field's understanding of social capital.

Or

Step 1B: Indicating a gap
While many studies have pointed to dramatic increases in computer use in education, little research exists on the effectiveness of such use.

Or

Step 1C: Question raising
Scholars of Soviet History have documented the inhumane treatment of prisoners in the Gulag, with many characterizing the labor camps as little more than death camps. Many camps, however, invested significant resources into cultural rehabilitation efforts, and recently opened records reveal that millions of prisoners, even political prisoners, were released after serving their terms. These facts, taken together, raise the question of whether or not rehabilitation was an earnest goal of the Soviet Gulag.

Or

Step 1D: Continuing a tradition
Research on knee pain has long sought to clearly define the terminology relative to the different causes of anterior knee pain. By screening out anterior knee pain caused by a variety of well-defined pathologies, this study suggests the remaining presentations of anterior knee pain may be classified as patellofemoral pain syndrome.

Move 3: Occupying the Niche

Now that the controversy is clearly defined according to the field's interests, the final move in the CARS model is to indicate how the current research responds to the controversy.

Step 1A: Outlining purposes
The purpose of this study is to determine the extent to which federal forest management mitigates fire risk in California.

Or

Announcing present research
This study measured the effects of different wavelengths of light on the production of saliva melatonin.

Step 2: Announcing principal findings
The shorter wavelengths of 470, 495, and 525 nm showed the greatest melatonin onset advances ranging from approximately 40 to 65 min, while the longer wavelengths produced no significant phase advance.

Step 3: Indicating article structure
The first section of this article examines attitudes toward language diversity among primary teachers. Next, we examine attitudes toward

language diversity among secondary teachers. The third section compares and contrasts the results in these two categories, and we conclude
by suggesting what factors may account for these differences.

Conclusion

You have most likely been introduced to many academic arguments already and have
no doubt made several of your own. The subject matter of academic disciplines—
from anthropology to zoology—is an accumulation of arguments responding to controversies and controversies arising out of new arguments. The value of arguments in
academic fields is not so much that they end controversies but that they give rise to
new important questions, questions that drive scholarly inquiry in those fields.

One of the most important things to understand as a student, then, is your
own role in academic argument: that you are not simply to memorize and recite
arguments in the field but look for ways to engage them, to consider new controversies, ask new questions that are valuable to the field. Of course, this is difficult to do when you are just learning the basics of a discipline. How can you
be expected to identify and respond to a new controversy in biology when you've
only taken a single course or two? Even if you are nearly finished with your major,
you will still not have the level of knowledge that you would with further study.

Regardless of your content knowledge, however, understanding that knowledge
is produced in academia through argumentation helps you recognize that your goal
is to participate in that argumentation. This means you are expected to gather or
identify sources of data, notice patterns in that data, make reasonable and relevant
interpretations, and test those interpretations by making claims based on them.
The tools provided in this chapter should make useful reference guides as you work
to understand and make arguments in various disciplines, though of course they
cannot be thorough representations of argumentation in so varied a field.

PROBE

How far can you take Sowinska's argument that personal experience should
be a relevant source of evidence or data in academia? Is personal experience relevant in sciences like physics or biology, for example? You may
choose to review the resources provided by the Underrepresentation Curriculum Project (underrep.com) as you reflect.

Chapter 17
Politics, Argumentation, and Democracy

Key Terms

anaphora

public sphere

kairos

partisanship

petition

tenacity

authority

a priori correspondence

verification

replicate

epistemic function

Key Points

- Argumentation is fundamental to democracy because it helps constitute and maintain a healthy public sphere.
- Argumentation in the public sphere has two main characteristics: it must be accessible to everyone, and it affects everyone.
- The public sphere has several characteristics that distinguish it from both the personal and technical spheres.
- Argumentation can help produce knowledge about things, like cultural values, that are not independently verifiable.
- A major challenge to argumentation in the public sphere is the erosion of trust.

PRIME

What have you heard about the state of argumentation in politics in the news or in conversation with others? Do you agree or disagree with these assessments?

What I Heard about Iraq

Eliot Weinberger (2005)

In 1992, a year after the first Gulf War, I heard Dick Cheney, then secretary of defense, say that the US had been wise not to invade Baghdad and get "bogged down in the problems of trying to take over and govern Iraq." I heard him say: "The question in my mind is how many additional American casualties is Saddam worth? And the answer is: not that damned many."

In February 2001, I heard Colin Powell say that Saddam Hussein "has not developed any significant capability with respect to weapons of mass destruction. He is unable to project conventional power against his neighbours."

That same month, I heard that a CIA report stated: "We do not have any direct evidence that Iraq has used the period since Desert Fox to reconstitute its weapons of mass destruction programmes."

In July 2001, I heard Condoleezza Rice say: "We are able to keep his arms from him. His military forces have not been rebuilt."

On 11 September 2001, six hours after the attacks, I heard that Donald Rumsfeld said that it might be an opportunity to "hit" Iraq. I heard that he said: "Go massive. Sweep it all up. Things related and not."

I heard that Condoleezza Rice asked: "How do you capitalise on these opportunities?"

I heard that on 17 September the president signed a document marked top secret that directed the Pentagon to begin planning for the invasion and that, some months later, he secretly and illegally diverted $700 million approved by Congress for operations in Afghanistan into preparing for the new battle front.

In February 2002, I heard that an unnamed "senior military commander" said: "We are moving military and intelligence personnel and resources out of Afghanistan to get ready for a future war in Iraq."

I heard the president say that Iraq is "a threat of unique urgency," and that there is "no doubt the Iraqi regime continues to possess and conceal some of the most lethal weapons ever devised."

I heard the vice president say: "Simply stated, there is no doubt that Saddam Hussein now has weapons of mass destruction."

I heard the president tell Congress: "The danger to our country is grave. The danger to our country is growing. The regime is seeking a nuclear bomb, and with fissile material could build one within a year."

I heard him say: "The dangers we face will only worsen from month to month and from year to year. To ignore these threats is to encourage them."

Each passing day could be the one on which the Iraqi regime gives anthrax or VX nerve gas or, someday, a nuclear weapon to a terrorist ally."

I heard the president, in the State of the Union address, say that Iraq was hiding materials sufficient to produce 25,000 litres of anthrax, 38,000 litres of botulinum toxin, and 500 tons of sarin, mustard and nerve gas.

I heard the president say that Iraq had attempted to purchase uranium— later specified as "yellowcake" uranium oxide from Niger—and thousands of aluminium tubes "suitable for nuclear weapons production."

I heard the vice president say: "We know that he's been absolutely devoted to trying to acquire nuclear weapons, and we believe he has, in fact, reconstituted nuclear weapons."

I heard the president say: "Imagine those 19 hijackers with other weapons and other plans, this time armed by Saddam Hussein. It would take one vial, one canister, one crate slipped into this country to bring a day of horror like none we have ever known."

I heard Donald Rumsfeld say: "Some have argued that the nuclear threat from Iraq is not imminent. I would not be so certain."

I heard the president say: "America must not ignore the threat gathering against us. Facing clear evidence of peril, we cannot wait for the final proof—the smoking gun—that could come in the form of a mushroom cloud."

I heard Condoleezza Rice say: "We don't want the 'smoking gun' to be a mushroom cloud."

I heard the American ambassador to the European Union tell the Europeans: "You had Hitler in Europe and no one really did anything about him. The same type of person is in Baghdad."

I heard Colin Powell at the United Nations say: "They can produce enough dry biological agent in a single month to kill thousands upon thousands of people. Saddam Hussein has never accounted for vast amounts of chemical weaponry: 550 artillery shells with mustard gas, 30,000 empty munitions, and enough precursors to increase his stockpile to as much as 500 tons of chemical agents. Our conservative estimate is that Iraq today has a stockpile of between 100 and 500 tons of chemical-weapons agent. Even the low end of 100 tons of agent would enable Saddam Hussein to cause mass casualties across more than 100 square miles of territory, an area nearly five times the size of Manhattan."

I heard him say: "Every statement I make today is backed up by sources, solid sources. These are not assertions. What we're giving you are facts and conclusions based on solid intelligence."

I heard the president say: "Iraq has a growing fleet of manned and unmanned aerial vehicles that could be used to disperse chemical or biological

weapons across broad areas." I heard him say that Iraq "could launch a biological or chemical attack in as little as 45 minutes after the order is given."

I heard Tony Blair say: "We are asked to accept Saddam decided to destroy
those weapons. I say that such a claim is palpably absurd."

I heard the president say: "We know that Iraq and al-Qaida have had
high-level contacts that go back a decade. We've learned that Iraq has trained
al-Qaida members in bomb-making and poisons and deadly gases. Alliance
with terrorists could allow the Iraq regime to attack America without leaving
any fingerprints."

I heard the vice president say: "There's overwhelming evidence there was a
connection between al-Qaida and the Iraqi government. I am very confident
there was an established relationship there."

I heard Colin Powell say: "Iraqi officials deny accusations of ties with
al-Qaida. These denials are simply not credible."

I heard Condoleezza Rice say: "There clearly are contacts between al-
Qaida and Saddam Hussein that can be documented."

I heard the president say: "You can't distinguish between al-Qaida and
Saddam."

I heard Donald Rumsfeld say: "Imagine a September 11th with weapons of
mass destruction. It's not three thousand—it's tens of thousands of innocent
men, women and children."

I heard Colin Powell tell the Senate that "a moment of truth is coming":
"This is not just an academic exercise or the United States being in a fit of pique.
We're talking about real weapons. We're talking about anthrax. We're talking
about botulinum toxin. We're talking about nuclear weapons programmes."

I heard Donald Rumsfeld say: "No terrorist state poses a greater or more
immediate threat to the security of our people."

I heard the president, "bristling with irritation," say: "This business about
more time, how much time do we need to see clearly that he's not disarming?
He is delaying. He is deceiving. He is asking for time. He's playing hide-and-
seek with inspectors. One thing is for certain: he's not disarming. Surely our
friends have learned lessons from the past. This looks like a rerun of a bad
movie and I'm not interested in watching it."

I heard that, a few days before authorising the invasion of Iraq, the Senate was
told in a classified briefing by the Pentagon that Iraq could launch anthrax
and other biological and chemical weapons against the eastern seaboard of
the United States using unmanned aerial "drones."

I heard Donald Rumsfeld say he would present no specific evidence of
Iraqi weapons of mass destruction because it might jeopardise the military
mission by revealing to Baghdad what the United States knows.

***

I heard the Pentagon spokesman call the military plan "A-Day," or "Shock and Awe." Three or four hundred cruise missiles launched every day, until "there will not be a safe place in Baghdad," until "you have this simultaneous effect, rather like the nuclear weapons at Hiroshima, not taking days or weeks but in minutes." I heard the spokesman say: "You're sitting in Baghdad and all of a sudden you're the general and thirty of your division headquarters have been wiped out. You also take the city down. By that I mean you get rid of their power, water. In two, three, four, five days they are physically, emotionally and psychologically exhausted." I heard him say: "The sheer size of this has never been seen before, never contemplated."

I heard Major-General Charles Swannack promise that his troops were going to "use a sledgehammer to smash a walnut."

I heard the Pentagon spokesman say: "This is not going to be your father's Persian Gulf War."

I heard that Saddam's strategy against the American invasion would be to blow up dams, bridges and oilfields, and to cut off food supplies to the south so that the Americans would suddenly have to feed millions of desperate civilians. I heard that Baghdad would be encircled by two rings of the elite Republican Guard, in fighting positions already stocked with weapons and supplies, and equipped with chemical protective gear against the poison gas or germ weapons they would be using against the American troops.

I heard Vice Admiral Lowell Jacoby tell Congress that Saddam would "employ a 'scorched earth' strategy, destroying food, transportation, energy and other infrastructure, attempting to create a humanitarian disaster," and that he would blame it all on the Americans.

I heard that Iraq would fire its long-range Scud missiles—equipped with chemical or biological warheads—at Israel, to "portray the war as a battle with an American-Israeli coalition and build support in the Arab world."

I heard that Saddam had elaborate and labyrinthine underground bunkers for his protection, and that it might be necessary to employ B61 Mod 11 nuclear "bunker-buster" bombs to destroy them.

I heard the vice president say that the war would be over in "weeks rather than months."

I heard Donald Rumsfeld say: "It could last six days, six weeks. I doubt six months."

I heard Donald Rumsfeld say there was "no question" that American troops would be "welcomed": "Go back to Afghanistan, the people were in the streets playing music, cheering, flying kites, and doing all the things that the Taliban and al-Qaida would not let them do."

I heard the vice president say: "The Middle East expert Professor Fouad Ajami predicts that after liberation the streets in Basra and Baghdad are 'sure to erupt in joy.' Extremists in the region would have to rethink their strategy of jihad. Moderates throughout the region would take heart. And our ability to advance the Israeli-Palestinian peace process would be enhanced."

I heard the vice president say: "I really do believe we will be greeted as liberators."

I heard Tariq Aziz, the Iraqi foreign minister, say: "American soldiers will not be received by flowers. They will be received by bullets."

I heard that the president said to the television evangelist Pat Robertson: "Oh, no, we're not going to have any casualties."

I heard the president say that he had not consulted his father about the coming war: "You know he is the wrong father to appeal to in terms of strength. There is a higher father that I appeal to."

I heard the prime minister of the Solomon Islands express surprise that his was one of the nations enlisted in the "coalition of the willing": "I was completely unaware of it."

I heard the president tell the Iraqi people, on the night before the invasion began: "If we must begin a military campaign, it will be directed against the lawless men who rule your country and not against you. As our coalition takes away their power we will deliver the food and medicine you need. We will tear down the apparatus of terror. And we will help you build a new Iraq that is prosperous and free. In a free Iraq there will be no more wars of aggression against your neighbours, no more poison factories, no more executions of dissidents, no more torture chambers and rape rooms. The tyrant will soon be gone. The day of your liberation is near."

I heard him tell the Iraqi people: "We will not relent until your country is free."

***

I heard the vice president say: "By any standard of even the most dazzling charges in military history, the Germans in the Ardennes in the spring of 1940 or Patton's romp in July of 1944, the present race to Baghdad is unprecedented in its speed and daring and in the lightness of casualties."

I heard Colonel David Hackworth say: "Hey diddle diddle, it's straight up the middle!"

I heard the Pentagon spokesman say that 95 per cent of the Iraqi casualties were "military-age males."

I heard an official from the Red Crescent say: "On one stretch of highway alone, there were more than fifty civilian cars, each with four or five people incinerated inside, that sat in the sun for ten or fifteen days before they were buried nearby by volunteers. That is what there will be for their relatives to come and find. War is bad, but its remnants are worse."

I heard the director of a hospital in Baghdad say: "The whole hospital is an emergency room. The nature of the injuries is so severe—one body without a head, someone else with their abdomen ripped open."

I heard an American soldier say: "There's a picture of the World Trade Center hanging up by my bed and I keep one in my Kevlar. Every time I feel sorry for these people I look at that. I think: 'They hit us at home and now it's our turn.'"

I heard about Hashim, a fat, "painfully shy" 15-year-old, who liked to sit for hours by the river with his birdcage, and who was shot by the 4th Infantry Division in a raid on his village. Asked about the details of the boy's death, the division commander said: "That person was probably in the wrong place at the wrong time."

I heard an American soldier say: "We get rocks thrown at us by kids. You wanna turn around and shoot one of the little fuckers, but you know you can't do that."

I heard the Pentagon spokesman say that the US did not count civilian casualties: "Our efforts focus on destroying the enemy's capabilities, so we never target civilians and have no reason to try to count such unintended deaths." I heard him say that, in any event, it would be impossible, because the Iraqi paramilitaries were fighting in civilian clothes, the military was using civilian human shields, and many of the civilian deaths were the result of Iraqi "unaimed anti-aircraft fire falling back to earth."

I heard an American soldier say: "The worst thing is to shoot one of them, then go help him," as regulations require. "Shit, I didn't help any of them. I wouldn't help the fuckers. There were some you let die. And there were some you double-tapped. Once you'd reached the objective, and once you'd shot them and you're moving through, anything there, you shoot again. You didn't want any prisoners of war."

I heard Anmar Uday, the doctor who had cared for Private Jessica Lynch, say: "We heard the helicopters. We were surprised. Why do this? There was no military. There were no soldiers in the hospital. It was like a Hollywood film. They cried 'Go, go, go,' with guns and flares and the sound of explosions. They made a show: an action movie like Sylvester Stallone or Jackie Chan, with jumping and shouting, breaking down doors. All the time with cameras rolling."

I heard Private Jessica Lynch say: "They used me as a way to symbolise all this stuff. It hurt in a way that people would make up stories that they had no truth about." Of the stories that she had bravely fought off her captors, and suffered bullet and stab wounds, I heard her say: "I'm not about to take credit for something I didn't do." Of her dramatic "rescue," I heard her say: "I don't think it happened quite like that."

I heard the Red Cross say that casualties in Baghdad were so high that the hospitals had stopped counting.

I heard an old man say, after 11 members of his family—children and grandchildren—were killed when a tank blew up their minivan: "Our home is an empty place. We who are left are like wild animals. All we can do is cry out."

As the riots and looting broke out, I heard a man in the Baghdad market say: "Saddam Hussein's greatest crime is that he brought the American army to Iraq."

As the riots and looting broke out, I heard Donald Rumsfeld say: "It's untidy, and freedom's untidy."

And when the National Museum was emptied and the National Library burned down, I heard him say: "The images you are seeing on television you are seeing over, and over, and over, and it's the same picture of some person walking out of some building with a vase, and you see it twenty times, and you think: 'My goodness, were there that many vases? Is it possible that there were that many vases in the whole country?'"

I heard that 10,000 Iraqi civilians were dead.

***

I heard Colin Powell say: "I'm absolutely sure that there are weapons of mass destruction there and the evidence will be forthcoming. We're just getting it now."

I heard the president say: "We'll find them. It'll be a matter of time to do so."

I heard Donald Rumsfeld say: "We know where they are. They're in the area around Tikrit and Baghdad, and east, west, south and north, somewhat."

I heard the US was building 14 "enduring bases," capable of housing 110,000 soldiers, and I heard Brigadier-General Mark Kimmitt call them "a blueprint for how we could operate in the Middle East." I heard that the US was building what would be its largest embassy anywhere in the world.

I heard that it would only be a matter of months before Starbucks and McDonald's opened branches in Baghdad. I heard that HSBC would have cash machines all over the country.

I heard about the trade fairs run by New Bridges Strategies, a consulting firm that promised access to the Iraqi market. I heard one of its partners say: "Getting the rights to distribute Procter & Gamble would be a gold mine. One well-stocked 7-Eleven could knock out 30 Iraqi stores. A Wal-Mart could take over the country."

On 1 May 2003, I heard the president, dressed up as a pilot, under a banner that read "Mission Accomplished," declare that combat operations were over: "The battle of Iraq is one victory in a war on terror that began on 11 September 2001." I heard him say: "The liberation of Iraq is a crucial advance in the campaign against terror. We've removed an ally of al-Qaida, and cut off a source of terrorist funding. And this much is certain: no terrorist network will gain weapons of mass destruction from the Iraqi regime, because the regime is no more. In these 19 months that changed the world, our actions have been focused and deliberate and proportionate to the offence. We have not forgotten the victims of 11 September: the last phone calls, the cold murder of children, the searches in the rubble. With those attacks, the terrorists and their supporters declared war on the United States. And war is what they got."

On 1 May 2003, I heard that 140 American soldiers had died in combat in Iraq.

I heard Richard Perle tell Americans to "relax and celebrate victory." I heard him say: "The predictions of those who opposed this war can be discarded like spent cartridges."

I heard Lieutenant-General Jay Garner say: "We ought to look in a mirror and get proud and stick out our chests and suck in our bellies and say: 'Damn, we're Americans.'"

And later I heard that I could buy a 12-inch "Elite Force Aviator: George W. Bush" action figure: "Exacting in detail and fully equipped with authentic gear, this limited-edition action figure is a meticulous 1:6 scale re-creation of the commander-in-chief's appearance during his historic aircraft carrier landing. This fully poseable figure features a realistic head sculpt, fully detailed cloth flight suit, helmet with oxygen mask, survival vest, G-pants, parachute harness and much more."

I heard that Pentagon planners had predicted that US troop levels would fall to 30,000 by the end of the summer.

***

I heard that Paul Bremer's first act as director of the Coalition Provisional Authority was to fire all senior members of the Baath Party, including 30,000 civil servants, policemen, teachers and doctors, and to dismiss all 400,000 soldiers of the Iraqi army without pay or pensions. Two million people were dependent on that income. Since America supports private gun ownership, the soldiers were allowed to keep their weapons.

I heard that hundreds were being kidnapped and raped in Baghdad alone; that schools, hospitals, shops and factories were being looted; that it was impossible to restore the electricity because all the copper wire was being stolen from the power plants.

I heard Paul Bremer say, "Most of the country is, in fact, orderly," and that all the problems were coming from "several hundred hard-core terrorists" from al-Qaida and affiliated groups.

As attacks on American troops increased, I heard the generals disagree about who was fighting: Islamic fundamentalists or remnants of the Baath Party or Iraqi mercenaries or foreign mercenaries or ordinary citizens taking revenge for the loss of loved ones. I heard the president and the vice president and the politicians and the television reporters simply call them "terrorists."

I heard the president say: "There are some who feel that conditions are such that they can attack us there. My answer is: bring them on! We have the force necessary to deal with the situation."

I heard that 25,000 Iraqi civilians were dead.

I heard Arnold Schwarzenegger, then campaigning for governor, in Baghdad for a special showing to the troops of *Terminator 3*, say: "It is really wild driving round here, I mean the poverty, and you see there is no money, it is disastrous financially and there is the leadership vacuum, pretty much like California."

I heard that the army was wrapping entire villages in barbed wire, with signs that read: "This fence is here for your protection. Do not approach or try to cross, or you will be shot." In one of those villages, I heard a man named Tariq say: "I see no difference between us and the Palestinians."

I heard Captain Todd Brown say: "You have to understand the Arab mind. The only thing they understand is force—force, pride and saving face."

I heard that the US, as a gift from the American people to the Iraqi people, had committed $18.4 billion to the reconstruction of basic infrastructure, but that future Iraqi governments would have no say in how the money was spent. I heard that the economy had been opened to foreign ownership, and that this could not be changed. I heard that the Iraqi army would be under the command of the US, and that this could not be changed. I heard, however, that "full authority" for health and hospitals had been turned over to the Iraqis, and that senior American health advisers had been withdrawn. I heard Tommy Thompson, secretary of health and human services, say that Iraq's hospitals would be fine if the Iraqis "just washed their hands and cleaned the crap off the walls."

I heard Colonel Nathan Sassaman say: "With a heavy dose of fear and violence, and a lot of money for projects, I think we can convince these people that we are here to help them."

I heard Richard Perle say: "Next year at about this time, I expect there will be a really thriving trade in the region, and we will see rapid economic development. And a year from now, I'll be very surprised if there is not some grand square in Baghdad named after President Bush."

***

I heard about Operation Ivy Cyclone. I heard about Operation Vigilant Resolve. I heard about Operation Plymouth Rock. I heard about Operation Iron Hammer, its name taken from Eisenhammer, the Nazi plan to destroy Soviet generating plants.

I heard that air force regulations require that any airstrike likely to result in the deaths of more than 30 civilians be personally approved by the secretary of defense, and I heard that Donald Rumsfeld approved every proposal.

I heard the marine colonel say: "We napalmed those bridges. Unfortunately, there were people there. It's no great way to die." I heard the Pentagon deny they were using napalm, saying their incendiary bombs were made of something called Mark 77, and I heard the experts say that Mark 77 was another name for napalm.

I heard a marine describe "dead-checking": "They teach us to do dead-checking when we're clearing rooms. You put two bullets into the guy's chest and one in the brain. But when you enter a room where guys are wounded, you might not know if they're alive or dead. So they teach us to dead-check them by pressing them in the eye with your boot, because generally a person, even if he's faking being dead, will flinch if you poke him there. If he moves, you put a bullet in the brain. You do this to keep the momentum going when you're flowing through a building. You don't want a guy popping up behind you and shooting you."

I heard the president say: "We're rolling back the terrorist threat, not on the fringes of its influence but at the heart of its power."

When the death toll of American soldiers reached 500, I heard Brigadier-General Kimmitt say: "I don't think the soldiers are looking at arbitrary figures such as casualty counts as the barometer of their morale. They know they have a nation that stands behind them."

I heard an American soldier, standing next to his Humvee, say: "We liberated Iraq. Now the people here don't want us here, and guess what? We don't want to be here either. So why are we still here? Why don't they bring us home?"

I heard Colin Powell say: "We did not expect it would be quite this intense this long."

I heard Donald Rumsfeld say: "We're facing a test of will."

I heard the president say: "We found biological laboratories. They're illegal. They're against the United Nations resolutions, and we've so far discovered two. And we'll find more weapons as time goes on. But for those who say we haven't found the banned manufacturing devices or banned weapons, they're wrong, we found them."

I heard Tony Blair say: "The remains of 400,000 human beings have been found in mass graves." And I saw his words repeated in a US government pamphlet, *Iraq's Legacy of Terror: Mass Graves*, and on a US government website which said this represented "a crime against humanity surpassed only by the Rwandan genocide of 1994, Pol Pot's Cambodian killing fields in the 1970s and the Nazi Holocaust of World War Two."

***

I heard the president say: "Today, on bended knee, I thank the Good Lord for protecting those of our troops overseas, and our Coalition troops and innocent Iraqis who suffer at the hands of some of these senseless killings by people who are trying to shake our will."

I heard that this was the first American president in wartime who had never attended a funeral for a dead soldier. I heard that photographs of the flag-draped coffins returning home were banned. I heard that the Pentagon had renamed body bags "transfer tubes."

I heard a tearful George Bush Sr., speaking at the annual convention of the National Petrochemical and Refiners Association, say that it was "deeply offensive and contemptible" the way "elites and intellectuals" were dismissing "the sowing of the seeds of basic human freedom in that troubled part of the world." I heard him say: "It hurts an awful lot more when it's your son that is being criticised."

I heard the president's mother say: "Why should we hear about body bags and deaths? Why should I waste my beautiful mind on something like that?"

I heard that 7 per cent of all American military deaths in Iraq were suicides, that 10 per cent of the soldiers evacuated to the army hospital in Landstuhl, Germany, had been sent for "psychiatric or behavioural health issues," and that 20 per cent of the military was expected to suffer from post-traumatic stress disorder.

I heard Brigadier-General Kimmitt deny that civilians were being killed: "We run extremely precise operations focused on people we have intelligence on for crimes of violence against the Coalition and against the Iraqi people." And later I heard him say that marines were being fired on from crowds containing women and children, and that the marines had fired back only in self-defence.

I heard Donald Rumsfeld say that the fighting was the work of "thugs, gangs and terrorists." I heard General Richard Myers, chairman of the Joint Chiefs of Staff, say: "It's not a Shiite uprising. Muqtada al-Sadr has a very small following." I heard that an unnamed "intelligence official" had said: "Hatred of the American occupation has spread rapidly among Shia, and is now so large that Mr. Sadr and his forces represent just one element.

Destroying his Mehdi Army might be possible only by destroying Sadr City."
Sadr City is the most populated part of Baghdad. I heard that, among the
Sunnis, former Baath Party leaders and Saddam loyalists had been joined by
Sunni tribal chiefs.

I heard that there were now thirty separate militias in the country. I heard
the television news reporters routinely refer to them as "anti-Iraqi forces."

I heard that Paul Bremer had closed down a popular newspaper, *Al Hawza*,
because of "inaccurate reporting."

As Shias in Sadr City lined up to donate blood for Sunnis in Fallujah,
I heard a man say: "We should thank Paul Bremer. He has finally united
Iraq—against him."

I heard the president say: "I wouldn't be happy if I were occupied either."

***

I heard Tony Blair say: "Before people crow about the absence of weapons of
mass destruction, I suggest they wait a bit."

I heard General Myers say: "Given time, given the number of prisoners
now that we're interrogating, I'm confident that we're going to find weapons
of mass destruction."

I heard the president say: "Prisoners are being taken, and intelligence is
being gathered. Our decisive actions will continue until these enemies of
democracy are dealt with."

I heard a soldier describe what they called "bitch in a box': "That was the
normal procedure for them when they wanted to soften up a prisoner: stuff
them in the trunk for a while and drive them around. The hoods I can understand, and to have them cuffed with the plastic things—that I could see. But
the trunk episode—I thought it was kind of unusual. It was like a sweatbox,
let's face it. In Iraq, in August, it's hitting 120 degrees, and you can imagine
what it was like in the trunk of a black Mercedes."

I heard a National Guardsman from Florida say: "We had a sledgehammer that we would bang against the wall, and that would create an echo that
sounds like an explosion that scared the hell out of them. If that didn't work
we would load a 9mm pistol, and pretend to be charging it near their head
and make them think we were going to shoot them. Once you did that they
did whatever you wanted them to do basically. The way we treated these men
was hard even for the soldiers, especially after realising that many of these
'combatants' were no more than shepherds."

I heard a marine at Camp Whitehorse say: "The 50/10 technique was used
to break down EPWs and make it easier for the HET member to get information from them." The 50/10 technique was to make prisoners stand for
50 minutes of the hour for ten hours with a hood over their heads in the

heat. EPWs were "enemy prisoners of war." HETs were "human exploitation teams."

I heard Captain Donald Reese, a prison warden, say: "It was not uncommon to see people without clothing. I was told the 'whole nudity thing' was an interrogation procedure used by military intelligence, and never thought much about it."

I heard Donald Rumsfeld say: "I have not seen anything thus far that says that the people abused were abused in the process of interrogating them or for interrogation purposes."

I heard Private Lynndie England, who was photographed in Abu Ghraib holding a prisoner on a leash, say: "I was instructed by persons in higher rank to stand there, hold this leash, look at the camera, and they took pictures for PsyOps. I didn't really, I mean, want to be in any pictures. I thought it was kind of weird."

Detainees 27, 30 and 31 were stripped of their clothing, handcuffed together nude, placed on the ground, and forced to lie on each other and simulate sex while photographs were taken. Detainee 8 had his food thrown in the toilet and was then ordered to eat it. Detainee 7 was ordered to bark like a dog while MPs spat and urinated on him; he was sodomised with a police stick while two female MPs watched. Detainee 3 was sodomised with a broom by a female soldier. Detainee 15 was photographed standing on a box with a hood on his head and simulated electrical wires were attached to his hands and penis. Detainees 1, 16, 17, 18, 23, 24 and 26 were placed in a pile and forced to masturbate while photographs were taken. An unidentified detainee was photographed covered in faeces with a banana inserted in his anus. Detainee 5 watched Civilian 1 rape an unidentified 15-year-old male detainee while a female soldier took photographs. Detainees 5 and 7 were stripped of their clothing and forced to wear women's underwear on their heads. Detainee 28, handcuffed with his hands behind his back in a shower stall, was declared dead when an MP removed the sandbag from his head and checked his pulse.

I heard Donald Rumsfeld say: "If you are in Washington DC, you can't know what's going on in the midnight shift in one of those many prisons around the world."

***

I heard that the Red Cross had to close its offices because it was too dangerous. I heard that General Electric and the Siemens Corporation had to close their offices. I heard that Médecins sans Frontières had to withdraw, and that journalists rarely left their hotels. I heard that, after their headquarters were bombed, most of the United Nations staff had gone. I heard that the cost of life insurance policies for the few remaining Western businessmen was $10,000 a week.

I heard Tom Foley, director of Iraq Private Sector Development, say: "The security risks are not as bad as they appear on TV. Western civilians are not the targets themselves. These are acceptable risks."

I heard the spokesman for Paul Bremer say: "We have isolated pockets where we are encountering problems."

I heard that, no longer able to rely on the military for help, private security firms had banded together to form the largest private army in the world, with its own rescue teams and intelligence. I heard that there were 20,000 mercenary soldiers, now called "private contractors," in Iraq, earning as much as $2,000 a day, and not subject to Iraqi or US military law.

I heard that 50,000 Iraqi civilians were dead.

I heard that, on a day when a car bomb killed three Americans, Paul Bremer's last act as director of the Coalition Provisional Authority was to issue laws making it illegal to drive with only one hand on the steering wheel or to honk a horn when there was no emergency.

I heard that the unemployment rate was now 70 per cent, that less than 1 per cent of the workforce was engaged in reconstruction, and that the US had spent only 2 per cent of the $18.4 billion approved by Congress for reconstruction. I heard that an official audit could not account for $8.8 billion of Iraqi oil money given to Iraqi ministries by the Coalition Provisional Authority.

I heard the president say: "Our Coalition is standing with responsible Iraqi leaders as they establish growing authority in their country."

I heard that, a few days before he became prime minister, Iyad Allawi visited a Baghdad police station where six suspected insurgents, blindfolded and handcuffed, were lined up against a wall. I heard that, as four Americans and a dozen Iraqi policemen watched, Allawi pulled out a pistol and shot each prisoner in the head. I heard that he said that this is how we must deal with insurgents.

On 28 June 2004, with the establishment of an interim government, I heard the vice president say: "After decades of rule by a brutal dictator, Iraq has been returned to its rightful owners, the people of Iraq."

This was the military summary for an ordinary day, 22 July 2004, a day that produced no headlines: "Two roadside bombs exploded next to a van and a Mercedes in separate areas of Baghdad, killing four civilians. A gunman in a Toyota opened fire on a police checkpoint and escaped. Police wounded three gunmen at a checkpoint and arrested four men suspected of attempted murder. Seven more roadside bombs exploded in Baghdad and gunmen twice attacked US troops. Police dismantled a car bomb in Mosul and gunmen attacked the Western driver of a gravel truck at Tell Afar. There were three roadside bombings and a rocket attack on US troops in Mosul and another gun attack on US forces near Tell Afar. At Taji, a civilian vehicle collided with a US military vehicle, killing six civilians and injuring seven others. At Bayji, a US vehicle hit a landmine. Gunmen murdered a dentist at the Ad Dwar hospital. There were 17 roadside bomb explosions against US forces in Taji, Baquba, Baqua, Jalula, Tikrit, Paliwoda, Balad, Samarra and Duluiyeh, with attacks by gunmen on US troops in Tikrit and Balad. A headless body in an orange jumpsuit was found in the Tigris; believed to be Bulgarian hostage Ivalyo Kepov. Kirkuk air base attacked. Five roadside bombs on US forces in Rutbah, Kalso and Ramadi. Gunmen attacked Americans in Fallujah and Ramadi. The police chief of Najaf was abducted. Two civilian contractors were attacked by gunmen at Haswah. A roadside bomb exploded near Kerbala and Hillah. International forces were attacked by gunmen at al-Qurnah."

***

I heard the president say: "You can embolden an enemy by sending a mixed message. You can dispirit the Iraqi people by sending mixed messages. That's why I will continue to lead with clarity and in a resolute way."

I heard the president say: "Today, because the world acted with courage and moral clarity, Iraqi athletes are competing in the Olympic Games." Iraq had sent teams to the previous Olympics. And when the president ran a campaign advertisement with the flags of Iraq and Afghanistan and the words "at this Olympics there will be two more free nations—and two fewer terrorist regimes," I heard the Iraqi coach say: "Iraq as a team does not want Mr. Bush to use us for the presidential campaign. He can find another way to advertise himself." I heard their star midfielder say that if he weren't playing soccer he'd be fighting for the resistance in Fallujah: "Bush has committed so many crimes. How will he meet his god having slaughtered so many men and women?"

I heard an unnamed "senior British army officer" invoke the Nazis to describe what he saw: "My view and the view of the British chain of command is that the Americans' use of violence is not proportionate and is over-responsive to the threat they are facing. They don't see the Iraqi people the way we see them. They view them as Untermenschen. They are not concerned about the Iraqi loss of life. As far as they are concerned, Iraq is bandit country and everybody is out to kill them. It is trite, but American troops do shoot first and ask questions later."

I heard Makki al-Nazzal, who was managing a clinic in Fallujah, say, in unaccented English: "I have been a fool for 47 years. I used to believe in European and American civilisation."

I heard Donald Rumsfeld say: "We never believed that we'd just tumble over weapons of mass destruction."

I heard Condoleezza Rice say: "We never expected we were going to open garages and find them."

I heard Donald Rumsfeld say: "They may have had time to destroy them, and I don't know the answer."

I heard Richard Perle say: "We don't know where to look for them and we never did know where to look for them. I hope this will take less than two hundred years."

***

I heard the president say: "I know what I'm doing when it comes to winning this war."

I heard the president say: "I'm a war president."

I heard that 1,000 American soldiers were dead and 7,000 wounded in combat. I heard that there was now an average of 87 attacks on US troops a day.

I heard Condoleezza Rice say: "Not everything has gone as we would have liked it to."

I heard Colin Powell say: "We did miscalculate the difficulty."

I heard an unnamed "senior US diplomat in Baghdad" say: "We're dealing with a population that hovers between bare tolerance and outright hostility. This idea of a functioning democracy is crazy. We thought there would be a reprieve after sovereignty, but all hell is breaking loose."

I heard Major Thomas Neemeyer say: "The only way to stomp out the insurgency of the mind would be to kill the entire population."

I heard the CNN reporter near the tomb of Ali in Najaf say: "Everything outside of the mosque seems to be totalled."

I heard Khudeir Salman, who sold ice from a donkey cart in Najaf, say he was giving up after marine snipers had killed his friend, another ice-seller: "I found him this morning. The sniper shot his donkey too. Even the ambulance drivers are too scared to get the body."

I heard the vice president say: "Such an enemy cannot be deterred, cannot be contained, cannot be appeased, or negotiated with. It can only be destroyed. And that is the business at hand."

I heard a "senior American commander" say: "We need to make a decision on when the cancer of Fallujah needs to be cut out."

I heard Major-General John Batiste, outside Samarra, say: "It'll be a quick fight and the enemy is going to die fast. The message for the people of Samarra is: peacefully or not, this is going to be solved."

I heard Brigadier-General Kimmitt say: "Our patience is not eternal."

I heard the president say: "America will never be run out of Iraq by a bunch of thugs and killers."

I heard about the wedding party that was attacked by American planes, killing 45 people, and the wedding photographer who videotaped the festivities until he himself was killed. And though the tape was shown on television, I heard Brigadier-General Kimmitt say: "There was no evidence of a wedding. There may have been some kind of celebration. Bad people have celebrations, too."

I heard an Iraqi man say: "I swear I saw dogs eating the body of a woman."

I heard an Iraqi man say: "We have at least 700 dead. So many of them are children and women. The stench from the dead bodies in parts of the city is unbearable."

I heard Donald Rumsfeld say: "Death has a tendency to encourage a depressing view of war."

***

On the occasion of Iyad Allawi's visit to the United States, I heard the president say: "What's important for the American people to hear is reality. And the reality is right here in the form of the prime minister."

Asked about ethnic tensions, I heard Iyad Allawi say: "There are no problems between Shia and Sunnis and Kurds and Arabs and Turkmen. Usually we have no problems of an ethnic or religious nature in Iraq."

I heard him say: "There is nothing, no problem, except in a small pocket in Fallujah."

I heard Colonel Jerry Durrant say, after a meeting with Ramadi tribal sheikhs: "A lot of these guys have read history, and they said to me the government in Baghdad is like the Vichy government in France during World War Two."

I heard a journalist say: "I am housebound. I leave when I have a very good reason to and a scheduled interview. I avoid going to people's homes and never walk in the streets. I can't go grocery shopping any more, can't eat in restaurants, can't strike up a conversation with strangers, can't look for stories, can't drive in anything but a full armoured car, can't go to scenes of breaking news stories, can't be stuck in traffic, can't speak English outside, can't take a road trip, can't say 'I'm an American,' can't linger at checkpoints, can't be curious about what people are saying, doing, feeling."

I heard Donald Rumsfeld say: "It's a tough part of the world. We had something like 200 or 300 or 400 people killed in many of the major cities of America last year. What's the difference? We just didn't see each homicide in every major city in the United States on television every night."

I heard that 80,000 Iraqi civilians were dead. I heard that the war had already cost $225 billion and was continuing at the rate of $40 billion a month. I heard there was now an average of 130 attacks on US troops a day.

I heard Captain John Mountford say: "I just wonder what would have happened if we had worked a little more with the locals."

I heard that, in the last year alone, the US had fired 127 tons of depleted uranium (DU) munitions in Iraq, the radioactive equivalent of approximately ten thousand Nagasaki bombs. I heard that the widespread use of DU in the first Gulf War was believed to be the primary cause of the health problems suffered by its 580,400 veterans, of whom 467 were wounded during the war itself. Ten years later, 11,000 were dead and 325,000 on medical disability. DU carried in semen led to high rates of endometriosis in their wives and girl-friends, often requiring hysterectomies. Of soldiers who had healthy babies before the war, 67 per cent of their postwar babies were born with severe defects, including missing legs, arms, organs or eyes.

I heard that 380 tons of HMX (high melting point explosive) and RDX (rapid detonation explosive) were missing from al-Qaqaa, one of Iraq's "most sensitive military installations," which had not been guarded since the invasion. I heard that one pound of these explosives was enough to blow up a 747 jet, and that this cache could be used to make a million roadside bombs, which were the cause of half the casualties among US troops.

I heard Donald Rumsfeld say, when asked why the troops were being kept in the war much longer than their normal tours of duty: "Oh, come on. People are fungible. You can have them here or there."

***

I heard Colonel Gary Brandl say: "The enemy has got a face. He's called Satan. He's in Fallujah and we're going to destroy him."

I heard a marine commander tell his men: "You will be held accountable for the facts not as they are in hindsight but as they appeared to you at the time. If, in your mind, you fire to protect yourself or your men, you are doing the right thing. It doesn't matter if later on we find out you wiped out a family of unarmed civilians."

I heard Lieutenant-Colonel Mark Smith say: "We're going out where the bad guys live, and we're going to slay them in their zip code."

I heard that 15,000 US troops invaded Fallujah while planes dropped 500-pound bombs on "insurgent targets." I heard they destroyed the Nazzal Emergency Hospital in the centre of the city, killing 20 doctors. I heard they occupied Fallujah General Hospital, which the military had called a "centre of propaganda" for reporting civilian casualties. I heard that they confiscated all mobile phones and refused to allow doctors and ambulances to go out and help the wounded. I heard they bombed the power plant to black out the city, and that the water was shut off. I heard that every house and shop had a large red X spray-painted on the door to indicate that it had been searched.

I heard Donald Rumsfeld say: "Innocent civilians in that city have all the guidance they need as to how they can avoid getting into trouble. There aren't going to be large numbers of civilians killed and certainly not by US forces."

I heard that, in a city of 150 mosques, there were no longer any calls to prayer.

I heard Muhammad Abboud tell how, unable to leave his house to go to a hospital, he had watched his nine-year-old son bleed to death, and how, unable to leave his house to go to a cemetery, he had buried his son in the garden.

I heard Sami al-Jumaili, a doctor, say: "There is not a single surgeon in Fallujah. A 13-year-old child just died in my hands."

I heard an American soldier say: "We will win the hearts and minds of Fallujah by ridding the city of insurgents. We're doing that by patrolling the streets and killing the enemy."

I heard an American soldier, a Bradley gunner, say: "I was basically looking for any clean walls, you know, without any holes in them. And then we were putting holes in them."

I heard Farhan Salih say: "My kids are hysterical with fear. They are traumatised by the sound but there is nowhere to take them."

I heard that the US troops allowed women and children to leave the city, but that all "military age males," men from 15 to 60, were required to stay. I heard that no food or medicine was allowed into the city.

I heard the Red Cross say that at least 800 civilians had died. I heard Iyad Allawi say there were no civilian casualties in Fallujah.

I heard a man named Abu Sabah say: "They used these weird bombs that put up smoke like a mushroom cloud. Then small pieces fall from the air with long tails of smoke behind them." I heard him say that pieces of these bombs exploded into large fires that burned the skin even when water was thrown on it.

I heard Kassem Muhammad Ahmed say: "I watched them roll over wounded people in the streets with tanks."

I heard a man named Khalil say: "They shot women and old men in the streets. Then they shot anyone who tried to get their bodies."

I heard Nihida Kadhim, a housewife, say that when she was finally allowed to return to her home, she found a message written with lipstick on her living-room mirror: FUCK IRAQ AND EVERY IRAQI IN IT.

I heard General John Sattler say that the destruction of Fallujah had "broken the back of the insurgency."

I heard that three-quarters of Fallujah had been shelled into rubble. I heard an American soldier say: "It's kind of bad we destroyed everything, but at least we gave them a chance for a new start."

I heard that only five roads into Fallujah would remain open. The rest would be sealed with "sand berms," mountains of earth. At the entry points, everyone would be photographed, fingerprinted and have iris scans taken before being issued identification cards. All citizens would be required to wear identification cards in plain sight at all times. No private automobiles would be allowed in the city. All males would be organised into "work brigades" rebuilding the city. They would be paid, but participation would be compulsory.

I heard Muhammad Kubaissy, a shopkeeper, say: "I am still searching for what they have been calling democracy."

I heard a soldier say that he had talked to his priest about killing Iraqis, and that his priest had told him it was all right to kill for his government as long as he did not enjoy it. After he had killed at least four men, I heard the soldier say that he had begun to have doubts: "Where the fuck did Jesus say it's OK to kill people for your government?"

***

I heard Donald Rumsfeld say: "I don't believe anyone that I know in the administration ever said that Iraq had nuclear weapons."

I heard Donald Rumsfeld say: "The Coalition did not act in Iraq because we had discovered dramatic new evidence of Iraq's pursuit of weapons of mass destruction. We acted because we saw the evidence in a dramatic new light, through the prism of our experience on 9/11."

I heard a reporter say to Donald Rumsfeld: "Before the war in Iraq, you stated the case very eloquently and you said they would welcome us with open arms." And I heard Rumsfeld interrupt him: "Never said that. Never did. You may remember it well, but you're thinking of somebody else. You can't find, anywhere, me saying anything like either of those two things you just said I said."

I heard Ahmed Chalabi, who had supplied most of the information about the weapons of mass destruction, shrug and say: "We are heroes in error . . . What was said before is not important."

I heard Paul Wolfowitz say: "For bureaucratic reasons, we settled on one issue, weapons of mass destruction, as justification for invading Iraq, because it was the one reason everyone could agree on."

I heard Condoleezza Rice continue to insist: "It's not as if anybody believes that Saddam Hussein was without weapons of mass destruction."

I heard that the Niger "yellowcake" uranium was a hoax legitimised by British intelligence, that the aluminium tubes could not be used for nuclear weapons, that the mobile biological laboratories produced hydrogen for weather balloons, that the fleet of unmanned aerial drones was a single broken-down oversized model airplane, that Saddam had no elaborate underground bunkers, that Colin Powell's primary source, his "solid information" for the evidence he presented at the United Nations, was a paper written ten years before by a graduate student. I heard that, of the 400,000 bodies buried in mass graves, only 5,000 had been found.

I heard Lieutenant-General James Conway say: "It was a surprise to me then, and it remains a surprise to me now, that we have not uncovered weapons. It's not from lack of trying."

I heard a reporter ask Donald Rumsfeld: "If they did not have WMDs, why did they pose an immediate threat to this country?" I heard Rumsfeld answer: "You and a few other critics are the only people I've heard use the phrase 'immediate threat.' It's become a kind of folklore that that's what happened. If you have any citations, I'd like to see them." And I heard the reporter read: "No terrorist state poses a greater or more immediate threat to the security of our people." Rumsfeld replied: "It—my view of—of the situation was that he—he had—we—we believe, the best intelligence that we had and other countries had and that—that we believed and we still do not know—we will know."

I heard Saadoon al-Zubaydi, an interpreter who lived in the presidential palace, say: "For at least three years Saddam Hussein had been tired of the day-to-day management of his regime. He could not stand it anymore: meetings, commissions, dispatches, telephone calls. So he withdrew . . . Alone, isolated, out of it. He preferred shutting himself up in his office, writing novels."

***

I heard the president say that Iraq is a "catastrophic success."

I heard Donald Rumsfeld say: "They haven't won a single battle the entire time since the end of major combat operations."

I heard that hundreds of schools had been completely destroyed and thousands looted, and that most people thought it too dangerous to send their children to school. I heard there was no system of banks. I heard that in the cities there were only ten hours of electricity a day and that only 60 per cent of the population had access to drinkable water. I heard that the malnutrition of children was now far worse than in Uganda or Haiti. I heard that none of the 270,000 babies born after the start of the war had received immunisations.

I heard that 5 per cent of eligible voters had registered for the coming elections.

I heard General John Abizaid say: "I don't think Iraq will have a perfect election. And, if I recall, looking back at our own election four years ago, it wasn't perfect either."

I heard Donald Rumsfeld say: "Let's say you tried to have an election and you could have it in three-quarters or four-fifths of the country. But some places you couldn't because the violence is too great. Well, so be it. Nothing's perfect in life."

I heard an Iraqi engineer say: "Go and vote and risk being blown to pieces or followed by insurgents and murdered for co-operating with the Americans? For what? To practise democracy? Are you joking?"

I heard General Muhammad Abdullah Shahwani, the chief of Iraqi intelligence, say that there were now 200,000 active fighters in the insurgency.

I heard Donald Rumsfeld say: "I don't believe it's our job to reconstruct that country. The Iraqi people are going to have to reconstruct that country over a period of time." I heard him say that, in any event, "the infrastructure of that country was not terribly damaged by the war at all."

I heard that the American ambassador, John Negroponte, had requested that $3.37 billion intended for water, sewage and electricity projects be transferred to security and oil output.

I heard that the reporters from the al-Jazeera network were indefinitely banned. I heard Donald Rumsfeld say: "What al-Jazeera is doing is vicious, inaccurate and inexcusable."

I heard that Spain left the "coalition of the willing." Hungary left; the Dominican Republic left; Nicaragua left; Honduras left. I heard that the Philippines had left early, after a Filipino truck driver was kidnapped and executed. Norway left. Poland and the Netherlands said they were leaving. Thailand said it was leaving. Bulgaria was reducing its few hundred troops. Moldova cut its force from 42 to 12.

I heard that the president had once said: "Two years from now, only the Brits may be with us. At some point, we may be the only ones left. That's OK with me. We are America."

I heard a reporter ask Lieutenant-General Jay Garner how long the troops would remain in Iraq, and I heard him reply: "I hope they're there a long time."

I heard General Tommy Franks say: "One has to think about the numbers. I think we will be engaged with our military in Iraq for perhaps three, five, perhaps ten years."

I heard that the Pentagon was now exploring what it called the "Salvador option," modelled on the death squads in El Salvador in the 1980s, when John Negroponte was ambassador to Honduras and when Elliott Abrams, now White House adviser on the Middle East, called the massacre at El

Mozote "nothing but Communist propaganda." Under the plan, the US would advise, train and support paramilitaries in assassination and kidnapping, including secret raids across the Syrian border. In the vice presidential debate, I heard the vice president say: "Twenty years ago we had a similar situation in El Salvador. We had a guerrilla insurgency that controlled roughly a third of the country . . . And today El Salvador is a whale of a lot better."

I heard that 100,000 Iraqi civilians were dead. I heard that there was now an average of 150 attacks on US troops a day. I heard that in Baghdad 700 people were being killed every month in "non-war-related" criminal activities. I heard that 1,400 American soldiers had been killed and that the true casualty figure was approximately 25,000.

I heard that Donald Rumsfeld had a machine sign his letters of condolence to the families of soldiers who had been killed. When this caused a small scandal, I heard him say: "I have directed that in the future I sign each letter."

I heard the president say: "The credibility of this country is based upon our strong desire to make the world more peaceful, and the world is now more peaceful."

I heard the president say: "I want to be the peace president. The next four years will be peaceful years."

I heard Attorney General John Ashcroft say, on the day of his resignation: "The objective of securing the safety of Americans from crime and terror has been achieved."

I heard the president say: "For a while we were marching to war. Now we're marching to peace."

I heard that the US military had purchased 1,500,000,000 bullets for use in the coming year. That is 58 bullets for every Iraqi adult and child.

I heard that Saddam Hussein, in solitary confinement, was spending his time writing poetry, reading the Koran, eating cookies and muffins, and taking care of some bushes and shrubs. I heard that he had placed a circle of white stones around a small plum tree.

PAUSE

Anaphora means using repetition for rhetorical effect. Weinberger's piece is a good example of anaphora at work. He repeats the phrase "I heard . . ." to characterize the way the Iraq War was portrayed by public figures. What impact does this repetition have on you as a reader?

Introduction

We've looked, in the previous two chapters, respectively, at argumentation in the personal and technical spheres. Now we're going to take a look at argumentation in the **public sphere**. You may think of argumentation in the public sphere as political argument. Often, public argumentation is political—presidential debates, arguments over tax policy, and arguments about the appropriate role of our military are all examples of arguments in the public sphere. But other arguments fall into the public sphere that you may not think of as political. Controversies like what is the best way to be a good neighbor and how we should raise money for our annual school trip are also examples of public argumentation.

> While scholars continue to debate and refine the term *public sphere*, including arguing about its suitability, a basic definition is a social space in which participants argue in response to controversies that go beyond their personal and technical interests. We build on this definition below.

So how do you know if an argument belongs in the public sphere or somewhere else? Argumentation in the public sphere has two main characteristics:

1. It is equally accessible to everyone in a given public. When we make arguments in the public sphere, our audience is the general public, regardless of whether we are making those arguments to a group of friends, a local newspaper or blog, or a national television audience. We are also arguing in the best interests of everyone, rather than for our own self-interests or for only a select group. I cannot successfully run for president of a country by arguing that becoming president will be great for me because I really need a job right now, or because I have lots of family members who would benefit from a high position in government. I would need to make the argument that my presidency would benefit everyone equally.

2. The decisions made based on argumentation in the public sphere affect everyone. If I make the argument that we should go to war, for example, I need to be aware that going to war will affect not just the people being sent to fight and the support operations at home but also everyone else who may have to pay higher taxes to fund the war or help heal physically and psychically wounded veterans, and who has an ethical stake in the decision to go to war. Not everyone is affected equally, but everyone is affected.

If an argument displays these two characteristics, then it belongs in the public sphere. However, what is meant by a general public, by everyone in this context, is not always clear.

What Is the Public Sphere?

When I say an argument in the public sphere must be equally accessible to everyone and affects everyone, who exactly do I mean by everyone? Everyone in the entire world? Everyone in a particular country or state? What if I am making an argument about something that should be done in my hometown, or just my block?

Consider these arguments, all of which are in the public sphere:

1. Liv is running for city council and makes the argument that a pedestrian bridge ought to be built over the river in the northeastern part of the city.
2. At a meeting of the school board, George makes the case that masks ought to be worn whenever COVID-19 transmission rates top a certain mark.
3. Veronika, writing an opinion piece for an online magazine, argues that anyone earning over the local median income should donate a third of their income to the developing world.
4. Julia argues before the United Nations that the largest climate polluters need to cut their emissions by 50 percent by 2030.

Even if Liv in number 1 makes their argument on their YouTube channel, for example, meaning it could potentially reach a wide viewership, they are nevertheless addressing their argument to those viewers who are likely voters in the upcoming city council election. Those potentially affected by their plan, too, are limited to residents of the city in which they propose to build the pedestrian bridge. In this case, "everyone" seems to include just residents of Liv's city.

In number 2, George's audience is made up of those attending the school board meeting. In today's digital age, any argument made related to a topic that has broad appeal may be recorded and seen by thousands worldwide, who may be considered the audience for that argument and may be affected by it. So, in George's case, "everyone" could potentially be anyone from just the people in his school district to a broad national or global population engaged in the debate over how schools should respond to the COVID-19 pandemic.

Veronika is making an argument that directly addresses anyone making over the local median income. But people making under the median income would certainly be interested in the argument, and certainly they would be affected by the policy the argument is proposing. So "everyone" in this case would likely be everyone worldwide.

Julia is making a self-consciously global argument to a self-consciously global body. Like in the example for number 3, "everyone" here would seem to include, genuinely, everyone.

So what exactly is the public sphere, and who makes up the public sphere? How can the residents of a small city and the population of the entire globe both be considered the public sphere, depending on the situation?

The Public Sphere Is a Social Space

The first thing to understand about the public sphere is that it is not necessarily a geographical space at all. In the old days, before mass media like newspapers, radio, and television, and certainly before the Internet, the public sphere would exist in a physical space called a public forum. Different cultures designated different spaces as their public fora. For the ancient Greeks, for example, it was the agora, a large open space typically centralized within a city, which functioned as a market and gathering place. Native American nations such as the Haudenosaunee held regular councils to maintain their complex participatory democracy. Regardless of the forum, people who wanted to (and were allowed to) participate in the discussion had to all be at the same place and at the same time.

Since the advent of mass media, however, people can communicate with one another with much less regard to time and space. A newspaper could be printed in the early morning and distributed throughout a city, state, or nation by breakfast time. Readers could respond to what they read in the paper by sending letters to the editor or writing op-eds. A radio broadcast could be syndicated throughout the country, and people could call in to share their points of view. The rise of the Internet and the multitude of platforms it supports has distributed the public forum even further. In the example of George's argument regarding masks at school, the public sphere is at least partially constructed through digital and broadcast news media, social networks, and more informal platforms such as YouTube.

So the public sphere is an imagined space in which people can freely exchange ideas and respond to problems or controversies with reasons.

The Public Sphere Must Meet Some Conditions

To function as a public sphere, this imagined space must meet five conditions.

1. People recognize a problem that affects them both individually and as a collective.

If my car breaks down and I can't get to work, that is a problem for, really, just me and anyone who counts on my labor. It is not typically considered a problem that belongs in the public sphere. On the other hand, if many people experience the same problem with the same car, the problem could be considered to belong in the public sphere. This is because the problem affects people both on the individual level and as a collective, or a group of people brought together by a shared interest, problem, or goal.

2. In order to address the problem, cooperative action is needed.

The second condition underlying the public sphere is that not only does the problem affect people collectively, but also the problem needs to be addressed on more than just the individual level. Again, if my car breaks down, I can fix the car myself, or have it towed to my mechanic, and be on my way. But if we decide this is a problem affecting the collective, I can't be expected to fix everyone's car. Rather, the collective, working together, would have to put legal and social pressure on the company to address the problem.

For another example, consider the wave of protests that erupted across the country in the wake of George Floyd's murder at the hands of a Minneapolis police officer. Why wasn't that handled on an individual level? Why not file charges and let the legal system deal with the injustice? Well, historically, Black people who have suffered from police violence have not had success getting justice on the individual level. It took a collective effort for the system to respond to this pattern of injustice. (In fact, it took decades of collective effort. Historians point to a series of cases similar to Floyd's, going back at least to the police killing of fifteen-year-old James Powell in 1964, which sparked the Harlem Riots.)

3. There is no self-evident solution.

Let's say a group of citizens gets together and decides, yes, there is a problem with this model of car, it's unsafe, and we need to do something about it. Well, from the perspective of the group the solution might be obvious: force the company to fix the vehicles and pay damages. But the auto company is probably going to see the solution differently—in fact, they may not agree that a problem exists in the first place. They may raise questions about driving habits or maintenance, calling for further investigation.

Similarly, what might be the solution to a pattern of racist policing practices that lead to disproportionate killing of Black men and women at the hands of police? Many protesters called for defunding the police, a movement to use some of the budget allocated to police departments to fund programs and services that address the root causes of crime, such as mental illness, addiction, and poverty. The call to defund the police became controversial as it gathered steam, with opponents raising the specter of cities without law enforcement and predicting rampant crime. Others, wishing to appear more moderate, called for police reforms.

Because we don't have complete information about the causes of these problems and what the consequences of proposed solutions might be, controversies in the public sphere lack self-evident solutions.

4. People must exercise subjective judgment.

To paraphrase Gorgias, from Chapter 2, because we do not have perfect under-standing of the conditions that have led to these problems, we do not all experi-ence the problems the same way, and because we do not have perfect knowledge of what the future will bring, we can never have complete agreement about what should be done. In public argumentation, as in argumentation in general, we must make inferential leaps, or judgment calls, to come to any conclusion about what ought to be done.

5. Nevertheless, a decision must be made.

Sometimes a lack of certainty can be used to indefinitely delay a tough decision. I imagine long lines at the ice cream shop, with customer after customer unable to decide whether they wanted vanilla or chocolate, led to the invention of the vanilla-chocolate twist. A car company may try to investigate a problem for years, until the public is no longer paying attention, to avoid making real reforms. Similarly, communities of color have long struggled to remove or reduce police presence in their neighborhoods, but lack of public consensus has continued to provide public figures cover for doing little or nothing.

Because change to public policies and institutions can be slow, arguments in the public sphere must often make the case for what Martin Luther King Jr. has called "the fierce urgency of now" and what classical Greek rhetoricians have called **kairos**: a consideration of the function of time in argumentation, which in the case of policy arguments means that they take into account the appropriate time for the policy to be adopted. Arguing in 1967 that more religious leaders needed to speak out against U.S. military involvement in Vietnam, King stated: "We are now faced with the fact that tomorrow is today. We are confronted with the fierce urgency of now. In this unfolding conundrum of life and history there is such a thing as being too late."

Trust in the Public Sphere

These conditions—that a problem affects people collectively, that they need to work together to address it, and that there is no self-evident solution and so people must rely on their own judgments to make a decision—mean that argumentation in the public sphere often relies on an underlying foundation of trust. People must trust that something like a collective is possible, which means they must see something like common ground as possible. On the one hand, **partisanship**, or unquestioned loyalty to a particular group identity, can undermine public trust when loyalty substitutes for civic engagement. On the other hand, the classical definition of partisanship is related

> Because it is a cooper-ative enterprise, argu-mentation cannot pro-ceed without a basis in trust.

to participation in political life; in fact, many see partisanship as the foundation of the public sphere.

Some argue that today, partisanship undermines the cooperative foundation of argumentation because it questions the fundamental motives of people who identify with a different political party. If you believe that members of an opposing political party are all liars who want to destroy America, you're not likely to engage in genuine argumentation with them. Others, however, argue that partisanship can lead to greater engagement in the public sphere because it plays a strong motivational role in political participation.

While partisanship can motivate political participation, argumentation in the public sphere depends on a threshold level of trust. For one thing, as we have seen throughout this book, argumentation is a cooperative enterprise. When we engage in argumentation with someone, we are working with them to make the best possible decision under the circumstances. We know that we cannot make the decision on our own, because we recognize that (1) this is a problem that affects many of us collectively, (2) we do not have enough power as individuals to address the problem, and (3) our individual point of view is necessarily limited. Even if we are very confident in our opinion (perhaps even more so when we are very confident in our opinion), we must recognize that our opinion could be wrong and that other opinions may be equally as or more reasonable.

These are hard assumptions to make, but they are necessary for argumentation in the public sphere to function.

It is also necessary to have trust in the system of argumentation—to believe that exchanging reasons is the best way to come to the best possible outcome. People won't participate in a system they don't believe in or that they think is fundamentally unjust. We can see this in situations where people lose trust in the voting system, for example. In the Jim Crow South the disenfranchisement of Black voters was a major contributor to the civil rights movement. Black people saw that their vote would not be counted, so they turned to alternate means, working cooperatively to make arguments and demonstrate for change. Because of changes to voting laws as a result of the civil rights movement, and I'm thinking here of the Voting Rights Act of 1965, protections were put in place to guarantee the right to vote regardless of race, and trust in the voting system was mostly restored. Recent attempts to delegitimize an election system that now does mostly work (though systematic disenfranchisement continues to play a role) are really not the same because they make claims without evidence. Though examples of buying votes, forging ballots, and voter intimidation can be found in U.S. history, there has been no fraud on anywhere near the scale necessary to have a meaningful impact on the outcome of a major election in the United States in the last several decades at least. The short-term effect of such baseless claims about election fraud is to energize supporters who believe they have been wronged; the long-term effect is to reduce enthusiasm for and participation in voting.

Like voting, argumentation depends on participation, which is undermined by a lack of trust in the potential of argumentation to make decisions effectively. Maybe you don't trust the person with whom you have a disagreement to engage in argumentation honestly, or maybe you don't believe the problem you are trying to solve can be addressed through argumentation. Because it is a cooperative enterprise, argumentation cannot proceed without a basis in trust.

Modes of Argumentation in the Public Sphere

Argumentation is a major foundation of democracy and democratic participation. A lot of the time, we think participating in democracy means voting every two or four years. Voting is important—it is a major way to participate in democracy, and perhaps the most firmly established in the U.S. system. For voting to work effectively, however, the voting public must be adequately informed on the relevant controversies and issues; they must be capable of building cases that respond to these controversies adequately to form an informed opinion. In other words, to be informed voters, people have to engage in argumentation—even if the arguments they make are only to themselves.

While voting is an important aspect of democracy, it is not the only method of participation we have. The principal purpose of argumentation is as a way of making decisions based on compelling reasons. Often the arguments do not come from elected representatives but from individuals and interest groups advocating for some cause or other. Other forms of direct participation in democracy open to those of us who do not hold a political office include the petition and demonstration. The right to **petition**, or to present requests to the government without fear of reprisal, is ensconced in the First Amendment to the U.S. Constitution—the same amendment that guarantees freedom of speech, press, and assembly, all of which were seen by the framers as central to the function of democracy. Petitions are, essentially, policy arguments that ask government bodies to adopt some course of action. They were seen as central to public participation in government—some believed them to be of greater importance than voting because of the opportunities they provided for the public to engage more directly in crafting public policy. Colonial-era records, for example, show petitions ranging from what sorts of products may be traded with Natives to the regulation of tobacco packaging. In fact, the petition led to more laws being passed in colonial America than any other means.

Prior to the mid-nineteenth century, political bodies and legal experts widely interpreted the right to petition to include not just the people's right to bring petitions but the right to have the petitions heard and responded to. In response to a growing number of petitions related to the abolition of slavery in the lead-up to the Civil War, however, both houses of the legislature adopted rules to limit their responsibility to read and respond to petitions. As a result, today it is rare for petitions to reach federal legislators directly, though ballot initiatives, which are similar, do play a role in various state governments.

Still, petitions are widely used to make a case to a general public today, or to generate public support for a cause. While the petitions themselves are rarely seen by federal legislators, the arguments they make may influence public policy if they gather enough support.

Public demonstration, too, offers the people the opportunity to be directly involved in political decision-making. A great example of this is the recent demonstrations in the wake of the murder of George Floyd to call for significant police and public policy reforms related to poverty and mental health. The movement made compelling arguments that police officers are coming into contact with people of color too often for things that police are not best positioned to handle. The increased police involvement leads to increased risk of death from police shootings. These public demonstrations led to significant movements to not only reform police departments and increase police officer training but also reconsider whether or not some funding currently going to police departments might be better off spent on mental health and medical first responders. Legislation like the George Floyd Justice in Policing Act of 2021, as well as local efforts in places like New York State and Minneapolis, represent direct impacts of these public movements.

Argumentation and Cultural Values

Argumentation is also a way of figuring out our beliefs and values. The philosopher C. S. Peirce describes four ways someone can come to know what they know, or to hold the beliefs that they hold. The first is what he calls **tenacity**, which is just holding on to the beliefs you develop first. These beliefs may come from your family or friends, or you may have come to them on your own, but with tenacity, once you develop a belief you don't let go of it, even if you are presented with evidence to the contrary. Tenacity, then, is unlikely to consistently lead to the best beliefs because it does not include any way to change your beliefs in response to new or better evidence.

The second way we come to believe we know something Peirce calls authority. When you come to your beliefs through **authority**, you uncritically accept what you are told by someone in a position of power or who is well known, or by a powerful institution. Beliefs that contradict those of the authority are either silenced or unfairly undermined. Authority, too, is unlikely to consistently lead to the best beliefs because it too does not have a good way to consider whether or not other beliefs and evidence might be better.

A priori correspondence, Peirce's third way of developing one's beliefs, involves using deductive reasoning. As we read in Chapter 2, a limitation of deductive reasoning is that, though it can be a useful way of rearranging knowledge, it does not lead to new knowledge.

Peirce's fourth method for developing knowledge is called verification, which we now call the scientific method. **Verification** involves testing beliefs through observation, using specific and transparent methods. Verification has several advantages over the other three approaches. For one, verification publicizes its methods, meaning that members of the public can review the methods and challenge them if they see fit. Second, verification uses transparent methods, meaning that any study can be checked by others. Anyone who doubts the results of a particular study, or wishes to see if the same study will have different results in different contexts, can **replicate** the study, or conduct the same study again using the same methods. Finally, unlike the other approaches, the methods used in verification are designed to produce the most reasonable knowledge under the circumstances. The conclusions arrived at through verification are the results of a well-designed study rather than chance.

However, there are significant limits to verification as a way of acquiring beliefs as well, particularly when it comes to beliefs that are not verifiable through observation. If verification were the only acceptable way to attain knowledge, then we would have no good way of knowing about ethical and cultural values, no good way to make predictions, and no good basis for making recommendations about what we should do going forward. Verification does not have a good answer for, say, the value of Toni Morrison's *Beloved*, or who will win the next presidential election, or how we should address rising tensions in East Asia.

Rather, argumentation provides better answers to these sorts of questions. Argumentation, too, is a way of knowing, one that has many of the same advantages over tenacity, authority, and a priori correspondence that verification has, but can lead to reasoned beliefs about things that are not empirically verifiable.

Argumentation, as a way to develop knowledge, runs parallel to verification. Like verification, there is a clear procedure to be followed, meaning that the methods of argumentation are likewise transparent. While argumentation does not allow for replication, the knowledge that all aspects of an argument can be challenged and alternatives provided motivates people to produce the best arguments they have available and makes it more likely that weak arguments will not gain long-lasting support. Like verification, the methods of argumentation are arrived at by design and are rooted in the values of cooperation and collaboration. Like verification, argumentation is designed to produce reasonable and reliable knowledge, based on transparency and agreement.

Recognizing that argumentation has an **epistemic function**, that is, that argumentation leads to knowledge rather than just packaging what we already know, tells us two important things about the nature of knowledge. One, when it comes to things that we cannot know with certainty, truth depends at least in part on point of view and is subject to change over time as new evidence and new arguments are discovered. This does not mean, however, that any truth is as good as any other, just as we know not every argument is as good as any other. Just because truth is relative in these ways does not mean that what a doctor knows about an illness is just as true as what your Uncle Joey knows about that illness by reading about it on social media. Rather, how truthful any knowledge is depends on the strength of the argument supporting that knowledge.

Two, knowledge is never developed in isolation. Everything we know, including about ourselves, we know by talking with and observing others.

Conclusion

Argumentation is fundamental to democracy because it helps constitute and maintain a healthy public sphere. Argumentation in the public sphere has two main characteristics: it must be accessible to everyone, and it affects everyone. When an argument cannot be settled in either the personal sphere or the technical sphere, it may be addressed in the public sphere. The public sphere, in turn, has five characteristics that distinguish it from both the personal and technical spheres: (1) People recognize a problem that affects them both individually and as a collective, (2) in order to address the problem, cooperative action is needed, (3) there is no self-evident solution, and so (4) people must exercise subjective judgment, but (5) nevertheless, a decision must be made.

A major challenge to argumentation in the public sphere is the erosion of trust in the bulwark entities that seek to preserve a viable public sphere: the government and mass media. The government guarantees access to the public sphere by securing the right to vote, to assembly, to free speech, and to other rights that facilitate participation in public deliberation. Mass media gives people access to the information they need to make well-informed decisions. While both government provisions and access to mass media are vital to public deliberation, they are less robust today than in the past. Argumentation, as a method for producing reasonable and reliable knowledge based on transparency and agreement, is fundamental to a functioning democracy.

PROBE

Consider which sources of information you find most trustworthy, and which sources you find least trustworthy. Why do you have the level of trust in these sources you do? What might make your level of trust increase? What might make your level of trust decrease?

Source Credits

Texts

P. 326　"What I Heard about Iraq" by Eliot Weinberger from *Oranges and Peanuts for Sale,* copyright © 2009 by Eliot Weinberger. Reprinted by permission of New Directions Publishing Corp.

Images

P. 129　"Global Average Temperature vs. Number of Pirates." Created by Andrei Rjkov (2011). From https://commons.wikimedia.org/wiki/File:Pirates-VsTemp(en).svg.

P. 159　"Queen Elizabeth I of England making her speech at Tilbury before the defeat of the Spanish Armada, 1588." Handcoloured copperplate engraving by Verico from Giulio Ferrario's *Costumes Ancient and Modern of the Peoples of the World,* Florence, 1847. Alamy Stock Photo by Florilegius.

P. 162　"Save Water" [Advertisement]. Created by Venfield (January 2005). From https://www.adforum.com/creative-work/ad/player/46527/save-water/venfield.

P. 165　Created by the National Parks Service (2017). From https://commons.wikimedia.org/wiki/File:Trump_Crowd_Size_IMG_0478.jpg.

P. 165　Created by the National Parks Service (2017). From https://commons.wikimedia.org/wiki/File:Trump_Crowd_Size_IMG_0480.jpg.

P. 200　"Smoking Him Out," lithograph by Peter Smith [Nathaniel Currier] (1848). From https://www.loc.gov/pictures/item/2008661511/.

P. 216　Created by John Snow (1854). From https://commons.wikimedia.org/wiki/File:Snow-cholera-map-1.jpg.